Qajar Iran

STUDIES PRESENTED TO PROFESSOR L. P. ELWELL-SUTTON

1800–1925

QAJAR
IRAN

Political, social and cultural change
1800–1925

Edited by

Edmond Bosworth and Carole Hillenbrand

Mazda Publishers

Costa Mesa, California U.S.A.

Library of Congress Cataloging-in-Publication Data

Qajar Iran:Political, Social, and Cultural Change, 1800-1925/
edited by Edmond Bosworth and Carole Hillenbrand.

      p. cm.

      Originally published: Edinburgh: Edinburgh University Press,
      © 1983.

       Includes bibliographical references and index.

      ISBN:0-939214-98-9 (paper)

      1. Iran-- history --Qajar dynasty, 1794-1925. 2. Iran-
      civilization--19th century. 3. Iran--Civilization--20th century.
      I. Bosworth, Clifford Edmond. II. Hillenbrand, Carole.

      DS298.Q34   1992

      955'. 04--dc20   92-6345
                                                 CIP

ISBN:0-939214-98-9

Mazda Publishers   **1992**   انتشارات مزدا

Contents

Contents

Preface

Laurence Elwell-Sutton once remarked to me that the Qajar period in Persian history had always interested him, and that he regretted that he had never written on it during his long career in Islamic studies. Typically enough, his statement was more modest than strictly accurate, as for instance his article on Ḳurrat al-ʿAyn in a recent fascicle of the *Encyclopaedia of Islam* bears witness. His chance comment nevertheless gave us the idea of the theme for this *Festschrift*.

Such a statement also sheds light on Laurence Elwell-Sutton himself. It is typical of him that, after more than half a century in the Islamic field, he should lay stress on what he claims he does not know rather than on the wide-ranging, often esoteric knowledge which he has acquired during his long and varied career as a publishing academic. As well as maintaining a catholic interest in modern Persian language, literature and history, he has published *The Persian metres,* which is a monument to his industry as well as to his scholarship, and latterly he has developed a deep interest in Islamic astronomy and astrology. His knowledge of Arabic, moreover, has been kept at a high level by, *inter alia,* his unusual skill in deciphering inscriptions and his nearly completed edition of al-Bîrûnî's treatise on the astrolabe, an edition compiled from six major manuscripts. He is also an accomplished calligrapher with a mastery of many different hands.

His productive scholarly life reveals, however, only one facet of a singularly complex personality. He is by no means just a narrow Orientalist. He is a devoted family man and he has always found occasion to indulge his favourite pastimes: amateur theatre, politics and travel. He has been a member of a leading amateur dramatic society in Edinburgh for over thirty years and has been involved in acting, stage manage ment and producing alike. Anyone who has seen him acting will never cease to be surprised and delighted at the transformations he can undergo. Like many a shy person he finds it exhilarating to act, and to act extremely well, be it as Shylock, Zeus or the villain in the Victorian melodrama *Down with Demon Drink*. Moreover, he expects the same high standards from those acting in plays produced by him, as I have recently learned to my cost – and benefit.

His political interests, which also span half a century of continuous involvement, reflect his deep conviction that 'small is beautiful' and that the individual is in danger of being engulfed in modern society. He is a long-standing member of the Kibbo Kift and has always sought to press the claims of the Social Credit movement.

As for his enthusiasm for travel, which his attendance at numerous far-flung conferences over several decades attests, it will be enough to outline *exempli gratia* his achievement in the autumn of 1983. My husband and I had the privilege and fun of going on a two-month trip with him, which included twelve days on the Trans-Siberian railway and another ten in Japan, with the rest of the time devoted to Soviet Central Asia, where his wife Alison joined us. During this fascinating journey, Laurence Elwell-Sutton savoured with great zest the wide variety of countries through which we travelled (and their diverse cuisines), showed remarkable resilience and dignity when things went wrong and was at once humorous and equable. In short, the ideal travelling companion.

Had it been possible, Laurence Elwell-Sutton would of course have spent at least some of his retirement in Persia, meeting all the friends he has there and enjoying the country he knows and loves best. He speaks with great nostalgia and warmth about his many visits there and is especially fond of Mâzandarân, an area in which he travelled widely in 1973 whilst gathering folk tales, another continuing interest of his. His recent trip to Russia, Japan and Central Asia was, however, some consolation. It also enabled us to get to know someone who is usually too shy and modest to reveal his quirky sense of humour, his refreshingly unconventional views, his adaptability, tolerance and above all his *joie de vivre*.

As head of the Department of Islamic and Middle Eastern Studies in the University of Edinburgh, Laurence Elwell-

Sutton was always punctilious, courteous and kind in the performance of what was often a difficult and time-consuming task. As hosts to staff and students, Laurence and his wife Alison have for many years been generous to a fault in providing hospitality, and in this they are a model to us all.

Now that he has retired, Laurence Elwell-Sutton's interest in scholarship remains as enthusiastic as ever. He has plans to write a biography of Reza Shah and a book on Islamic astronomy and astrology. He is currently fighting a serious illness with his usual unobtrusive courage and determination. Indeed, the proof of his indomitability is his embarking, despite his illness, on a translation of the massive *Kîmiyâ-yi Sa'âdat* of al-Ghazâlî. Now, as ever, he can be sure of the warmest affection and support from all his friends, both in the West and in Persia. We ask him to accept this *Festschrift* as a celebration of his scholarly career and as a token of that affection.

Carole Hillenbrand

ACKNOWLEDGEMENTS. The editors would like to acknowledge with gratitude and thanks the help of a number of people at various stages in the publication of his book. First, we are extremely grateful to the staff of the Edinburgh University Press for much encouragement and help. We should also like to thank Dr John Gurney for valuable advice and suggestions, Dr Fritz Hillenbrand for translating Professor Alavi's chapter from German, the translator of Professor Afshar's contribution in Persian (who wishes to remain anonymous), Dr Robert Hillenbrand for checking numerous points of detail, and Mrs Alison Elwell-Sutton for providing an index and for giving much selfless and unobtrusive help during the preparation of this book.

Principal abbreviations used in the present volume

BSOAS	Bulletin of the School of Oriental and African Studies
CHI	Cambridge History of Iran
*EI*¹	Encyclopaedia of Islam, first edition
*EI*²	Encyclopaedia of Islam, second edition
IJMES	International Journal of Middle Eastern Studies
JA	Journal Asiatique
JESHO	Journal of the Economic and Social History of the Orient
JNES	Journal of Near Eastern Studies
JRAS	Journal of the Royal Asiatic Society
JSS	Journal of Semitic Studies
MEJ	Middle East Journal
MES	Middle Eastern Studies
RCAJ	Royal Central Asian Journal
REI	Revue des Etudes Islamiques
SI	Studia Islamica
TLS	Times Literary Supplement
ZDMG	Zeitschrift der Deutschen Morgenländischen Gesellschaft

Transliteration

The editors of the present volume were asked by Edinburgh University Press to keep transliteration to a minimum. We have therefore not indicated any dotted consonants and, as requested, we have used the circumflex accent ˆ for long vowels and the signs ' for the *hamza* and ' for the *'ayn*. The Persian silent 'h' is transliterated as *a*; e.g. *nâma*.

The following system has been adopted for the vowels:

long	ا	â
	و	û
	ي	î
doubled	يّ	iyy (final form, î)
diphthongs	او	aw
	اى	ay
short	´	a
	ٔ	u
	ˌ	i

The Arabic definite article appears as *al-* and *'l* even before sun letters: e.g. Jalâl al-Dîn. The macron of Abû and Dhû is omitted before the article: e.g. Abu'l 'Abbâs.

Frequently used terms such as Qajar, Shah and Khan and well-known place-names such as Tehran, Isfahan and Kirman appear in this book without macrons. Similarly, Arabic or Persian words which have been provided with an English termination appear without macrons: e.g. Safavids.

Inevitably, any transliteration system will be found unsatisfactory by some. The editors, not the contributors, are responsible for the one used in this book, which is basically that employed in the *Cambridge History of Iran*. By definition the transliteration system adopted here cannot be said to reflect the pronunciation of modern spoken Persian.

List of contributors

I. AFSHAR, Tehran
B. ALAVI, East Berlin
F. R. C. BAGLEY, formerly of the
University of Durham
S. BAKHASH, Princeton University
A. BAKHTIAR, London
A. BAUSANI, Accademia Nazionale
dei Lincei, Rome
M. BAYAT, Harvard University
J. CALMARD, CNRS, Paris
P. CHELKOWSKI. New York University
M. ETTEHADIEH, Tehran
W. FLOOR, The Hague
R. HILLENBRAND, University of Edinburgh
G. LENCZOWSKI, University of
California, Berkeley
D. MACEOIN, University of
Newcastle-upon-Tyne
A. S. MELIKIAN-CHIRVANI, CNRS, Paris
S. H. NASR, Temple University
B. ROBINSON, formerly of the
Victoria and Albert Museum, London
J. M. SCARCE, Royal Scottish Museum, Edinburgh
B. SPOONER, University of Pennsylvania
G. M. WICKENS, University of Toronto
E. YARSHATER, Columbia University

Foreword

Laurence Paul Elwell-Sutton was born on 2 June 1912 at Ballylickey, Bantry Bay, Co. Cork, the eldest son of Lt-Cdr A. S. Elwell-Sutton, RN and Mrs Violet Elwell-Sutton; it was indeed the fact of his father's naval service that, by pure chance, caused him to be born in Ireland. After school at Winchester College, he studied at the School of Oriental Studies, University of London, and graduated in 1934 with First Class Honours in Arabic. There was nothing thus far to indicate an attachment to the land of Iran, where he was to live for many years and to whose literary and cultural heritage he was to devote so much subsequent attention.

However, employment with the Anglo-Iranian Oil Company at Abadan from 1935 to 1938, where he served in the staff and labour administration, introduced him to Iran and the Iranians. With the outbreak of war, he was back in London and attached to the Ministry of Information as a Middle East specialist, at the same time lecturing in Arabic at the School of Oriental and African Studies from 1939 to 1940 and then working with the BBC as a Persian specialist and as editor of *al-Mustami' al-'Arabî* (*The Arabic Listener*). In 1943 he returned to Iran, where he worked as Press Attaché, Broadcasting, until 1947. It was in this capacity that he acquired a particular interest in the Iranian press at a time when, in the years after Riza Shah's abdication in 1941 and the uncertain early years of the young Muhammad Riza Shah's reign, the local press enjoyed a remarkable efflorescence and expressed a multitude of political and cultural viewpoints; these publications, many of them very obscure and ephemeral, Elwell-Sutton was carefully to tabulate and describe in a later article (see *Bibliography*, below, p.xv). After returning to the BBC he spent the next four years as Arabic and Persian language supervisor and took up once again the editorship of *al-Mustami' al-'Arabî*, punctuated by a summer semester at the Department of Near Eastern Studies, University of Michigan, Ann Arbor (1950).

His connection with Edinburgh University began in 1952 when he was appointed Lecturer in Persian. This was the period of expansion in oriental studies which came in the wake of the report of the Scarbrough Committee (1948), and as in other universities like Manchester and Durham, a post specifically in Persian was an innovation at Edinburgh. During the thirty years in which he was responsible for Persian – for the first decade or so as the sole teacher of the language and its literature – he progressed through the university hierarchy of posts, until in 1976 he was promoted to a personal chair in Persian. This was undoubtedly due recognition for his achievements as a Persian scholar (these will be touched upon below), but also for his equally significant achievement in raising Persian studies from what was originally an adjunct of other Middle Eastern languages to an independent Department within the University and one in which Persian could be studied as a major honours subject; it continues now as an integral part of the Department of Islamic and Middle Eastern Studies at Edinburgh. By the time of his retirement in 1982 he had the invidious distinction, in the present period of retrenchment and freezing of posts, of being the sole surviving Professor of Persian Studies in the United Kingdom, and his subject had during the preceding years attracted an increasing number of students, in particular, of postgraduate students from Iran and the Indo-Pakistan subcontinent, attracted by his internationally known stature in the field.

The extent and breadth of Elwell-Sutton's published works can be gauged by the *Bibliography* given below at pp.xv–xxi. They can be divided roughly into five categories: Persian language; Persian literature; modern Iranian history and politics; folk lore; and Islamic science, in particular, astronomy and astrology. Within the first group, his *Colloquial Persian* (1941) and *Elementary Persian Grammar* (1963) have always remained in print as standard works. In the second, one finds translations like that of a Persian life of the Prophet Muhammad, *Payâmbar – the Messenger* (1964–6), and of the contemporary novelist and short story writer Ali Dashti's *In Search of Omar Khayyam* (1971), together with what is probably his most technical and closely-argued work, *The Persian Metres* (1976). In this detailed examination of a highly abstruse question, he shows the futility of an approach to these metres from the classical Arabic rules of prosody or *'arûd* and demonstrates the Persian metres as an indigenous tradition which has been used by Iranian poets, without major innovation, for a millennium. In the third catgory, his *Modern Iran* (1941) was a pioneer study of the régime of the Iranian ruler Riza Shah (to whom he is now returning, as the subject of a full-scale biography, in his retirement), whilst his *Persian Oil: a Study in Power Politics* (1955) stirred up considerable controversy at the time in such places as the correspondence columns of *The Listener* and in the *Times Literary Supplement* because of its critical attitude towards his former employers, the Anglo-Iranian Oil Company; perhaps not surprisingly, it was shortly afterwards translated into Russian and Chinese. The fourth sphere of scholarship, that of folk lore, has been a particular interest of his, and he has utilised his periods of residence in Iran and later visits to collect and record the folk heritage of Iran, a heritage under pressure, as elsewhere, from the levelling and standardising processes of modern education and communications; his translation of the collection of Persian folk tales by Mashti Galeen Khanom, *The Wonderful Sea-horse and other Persian Tales* (1950), illustrates this enthusiasm. Fifthly, his study of science has recently borne fruit in *The Horoscope of Asadullah Mirza: a Specimen of Nineteenth-century Persian Astrology* (1977). Finally, one should certainly mention his careful and judicious editorship of the recent *Bibliographical Guide to Iran* (1983). This gives coverage for the Iranian world parallel to that for the Arab world and for Islam in general as an institution provided by the Middle East Library Committee's guide *Arabic Islamic Bibliography* (1977) and to J. D. Pearson's *Bibliography of Pre-Islamic Persia* (1975). Elwell-Sutton's new work is in some ways a much-enlarged and improved version of the *Guide to Iranian Area Study* for which he was solely responsible thirty years previously.

It falls to the exiguous band of senior orientalists in Britain to shoulder considerable burdens in the way of membership of and assistance to learned societies, associations, etc., and here Elwell-Sutton has given faithful service, with active participation in bodies as varied as the Folklore Society and the British Society for Middle East Studies.

All who have ever had contact with Laurence Elwell-Sutton will recall with pleasure this modest and kindly man, ever ready to extend help and hospitality to fellow-enthusiasts or to beginners in oriental studies; many of us have shared in conviviality within the welcoming portals of 5 Merchiston Gardens. In retirement, he and his wife Alison have continued to extend their horizons both spatially and mentally, with a recent trip to Central Asia and to the International Congress of Orientalists at Tokyo via the Trans-Siberian Railway. We wish him now, with these studies, an enjoyable and fruitful retirement *ad multos annos*.

The present collection of articles contributed by friends, former colleagues and wellwishers, deals with a period when Iran was ruled by a distinctly unattractive dynasty, the Qajars, but when the country had to face a series of crises in the nineteenth and early twentieth centuries from external encroachment on its sovereignty, one interfering with the internal functioning of the country as well as appropriating its territory outright, and with internal crises generated in a conservative Islamic society by attempts, with varying degrees of enthusiasm, to come to terms with the contemporary modern world. It is a cliché to characterise the present revolutionary ferment in Iran as a response to over-hasty westernisation, yet equally sharp adjustments to the challenge of modernisation were successfully accomplished in late nineteenth-century Japan and in China and Japan in the earlier part of the present century. It is not the aim of this book to deal with contemporary Iranian history, and it is now nearly sixty years since a Qajar sat on the throne in Tehran. Rather, it is hoped that the constituent articles will illustrate some of the processes of change which were already at work in nineteenth and early twentieth-century Iran, whether in the administrative and military structures, in literature and culture, in the mentalities of Shahs who travelled in the West and saw its strange wonders, or in the diffusion of a simple technical gadget like a camera. Perhaps with the aid of such studies as these we shall be helped towards a clearer understanding of recent events and the explosion there of violence and fanaticism, and towards a calmer estimate of the inter-vening Pahlavi period, when many of the Qajar period trends came to fruition.

C. E. Bosworth, *Manchester, November 1983*

A bibliography of the works of
L. P. ELWELL-SUTTON

1940

1) Review of A. J. Arberry, *Specimens of Arabic and Persian palaeography*, in *BSOAS*, x (1940–2), 802.

2) Review of E. Rossi, *L'Arabo parlato a Ṣanʿāʾ*, in *ibid.*, 801–2.

1941

3) *Colloquial Persian*, London 1941.
4) *Modern Iran*, London 1941.
5) 'Iranian routes to Russia', *Manchester Guardian*, 30.12.41, 4 and 6.

1942

6) 'Iran in the modern world', *RCAJ*, xxix (1942), ii, 120–8.

1943

7) Review of three Persian magazines from Delhi, *RCAJ* (1943), xxxi, 125.

1947

8) *Irān-i naw*, Persian translation of *Modern Iran* by A. Javāhir Kalām, Tehran 1947.

1948

9) 'The press in Iran today', *RCAJ*, xxxv (1948), iii/iv, 209–19.

1949

10) 'Political parties in Iran', *MEJ*, iii (1949), i, 45–62.

1950

11) *The Wonderful Sea-horse and other Persian Tales*, London 1950.

Bibliography

1952

12) *A Guide to Iranian Area Study,* Washington 1952.

1953

13) 'Arabia (history)', in *The Middle East, a Survey and Directory of the Countries of the Middle East,* London 1953, 23–5.

14) 'Jordan (history)', in *ibid.,* 189–90.

1954

15) *Persian Proverbs,* London 1954.

16) Review of A. J. Arberry, ed., *The Legacy of Persia,* in *Journal of the Iran Society,* I (1954), 5, 209.

1955

17) *Persian Oil: a Study in Power Politics,* London 1955.

1956

18) *Iranskaya neft,* Russian translation of *Persian Oil* by N. Paisov, Moscow 1956.

19) *Riẓā Shāh-i Kabīr yā Irān-i naw,* Persian translation of *Modern Iran* by A. A. Sabūrī, Tehran 1956.

1957

20) 'A short history of the theatre in Iran', *Sukhan* (Tehran), VII (June/July 1957), 288–92 and 383–91.

21) 'Journey in Persia', *Gordonstoun Record Annual* (1957), 11 (December), 68–75.

1958

22) *Yilang shiyou,* Chinese translation of *Persian Oil* by D. Zheng, Beijing 1958.

23) Review of G. Levi Della Vida, *George Strachan: Memorials of a Wandering Scottish Scholar of the Seventeenth Century,* in *Scottish Historical Review,* XXXVII (1958), 83–5.

24) Review of J. C. E. Bowen, *The Golden Pomegranate,* in *RCAJ,* XLV (1958), 94–6.

25) 'Nationalism and neutralism in Iran', *MEJ,* XII (1958), 20–32.

26) 'Arab nationalism vs. the oil international', *Nation* (April 1958), 313–16.

27) 'Academic freedom in Iran', *Science and Freedom,* 12 (October 1958), 13–18.

Bibliography

1959

28) 'The Persian metres', in *Akten des 24sten internationalen Orientalisten-Kongresses München,* ed. H. Franke, Wiesbaden 1959, 307–9.

29) 'Dāstānhā-yi 'āmmiyāna-yi Irān', in *Sapīda-yi fardā,* VI (March/April 1959), 57–66.

1962

30) *Afsānahā-yi Irānī,* Persian translation of *The Wonderful Sea-horse and other Persian tales* by A. Javāhir Kalām, Tehran 1962.

31) 'Ḥāfiẓ', *Encyclopaedia Britannica,* XI, 72.

32) 'Jāmī', *ibid.,* XII, 867.

33) 'Jalāl al-Dīn Rūmī', *ibid.,* XII, 870–1.

34) 'Niẓāmī', *ibid.,* XVI, 475–6.

35) 'Sanā'ī', *ibid.,* XIX, 927.

36) 'Parleying with the Russians in 1827', *RCAJ,* XLIX (1962), 183–7.

37) 'Der iranische Nationalismus', *Bustān* (Vienna), 3 (September 1962), 10–13.

38) 'The Persian novel' (Parts I and II), *Paymun* (Iranian Students' Society, Leeds University), II (March/April 1962), 6–11, 20–3.

1963

39) *Elementary Persian Grammar,* Cambridge 1963.

40) 'An eighteenth-century (?) Caspian dialect', in *Mélanges d'orientalisme offerts à Henri Massé,* Tehran 1963, 110–40.

1964

41) *Payāmbar – the Messenger,* English translation of Z. Rahnema, *Payāmbar,* Lahore 1964, I.

42) 'The Vafsi dialect (north-western Persia)', in *Trudy Dvadtsat'pyatogo Mezhdunarodnogo Kongressa Vostokovedov,* Moscow 1964, II, 314–9.

43) 'Persian manuscripts in Scotland', *Rahnāma-yi Kitāb,* VII (1964), 1, 36–44.

1965

44) *Payāmbar – the Messenger,* English translation of Rahnema, *op. cit.,* II.

45) Review of A. D. Hytier, *Les dépêches diplomatiques du Comte de Gobineau en Perse,* in *Oriens,* XVIII (1965), 281–3.

Bibliography

46) Review of B. G. Martin, *German-Persian Diplomatic Relations, 1873–1912,* in *Oriens,* XVII (1965), 281–3.

47) Review of R. Frye, *The Heritage of Persia,* in *English Historical Review,* LXXX (1965), 629–30.

1966

48) *Payāmbar – the Messenger,* English translation of Rahnema, *op. cit.,* III.

49) 'Scaldheads and thinbeards in Persian folk-tale literature', in *Fourth International Congress for Folk-narrative Research: Lectures and Reports,* ed. G. A. Megas, Athens 1966, 105–8.

50) Review of H. Kamshad, *Modern Persian Prose Literature,* in *JSS,* XI (1966), 2, 282–3.

51) Review of E. Rosenthal, *Islam in the Modern National State,* in *RCAJ,* LIII (1966), 3, 352–4.

1967

52) 'Animal stories in Persian literature', in 'Ḥayawān', *EI²,* III, 313–14.

1968

53) 'The Iranian press, 1941–47', *Iran,* VI (1968), 65–104.

54) 'The Omar Khayyam puzzle', *RCAJ,* LV (1968), ii, 167–79.

55) Review of R. A. Nicholson, *Studies in Islamic Mysticism,* in *The Aryan Path,* XXXIX (1968), 494–5.

1969

56) 'The unfortunate heroine in Persian folk-literature', in *Yād-nāma-yi Irānī-yi Minorsky,* eds. M. Minovi and I. Afshar, Tehran 1969, 37–50.

57) 'The role of the dervish in the Persian folk-tale', in *Proceedings of the 26th International Congress of Orientalists,* ed. A. Ghosh *et al.,* Delhi 1969, II, 200–3.

58) Review of R. Graves and O. Ali-Shah, *The Original Rubaiyat of Omar Khayyam,* in *Delos,* 3 (1969), 170–90.

1970

59) Review of R. Levy, *An Introduction to Persian Literature,* in *Asian Affairs,* 57 (I) (1970), 1, 86.

60) Reviews of H. Corbin, *Creative Imagination in the Sufism of Ibn 'Arabī,* I. Shah, *The Way of the Sufi* and *idem, Tales of the Dervishes,* in *New York Review of Books,* XV, I (July 1970), 35–7.

Bibliography
1971

61) *In Search of Omar Khayyam,* London 1971, English translation of A. Dashtī, *Damī bā Khayyām,* Tehran 1969.

62) 'The influence of folktale and legend on modern Persian literature', in *Iran and Islam: in Memory of the Late Vladimir Minorsky,* ed. C. E. Bosworth, Edinburgh 1971, 247–54.

63) 'Omar Khayyam', *Man, Myth and Magic,* 74 (1971), 2061–3.

64) With J. M. Scarce, 'A problem piece of Kashmiri metalwork', *Iran,* IX (1971), 71–85.

65) 'Magic and the supernatural in Persian folk literature', *Actes du Ve congrès international d'Arabisants et d'Islamisants, Correspondance d'Orient,* Brussels 1971, II, 189–96.

66) 'Supra-nationalism and nationalism in the Persian Gulf', *Liberation,* XV (1971), 3, 10–15.

67) 'Persian armorial inscriptions', in *Actas IV congresso de estudos árabes e islâmicos 1968,* Lisbon 1971, 573–6.

68) Review of R. Russell and K. Islam, *Ghalib 1797–1869, Vol. 1: Life and Letters,* in *The Aryan Path,* XLI (1971), 4, 195–6.

69) Review of E. H. Palmer, *Oriental Mysticism,* in *The Aryan Path,* XLI (1971), 6, 288.

70) Reviews of G. von Grünebaum, *Classical Islam; The Cambridge History of Islam;* M. Fakhry, *History of Islamic Philosophy; The Fihrist of al-Nadim,* trans. B. Dodge; and O. Pound, *Arabic and Persian Poems,* in *New York Review of Books,* XVI (1971), 7 (April), 51–5.

71) Review of H. M. Balyuzi, *Edward Granville Browne and the Baha'i Faith,* in *Asian Affairs,* 58 (1971), 1 (February), 123.

72) Review of R. Levy, *An Introduction to Persian Literature,* in *JRAS,* 1 (1971), 69–70.

1972

73) 'Recent developments in Persian literature', *Bulletin of the British Association of Orientalists,* 5 (1972), 12–18.

74) Review of M. Rodinson, *Mohammed,* in *New York Review of Books,* XVII (1972), 12 (27 January), 22–5.

Bibliography

75) Review of *Iran Faces the Seventies,* ed. E. Yar-Shater, in
    Iranian Studies, IV (1972), 4, 167–71.

1973

76) 'The 2,500th anniversary of the Persian empire', *Bulletin
    of the British Association of Orientalists,* 6 (1973),
    20–3.

77) Review of H. M. Balyuzi, *Edward Granville Browne and
    the Baha'i Faith,* in *JRAS,* 1 (1972), 70–1.

78) Review of A. Christensen, *Etudes sur le persan con-
    temporain,* in *JRAS,* 2 (1972), 155–6.

78) Review of C.-H. de Fouchécour, *La déscription de la
    nature dans la poésie lyrique persane du XIe siècle,*
    in *JRAS,* 2 (1972), 156–7.

80) Review of H. M. Balyuzi, *'Abd al-Bahā': the Centre of
    the Covenant of Bahā'allāh,* in *JRAS,* 2 (1973),
    166–8.

1974

81) Review of S. H. Nasr, *Sufi Essays,* in *The Aryan Path,*
    XLIV (1974), 5, 228–9.

1975

82) 'The Rubā'ī in early Persian literature', in *The
    Cambridge History of Iran,* Cambridge 1975, IV,
    633–65.

83) 'Sufism and pseudo-Sufism', *Encounter,* XLIV (1975), 5,
    9–17.

84) 'The foundations of Persian prosody and metrics', *Iran,*
    XIII (1975), 75–97.

85) Review of H. Algar, *Mīrzā Malkum Khān,* in *JRAS,* 1
    (1975), 65–7.

86) Review of H. M. Balyuzi, *The Báb: the Herald of the
    Day of Days,* in *JRAS,* 1 (1975), 67.

87) Review of B. Utas, *Ṭarīq al-taḥqīq,* in *JRAS,* 1 (1975),
    64–5.

1976

88) *The Persian Metres,* Cambridge 1976.

89) 'Mountain and plain: contrasts in Persian folk-litera-
    ture', *Folk Narrative Research* (1976), 20, 330–7.

90) 'Family relationships in Persian folk-literature',
    Folklore, 87/2 (1976), 160–6.

91) 'Al-Bīrūnī on the astrolabe', in *Commemorative Volume
    of the Bīrūnī International Congress in Tehran: B.
    English and French Papers,* Tehran 1976, 113–27.

92) Review of *Sufi Studies,* ed. R. Williams, in *Folklore,*
    87/1 (1976), 120–1.

93) Review of *Introduction to Islamic Civilisation,* ed.
    R. M. Savory, in *TLS,* 24 December 1976, 1620.

94) Review of G. M. Wickens (trans.), *Morals Pointed and
    Tales Adorned. The Bustān of Saʿdī,* in *Iranian
    Studies,* ix/1 (1976), 67–75.

1977

95) *The Horoscope of Asadullah Mirza: a Specimen of Nine-
    teenth Century Persian Astrology,* Leiden 1977.

96) Review article, 'No place for the poets', *TLS,* 18 March
    1977, 295.

97) Review of W. M. Miller, *The Baha'i Faith: Its History
    and Teaching,* in *JRAS,* 2 (1976), 157–8.

98) Review of P. Morewedge, *The Metaphysics of Avicenna,*
    in *The Aryan Path,* xlvi (1975), 4, 179.

99) Review of M. H. Tabatabai, *Shiʿite Islam,* in *Expository
    Times,* lxxxviii (1977), 5, 152–3.

1978

100) 'Reza Shah the Great: founder of the Pahlavi dynasty',
     in *Iran Under the Pahlavis,* ed. G. Lenczowski,
     Standford 1978, 1–50.

101) 'The Pahlavi era', in *Persia: History and Heritage,* ed.
     J. A. Boyle, London 1978, 49–64.

102) Review of H. M. Balyuzi, *Muhammad and the Course of
     Islam,* in *JRAS,* 2 (1977), 208.

103) Review of *Twentieth Century Iran,* ed. H. Amirsadeghi,
     in *Maghreb Review,* iii (1978), 5/6, 36–8.

104) Review of C. E. Bosworth, *The Later Ghaznavids,* in
     British Book News, April 1978, 342.

1979

105) 'The Iranian revolution', *International Journal,
     Toronto,* xxxiv/3 (1979), 391–407.

106) 'The literary sources of the taʿziyeh', in *Taʿziyeh: Ritual
     and Drama in Iran,* ed. P. Chelkowski, New York
     1979, 167–81.

107) 'Persian armour inscriptions', in *Islamic Arms and
     Armour,* ed. R. Elgood, London 1979, 5–19.

108) Review of D. Stronach, *Pasargadae,* in *Asian Affairs,*
     x/2 (1979), 197–9.

109) Review of P. W. Avery, *The Rubaʿiyyat of Omar
     Khayyam,* in *British Book News,* November 1979,
     960.

Bibliography

110) Obituary of J. A. Boyle, *Folklore,* 1979/i, 105–6.

1980

111) 'Adīb Pīshāvarī', *EI²*, Supplement 1/2, 41.
112) 'Amīrī', *ibid.,* 73.
113) ''Ārif', *ibid.,* 83–4.
114) 'Ashraf', *ibid.,* 91–2.
115) 'Ḳiṣṣa', *EI²*, v, 197–201.
116) 'The Persian "passion play"', in *Folklore Studies in the 20th Century,* ed. V. J. Newall, London 1981, 188–91.

1981

117) 'The Iranian revolution: triumph or tragedy', in *The Security of the Persian Gulf,* ed. H. Amirsadeghi, London 1981, 231–54.
118) 'Ḳurrat al-'ayn', *EI²*, v, 502 (with D. MacEoin).
119) 'Čay-khāna', *EI²*, Supplement 3/4, 169–70.
120) Review article, 'Fundamentalism in flood'; review of H. Katouzian, *The Political Economy of Modern Iran* and B. Rubin, *Paved with Good Intentions,* in *TLS,* 4091, 28 August 1981, 987.

1982

121) 'Ābādān: history', *Encyclopaedia Iranica,* I, Fasc. 1, 51–3.
122) 'Collecting folktales in Iran', *Folklore,* 93/1 (1982), 98–104.
123) 'The Islamic world', in *Legends of the World,* ed. R. Cavendish, London 1982, 113–24.
124) 'A narrator of folktales from Iran', in *ARV, Scandinavian Yearbook of Folklore 1980,* 36, Uppsala 1983, 201–8.
125) Review of W. Behn, *Islamic Revolution,* in *British Society for Middle Eastern Studies Bulletin,* 8/2 (1981), 150–1.

1983

126) (Ed.) *Bibliographical Guide to Iran,* Brighton and Totowa 1983.
127) *'Adab'* (Persian periodicals), *Encyclopaedia Iranica,* Fasc. 4, 444–5.
128) *''Adālat'* (Persian periodicals), *ibid.,* 447.
129) *'Ādamiyat'* (Persian periodicals), *ibid.,* 448.
130) 'Sufism and pseudo-Sufism', in *Islam in the Modern World,* ed. D. MacEoin and A. al-Shahi, London 1983, 49–56.

Bibliography

131) 'Arthur Emanuel Christensen', *British Society for Middle Eastern Studies Bulletin,* 10/1, 59–68.

132) Reviews of Abu Bakr Mahmud bin Tufail, *The Journey of the Soul* and S.-S. Orbeliani, *A Book of Wisdom and Lies,* in *Asian Affairs,* xiv/1 (February 1983), 88–9.

133) Review of S. C. Roy, *The Birhors: a Little-known Jungle Tribe of Chota Nagpur,* in *Folklore,* 94/1 (1983), 129.

134) 'A royal Timurid nativity book', in *Logos Islamikos: Studia Islamica in honorem George Michael Wickens* (forthcoming).

PART

1

Political History

1

Observations on Nâsir al-Dîn Shah

Nâsir al-Dîn Shah reigned for nearly half a century, from 1264/1848 to 1313/1895. Although by virtue of the length of his rule and the relative abundance of available materials pertaining to his life and time he presents the most vivid picture among the Qajar kings, a full-scale documented biography of him is still lacking. In recent years a number of documents, including memoirs, letters and biographies, have been published which enlighten us further on Nâsir al-Dîn's character and administration. The most extensive, as well as the most informative, of these is Mîrzâ Hasan Khan I'timâd al-Saltana's *Rûznâma-yi Khâtirât*.[1] M. Bâmdâd's short account of Nâsir al-Dîn,[2] which draws heavily on this diary, remains a somewhat uneven, if valuable, sketch.

The latest documents to appear in this field are contained in volume IX of Dr. Qâsim Ghanî's *Yâddâshthâ*, 'Notations', edited by Professor M. J. Mahjûb and published through the commendable efforts of the author's son, Cyrus Ghanî. The volume comprises items of correspondence pertaining to the first decade of Nâsir al-Dîn's reign, notably by Sultân Murâd Mîrzâ Husâm al-Saltana (1233/1818–1300/1883), the thirteenth son of 'Abbâs Mîrzâ and a paternal uncle of Nâsir al-Dîn. He was in charge of the Persian army in the siege and capture of Herat in 1273/1856, which he reluctantly abandoned and ceded to the Afghans following the orders of the government as a result of British intervention. Professor Mahjûb provides a listing of these letters, together with some comments on their significance. A second batch of notes and documents belongs to the latter period of Nâsir al-Dîn's rule, and includes five letters – four of them extensive – from Muhsin Khan Mushîr al-Dawla (c. 1235/1820–1317/1899), who after having been the Persian ambassador in Istanbul for eighteen years was placed in charge of the Ministry of Justice (*Dîvân-khâna-yi 'Adliyya-yi A'zam*) and the Ministry of Commerce in 1309/1891. His letters deal chiefly with the difficulties he encountered in carrying out his charge, especially the paralysing meddling by other divisions of government and men of rank and influence in the administration of justice.

The most interesting documents in the collection, insofar as an assessment of Nâsir al-Dîn's character and conduct is concerned, are a series of hand-written notes by Nâsir al-Dîn containing decrees and comments generally in response to letters and reports presented to him. Of these, fourteen are addressed to Kâmrân Mîrzâ Nâ'ib al-Saltana, his third and favourite son, and four to Muhsin Khan Mushîr al-Dawla. Three entries from the diary of Nâsir al-Dîn's brother, 'Abd al-Samad Mîrzâ 'Izz al-Dawla (1261/1845–1348/1929), also contain critical comments on the Shah's conduct and personal habits.

It may be briefly recalled that, except for the loss of Herat, a general shrinking of Persian borders caused by Russian and British expansionist policies, and a series of Turkoman inroads into Khurasan, Nâsir al-Dîn's long reign was relatively peaceful and free from unsettling external events. Internally, the rise of the Bâb and the persecution of his followers, and the disturbances following the aborted concession of the tobacco monopoly to a British company, were the two notable events threatening the status quo of the social order. The latent development of Persian aspirations, however, and the increasing awakening of a national consciousness among patriots – chiefly as a result of growing contact with the West – were salient features of Persian social and intellectual development during the second half of the nineteenth century; in fact, Nâsir al-Dîn lost his life on account of rising popular discontent.

It is obvious from the materials in the Ghanî volume and elsewhere that Nâsir al-Dîn was by no means devoid of concern about the prestige and good name of the country, the application of justice, and a well-regulated administration. In a note addressed to Kâmrân Mîrzâ[3] he complains about the government's inefficiency in adopting reforms, saying: 'I cannot understand what misfortune has befallen the Iranian state that, however much it tries to bring some order to its affairs and endow its offices and privileges (*imtiyâzât*), etc., whether in the army or elsewhere, it does not succeed'.[4] In a chiding tone in the same note, he shows his displeasure at the proliferation of titles: 'Don't you see that the Persian government's prestige has been ruined through the bestowing of unreasonable (*bîjâ*) titles, offices, and medals (*nishân*)? By God, it has come to the point that no one gives so much as a farthing for your offices, medals and titles. A government whose honours (*iftikhârât*) and offices should sink so low and become so worthless, what dignity and prestige will it have? I wanted to establish a council (*majlis*) and lay a foundation for [the granting] of civilian and military titles and ranks, so as first to do away with intermediaries and pressures and insistences, and so that people would recognise their limits and know that if they want an office or title or medal, a few people should sit down and see if it is fitting, warranted and merited; [if so, then] the government should bestow it, otherwise refuse it. And second, [so that] once an office or title has been granted, people would not subject it to sarcastic remarks (*madmûn na-gûyand*), such as "the government has made such and such a child or good-for-nothing person a brigadier general (*sartîp*), or has given him the title of *iqbâl al-dawla* (the Fortune of the State) or *janâb* (Excellency)," but that they should say that such and such rank was given according to merit and by the approval of [some] twenty notables of the government. I swear to God that if this had not been advertised in the Journal,[5] by now all the attendants (*pîshkhidmat*) and the servants of the private quarters (*farrâsh-i khalvat*) would have received, through intermediaries from the outside or from the women's quarters, the title of *janâb*.' He ends this note with a sullen remark in a sarcastic tone: 'If you want everything to be without dignity and stature as before, that is all right too; let it be as it has been for years'.[6]

In another note to Kâmrân Mîrzâ,[7] he again chides him in a well-intentioned, fatherly fashion for having taken umbrage at some remarks directed to him by the Shah, and confirms his concern for the good working of the government apparatus: 'Some messages were sent to His Excellency the Sipahsâlâr,[8] all for establishing peace among the officers (*nawkarân*) of the government and the Court, [protesting] why they were causelessly at each other's throats, [and requiring] that they join hands and attend to the good working of the government (*nazm-i dawla*).' Again he ends this note with a characteristically sullen remark: 'If it is all right that they should abandon the good working of the government and [their] solidarity (*ittifâq*) and quarrel day and night, very well then, I have nothing to say; all [other] governments are advancing, whereas we should be ruining each other day by day.'

In 1309/1892 Nâsir al-Dîn appointed Muhsin Khan Mushîr al-Dawla as the Minister of Justice in charge of the '*Adâlat-Khâna* (House of Justice), and no doubt he intended him to establish equitable procedures in settling claims and disputes and in the administration of justice. This was when, in an effort to promote more consultation in deciding major issues, he had formed several ministries as well as a Council of Ministers (*Majlis-i Vuzarâ'*).[9] Responding to a letter in which Mushîr al-Dawla declares that he cannot continue in his job if men of rank and influence continue to sabotage his efforts, the Shah writes from Sâva[10] in order to assuage him, saying that his complaints are justified and that had he, the Shah, been in the capital such breaches of justice would not have happened; he promises to strengthen the position of the *Dîvân-Khâna* upon his return. In another note[11] responding to one of Mushîr al-Dawla's reports on the Ministry, the Shah expresses his complete satisfaction at the care exhibited in the affairs of the *Dîvân-Khâna* and asks to be sent such reports regularly.

In a number of other (albeit less significant) matters, Nâsir al-Dîn also shows a sense of propriety as well as concern for the interests, independence, and reputation of the state. From a note to Kâmrân Mîrzâ,[12] it appears that the French Minister in Tehran had requested permission for French to be taught at some private schools. The Shah strongly objects to the idea, which he sees as entailing many problems, and confirms that French may be taught to Persian children only at state schools such as Dâr al-Funûn (the Polytechnic) and the Military School, pointing out that 'otherwise the next day the Catholics and the Protestants will ask for the same thing in other schools in Tehran, Tabriz, Urmia, Khûy, Salmâs, Julfâ in Isfahan, Hamadan, etc., and this will lead to uprising among the people (*shûrish-i 'âmma*).' He unequivocally rejects the request.

In another hand-written note to Kâmrân Mîrzâ,[13] he emphasises that Muslim (Persian) women were not to have relations with Westerners (*farangîhâ*). He approves whole-heartedly of the arrest of a character who seems to have engaged in procuring women for foreigners, ordering his exile to Kirman. 'Another matter,' he writes in the same note, 'which is more important than all this is these women who go to the embassies and frequent the Westerners, and are repeatedly reported in a precise manner (*bâ ism-u rasm*) in secret reports, like Hâjar Qumî, etc. You must appoint persons [to look into this] . . ., and when you learn that a woman has relations with the Westerners, and when she leaves the house of a Westerner, have her seized the next day under some other pretext, [and] order her to be thrown into a sack (*javâl*).' Continuing with a touch of royal wrath and customary arbitrariness, he writes that 'two or three of them should be strangled and killed right in the sacks; others are to be severely punished, fined, and banished from the city once and for all.'

In yet another note to Kâmrân Mîrzâ[14] invoking royal dignity, he disapproves of installing his statue in the streets in front of the Lâlazâr-i Kont,[15] where it might be subjected to disrespectful behaviour. '[Placing] our image (*sûrat*) in the streets and where people, children, etc., come and go,' he writes, 'would eventually occasion some problems and cause regret and rumours. Have the statue removed, have it replaced by a flower-vase, and have it transferred to the hall of your own house or a similar location; it is not desirable in a public place.' Obviously the Shah was not unaware of the people's discontent, and the abuse that his statue could be subjected to in public places; this hand-written note was probably composed after the uprising which followed the tobacco monopoly fiasco.

What we can infer of Nâsir al-Dîn's interest in reform, the good name of the state, the establishment of a viable legal system and the introduction of modernising methods from this collection of letters is confirmed by other sources and documents that we possess on his reign.[16] His good intentions can be seen in a number of his actions as Shah: his support of Amîr-i Kabîr's reformist acts in the early years of his rule despite continual intrigues against the Amîr by courtiers and dignitaries (especially Mahd-i 'Ulyâ, the Shah's mother); the formation of the Council of Ministers in 1275/1859 and the State Council in 1288/1871; the establishment of justice boxes (*sandûq-i 'adâlat*) in 1283/1866 in which people

6

could drop their complaints;[17] his choice of the reform-minded and able Mîrzâ Husayn Khan Mushîr al-Dawla as Prime Minister in 1288/1871;[18] his support of a number of modernising efforts following his trips to Europe in 1290/1873, 1295/1878 and 1306/1889; his formation of the Cossack Brigade in 1299/1882; his regular visits to the Dâr al-Funûn and his encouragement of its staff (before he became disappointed in the lack of absolute loyalty among its graduates); his support of a fairly extensive publication programme and finally, his despatch of students to Europe to learn modern sciences.[19]

The benefits of all such measures were, however, subject to qualification. Their efficacy was limited by the Qajar system of government and the Shah's whims and idiosyncrasies. Their purposes were often subverted by adverse conditions prevailing at court, and at times the Shah himself acted against them. Although a number of modernising measures were carried out during Nâsir al-Dîn's reign, and a series of commendable reforms was instituted by Amîr-i Kabîr, Husayn Khan Mushîr al-Dawla, 'Alî Khan Amîn al-Dawla and even Amîn al-Sultân and others, the net result of his rule does not measure up to the opportunity that Persia was afforded in the half-century of relative peace during his kingship. In fact, Persia's inner erosion and moral and cultural decline continued under his rule; his reformist measures were hardly adequate enough to stop a decline which had its roots in Persia's past. In fact, Nâsir al-Dîn's long reign only exacerbated the realities of Persian social and political conditions. Oppression of the people and abuse of power and privileges were accelerated in the last decade of Nâsir al-Dîn's reign, when he had lost heart and began to leave most matters to 'Alî Asghar Amîn al-Sultân (1275/1858–1325/1907), a shrewd and able courtier who was indifferent to reform, Kâmrân Mîrzâ Nâ'ib al-Saltana, a mediocre and greedy prince in charge of the War Ministry and the northern provinces, and Mas'ûd Mîrzâ Zill al-Sultân, his eldest son and an avid despot, thus paving the way for the overthrow of the dynasty.

Nâsir al-Dîn did not have the ability or the dedication of his grandfather, 'Abbâs Mîrzâ, but neither was he as weak and uninformed as his father, Muhammad Shah, or his son and successor, Muzaffar al-Dîn. Nevertheless, and in spite of his good intentions and reformist measures, Nâsir al-Dîn's primary interest in life lay in having a good time rather than a good government. Although he made some sensible decisions – when they did not conflict with the interests of his purse or his power – he hardly ever followed them through. He lacked application and tenacity of purpose where reform, social justice, and good government were concerned. His absorbing passions were eating, drinking, sex, hunting, riding, and money;[20] his dedication to them is referred to in a number of entries in the Diary of I'timâd al-Saltana. We read, for instance, the following in the entry for 6 Ramadân 1302: 'Today I went to the Court. At lunch suddenly

[His Majesty] had a spell of dizziness. He was very frightened. May God preserve [him]; this is all the effect of Shiraz wines, too much sexual intercourse (*jimâ'*) and senseless riding. . . . At his age, excess is harmful in all matters, especially in these three things. It was decided to apply leeches on Monday.' He was gluttonous and ate ceaselessly;[21] a sidelight on his gastronomical delights is provided by a hand-written note[22] addressed to Kâmrân Mîrzâ, in which the Shah acknowledges with profuse acclaim the receipt of some delicious pineapples sent to him by the prince. He ends the note with: 'I hope (*inshâ' Allâh*) you will be sending this good fruit repeatedly in our presence.' He was by no means, however, a gourmet, and was apparently satisfied with simple food.[23] I'timâd al-Saltana refers in a number of entries to his drinking (mostly Shiraz wine and Bordeaux),[24] and Bâmdâd has published a number of photographs showing the Shah in a drunken state.[25]

His passion for women, which found expression in the large number of his wives and the extent of his harem, was outdone only by his great-grandfather, Fath 'Alî Shah. Eighty-five of his wives survived him, and his harem probably had close to 1,600 persons, including employees and eunuchs.[26] During his third trip to Europe, since he could not take any of his Muslim wives with him (veiling being a problem),[27] from Moscow he ordered his ambassador to Istanbul (Mîrza Muhsin Khan, Mu'în al-Mulk, whom he later made Minister of Justice) to purchase two Circassian concubines and have them clad as men and sent to him.[28] After the ascendancy of Amîn al-Sultân and the Shah's relaxation of his interest in reform and the routine of government, his indulgence of his private interests and hobbies increased.

Enriching himself remained a focus of attention all his life, and often coloured both his foreign and domestic dealings. The concessions he granted, the appointments he made, and the privileges he conferred on relatives, courtiers and men of means were often prompted by the prospect of gifts – both in money and material goods – which he expected and received.[29] I'timâd al-Saltana mentions numerous instances of this,[30] sometimes with a sense of shame and embarrassment. Neither did Nâsir al-Dîn shrink from claiming some of the wealth of his rich appointees once they fell from favour.[31] When Qamar al-Saltana, the wife of his former Prime Minister, Husayn Khan Sipahsâlâr, died in 1309/1892, the Shah lost no time in returning to the capital and ordering her property sealed; he knew of her excellent jewellery, which he appropriated together with a large number of gold coins.[32] Earlier, he had taken hold of some of the wealth of her husband, who had died in 1298/1881 while in disfavour. The Shah used to carry a 70-carat diamond which had belonged to Sipahsâlâr in his pocket and play with it. For years he entertained a craze for extracting gold, and later precious stones, from Persian mountains and spent a great deal of time examining various sample stones.[33]

An account of Nâsir al-Dîn's passions would not be complete without a mention of his inordinate and almost unaccountable attachment to Malîjak, 'Azîz al-Sultân, a nephew of his favourite wife Amîna Aqdas. His craze for this spoiled and wanton boy of rustic origins, which has been discussed by various authors[34] and forms one of the most bizarre chapters of Qajar history, eloquently mirrors the wantonness of autocratic rule. It is clear that nothing could quite retain the Shah's attention when Malîjak was involved. He was made a brigadier general (*sartîp*) at the age of eight. In some official ceremonies he preceded the Prime Minister; his retinue, pomp, and fanfare were a replica of – and second only to – the King's. Nâsir al-Dîn betrothed his daughter Akhtar al-Dawla to him when she was eight.[35] Dignitaries had to pay homage to him, on account of the Shah, even though he was hated by all. Mîrzâ Ridâ Kirmânî – who shot Nâsir al-Dîn – mentioned him in the course of his interrogation as an example of corruption and the waste of the country's revenues.

An autocrat brought up in the monarchical tradition, Nâsir al-Dîn followed his wishes and whims with little restraint. Although a fairly sensible man most of the time, with a good measure of royal dignity, and rather clever at manipulating his courtiers and holding the reins of power, nevertheless his pursuit of pleasure showed a childlike directness and impatience. I'timâd al-Saltana shows us an instance of this adolescent attitude when he writes that one afternoon, the Shah awoke him from his siesta to inform him proudly that he had shot a leopard; he then cancelled his overnight stay, had his whole train packed up, and hastened back to the capital in order to show off his prowess to the members of his harem.[36] The unrestrained affection and favours and the astonishing concessions he made to Malîjak provide another glaring example of this aspect of his character.

His reasonable and reformist decisions in state matters were frequently undermined by his own capricious and arbitary acts. His above-quoted admonition to Kâmrân Mîrzâ about the necessity of granting titles on the basis of rules and regulations must be viewed in light of his own contrary practice. He had named, for instance, that same Kâmrân Mîrzâ as governor of Tehran at the age of six, and made him viceroy at the age of eleven, commander-in-chief of the army at thirteen, and honoured him with the title of *amîr-i kabîr* at fourteen.[37] Malîjak was made an *amîr tûmân* (major-general)[38] at the age of nine, with all the paraphernalia which accrued to the rank; and the respected Finance Minister, Mîrzâ Yûsuf Âshtiyânî, had his seven-year-old son Hasan appointed to his own post with the title of *mustawfî al-mamâlik*. I'timâd al-Saltana, when recording the conferment of brigadier-generalship (*sartipî*) and the title of Mu'tamad al-Sultân on the eight-year-old Malîjak, makes the following comment: 'His Majesty has defecated on [all] ranks and privileges;

may God keep him in good health.'[39]

The above remarks are confirmed by the critical account given of Nâsir al-Dîn's personal habits and idiosyncrasies by his uncle, 'Abd al-Samad Mîrzâ 'Izz al-Dawla, in his diaries:[40] 'I very much tried to turn away my pen from this subject and not approach it, [but] the inappropriate manners and movements [that I have observed] did not let me. An age like this, when there are no criteria (*qâ'ida*),[41] and everybody's job depends on flattery and visits to rootless and shameless people . . . deserves reproach. The king is busy day and night living in pleasure (*'aysh-u nûsh*). His attention (*himmat*) is devoted to the care of his several cats;[42] in his trips they are taken along in cages. Hunting is his utmost desire. He avoids (*vahshat dârad*)[43] meeting people and does not like them.[44] Except in some festivals (*a'yâd*) there are no *salâms* (official group audiences), and even such audiences last [only] a quarter of an hour. . . .[45] He is exceedingly infatuated with women. Every day he marries one; currently he has fifty wives. His conversation and inclination is with roguish (*lutî-manish*) and inane servants or else young pages (*ghulâm bachcha*). He has no desire for the companionship of other than them. He is excessively desirous of food and victuals; especially fruits, which he eats incessantly. He is very much given to primping himself up (*khud-ârâ*). At all times he is accompanied by a mirror and a comb, which [the servants] carry around with him in gardens or rooms. I swear to the divine pure Essence that I have written down [only] a few of the many of his manners and attitude . . .' He ends this entry with the following remark: 'It is a pity that the king has no eyes for truth; it is not significant affairs which are the subject of his interest and preoccupation; he has contented himself with some trifles (*juz'iyyât*)'.

Perhaps this judgement of Nâsir al-Dîn Shah is too harsh; it may have been coloured by personal grievances on the part of 'Izz al-Dawla, who was somewhat neglected and whose own record is not above reproach.[46] The verdicts passed on Nâsir al-Dîn have, as expected, depended on the writers' viewpoints and criteria. Hidâyat, with an eye on his attempts at modernisation, his enlightened notes and decrees, and some of the digni-fied and lenient aspects of his character, considers him 'a great man, a lover of his nation and a patriot',[47] whose aspirations for Iran were dashed by his enemies and the insidious intentions of Britain and Russia. Bâmdâd, on the other hand, draws a completely negative picture of him, showing him as a pleasure-seeking despot with no commitment to remedying the ills of Persian society but rather subverting the cause of needed reform by his superficiality and capricious decisions. 'Abd Allâh Mustawfî comes perhaps closer to the truth by showing Nâsir al-Dîn as a man both of foibles and strengths; somewhat against the general trend followed by historians of the Pahlavi period, he draws attention also to his efforts at reform.[48]

In assessing Nâsir al-Dîn Shah's character and achievements, it is helpful to bear two points in mind. One is that while the mettle and the ideals of an autocratic monarch have an important bearing on the affairs of his nation, much also depends on the nation itself. The other is that a Shah, like others, goes through changes and develops over the course of a lifetime. Nâsir al-Dîn appears to have started as a promising youth, showing himself adept at developing an enthusiasm for modernisation, the rule of law, and the dignity of the state. Militating against the fulfilment of such wishes were the entrenched political and administrative structure of Qajar society, the Shah's suspicious nature, the resistance offered by the conservative elements of his court and the clergy, the constant intervention of Russia and Britain in Persian affairs, and finally the Shah's love of personal pleasures. Towards the end of his reign he began to show signs of disappointment, disheartening, and weariness,[49] and allowed the business of state to drift according to the dubious wisdom of his shrewd, self-seeking, and extravagant Prime Minister, 'Alî Asghar Amîn al-Sultân.

It is Nâsir al-Dîn's image from this period of his rule, full of abuse and corruption, which is most frequently remembered in the histories; it was the spreading of popular discontent which arose from worsening oppression and increasing disillusionment which, in the end, cut his life short and paved the way for the Constitutional Revolution.

NOTES AND REFERENCES

1. Ed. I. Afshâr, Tehran 1350/1971.
2. M. Bamdâd, *Sharh-i hâli rijâl-i Irân dar qarn-i 12 va 13 va 14 hijrî* (Tehran 1968-72), IV, 246-325.
3. Q. Ghanî, *Yâddâshthâ* (London 1982), IX, 414-5. Nâsir al-Dîn's style of writing in these notes is plain, sometimes colloquial, and not always immune from stylistic or grammatical lapses.
4. Cf. an expression of total despair by him in this respect as cited by Mahdî Qulî Hidâyat, *Khâtirât va khatarât*, Tehran 1950, 74.
5. The *Rûznâma-yi 'Illiya-yi Irân*, the official journal published by the government.
6. This and the following notes were written when the Shah was encouraged to institute reforms by his Prime Minister, Mîrzâ Husayn Khan Mushîr al-Dawla Sipahsâlâr (1243/1827-1298/1881).
7. Ghanî, *op. cit.*, 412-14.
8. Mîrzâ Husayn Khan Mushîr al-Dawla, the Prime Minister.
9. See 'Abbâs Iqbâl, *Târîkh-i Mufassal-i Îrân*, ed. M. Dabîrsiyâqî, Tehran 1968, 832; Bâmdâd, *op. cit.*, 259-60.
10. Ghanî, *op. cit.*, 422.
11. *Ibid.*, 445.
12. *Ibid.*, 409.
13. *Ibid.*, 409-10.
14. *Ibid.*, 411.

15. Gardens named after the Comte de Monte Forte, an Italian officer who entered the employment of Iran in 1878 and headed at different times the police and the gendarmerie (among other officers) for twelve years; see Bâmdâd, *op. cit.*, 273, n.1.
16. For a judicious presentation and critical evaluation of reformist measures under Nâsir al-Dîn, see S. Bakhash, *Iran: Monarchy, Bureaucracy and Reform under the Qajars, 1858-96,* London 1978, chs 2 and 3.
17. See 'Abd Allâh Mustawfî, *Sharh-i Zindagânî-yi Man,* Tehran n.d. [1964], ı, 135ff.
18. See particularly Nâsir al-Dîn's letters to the Sipahsâlâr when he was trying to reinstate him in office, in Mahmûd Farhâd Mu'tamid, *Sipahsâlâr-i A'zam* (Tehran 1947) *apud* Bakhash, *op. cit.*, 186ff.
19. See I'timâd al-Saltana's Diary, entry of 14 Jumâdâ ıı, 1307.
20. He was also interested in reading novels, history books and newspapers, or rather having them read to him. Cf. ı. Afshar's introduction to I'timâd al-Saltana's Diary, 22, for a list of the books he read.
21. See Bâmdâd, *op. cit.*, 265-7.
22. Ghanî, *op. cit.*, 412.
23. See, for example, I'timâd al-Saltana's Diary, the entry of 3 Jumâdâ ıı, 1298.
24. Cf. the entries of 29 Rajab, 1301; 2 Sha'bân, 1304; 21 Ramadân, 1306. He must have been a heavy smoker of the *qalyân* (nargila), judging by the number of photographs showing him smoking it. He also used snuff.
25. *Op. cit.*, 256-7 and 260.
26. Some estimates are as high as 3,000; see Bâmdâd, *op. cit.*, 248ff., and G. N. Curzon, *Persia and the Persian Question,* London 1892, ı, 410-1.
27. I'timâd al-Saltana's Diary, the entry of 13 Sha'bân, 1306; Bamdad, *op. cit.*, 278.
28. *Ibid.*, the entry of 18 Ramadân 1306.
29. See Bâmdâd, *op. cit.*, 308ff., for some examples.
30. Afshâr lists a number of these cases in his introduction to the *Rûznâma-yi Khâtirât,* 20.
31. See, for instance, Bâmdâd, *op. cit.*, ı, 422ff.
32. I'timâd al-Saltana's Diary, the entry of 18 Jumâdâ ıı, 1309.
33. *Ibid.* See the index under *ma'dan*.
34. Most fully in Bâmdâd, *op. cit.*, ııı, 20-50. See also Curzon, *op. cit.*, ı, 400.
35. See Mustawfî, *op. cit.*, ı, 498-500, and Bâmdâd, *op. cit.*, ııı, 42, for the extravaganza of their wedding.
36. The entry of 16 Jumâdâ ıı, 1298.
37. See Bâmdâd, *op. cit.*, ııı, 150-1.
38. One year after he had been made a brigadier-general. Curzon translates this somewhat exaggeratedly as field-marshal (*op. cit.*, ı, 400).
39. The entry of 1 Jumâdâ ıı, 1303.

40. Ghanî, *op. cit.*, 475-6.
41. Lit., 'basis'.
42. Curzon notes that Amîna Aqdas was in charge of his beloved cat before she was given weightier responsibilities in the harem (*op. cit.*, I, 410).
43. Lit., 'is terrified'.
44. Could be understood also as 'does not like it'.
45. This is in sharp contrast to M. Q. Hidâyat's remark which must pertain to the earlier part of his reign: 'Nâsir al-Dîn Shah wished to be in contact with all classes. Every day a group of the bureaucratic class would gather in the Gulistân Garden Palace; when the Shah emerged from the private quarters, they would make a bow, and the Shah would address some' (*Khâtirât va khatarât*, 124).
46. See Bâmdâd, *op. cit.*, 268ff.
47. *Op. cit.*, 131. He chooses to forget, however, the cruel treatment of the Bâbîs by Nâsir al-Dîn's consent and encouragement (cf. Ghanî, *op. cit.*, 411) and finds extenuating excuses for his hanging 9 soldiers who had inadvertently caused the horses of his carriage to shy (*Khâtirât*, 130).
48. Mustawfî, *op. cit.*, I, 111, 115-16, 147.
49. *Ibid.*, 490.

2

The failure of reform:
the Prime Ministership of Amîn al-Dawla, 1897–8

In April 1897, a year after his accession to the throne, Muzaffʳⁿ al-Dîn Shah named Mîrzâ 'Alî Khan Amîn al-Dawla as his prime minister.[1] Amîn al-Dawla's tenure was brief. Within 14 months, he was ousted from office. Yet his prime ministership is not without its interest. Amîn al-Dawla was a member of one of the wealthy and important bureaucratic families in Qajar Iran. His father, Muhammad Khan Majd al-Mulk, had been private secretary to Muhammad Shah's mother and, under Nâsir al-Dîn Shah, a minister of pensions and endowments and a member of the *majlis-i shawra-yi kubrâ,* the shah's consultative council. Amîn al-Dawla himself, for over 20 years, was private secretary to Nâsir al-Dîn Shah. He held the ministry of posts as a sinecure, which he later passed on to his son. He served also as minister of pensions and endowments, a position he passed on to his brother. He filled numerous other important positions.

Amîn al-Dawla even in his own time was regarded as an enlightened official. He was familiar with Europe; he was an advocate of change in the system of government along European lines. In the 1880's, in close collaboration with Malkam Khan, he had sought to induce Nâsir al-Dîn Shah to introduce governmental reforms. He was among the pioneers of the movement for educational reform in pre-constitutional Iran. He numbered Shaykh Hadî Najmâbâdî and Sayyid Muhammad Tabâtabâ'î, two leading constitutionalists among the 'ulamâ' as his friends.

His appointment as prime minister marked the end (albeit temporarily) of Amîn al-Sultân's long tenure of the post, a period during which Amîn al-Sultân's increasing commitment to the *status quo* effectively ruled out any possibility of change. His appointment also saw the return, perhaps for the first time since the dismissal of Mîrzâ Husayn Khan Mushîr al-Dawla from the prime ministership in 1873, of the 'reform party'[2] to power. His achievements as prime minister were meagre. His many reforms proved abortive. These measures, given hindsight, were more in the nature of palliatives, far removed from the fundamental changes that would have been necessary to ward off the revolution that came within a decade of Amîn al-Dawla's fall from power.

Nevertheless, his brief ministry deserves study for at least three reasons. First, it provides an insight into the fragmented nature of the Qajar ruling classes at the end of the nineteenth century and the irresponsible – and, for the Qajar, the ultimately disastrous – character of court and bureaucratic politics in the years just preceding the constitutional revolution. Secondly, his ministry provides a glimpse of the powerful currents that were already sweeping society. Finally, it indicates the measures which the most enlightened men within the Qajar ruling classes considered necessary to stave off disaster. That these measures proved totally inadequate confirmed the growing belief that significant change could not come from within the government.

Amîn al-Dawla's failure was due to the interplay of several factors: the untrammelled authority of the crown; the factionalism of a bureaucracy committed primarily to personal gain and interest; powerful vested interests which opposed reform; great-power rivalry which – whatever the particular intentions of the two adversaries – was in the final analysis divisive and debilitating in its impact on Iran. Then there was the man himself. Amîn al-Dawla understood better than most of his countrymen the urgent necessity for reform. But he was linked by a complex skein of marriage and family ties to the other great bureaucratic families, and, later, to the royal family itself. His considerable financial interests were woven into the fabric of the existing governmental system. It is hardly surprising that he did not effect a cleaner break with the past.

The 'Turk' party

Muzaffar al-dîn Shah's accession in May 1896 had two immediate effects: it placed a much weaker ruler on the throne and it injected a new element – the 'Turk' or 'Tabriz' party – into the factions competing in Tehran for the privileges of office. Nâsir al-Dîn Shah, by the close of his reign, had become a much less effective ruler than he had been at its beginning. Nevertheless, he was a strong Shah whose authority was not often questioned. Muzaffar al-Dîn was, by contrast, inexperienced and weak. As crown prince, he was already held in public contempt. 'I am told,' the British minister, Sir Mortimer Durand, wrote a year before Muzaffar al-Dîn's accession, in a commentary on Nâsir al-Dîn Shah's three sons, 'that according to the politicians of the teashops, the old lion of Persia [Nâsir al-Dîn] will leave behind him when he dies a panther, a fox, and an ass. The Zil-es-Sultan, cruel and treacherous, is the panther; the Naib-es-Saltaneh, who has the reputation of being a sneak and a coward, is the fox; the ass is the Valiahd [Muzaffar al-Dîn].'[3]

Although only 43 when he became Shah, Muzaffar al-Dîn was ailing in health. Thunderstorms sent him terror-stricken to his cellars. He managed to turn every attempt at serious discussion into a conversation about hunting rifles and shooting excursions. When not hunting, he liked to take rifle practice by firing at his courtiers' *kulâhs,* or hats. His long governorship of Azerbaijan was characterised primarily by its ineptness. Effective control of the province was often entrusted by Nâsir al-Dîn Shah to other hands.[4]

While his courtiers amassed great fortunes, he was not a wealthy man and squandered what he had by an over-zealous generosity. The Austrian instructor to his troops in Tabriz, General Wagner, told the British consul-general that 'in his own palace he had barely the necessities of every-day life, and lived literally from hand to mouth'. He was already in debt as crown prince and at his accession had to postpone going to the capital until money to pay the troops and to finance the southward journey could be found. These financial difficulties led to a rapid depletion of the treasury once Muzaffar al-Dîn arrived at the capital.

Around him in Tabriz had grown up a sizeable court of officials and retainers in whose hands the crown prince was a virtual prisoner. Though its members would at times act in concert against 'outsiders', they were split up into two or three great factions, the members in each group being linked together by a complex network of blood and family ties and other relationships.[5]

One of these factions was led by 'Abd al-Husayn Mîrzâ Farmânfarmâ, a cousin, son-in-law and brother-in-law of Muzaffar al-Dîn's. A Qajar prince, he had married a daughter of the crown prince, while Muzaffar al-Dîn had married Farmânfarmâ's sister. A second faction was led by 'Abd al-Majîd Mîrzâ 'Ayn al-Dawla, grandson of Fath 'Alî Shah and another of Muzaffar al-Dîn's sons-in-law. By far the largest, and for a time the most powerful, faction centred on the Tabâtabâ'î family of Azerbaijan. Members of this family had amassed considerable wealth by farming *khâlisa* land in the Azerbaijan area, where many villages had come into their direct possession. They had also established a formidable corner on grain. Their grain-hoarding led in 1895 to large-scale riots in Tabriz.

The leader of the Tabâtabâ'î clan, Mîrzâ Rafî' Nâzim al-'Ulamâ', had managed to secure for members of his family many of the important posts in the crown prince's court. A host of these relatives – brothers, sons-in-law, nephews, cousins – and other retainers were to be found in every branch of the crown prince's service. Mîrzâ Rafî' himself acted as Muzaffar al-Dîn Mîrzâ's principal adviser; a brother was his private secretary; two other brothers alternated between the crown prince's court and ambassadorships in Constantinople and St Petersburg; a son-in-law, 'Abd al-Rahîm Qâ'im Maqâm, was for many years governor of the province; Qâ'im Maqâm's own son-in-law was for some time *Beglerbegi* of Tabriz; other members of the family held posts in the Azerbaijan army, in the crown prince's secretariat and in the foreign ministry office at Tabriz.

All the three great factions were linked together by marriage ties. The factions were thus to a degree unstable. They constituted a number of 'poles' around which members of the court clustered in a series of shifting alliances. This situation not only further fragmented the bureaucracy once the 'Turk' party arrived in Tehran. It also made the Azerbaijanis susceptible to advances from the rival factions in the capital – a factor which was to prove relevant both in Amîn al-Dawla's appointment as prime minister and his later dismissal.

Almost this entire court joined the new Shah when he left Tabriz for Tehran in June, each official determined to be close at hand when the important posts were distributed in the capital by Muzaffar al-Dîn. The frenzied nature of this determination and the atmosphere of the Shah's camp on the southward journey were graphically described by Cecil Wood, the British consul-general in Tabriz, who accompanied the royal suite. Initially it was intended that the Shah should spend the night of the 7th at Yaftabad, six miles outside the capital, and make a ceremonial entry into Tehran on the morning of 8 June. Amîn al-Sultân, however, fearing for the Shah's life, secretly arranged for Muzaffar al-Dîn to proceed directly and quietly to Tehran from Yaftabad on the 7th leaving the rest of the camp behind. On 7 June, Wood and his Russian counterpart arrived at Yaftabad to find that the Shah had already gone:

> On the Shah's sudden decision becoming known all previous order ceased. Everybody, even the mule drivers, seemed to be animated with but one insane desire, and that was to enter Tehran with His Imperial Majesty. The cavalry actually charged along the road with loose reins, and the rush of empty carriages, which had been abandoned by their owners for the greater freedom and safety of the saddle, became appalling. . . . My Russian colleague's carriage and mine were soon separated by struggling companies, which the Ain-ed-Dowleh and the Hakim-ul-Mulk, both on horseback and abandoned by their attendants, vainly endeavoured to hold back.[6]

The 'Turks' in office

Upon his accession and while still at Tabriz, Muzaffar al-Dîn had confirmed Amîn al-Sultân in his post as *sadr-i aʿzam*. Almost alone among Iranian officials, Amîn al-Sultân had at Nâsir al-Dîn Shah's death maintained a cool head, prevented disorder at the capital and, with the support of the British and Russian ministers, ensured a smooth transfer of power. But with the appearance of the Shah's entourage in the capital, two parallel struggles got under way. Amîn al-Sultân sought to consolidate his own position by maintaining as extensive a control as possible over the administration. At the same time, the Tabriz party worked to secure for themselves the lucrative positions that had long counted as the prime minister's prerogatives.

17

Initially, Amîn al-Sultân's position appeared unshaken. Kamrân Mîrzâ, the new Shah's brother, lost his highly profitable position as minister of war and as governor of Tehran. Amîn al-Dawla, the *sadr-i a'zam*'s chief rival and a candidate for the prime ministership, was sent to Tabriz as *vazîr* to the new crown prince. 'Ayn al-Dawla, a close confidant to the shah, was sent to semi-exile as governor of Mazandaran. Amîn al-Sultân did make some concessions to the newcomers.[7] Several court positions, the governorship of Tehran and, eventually, the governorship of Fars, went to the Tabriz party. However, these slim pickings did not satisfy the 'Turks'. A move to oust the prime minister quickly gathered force.

The leader of this movement was the Farmânfarmâ.[8] He was made governor of Tehran and given the command of six regiments. But his ambition was to become minister of war, Sardâr-i Akram, a post which Amîn al-Sultân retained in his own hands, naming his son-in-law as commander-in-chief. Farmânfarmâ was able to form a powerful coalition against the *sadr-i a'zam* by uniting several disparate elements: members of the Tabriz party, several of the prime minister's enemies such as Kâmrân Mîrzâ, Amîn al-Dawla and Mushîr al-Dawla, and important older bureaucrats like Mukhbir al-Dawla. He received support from the harem through his sister, Hazrat 'Ulyâ, the new Shah's favourite wife.[9]

Amîn al-Sultân's position was further weakened by the financial situation.[10] In the disorder following the change of rulers, and possibly because of Amîn al-Sultân's own uncertain position, provincial governors held back the revenue. The excessive corruption of the prime minister's brother, Amîn al-Mulk, at the treasury, and Amîn al-Sultân's own indiscreet drinking appear to have been used against him.[11] On 24 November, the Shah dismissed Amîn al-Sultân, permitting him to spend his exile in Qum. The Shah did not immediately appoint a new *Sadr-i a'zam*. Instead, he constituted the ministers into a loose cabinet, that began to meet, but without regularity, in December.[12]

The new cabinet was a patchwork ministry and was not designed to last. As Durand observed, 'It seems doubtful that the Tabriz party will be satisfied with their share of the posts . . . and as the combination had nothing more in common than a wish to upset the Sadr-i-Azam, further intrigue may be expected.'[13]

In the meantime, the Tabrizis, 'like hungry vultures fallen on the carcass of the kingdom.'[14] set about lining their pockets. The Shah was influenced to confer recklessly high pensions and salaries on his favourites, while Farmânfarmâ, Hâkim al-Mulk and others secured the farms of valuable *khâlisa* land at ridiculously low prices, often at a fraction of even the nominal value.[15] There was a purge of the middle ranks of the bureaucracy, as the new ministers sought to place their favourites in desirable posts or to make money by selling positions.[16] Although at his accession Muzaffar al-Dîn announced he would refrain from the time-honoured practice of putting up provincial governments for sale, his courtiers freely engaged in the practice. The appointment of wholly incompetent governors exceeded even the usual scale. 'If there was a madman who wanted a Governorship and had the money,' one notable told the British chargé, Charles Hardinge, 'he would get it'.[17]

In this scramble, the most prominent figure was Farmânfarmâ, the man whom Col. H. Picot, the British Military Attaché, had described as one of Britain's two 'best friends in Persia'.[18] It was at Farmânfarmâ's request that, after the fall of Amîn al-Sultân, Durand called on the new foreign minister even before the cabinet had been received by the Shah, as a mark of British support for the incoming cabinet.[19]

Farmânfarmâ proved the most avaricious of the new ministers. He demanded money for appointments not only in his own ministry but for appointments in other departments as well.[20] When the former treasury minister, Amîn al-Mulk, was arrested and was being squeezed for a fine of £200,000, Durand wrote, the question was settled

> by the payment by the Amin ul-Mulk of a sum of 300,000 tomans (£60,000), the transfer of a valuable village near Tehran from the estates of the Amin ul-Mulk to the sister of the Firman Firma and wife of the Shah, and by the distribution of some 25,000 tomans (£5,000) amongst various high officials of the State.[21]

Farmânfarmâ intrigued against Kamran Mîrzâ and his cabinet colleagues.[22] He interfered in the affairs of every department.[23] He sought to weaken the Cossack Brigade, whose commander was an ally of Amîn al-Sultân's; and according to one source, he on several occcasions sought to have the former *sadr-i a'zam* murdered.[24] These various activities now resulted in a coalition directed against Farmânfarmâ. The Shah was urged to appoint a strong prime minister. In March, in the teeth of Farmânfarmâ's opposition,[25] Amîn al-Dawla was recalled from Azerbaijan to head a new cabinet.

Amîn al-Dawla in office: the finances

Upon coming into office, Amîn al-Dawla addressed himself to the many problems facing the country: in revenue administration and the administration of the mint and the customs, and in the assertion of central control at a time when the government's authority seemed to be breaking down. The most pressing question facing the country was the parlous state of the finances. The £500,000 debt incurred as a result of the cancellation of the tobacco regie had imposed an intolerable burden on the government. As Durand pointed out in 1895, there was striking agreement between a budget deficit then averaging £50,000 a year and the annual regie debt repayment of £40,000.[26]

A second factor was the perennial one of court extravagance. Already under Nâsir al-Dîn Shah mounting difficulties had necessitated the sale of *khâlisa* land;[27] the pension lists had grown; and the public debt had been increased by borrowing from the Imperial Bank of Persia. The reckless granting of pensions and the alienation of *khâlisa* land has already been mentioned. Large withdrawals were made from available funds shortly after Muzaffar al-Dîn Shah's accession. A sum of £60,000 had been borrowed from the Imperial Bank to finance the new Shah's journey from Tabriz to Tehran. This had to be repaid, along with £125,000 in older government debts owed to the bank. Between £80,000 and £120,000 were paid to the bank to cover the recall of copper coin.[28]

Thirdly, the tax collecting machinery appears to have broken down. The disorders following Nâsir al-Dîn Shah's assassination, the weakness of the new government and the irresponsible factional rivalries of officials in the capital encouraged governors to withhold tax revenues. The rapid turnover in governors, even before they had settled their accounts, and the general disorder, aggravated the situation. According to Mustawfî and Kosogovskii, the failure of the revenues to come in is attributable to a general collapse of central authority.[29] Kosogovskii adds that the non-payment of troops led the soldiers to transfer their allegiance to provincial governors and local commanders.[30] The government thus lost even the limited coercive power it had previously possessed.

Amîn al-Dawla sought to deal with this situation by changes in the administration of the customs, the mint and the financial system, and by securing a foreign loan. For the reorganisation of the customs, he turned to foreign administrators. A team of three ranking members of the Belgian customs department were employed, and arrived in April. They proposed a plan to abolish the farming of the customs, centralise customs administration directly under the government, abolish differentials in duties paid by Iranian and foreign merchants, establish a uniform five per cent duty for all merchandise, and eliminate the internal *octroi* or gate tolls.[31]

Amîn al-Dawla resigned before the Belgian plan could be carried out. But the soundness of the scheme, and the losses incurred by the government under the previous arrangement, are evident from the rapid rise in revenues under the new administration. Amîn al-Sultân, as customs farmer, paid the Shah £200,000 annually and was estimated to pocket another £50,000 himself. In 1900, just a year after the new administration went partially into effect, customs revenues stood at between £350,000 and £400,000.[32]

The mint, also farmed, was one of the major causes of the country's financial ills.[33] In the second half of Nâsir al-Dîn Shah's reign the mint was almost invariably in the hands of Amîn al-Sultân or his friend and ally, Amîn al-Zarb, a wealthy and enterprising merchant. The two men paid the Shah a rent of 25,000 tomans a year and made a large profit by issuing defective silver coin and excessive amounts of copper coin. The Shah's avarice further aggravated the situation. In 1893, he raised the cost of the farm of the mint to 125,000 tomans a year. As the Imperial Bank manager, Joseph Rabino, pointed out at the time, it was impossible to run the mint profitably at such a high rent without issuing a disastrously large amount of copper coin.[34]

The depreciation in the value of silver and copper coin rapidly accelerated. The silver *kran*, worth 29 *krans* to the pound sterling in 1893 fell to 50 *krans* to the pound in 1896. (The depreciation of silver coin was also due to the fall in international silver prices.) The depreciation of copper was even more severe. Nominally set at 20 *shâhîs* to the silver *kran*, the exchange value fell to 40, 50 and even 60 *shâhîs* to the *kran*. Since copper was the universal medium of exchange of the lower classes, and the coin in which the troops were paid, the effect was especially damaging on those who could least afford it.

Periodically, commissions would be convened, the mint farmers taken to task, copper called in, or its further issue forbidden altogether. The results were always the same. A period of slight improvement would be followed by further clandestine issue of copper and renewed depreciation, leading to riots and general unrest. Another crisis was brewing on the eve of Nâsir al-Dîn's death. When the new Shah arrived in Tehran, the Imperial Bank was authorised to call in the copper coinage in sufficient quantity to restore a reasonable balance between copper and silver money. At the same time, the Amîn al-Zarb and his son were arrested and the ex-farmer was fined 800,000 tomans (£160,000). Meantime, the bank began to buy up copper.

A new mint-master, Sanî' al-Dawla, was named in November 1896 and there were high hopes that the currency would be stabilised. This programme was already under way when Amîn al-Dawla became prime minister in April 1897. Only limited success had been achieved. In August, after the expenditure of nearly £100,000 on the recall of copper coin, copper was still 50 per cent below its nominal value. In July, Amîn al-Zarb succeeded, possibly by well-placed inducements, to secure a *farmân* from the Shah permitting him to enter into a partnership with Sanî' al-Dawla in the administration of the mint. Amîn al-Dawla and the British chargé d'affaires, Hardinge, strongly opposed the appointment and prevailed on the Shah to revoke it.[35]

Amîn al-Dawla used this breathing space to attempt a more thoroughgoing reform of the coinage. A plan was drawn up at his request by Picot and Rabino. It called for the hiring of foreign engineers, assayers and technicians to run the mint, and the appointment of a board to control the issue of copper and the purity of silver coin. Hardinge promised further British support. If the mint were reorganised, he told Amîn al-Dawla, 'it would serve as an encouragement to Her Majesty's Legation to assist the

Persian Government towards the realization of any further reforms which they might propose to undertake'.[36]

Amîn al-Dawla did not, however, have a chance to put his plan into operation. In October, there was another serious depreciation in the value of copper coin, this time apparently engineered by a group of native bankers and money-changers, and possibly acting in concert with Amîn al-Zarb. A group of 200 women accosted the Shah's carriage in the street, poured dust on their heads and insulted the monarch. At a subsequent meeting called by the Shah, a group of merchants and money-lenders, along with Amîn al-Zarb, undertook to administer the mint and to prevent depreciation below a certain level. On 24 October, against Amîn al-Dawla's wishes, the Shah agreed to turn over the mint to the group. The attempt to reform the mint had thus failed.[37]

British concern over the condition of the mint reflected a desire to stabilise the coinage. But it also reflected anxiety for the Imperial Bank, which suffered from the instability of the currency, the depreciation of silver, the dearth of silver coin and interruptions in the operations of the mint.

The bank, deprived of coin, was in a vulnerable position. Money-changers in Tehran, clearly acting in concert, refused to accept its notes and there was a run on the bank's paper money. Within 10 days, £95,000 of the bank's £125,000 worth of notes in circulation were encashed. The bank had gold and silver to cover all its note issue – but in bars. A catastrophe was averted only by the energetic action of Amîn al-Dawla, who made £40,000 in gold coins from the royal treasury available to the bank.[38]

There is evidence that enemies of Amîn al-Dawla, including Farmân-farmâ and possibly the Russian legation, helped organise the run.[39] Nevertheless, the situation was more complex. The establishment of the Imperial Bank took business away from native bankers and money-changers. By 1895, borrowing by the government and high officials had swung away from the bazaar to the Imperial Bank. In addition, a number of Iranian firms issued their own bills of exchange. Known as *bijaks*, the bills passed as money. But the Imperial Bank had been given a monopoly over note issue, and the Russian legation brought pressure on the government to suppress the circulation of *bijaks*.[40] There was thus an element of genuine grievance in the opposition to the government.

The lack of money proved an intractable problem. Reviewing the prime minister's many difficulties in the spring of 1898, Durand wrote to Salisbury that 'the most disquieting feature of the whole situation is the absolute emptiness of the Treasury, which hampers the Sadr-i-Azam at every turn'.[41] In addition to the breakdown of the tax-collection machinery, many abuses had crept into the system. Officials pocketed the revenues. Pension and salary lists had been inflated by the names of both the living and those who had long been dead. The tax lists were hopelessly out of date, and a new assessment was long overdue.[42]

Amîn al-Dawla selected Abu'l Qâsim Nâsir al-Mulk, an advocate of reform, to undertake a reordering of the finances. Hardinge, though expressing concern over Nâsir al-Mulk's timidity and inexperience, was pleased with the appointment: 'The Nasr-ul-Mulk's appointment,' he wrote, 'has been received as an unmistakable sign of the intention of the present Government to execute reforms in the Administration, and considerable consternation is felt amongst the crowds of officials and hangers-on of the Ministry of Finance in Tehran and elsewhere in the country, who live by speculation and the misappropriation of the revenue'.[43]

Nâsir al-Mulk attempted to centralise the treasury accounts and to end the issuing of *barâts,* or assignments, on provincial revenue, a practice open to widespread abuses. The measure was opposed by the account-ants, who padded pension lists and extracted commissions for the *barâts* they cashed. It was also opposed by influential officials who found it easier to extract money from provincial rather than from the central treasury, and who bought up *barâts* at a discount and used influence to cash them at their full value.[44] Nâsir al-Mulk also attempted to cut down on the privileges of court officials and ministers, to extend treasury control over military funds and to establish a regular budget. Amîn al-Dawla attempted to limit the Shah to a fixed salary.[45] The reaction to these measures (see below) was severe.

Amîn al-Dawla and Britain
While these long-term measures were under way, Amîn al-Dawla sought to meet his immediate needs through a foreign loan. The details of these loan negotiations have been described elsewhere.[46] In brief, Amîn al-Dawla attempted to raise a loan in Holland, then Belgium. Both these measures were blocked by the British, who objected to the southern customs being pledged to a foreign country. The prime minister next turned to England itself. But Iran's credit on the London market was poor, a loan of £400,000 would require a firm guarantee from the British government, and Salisbury did not feel parliamentary approval for such a guarantee could be secured. Eventually, Amîn al-Dawla had to make do with a £50,000 loan from the Imperial Bank.

Though disappointed in the loan negotiations, Amîn al-Dawla con-tinued to hope for greater British support. He appealed directly to Salisbury. In a letter to the British foreign minister, Amîn al-Dawla reaffirmed his own and the Shah's determination to push through reform, especially of the finances and the army. But a large class of people interested in the continuation of present abuses, he said, opposed his government. They had secured Russian backing and had attempted to use opposition to the British loan to unseat him. He hoped for British support against these machinations.

Salisbury, in his reply, emphasised the need for reform and said the British legation in Tehran would always be prepared to give 'the best advice in their power'; but he rejected the idea of British action against Russia's obstructive tactics. 'I should deprecate,' he said, 'any appearance of conflict between the lines of policy pursued by Great Britain and Russia . . . our efforts should be directed at promoting harmonious action.'[47] This was less than Amîn al-Dawla expected, or needed.

In Tehran, Durand and Hardinge both thought highly of Amîn al-Dawla and were eager to see his reforms succeed. Hardinge, who had established links with some of the leading 'ulamâ', used his influence with Sayyid 'Abdallâh Bihbihânî to soften clerical opposition and incitement against the prime minister.[48] He sought to prevent Farmânfarmâ from intriguing against Amîn al-Dawla and to patch up differences between the two men.[49] On the other hand, some of the legation's actions hurt the prime minister and badly compromised his position. Britain treated the south as a domain of British primacy, from which other foreign countries should be excluded. Unwillingness to permit any other country to secure a pledge on the southern customs blocked Amîn al-Dawla's hopes of raising a loan in Europe. Britain interfered in the appointment of officials to the ports area.

In 1897, desperate for funds, Amîn al-Dawla farmed out the customs of the southern ports to Sa'd al-Mulk, an official to whom the British objected. Two years earlier, the legation had obtained from the Iranian government an oral pledge not to give Sa'd al-Mulk *any* position for a five year period. Hardinge now forced Amîn al-Dawla to cancel Sa'd's appointment and to renew the pledge, this time in writing. This meant a considerable loss of prestige for the government.[50] When disturbances grew common in the south, the British, to protect their interests, landed 150 Indian troops, under British officers, at Jask and Châhbahâr. Amîn al-Dawla could hardly protest.[51] But this disregard for Iranian sovereignty, and the presence of foreign troops on Iranian soil, further undermined the prime minister's position.

As a condition for extending the £50,000 loan to the government, the Imperial Bank demanded the right to place its agents as receivers in the customs houses at Kirmanshah and Bushire. Amîn al-Dawla was forced to agree. This proved an especially damaging concession. The presence in the customs of British agents was extremely unpopular with both the Iranian merchants and Iranian officials at headquarters. 'The Sadr-i-Azam,' Durand wrote in an assessment a year later, 'was loudly denounced for having "sold Bushire to the English", and in a few weeks he was dismissed from office.' Durand recalled that he had advised against the measure. His memorandum to Salisbury depicts the dilemma facing

British policy-makers: non-interference generally meant permitting a further slide into chaos; insistence on reform often had even more disastrous results:

> In my memorandum of 1895 I explained the great difficulty in effecting reforms, notably in the customs system, and I added: 'By pressing for them inconsiderately, we run the risk, not only of failure, but of making ourselves disliked by the Shah and the Sadr-i-Azam, and other influential persons, and of driving them into the arms of Russia'. These words are just as true now as they were in 1895, and I would earnestly recommend that we act with great caution in these matters.[52]

The opposition

Almost immediately after Amîn al-Dawla assumed office, movements were initiated both inside and outside the government to unseat him. The opposition came from political rivals, from those hurt by Amîn al-Dawla's proposed measures of reform, and by their allies among the clerical and merchant classes. But it was fuelled also by genuine opposition to the growth of foreign influence, by economic unrest and by growing dissatisfaction with Qajar misrule.

Inside the government, the intrigue against the prime minister was led by Farmânfarmâ, who set out to prove that nothing could be accomplished without his acquiescence. With the assistance of Vakîl al-Mulk, a member of the Tabriz party and the Shah's private secretary, he blocked all business sent before the Shah by Amîn al-Dawla and the foreign minister, Mushîr al-Dawla. His obstruction grew sufficiently acute for Hardinge to send the Farmânfarmâ word he would not permit further delays on affairs of interest to the legation.[53] But there were signs that the Farmânfarmâ's position with the Shah was weakening. The Shah in August 1897 gave Amîn al-Dawla the title of *vazîr-i a'zam,* with authority over all the departments, including the war ministry, which even under Amîn al-Sultân had been excluded from the prime minister's jurisdiction. 'Ayn al-Dawla was recalled from Hamadan and Amîn Khan Sardâr from London, where he was representing the Shah at the Queen's Jubilee. (Amîn Khan Sardâr was later named minister of war.)

With his dismissal imminent, Farmânfarmâ resigned the war ministry in September. In a despatch,[54] Hardinge attributed his fall from power to his intrigues, his interference in other departments and his insatiable appetite for money. Farmânfarmâ, he said, was reported to have received £100,000 in bribes during his nine months in office and to have made another large sum by diverting the pay of the troops. He was also rumoured to have conspired to have the crown prince, Muhammad 'Alî Mîrzâ, set aside in favour of Nâsir al-Dîn Mîrzâ, the son of his sister, Hazrat 'Ulyâ. Eager to get him out of the capital, the Shah and the prime minister persuaded him to accept the governorship of Fars. He first delayed leaving the capital, and when at the end of October he at long last departed, it was only to make camp in a village six miles outside the capital, where he began to intrigue against Amîn al-Dawla.[55]

The Shah indicated his continuing support for the prime minister by finally giving him the title of *sadr-i a'zam* in December. In February 1898, Amîn al-Dawla further consolidated his position by arranging for his son, Mu'in al-Mulk, to marry the daughter of the Shah by Hazrat 'Ulyâ. There was, however, an undertone of unpleasantness to the marriage. Hazrat 'Ulyâ was believed to have sought the marriage to enlist the prime minister's support to have her infant son named heir apparent. Mu'in al-Mulk, moreover, was already married. In order for the royal marriage to take place, he had to divorce his wife, who happened to be the daughter of the foreign minister, Mushîr al-Dawla, one of Amîn al-Dawla's closest friends. The prime minister's opportunism did little to enhance his reputation among his countrymen. Furthermore, while Mushîr al-Dawla, in a somewhat macabre situation, played an active part in the betrothal of his former son-in-law, Amîn al-Dawla had earned himself another enemy.[56]

A disparate coalition was forming against the prime minister. Durand discovered that Farmânfarmâ was in touch with the former *sadr-i a'zam*, Amîn al-Sultân, who was working to have Amîn al-Dawla overthrown.[57] The British legation believed that Amîn al-Sultân was working with the Russians to stir up opposition to the projected British loan.[58] Both Amîn al-Sultân and Farmânfarmâ were in touch with elements among the clerical community. In May, the enemies of Amîn al-Dawla gained another adherent. Zill al-Sultân, the Shah's brother and powerful governor of Isfahan, arrived in Tehran. Durand called on him and discovered that he wanted the command of the army. Durand also learned that Zill al-Sultân had already been sounded out by some of the 'ulama' and others to join a conspiracy to overthrow the prime minister. 'I advised him to do nothing of the kind,' Durand wrote home, 'but loyally to support the Minister, who had the support of the Shah, which he promised to do.'[59] But Zill al-Sultân had no intention of keeping his promise. When Amîn al-Dawla sent him back to Isfahan empty-handed, he too joined the forces of the opposition. In a report two months earlier, Durand had noted that

> their (sic) is a very strong anti-reform party, composed chiefly of court officials who have come from Tabreez with the Shah and form His Majesty's principal surroundings. These have allied themselves to the party of the late Sadr Azam and to the many sections of officials and employés who forsee in the introduction of reforms an end to many sinecures and other sources of unearned profit. Within the last fortnight an attempt was made to discredit the Sadr Azam by

26

the presentation to the Shah of a Petition full of abuse, but the Shah insisted upon the authors being discovered, and eventually it was traced to several personages of position, amongst them being the Kawam-i Daftar, who was immediately exiled in chains to Ardebil.[60]

Amîn al-Dawla also managed to alienate members of the merchant community. He ordered the arrest of Nasr al-Saltana for intriguing against the government. He also had the Malik al-Tujjâr, a wealthy merchant, seized and exiled to Ardabil.[61] Nasr al-Saltana, a protégé of the Shah's brother, Kâmrân Mîrzâ, was enmeshed in court politics and had apparently turned against the government after losing the farm of the customs. But Malik al-Tujjâr was a highly respected merchant and had close ties with the religious classes. His involvement in anti-governmental activity would suggest deeper causes of malaise among the merchant and religious classes.

Mention of the religious classes is scattered throughout British embassy dispatches and in contemporary Persian accounts of opposition activity against Amîn al-Dawla. The clerics are mentioned as being in contact with Farmânfarmâ, Amîn al-Sultân, Zill al-Sultân and others. No doubt, some of their involvement in opposition activity was venal in nature. But it also reflected much wider unrest in the society. Even before Amîn al-Dawla's appointment, there had been signs of clerical opposition. In March 1898, crowds led by the 'ulamâ' in Shushtar were involved in a severe clash with the troops of the new governor, who had bombarded the town. The governor resigned, but the clerical leaders were now demanding his head.[62] In Tehran, another cleric, Shaykh Rîhânallâh, incited the populace against the Jews.[63] By October 1897, clerical agitation had focused against the projected foreign loan. The walls were repeatedly plastered with posters attacking Amîn al-Dawla and Mushîr al-Dawla as traitors and as destroyers of religion. There was an attempt to incite a massacre of the Jews in order to discredit the government. According to a British legation despatch, 'the four leading moolahs of Tehran also addresssed two petitions to the Shah bearing the signatures of many others in which they demanded in a preemptory manner the dismissal of the Amin-ud-Dowleh, while in the bazaars they openly spoke of their intention to upset the government, and even went so far as to discuss dethronement of the Shah'.[64]

The British legation thought the agitation that was mounting against the foreign loan was merely a cover for the attempt to bring down the government, and that the religious leaders resented the prime minister's indifference to their aims and to their demands for money.[65] In Amîn al-Dawla's own memoirs, it is claimed that the anti-government movement among the 'ulamâ' was led by the prominent cleric, Mîrzâ Hasan Ashtiyânî, whose son had received more than 12,000 tomans in pensions for himself and his retainers during Amîn al-Sultân's prime ministership.

The clerics, the memoirs say, remembered Amîn al-Sultân's former largesse, while the Amîn's brother was continuing to provide the 'ulamâ' with pecuniary inducements.[66]

But there was widespread public dissatisfaction on which the religious leaders could work and which they to a degree reflected. There was concern that the projected foreign loan would place Iran further under the thumb of the great powers, only to provide funds for court prodigality. The presence of British, then Belgian, agents at the customs was regarded as a sign that the country was being sold to foreigners. Misgovernment was widespread and economic problems were mounting. Yet Amîn al-Dawla showed himself insensitive to clerical sensibilities. A servant of Mîrzâ Hasan Ashtiyânî was bastinadoed for insulting a passerby in the street.[67] In March 1898, 'for the first time in Persian history', the sanctity of refuge at the shrine of Imâm Rizâ at Mashhad was violated. Amîn al-Dawla had his officers enter the shrine to arrest a prisoner who had taken refuge there; the man was later punished.[68]

In the meantime, the treasury was virtually empty.[69] In May 1898 there were open signs of revolt among the troops. Durand reported that 'even the long-suffering Persian soldiers have begun to use strong language . . . Some of the men have received no pay for three years, and their patience is becoming exhausted'.[70] Placards of a threatening nature were posted near the barracks. The prime minister and the Shah did not dare ignore the troops any longer, obtained a small loan from the local market and paid the soldiers a small instalment on their arrears.

It was this inability to raise money that appears to have finally induced the Shah to give in to the opposition to Amîn al-Dawla. Throughout the winter and spring, Amîn al-Dawla had sought to raise a further British loan of £200,000. But the negotiations became bogged down over the usual problems of guarantees and customs control. In the meantime, Amîn al-Sultân in semi-exile in Qum, had entered into secret negotiations with the Russians who promised to make the necessary money available to him. This inducement proved decisive with the Shah.[71] In the first week of June, Salisbury telegraphed new, somewhat easier conditions for a British loan. But the die had already been cast. 'Our offer,' Durand telegraphed back, '. . . has come too late. Today the Sadr-i-Azam was dismissed, and the Government has been intrusted to a Cabinet under the Presidency of the Mushir od-Dowleh.'[72]

Summing up the events leading up to Amîn al-Dawla's dismissal later that month, Durand wrote:

> Various reasons contributed to bring about his downfall. He had offended the Mullahs by not giving them money, and generally by keeping them in order. He had, I fear, turned the Zil-es-Sultan against him by letting his Royal Highness leave Tehran with nothing to show for his visit. He had allowed his son to make large sums of

money by improper means, and also to divorce the daughter of the Mushir-ed-Dowleh, the Foreign Minister, in order to marry a daughter of the Shah. Above all, he had failed to raise money.[73]

Conclusion

During his stormy 14 months in office, Amîn al-Dawla undertook a range of reforms. Perhaps the most important of these was the attempt to reorganise the finances and the revenue system. But he also sought to introduce a new administration into the customs, to place the country's depreciated currency on a sound footing and to establish a gendarmerie to safeguard trade and caravans plying between cities. He set up several small committees to discuss and propose reform measures. These reforms had a broader implication: the assertion of central control over a fragmented bureaucracy, and a substitution of central direction for the farming system that prevailed in virtually every branch of the administration.

To achieve his aims, Amîn al-Dawla had recourse to various stratagems. He attempted, although to a very limited degree, to bring what were considered to be more competent men, like Abu'l Qâsim Nâsir al-Mulk, into his administration. He utilised foreign advisers. He sought to secure his position by seeking the support of the Shah and establishing a marriage link between the royal family and his own. He appears to have sought also to escape the tutelage of the great powers by turning to third countries. He applied to Holland, then to Belgium, for a loan; he employed customs administrators in Belgium, a gendarmerie officer in Italy, a physician for the ailing Shah in Germany.

The third country strategy did not work and Amîn al-Dawla sought, and increasingly leaned, on British support, partly from personal predilections, partly because of Russian support for his rivals. In many areas, such British support was forthcoming. But on the one issue that in the short run mattered most – a foreign loan – England was unable to help Amîn al-Dawla. Moreover, British support was a mixed blessing. British officials were not always sufficiently sensitive to the domestic pressures faced by the prime minister. They demanded, and received, concessions which further compromised his position in the eyes of his countrymen. Moreover, the Russians, believing him to be pursuing a pro-British policy, threw their support to Amîn al-Dawla's enemies.

The opposition he had to face ranged across a broad spectrum. It was led, in the first instance, by rivals like Amîn al-Sultân and Farmânfarmâ whose principal aim was to unseat him and take his place. Their efforts were supported by other influential individuals – those for example who made fortunes farming the customs and the mint – whose financial interests were threatened by Amîn al-Dawla's proposed reforms. His measures to centralise revenue administration and cut down on expenditure touched on the interests of a much wider spectrum of government officials and their retainers and for this reason aroused a wider opposition. Moreover, Amîn al-Dawla was not above using office for personal benefit, or at least for the benefit of members of his family. His financial measures also hurt members of the clerical classes.

Not all the opposition was selfishly motivated. Many were genuinely concerned with the growth of foreign influence. A rising merchant class, engaged in legitimate trade, felt threatened by the competition from European firms, who enjoyed the support of their legations. Foreign customs administrators were disturbing traditional relationships between traders and local officials; the British-owned Imperial Bank was cutting into business previously controlled by native bankers. Merchants had little protection, as the central authority weakened, against the exactions of governors and provincial officials. Financial disorder and government weakness created an intolerable situation for the mass of the people, who were prey to high prices, the depreciation of the currency and the extortion of officials, and who began to see a relationship between the nature of the governmental system and their own condition.

As in the tobacco protest movement of 1891–2 there was, in the agitation against Amîn al-Dawla, a mixture of private interests and public grievances, of internal and external forces. In time, these various streams coalesced. Members of the official and ruling classes, some enjoying Russian support, along with 'ulamâ' and merchants were able to harness public dissatisfaction to their advantage and to unseat the prime minister.

NOTES AND REFERENCES

1. Amîn al-Dawla did not immediately receive the title of *sadr-i a'zam*. He was initially given the title of *ra'îs al-vuzarâ'*, or president of the council of ministers. He was named *vazîr-i a'zam* in August 1897 and *sadr-i a'zam* only in December of that year.

2. Contemporary accounts held out high hopes of what Amîn al-Dawla would do. See 'Abd allâh Mustawfî, *Sharh-i Zindigânî-yi Man*, II (Tehran, n.d.), 19-20; and 'Abbâsqulî Jelli (translator), *Khâtirât-i Colonel Kosogovskii* (translation of V. S. Kosogovskii, *Iz tegeranskogo dnevnika*) (Tehran, 1344/1965-6), 109.

3. Durand to Kimberley, No. 26 (3), Tehran, 13 January 1895: FO 539/69.

4. There are several assessments of Muzaffar al-Dîn Mîrzâ, all in much the same tenor, in the British and Iranian sources. See, for example, Mahdîqulî Hidâyat, *Khâtirât va khatarât* (Tehran, 1344/1965-6), 97; Mustawfî, II, 10; Enclosure in Lascelles to Rosebery, No. 45 (22), Confidential, Tehran, 26 January 1894: FO 539/66; and Enclosure 2 in Greene to Kimberley, No. 116 (225), Secret, Tehran, 5 November 1894: FO 539/68.

5. The factions and intricate family alignments in the crown prince's court are described in Wood to Durand, No. 35, Tabriz,

6 August 1896, F O 248/633 and in Enclosure 2, Greene to Kimberley, No. 116 (225), Secret, Tehran, 5 November 1894: F O 539/68.

6. Enclosure in Durand to Salisbury, No. 7 (42), Gulhek, 11 June 1896: F O 539/75.

7. Mustawfî, II, 10.

8. Both Hidâyat, 98, and Amîn al-Dawla, *Khâtirât* (Tehran, 1341/1962-3), 228, claim that it was Amîn al-Sultân who, against the advice of Muzaffar al-Dîn Shah, recalled Farmânfarmâ to Tehran, using him to get rid of 'Ayn al-Dawla and other rivals. If true, this would be the first of the short-lived alliances of this period.

9. Hidâyat, 98; Kosogovskii, 124; and Enclosure in Durand to Salisbury, No. 49 (66), Tehran, 26 November 1896: F O 539/75.

10. Enclosure in same to same, No. 47 (64), Tehran, 24 November 1896: F O 539/75.

11. Kosogovskii, 127-30. Kosogovskii also claims that Amîn al-Sultân was carrying on an illicit relationship with one of the former Shah's wives which, to his discredit, became public knowledge. The story also appears in Amîn al-Dawla, 189.

12. F O 248/637, Memo. by Col. H. Picot, dated 7 December.

13. Durand to Salisbury, No. 47 (64), Tehran, 24 November 1896: F O 539/75.

14. Amîn al-Dawla, 229.

15. Mustawfî, II, 11-12.

16. Enclosure in Durand to Salisbury, No. 6 (4), Tehran, 18 January 1897: F O 539/76.

17. Hardinge to Salisbury, No. 52 (48), Tehran, 17 April 1897: F O 539/77.

18. Enclosure in Durand to Salisbury, No. 47 (64), Tehran, 24 November 1896: F O 539/75.

19. Enclosure in Durand to Salisbury, No. 49 (66), Tehran, 26 November 1896: F O 539/75.

20. Hardinge to Salisbury, No. 39 (27), Tehran, 17 March 1897: F O 539/76.

21. Hardinge to Salisbury, No. 73, Tehran, 2 June 1897: F O 60/584.

22. Same to same, No. 52 (48), Tehran, 17 April 1897: F O 536/77.

23. Hidâyat, 102.

24. Kosogovskii, 188-90.

25. Mustawfî, II, 14; Hardinge to Salisbury, No. 41, Tehran, 12 April 1897: F O 60/584.

26. Memorandum by Sir M. Durand on the situation in Persia: F O 60/581.

27. A. K. S. Lambton, *Landlord and Peasant in Persia*, Oxford 1969, 153.

28. Durand to Salisbury, No. 5 (61), Telegraphic, Gulhek, 6 July 1896; and enclosure in same to same, No. 47 (64), Tehran, 24 November 1896: F O 539/75.

29. Mustawfî, II, 23; and Kosogovskii, 95-7.

30. Kosogovskii, 114.

31. Enclosure in Hardinge to Salisbury, No. 73 (53), Tehran, 29 May 1898: FO 539/78.
32. Compare Memorandum by Sir M. Durand on the situation in Persia: FO 60/581 with enclosure in Spring Rice to Salisbury, No. 110 (89), Tehran, 18 September 1900: FO 416/4.
33. For an account of the administration of the mint see 'Report on the possibility of reform of the currency in Persia', by J. Rabino, enclosed in Greene to Kimberley, No. 146, Secret, Gulhek, 22 June 1894: FO 60/558.
34. Lascelles to Salisbury, No. 20, Tehran, 31 January 1893, and Enclosure: FO 60/542.
35. Hardinge to Salisbury, No. 28 (101), Confidential, Gulhek, 1 August 1897: FO 539/77.
36. Same to same, No. 46 (122), Gulhek, 13 September 1897: FO 539/77.
37. Same to same, No. 58 (143), Tehran, 24 October 1897: FO 539/77.
38. Hardinge to Salisbury, No. 33 (113), Gulhek, 28 August 1897 and same to same, No. 43 (119), Gulhek, 8 September 1897: FO 539/78.
39. Hardinge to Salisbury, No. 45 (121), Gulhek, 12 September 1897: FO 539/77.
40. For the change in borrowing habits, see 'Report on the working of the Bank' by J. Rabino, enclosure in Hardinge to Salisbury, No. 38 (24), Tehran, 15 March 1897: FO 539/76. For the trade in *'bijaks',* see correspondence in FO 60/598.
41. Durand to Salisbury, No. 63, Tehran, 29 April 1898: FO 539/78.
42. Mustawfî, II, 23-5.
43. Hardinge to Salisbury, No. 53 (29), Tehran, 12 February 1898: FO 539/78.
44. Mustawfî, II, 24-5.
45. Nâzim al-Islâm Kirmânî, *Târîkh-i Bîdâri-yi Îrâniyân,* Tehran 1332/1953-4), 124-5 and Amîn al-Dawla, 263.
46. Firuz Kazemzadeh, *Russia and Britain in Persia: 1864-1914,* New Haven 1968, 307-18.
47. Salisbury to Hardinge, No. 9 (8a), Confidential, Foreign Office, 25 January 1898: FO 539/78.
48. Enclosure in Hardinge to Salisbury, No. 74 (58), Tehran, 7 May 1897 and No. 83 (70), Tehran, 26 May 1897: FO 539/76.
49. Same to same, No. 12 (83), Gulhek, 3 July 1897: FO 539/77.
50. Same to same, No. 47 (124), Gulhek, 17 September 1897: 539/77.
51. Hardinge to Salisbury, No. 13 (27), Tehran, 24 January 1898: FO 539/78.
52. Durand to Salisbury, No. 16, Tehran, 12 February 1899: FO 60/608.
53. Hardinge to Salisbury, No. 12 (83), Gulhek, 3 July 1897: FO 539/77.
54. Same to same, No. 45 (21), Gulhek, 27 August 1897: FO 539/77.
55. Draft, same to same, No. 151, Tehran, 16 November 1897: FO 248/647.

56. Same to same, No. 17 (29), Tehran, 1 February 1898: FO 539/78.
57. Same to same, No. 31 (10), Gulhek, 27 August 1897: FO 539/77.
58. Same to same, No. 65 (152), Tehran, 17 November 1897: FO 539/77.
59. Durand to Salisbury, No. 70 (115), Tehran, 20 May 1898: FO 539/78.
60. Hardinge to Salisbury, No. 52 (72), Tehran, 29 March 1898: FO 539/78.
61. Hardinge to Salisbury, No. 65 (152), Tehran, 17 November 1897: FO 539/77; and No. 2 (161), 8 December 1897: FO 539/78.
62. Same to same, No. 12 (83), Gulhek, 3 July 1897: FO 539/77.
63. Same to same, No. 83 (70), Gulhek, 26 July 1897: FO 539/77.
64. Same to same, No. 65 (152), Tehran, 17 November 1897: FO 539/77.
65. *Ibid.*
66. Amîn al-Dawla, 237-8.
67. Hardinge to Salisbury, No. 7 (17), Confidential, Tehran, 6 February 1898: FO 539/78.
68. See footnote 60.
69. Durand to Salisbury, No. 58 (77), Tehran, 12 April 1898: FO 539/78.
70. Same to same, No. 73 (117), Gulhek, 1 June 1898: FO 539/78.
71. Kazemzadeh, 318-19.
72. Durand to Salisbury, No. 102 (65), Gulhek, 5 June 1898: FO 539/78.
73. Same to same, No. 83 (41), Gulhek, 30 June 1898: FO 539/78.

3

Shah Muzaffar Al-Dîn's European tour, A D 1900

The figure of the 'Oriental' reacting to the encounter with Europe is a staple of Western literature from at least the eighteenth century onwards. With the growth of interest in social and political analysis on the home-front and in the clash of cultures the world over, this situation was seen to be one that was particularly apposite, rich and piquant. To confine onself solely to the utilisation of Persians as the vehicle of such multi-purpose and multi-faceted satires or studies, and only to two of the best examples in the field, one may cite Montesquieu's *Lettres persanes* and James Morier's two books on the adventures of Hajji Baba.[1] There are, however, many others, mostly fictional, some with a basis in reality, a few on the level of straightforward, unselfconscious reporting. Among the most factual examples of the last category are the three European travel-diaries of Nâsir al-Dîn Shah, two of which, excellently and promptly rendered into English, were fashionable reading in Britain between about 1875 and 1890.[2]

We are concerned here with the European journal kept by the son of this ruler, Shah Muzaffar al-Dîn, on his first visit to Europe in the year 1900. It is very possible that western taste for *orientalia*, at base somewhat aristocratic and leisurely, had vanished abruptly by the turn of the century; for Muzaffar al-Dîn's records, unlike the two of his father, were never translated into English, or – so far as I have been able to discover – into any European language at all. Indeed, copies of the work in Persian itself are very difficult to come by: the standard bibliographical authority, the late C. A. Storey, knows of only one Persian edition, that published at Allahabad, in India, in 1915, fifteen years after the journey itself and eight years after the death of the author.[3] My own copy, published also in India, in Bombay, in 1903, is unknown to this authority, though it was noted in the 1950s for inclusion in his next *addenda*. As Storey himself put it, your 'edition seems to have escaped registration under the Indian Copyright Act and consequently to be absent from the British Museum and the India Office Library'. The fact that I can no longer recall when, where or how I obtained my copy occasions me some frustration, but – I rejoice to say – no apprehension of subconscious guilt-feelings.

There is, one cannot help suspecting, some minor mystery enveloping this diary. This particular Shah – and one is surely allowed to speak other than good of the dead if they are Shahs – was a not altogether popular figure in Persia, a dull though decent man, a characteristic eleventh-hour reactionary of the type familiar and frequent in Europe from the English Civil War onwards. But dullness and unpopularity have rarely been obstacles to appearance in print, and they alone would certainly not have deterred an Oriental potentate with a private press at his disposal. Moreover, even if my 1903 edition were not the first, its printing in India at all is difficult to account for: inflammatory material by the Shah's enemies was frequently set up on the presses of Persian-speaking areas outside Persia itself, but such measures would have been pointless in the case of an innocuous little composition by the Head of State in person. There are reasonable presumptions that an edition printed in Persia did in fact appear; but whether it was limited in quantity, or involved in some disaster such as a warehouse fire, or otherwise prevented from general circulation, must for the moment, and perhaps for always, remain a subject for conjecture. As far as the work's failure to get translated is concerned, I have already suggested one contributory factor – a fundamental change in European taste and preoccupation; other undoubted reasons were, first, the Shah's unpopularity in liberal-minded Britain, particularly in the picture repeatedly drawn of him by the then much-heeded Lord Curzon, and also by the Cambridge scholar, E. G. Browne, that legendary, large-hearted and influential English gentleman, universally known as 'Johnny ('Persian') Browne'. A second, and closely associated, factor was the Shah's intermittent tendency to place one of his gout-stricken feet more firmly and more often in the Russian camp (at that time, of course, it was the Tsarist Russian camp) than in the British.

The Shah at this time was 47 years old, and had seven more years of life before him. On his father's assassination, four years earlier, in 1896, he had – contrary to the expectations of some – succeeded in ascending the throne, his main preparation for this office being many years in the traditional governorship of Azerbaijan, the large but isolated province in northwestern Persia bordering on Russia and Turkey. Thus, in middle life, and with very limited experience, he had inherited a backward and disgruntled realm, with a treasury as empty of resources as his own plate was full of unsolved, and probably insoluble, problems.

What, in this case, were the reasons, one may ask, for this visit of the Shah to Europe, apart from the fact that such trips had, by the end of the nineteenth century, become somewhat the accepted thing? Browne suggests, with his generous, but often rather unsubtle, bluntness, that the trip was partly a fund-raising tour, partly a mark of respect to the lenders of funds already consumed – chiefly Russia – and partly an expensive and unnecessary holiday.[4] However large the grain of truth in any or all of these reasons, it comes as no surprise to find none of them mentioned by the Shah himself. On the contrary, he is quite explicit, from the very outset, that he travelled partly to establish or to preserve good relations with foreign rulers, and partly to bring the benefits of modern discoveries to his own country.[5] If Pontius Pilate was shy of a definition of truth, our own age has gone the one better of characterising as invalid the question of sincerity: nevertheless, and even at the hazard of incurring the charge of eccentricity, I would suggest that there may have been as much truth in Muzaffar's naive and cheerful profession of noble purposes as there was in Persian Browne's tough, debunking analysis of his motives. Certainly, the Shah often seems overwhelmed by a powerful sense of almost mystical kinship with his royal cousins in Europe; equally surely, he has nothing in common with his countryman whom Montesquieu makes declaim: 'Heureuse l'ignorance des enfants de Mahomet!' Shah Muzaffar's interest in science is in fact often somewhat childish and selfish, but it is none the less compelling for that. Another of the motives for his journey, and one that is at least implicit in the diary – one also that partly dictated his peculiarly circuitous route – was the need he had to combine a seasonable 'taking of the waters' at certain fashionable spas with official and unofficial visits to European capitals at times convenient to the various princes concerned. He is from time to time at pains to mention that the expenses of the journey were borne by him personally (whatever we take that to mean in terms of real accounting) whenever, at given points, the visit became unofficial and did not therefore entitle him to receive the hospitality of the country in question.

What of the year in which the Shah made his trip? Viewed from the Western standpoint, he could scarcely have chosen a less auspicious one. Yet, if change and decay were clearly to be seen on every hand, the Shah and his advisers seem no more to have apprehended the situation in advance than they realised it later, when confronted with several unpleasant facts of a portentous bearing. In the first place, although there is not the slightest hint thereof in the diary, the Boer War was beginning seriously to unsettle Britain's domestic politics as well as her relations with much of the rest of the world. It was a frightening time, both in itself and in its forebodings, and such cheerfully impudent pieces of personal enterprise as the young Winston Churchill's recent escape from Boer captivity in Pretoria no longer had the spirit-raising effect they would surely have produced in, say, Nelson's time. In my own country, Canada, at just about the time the Shah was setting out from Persia, Sir Wilfred Laurier had succeeded in gaining one of those few, but fateful, votes of confidence on Canadian participation in a war overseas. In the Far East the Boxer Rebellion was occasioning the first tremor for many years to the great edifices of imperial power: even the Shah mentions on a number of occasions the impending or actual departure of Prussian and other officers to bear a hand in these distant troubles. (As a contrast with the present day, it may be mentioned that the Persian monarch displays no trace of sympathy for his fellow-Asians in their conflict with the West: indeed, the case is quite the contrary.) Later in the same year British shipyards were to launch a Japanese battleship, for a time the largest in commission. But if these events signified little or nothing to the Shah, he would draw no direr prophetic conclusions from the several royal deaths and disasters of the period: the great passing of Victoria, like the assassination of President McKinley, was still a year or so hence, but the Shah's very departure from Persia coincided with an attempt on the life of the Prince of Wales in Brussels; while he was still on the way, the King of Italy was assassinated; on his return journey he learned with relief of the Kaiser's escape from an assassin's hand; and his projected inclusion in his tour of a visit to Britain had to be abandoned suddenly when the court went into mourning for the death of the Queen's fourth child, the Duke of Saxe-Coburg and Gotha (this, it may be added, was a cancellation that, though inevitable, did nothing to improve Anglo-Persian relations). Last, but far from least, the climax of the tour itself was in many ways the armed attack made in Paris, by a French anarchist stooge, on the Shah himself; but even this event, prone though he was to tell it over and over again in detail, seems to have caused him less real anxiety and alarm than did his first entry into a tunnel, or the speed of the European trains, or the giddy precipices he traversed in the Balkans and the Caucasus. Yet it should not be thought that the Shah had no concern for the future; he had, but like each of us, he had it in his own particular way, as the following passages may show. On his way through Russia, a Russian officer had presented him with a few leaves of the Koran, salvaged from the wayside and bound in the traditional Muslim colour of green; the Shah writes: 'Taking this as a very good omen, we opened it in reference to our journey; this blessed verse was at the top of the page, "When they shall not ward off the fire from their faces nor their backs, neither shall they be helped".[6] For some time we mused on these pages of the Koran'. Three days later the Shah was untying a pile of books, among which he found the poems of Hâfiz; he goes on: 'We gave it to the Imperial Minister to cast an augury for this journey of ours. He turned up the ode that begins, "At dawn when the Lord of the East set his standard on the mountain-tops, my Beloved, with the hands of pity, knocked at the door of the hopeful ones".[7] This was amazing [says the Shah] for in 1308, that is to say ten years ago, when we consulted this same Master Hâfiz on our affairs, this very same ode came up, and we noted it down in our own hand'.

Clearly, the Emperor was as concerned about the future as the next man, and he was no doubt conscious to some degree that the world might be passing through a bad patch. But, at the level of the eternal verities, there were banquets to attend, orders and decorations to give and

receive, and troops to review; there was the fascinating round of existence at the great European watering-places; the Paris International
Exposition, and still fairly novel Eiffel Tower; there were knick-knacks
of all kinds to buy and gadgets to try out; there was – and this, if nothing
else, should qualify him for the sympathy and respect of large sections of
our society – there was one's health to worry about. Finally, there were
pathetic and even now still unrealised, dreams to cherish of the prosperity
Persia would enjoy when certain great schemes were put into effect, 'after
our return'.

The Shah's journey, from palace gates back to the Imperial portals,
lasted some eight months, from April to December 1900. In a carriage, on
horseback, and by train – with the occasional services of a boat or a
motor-car – it took him to Russia, Germany, France, Austria-Hungary
and the Balkans generally, Turkey, and Belgium and Holland. As I have
already indicated, some of these countries were visited more than once,
so that the route as traced on a map looks like nothing so much as a skein
of wool after the attentions of a playful kitten.

This constant back-tracking, this going round in circles, fortunately
relieves us of any sense of obligation to try to trace the journey in
sequence. More profitable, it might seem, is to select some of the high-
lights of the trip, those incidents and situations that, either in themselves
or as pointers to something larger, appear as of special interest or significance. Above all, I propose, of course, to comment on, or to translate,
some passages which seem to tell us most about the man himself, or about
his reactions to the novel situations in which he finds himself involved.

The diary, in my edition, runs to 270 Imperial octavo pages – that is, on
average, just over a page per day – and treats practically each day of the
journey in a separate section according to the Muslim lunar calendar. It
should, however, be remarked that it was not always written up day by
day, but was dictated – often three or four days at a time, as the Shah
himself observes – to one or other of the courtiers, as opportunity served.
Such a procedure was not imposed by any real physical handicap, still less
by personal illiteracy – indeed, the Shah seems, like his father, to have
had considerable feeling for style, evolving an expression that subtly
blends moderately educated speech with recognisable literary tradition.
The simple fact is undoubtedly is that His Imperial Majesty, no less than
the modern business tycoon, – indeed, like the great at almost all times –
would have tended to feel the actual day-to-day task of writing to be
somewhat beneath him. It will be obvious, however, that a diary composed in this manner, even had the Shah been other than he was, is
unlikely to provide sensational scoops, or spiteful opinions on his retinue
or on his various individuals with whom he came into contact: with few
exceptions – and these are naturally of some interest – all his observations
are in the full tradition of much Persian historiography and literary

criticism: all the men worth mentioning are intelligent and kind, brave and self-sacrificing; the women, few as they are, are chaste, beautiful and gracious. This is something at once more frustrating to the investigator and altogether more subtle than the polite clichés of official reports as we know them in the West.

But what the diary lacks in what we may, perhaps, without impropriety term 'spice', it more than makes up for in terms of solidity and fullness. Statistical details of fantastic accuracy – and often of stark insignificance – abound throughout the whole work, covering such things as distances traversed, the population and size of places visited, the number and the proportions of rooms in hotels or palaces where the royal party stayed, the exact placing of guests at table, the dimensions of the main railway-station in Cologne or of the St Sophia cathedral-mosque at Istanbul. We learn that the Shah washed, said his prayers and breakfasted most days on rising, we are reassured that on no evening did he go supperless to bed. Here, in one important sense, we have the measure of the man: a conscientious dullard, with a mind that sought refuge in detail and precision, but balked at judgement, discretion and selection. Yet perhaps 'balked' is not a just term, for whatever the subconscious psychological implications of the Shah's attitude, there is certainly no flinching from experience in the fullest sense of the word: one astonishing revelation, in an age inclined to pity royalty for what it has to endure in the way of speechmaking, and handshaking, and the rest, – one truly alarming discovery, is how much at least one prince seems richly to have enjoyed every moment of his tour.

However, whether or not the Shah was what my psychiatric colleagues apparently call a 'compulsive', he was most certainly a hypochondriac; but, like the man in the *New Yorker* cartoon, he was a hypochondriac with a real malady, an affection of the kidneys from which he was to die at only 54 years of age.[8] The supposed treatment of this disease occasioned his longest single stay in one place throughout the whole journey, a sojourn of one month in the now somewhat unfashionable spa of Contrexéville, near Épinal, just west of the Vosges. (A somewhat shorter stay, with the same end in view, was made at the Bohemian spa of Marienbad, *alias* Mariánské Lázně.) This, to Muzaffar al-Dîn, was the most truly delightful part of his journey, the period to which, in later conversations with his courtiers, he would again and again revert, as to some precious memory of an age that, if not golden, was certainly gilt. The life of contrived amusement, the daily round dedicated to the sociability of controlled and moderate suffering – these things suited him as nothing else could. Here, in my translation, are some typical extracts from the diary at this period:

> We were still in bed this morning when the Court Minister and
> Dr. Adcock arrived to suggest that we ought to begin to-day to drink

the mineral waters. As they made this suggestion, it seemed to us a
hard and difficult thing to have to begin to-day. However, we got up
and, without taking any tea, came to the well and drank half-a-glass
of water. Then we began to walk about . . . Meanwhile the actresses
[here he tries to explain the word in Persian for an audience to
whom, at that time, the theatre – in the Western sense – was an
unknown concept] – meanwhile the actresses, who appeared at the
theatre last night, and who looked very fine from a distance, had
arrived. Now that we saw them close-to, they were nothing special.
As they say in the old tale : at night cats look like sables . . . Then we
went to a place for shooting. We fired several rounds, hitting eggs
and other objects . . . We went back to the shop kept by the girl who
sold rings; she had one with an emerald, which she priced at 2700
francs. 'Alâ' al-Mulk [one of the retinue] bought it and presented it
to us as an offering . . . There is a device here which weighs people.
We stood upon it to-day and discovered that our weight was 80kgs
. . . At sunset we went to the theatre. It was a very fine and beautiful
place, and the play was not bad either. It was the story of three
riflemen, called [here the Shah also attempts to write 'Trois Mous-
quetaires' in Persian characters], and the book [he goes on to say] is
well known. It was a good tale, and we stayed right to the end of the
play . . . A doctor staying here came to see us and listened to our
heart. Praise be to God!, he said we had no illness or ailment, and
indeed, by God's grace, we do feel well [all this is, of course, the
royal rather than the medical 'we'!] . . . To-day we saw a person of
the English race; he was very tall and had an extremely long beard,
but, having shaved off his moustaches, he presented a strange and
wonderful aspect and appearance . . . We bought three pairs of silver
scissors . . . then a watchmaker came, bringing several watches, of
which we approved. . . then a tailor, whom we had sent for from
Paris, was brought into our presence: we ordered several suits of
clothes, both official and unofficial . . . We went downstairs where a
person had made ready an automobile [the Shah uses this word in its
native, unrefined form]. We ordered Nâsir Khâqân to sit by him and
to take a short trip . . . Truly, we have grown tired at the hands of the
photographers here, they will not leave us in peace for a moment . . .
We went downstairs and studied the motor-car, which had come
from Paris in fourteen hours. We had originally intended to buy it,
but as it was shaped like a wagon we did not; it has room for four
persons, and they are able to sit down. We ordered Nadîm al-Sultân
and Amîn Hazrat to climb aboard and ride up and down for a while
before us. Then we commanded Nâsir Khâqân to do likewise, and he
was taken away outside the park to a considerable distance. When he
returned, he submitted that the motion was very pleasant and com-

fortable.

One could with pleasure continue to quote at length from this section, particularly as it offers, in the course of its 25 pages, at least one example (and often many more) of some important secondary aspects of the Shah's character and personality. I must, however, content myself now with listing some of these aspects, both as they appear in the foregoing quotations as well as elsewhere in this same period. Where appropriate, I propose also to refer to relevant instances from other stages of the journey.

I have already touched on some facets of the Shah's hypochondria. There are others. For one thing, despite his uncertain health, he seems to have been an excellent trencherman, frequently commending the fine meals set before him, even the doubtless fearsomely heavy fare common at public banquets at that period. Yet it must be remarked that on almost no occasion does he indulge his passion for cataloguing to the extent of actually recording the dishes served: this general omission may well have been a consequence of his uncertainty as to what he was actually eating, for the only exceptions to it are the rare instances where his hosts favoured him with meals in Persian style. Fortunately, if surprisingly, – like the Persian music often performed in his honour by European orchestras and soloists – these seem to have been very much to his liking.

Like many of his temperament, the Shah was a helpless victim of motion-sickness, and he freely admits his terror of speeds much in the excess of 20 m.p.h. The diary has several instances of his abruptly stopping the special train in France, Germany and elsewhere because the driver was touching something more like twice this velocity. In the face of this grave handicap, schedules were maintained only by travelling at high speed through the night, while the royal head possibly lay more easily. However, as the Shah always had difficulty in getting to sleep in any case, and was certainly unable to do so while the train was actually moving, these night journeys must have involved much delicate contact and flexible improvisation as between his housholds and the European railway authorities concerned. Perhaps the most pathetic instances of his suffering in this respect, if only in imagination, occurred at St Petersburg. The Tsar of Russia had projected an extensive tour by launch of the great naval base at Kronstadt, but the weather in the Baltic turned very rough for several days on end, and the trip was constantly postponed. Day after day, the Shah records, almost as a prayerful litany, that it may well prove impossible to make the trip at all if no rapid improvement sets in. In the event, the tour of inspection was carried out before he left, with less discomfort than the unfortunate man had so long dreaded, but sufficient, nevertheless, to render him very chary, at a later date, of a little pleasure-cruise on the Danube. (A propos of this Kronstadt visit, it may be mentioned that the great powers, eighty years ago, seem to have had no misgivings whatsoever at showing a foreign ruler – at least, in the case of an Asian Emperor – over their arsenals, their training grounds and their fortifications. In France and Germany, for example, the Shah, who prided himself on his military expertise, made (in person or by proxy) exhaustive tours of such key military installations as Épinal, Nancy and Lille, and Metz, noting down the location, calibre and number of the big guns, the strength of forces in garrison, and even working out a rough sort of order-of-battle. Fortunately or otherwise, such information seems to have remained virtually locked away in Persia until it no longer was of value. In this respect it was obvious that, as at the present time, the overriding concern of the hosts was to impress the visitor with their strength and efficiency, and also to induce him to place orders and commissions with their respective general-staffs and arsenals. The greatest measure of success in this connection was achieved, as it happens, by Austria-Hungary, though Germany came a close second.)

To revert once more to the Shah's person, it is difficult, I think, not to be struck, in the Contrexéville passages I quoted earlier, by the Emperor's attitude to his courtiers and servants. The constant use of these, often elderly, unfortunates as guinea-pigs to try out some new device, such as the motor-car, naturally has for us a strong element of the richly comic. But there can have been few situations more degrading to human dignity than theirs, as the functionaries of a man who was not only morbid and selfish, but also equipped with the absolute authority of Oriental power. Unlike his successor of 30 years later, he never liquidated his retainers, but at one point he has them combing the beach at Ostend for pretty shells, at another they are sent forth in a blinding Armenian storm to collect hailstones; the courtiers who were made to ride in the car came off lightly beside those who were put to manage obstreperous bicycles or wicked-tempered horses. Not that there seems to have been anything cold or calculated about these subjections to discomfort: the Shah is often grateful, as grateful for the prettiest shell or the biggest hailstone as he is uproariously amused by his followers' Chaplinesque attempts at controlled locomotion.

The Shah's sense of humour, incidentally, is most often very broad, but occasionally quite subtle. In the theatre, next after juggling and conjuring acts, he loves knockabout comedy without stint of custard-pies or broken heads. It is quite another man, however, who records his satisfaction one morning at having himself woken his doctor, whose waking of him has hitherto been the unvarying *introit* of the Shah's daily round. Then, again, there is his own quiet amusement at the imperfectly concealed gazes and stares his appearance provokes among those he meets, with the repeated, but ever-charitable observation: 'I am probably the first Persian they have ever seen'. Again, though his style allows him no shadow of caricature, there is something of the bite of Thackeray in his references to the (doubtless very prudent) hovering of bill-collectors whenever the Imperial party is about to break camp and move on.

Let us pass over the Shah's evident eye for a pretty woman: it is clearly always open, but apparently never covetous. (In this connection, it may be mentioned that the royal harem accompanied him as far as the Persian frontier, where it awaited him again on his return.) Let us touch but lightly, too, on his professed regard for the arts and sporting pastimes: music and literature, marksmanship and horseriding (as well as horse-racing) he seems genuinely to have loved; European sculpture and painting seem to have impressed him more by their quantity, their size and their photographic accuracy than by any other consideration; to his theatrical preferences I have already alluded, to the rather ironical situation of the so-called mysterious and cunning Oriental sitting spellbound before European sleight of hand and acrobatic skill. His intellectual attainments in the strictest sense were not impressive by any standard of East or West: he seems, for example, to have had no real grasp of any foreign language, not even Turkish or Russian (and this despite many years in North Persia, where Russian is widely used, while Turkish is at least equal in status and currency to Persian); admittedly, the position here is somewhat obscure, and it would appear that he occasionally caught the drift of conversations in French, but what is certain is that no words passed between himself on the one hand, and his hosts or various casual acquaintances on the other, save through interpreters. (Usually these were drawn from the then rather thin ranks of Persians with any sort of Western training, but on one occasion, in Budapest, he was happy to avail himself of the skill of the celebrated Hungarian orientalist, Arminius Vambéry.) His scientific knowledge was equally sketchy: there is something peculiarly modern in a passion for gadgetry that rests on a profound ignorance of basic scientific concepts. He remains, for example, puzzled but impressed that the St Sophia mosque, which – as an originally Christian church – should have been laid on Jerusalem, in fact seems to have anticipated its later Muslim utilisation by orientation on Mecca. Nobody seems to have told him – at least, no one seems to have succeeded in making clear to him – that from the bearing of Istanbul the two places are in approximate alignment. (A journey to the southern hemisphere, one feels, might well have shaken his faith to its very foundations.) Again, on his outward journey, he seems to have only an imperfect understanding why the spring arrives later in northern latitudes than it does in Persia, and imperfection of understanding gives way to utter confusion when the complicating factor of elevation has also to be taken into account. Yet, in keeping with much else in his character, and like so many monarchs skilled in ceramics or entomology or what have you, he displays no mean knowledge of botany and horticulture. One unlikely aspect of Paris, for example, that continually catches his eye is the plane-tree, which he contrasts learnedly with its Persian counterpart; and whenever he is able to visit a botanical garden – in Vienna, or St Petersburg or Warsaw – he taxes all the resources of his interpreters in long conclaves with the gardeners, making arrangements to ship seeds and plants and cuttings to Persia.[9] It is difficult, for this reason, to doubt the sincerity of his regret at the relative infertility of southeastern Europe and his own part of Asia, or the genuineness of his concern for large-scale irrigation works designed to restore to Persia something of her ancient prosperity. Sometimes his interest in cultivation puts him on the track of unexpected knowledge; throughout his tour he makes clear that as a good Muslim he drinks his toasts in sherbet and not in wine, but he savours over and over again, in a sort of delighted horror, the information that the huge German potato crop is produced largely to make high-grade alcohol for the citizens of the USA. Another topic on which he displays more than commonplace knowledge is that of gold-mining, and his excitement is considerable when he learns that some European prospectors have uncovered in North Persia a vein that may yield well above the minimum economic fraction. At the same time, it is he (and not they) who immediately assesses the many factors that did eventually render the find unworkable.

Apart from these few instances, however, his scientific knowledge remains on a par with that of A. W. Kinglake's legendary Turkish pasha of half-a-century earlier, who is constantly made to cry in admiration at Western achievement: 'Whirr, whirr, all by wheels; whizz, whizz, all by steam!'[10] Like so many rulers from the 'timeless East', he is fascinated by clocks and watches, of which he buys a great profusion during his journey; cameras, too, and binoculars exercise their own charm, so that in one respect the Shah's homecoming must have resembled that of a Russian soldier returning from the liberated Eastern Europe of the mid-1940s. At one period, all motion sickness forgotten, he is enthralled by rides in the elevators of a European hotel; at another, in a palace of Catherine the Great, he devotes all his attention to an ingenious dumb-waiter table, which rises fully laden through the floor, and silently disappears in the same manner when the meal is over: the advantages in terms of conversations uninterrupted by the coming and going of servants are immediately apparent to a monolingual ruler like himself, and he notes his intention to have one installed without delay in Tehran. Constantly, as may be imagined, his passion for gadgets and his hypochondria are both fully engaged by the numerous machines on the market at the time for slimming or toning up the liver or developing the chest. Yet, again, he can at times show a surprising, if limited, practical sense, as when he minutely examines and records the details of, the bright naphtha lamps in Kharkov station, in order that similar models may be brought to Persia as soon as possible.

Kind and sentimental though he was fundamentally, the Shah was certainly no man of the people. His efforts to strike up an acquaintance with peasants and others along his route are stilted and awkward, and always stultified by the language problem – for even an Oxford-trained Persian courtier will find himself somewhat at a loss when called upon to turn an oriental figure of speech into one of the rarer dialects of Bohemia. A wild-west show in the Paris Exposition greatly took the Shah's fancy, but he could never have himself imitated the ride by his successor, a few years ago, down the main street of American cities, seated on the rolled-back top of a convertible and waving a cowboy's hat. (In other respects, I would say that the two monarchs were not so different.) His view of the proper order of things as between himself and other men is more nearly shown by his purchase of black slaves in Istanbul, or by his paternal chiding of the North Persian bourgeoisie, who met him, requesting the political panacea of that day and ours – a constitution. Indeed, his velvet glove might be suspected at times of sporting a mild sort of knuckle-duster: he comments, for example, when meeting the then Prince Metternich, on the neat and efficient arrangement that will obtain in the state when the Prince's daughter has succeeded in gaining the Austrian Chief-of-Police as a husband.

I explained earlier why I would not attempt to follow the Shah's journey in any sequence. I have in the main not pursued him in any detail either. Other travellers besides Muzaffar have noted, for example, with all the infuriating truth of a truism, that 'Paris is a fine city, with many splendid buildings and wide streets'. Actually, the Shah and members of his retinue were strenuously divided on the relative merits of the Ville Lumière and Berlin, and I am afraid – though, all things considered, scarcely surprised – that the Kaiser's capital appealed to the majority. But the example will serve.

What I have tried to show is the Shah's tour against a background, and the Shah's response, or lack of it, to a novel, complicated and pregnant situation.

The basic feature of the background was, of course, Anglo-Russian rivalry for spheres of influence in the Middle East; but, for reasons I have given, Britain in fact hardly comes into the picture at all as regards the tour, apart from the constant irruption, at every major halting-place, of the various British representatives, hard on the heels – but never ahead – of their Russian counterparts. Meanwhile, the British failure to give the Shah, even by proxy, a decoration he much coveted,[11] let alone to offer him tangible rewards for friendship, – this failure must be set against a fairly successful all-out effort to bribe and to entertain him by the Russians. It is ironical to see, even at this early date, how the Russian ballet and Russian culture generally were used with telling effect in the initial softening-up process of an intended victim.

As for the Shah's general level of reaction, it is, I think, most strikingly seen in relation to three material phenomena: the station oil-lamps at Kharkov, the motor-car he finally purchased after much shopping-around, and the Russian oil-wells he visited in Baku. He reacts to each of the three personally, and without any intuitive grasp of their inter-connection in a more ample sphere. The oil-lamps were a cheap, simple, obvious and effective improvement in material standards, and on which, in its limited scope, contained no disturbing suggestion of large-scale social change or economic upheaval. The car, which he finally brought himself to sit in when nearly back to Tehran, was a mere toy – something in which to drive around the palace-grounds when other amusements flagged: its ingenuity alone was admired, but it was not, like the lamps, felt to confer any personal or general advantage, nor – consequently – were its eventual drawbacks at all manifest. The oil-wells (he describes the derricks as being a sort of huge ballista or catapult) were seen in stark terms of personal discomfort, inasmuch as His Majesty could breathe and eat and drink nothing uncontaminated by oil all the time he was in Baku. Why the oil was being extracted, what its relation might be to the car and the lamps, what effect all three were to have on the life of Persia and the world at large – these were questions he was not moved to formulate even in the vaguest of terms, despite his professed preocupation with Western-isation and scientific progress. Yet both he and his father had given the Russians rights to drill in North Persia (rights never in fact used, though later made the pretext for several Russian escapades in the area), and negotiations were already in train for the agreement by which the British would eventually create the huge oil industry of southwestern Persia which lingers into our own day.

One supreme irony of the situation is that the Shah's scale of values had its own authentication. All the changes and upheavals in principalities and powers, all the refusals and grantings of constitutions and powers in Iran itself, all the gushing oil and hissing lamps and rushing motor-cars – all these were to leave Persia very much what it was in essentials, and the Persian throne one of the few in the world still virtually intact for another 80 years. Then it would be lost by a monarch who understood very well the inwardness of Westernisation, in everything but human terms.

Shah Muzaffar, like most Persians, probably did not rate very highly the poetry of 'Omar Khayyâm, and – even had he known English – he might have had difficulty in recognising him in Fitzgerald's dress. Yet he would surely have found his attitude to life epitomised in the idea of taking the cash and letting the credit go. Certainly he never heeded the rumble of a distant drum. . . .

NOTES AND REFERENCES
1. Paris 1721; London 1824 and 1828, respectively.
2. The first, translated by J. W. Redhouse, London 1874; the

second by A. Houtum Schindler and Baron L. de Norman, London 1879. The record of the third trip (that of 1889) apparently did not get translated, for reasons on which one can only speculate (but see the comments in the following paragraphs of the text in immediate reference to the present work).

3. *Persian literature,* 347. Two later journeys (1902 and 1905) did not apparently generate travel-diaries.
4. *The Persian revolution of 1905-9,* Cambridge 1910, *passim* and several allusions in Browne's writings generally.
5. Since both my edition and the one noted by Storey are so rare, I have not given page-references, but would be glad to identify any item on request.
6. XXI, 40.
7. *sahar chûn khusraw-i khâvar 'alam bar kuhsârân zad/ba-dast-i marhamat yâram dar-i ummîdvârân zad* (Qazvînî-Ghanî, 104).
8. 8 January 1907.
9. Persian was at that time, and in general still is, notoriously ambiguous and confusing in its terminology relating to flora (and fauna and minerals).
10. See *Eothen,* London 1844, and very many reprintings.
11. This happened (or failed to happen) again on his next trip (see P. M. Sykes, *History of Persia,* II, 505).

4

New light on the Iranian constitutional movement

The Iranian lawyer and scholar Farîdûn Âdamiyyat became known for his books entitled *The Bahrein Islands*,[1] *Amîr-i Kabîr va Îrân*[2] and *Fikr-i âzâdî dar muqaddama-yi nahzat-i mashrûtiyyat-i Îrân* ('The concept of freedom in the period in the period preceding the Iranian constitutional movement,').[3] These were followed by monographs on the reformist ideas of Fath-'Alî Âkhûndzâda, Sipahsâlâr, Âqâ Khân Kirmânî, and 'Abd al-Rahîm Tâlibov. More recent products of Mr Âdamiyyat's research are *Fikr-i dimûkrâsî-yi ijtimâ'î dar nahzat-i mashrûtiyyat-i Îrân* ('The concept of social democracy in the Iranian constitutional movement'),[4] and *Îdi'ûlûzhî-yi nahzat-i mashrûtiyyat-i Îrân* ('The ideology of the Iranian constitutional movement').[5] As the title indicates, *Îdi'ûlûzhî-yi nahzat-e mashrûtiyyat* is a study of ideas, not events, but it throws new light on many events and brings hitherto accepted appraisals into question. The author has made extensive use of the Majlis records and also of the British Legation reports in the London Public Records Office. The period covered is from 1897 to the first phase of the Second Majlis (October 1909–July 1910). Sections from the first half of *Fikr-i dimûkrâsî-yi ijtimâ'î* are incorporated in *Îdi'ûlûzhî-yi nahzat-i mashrûtiyyat*. At the end of the last-named book, a sequel is promised. In the present article, the salient themes of *Îdi'ûlûzhî-yi nahzat-e mashrûtiyyat* are outlined, some comments are offered, and a few words about the contents of *Fikr-i dimûkrâsî-yi ijtimâ'î* are added.

The first theme is the failure of the reforms which were attempted in the reign of Muzaffar al-Dîn Shah. Reforms on much the same lines were enacted by the first two parliaments and implemented after the First World War. Mr Âdamiyyat discusses the economic background of the Qajar government's financial weakness and the growing social unrest. Increasing importation of foreign manufactures to the detriment of indigenous handicrafts coincided with depreciation of the silver currency due to the fall in the world value of silver in the 1890s. These factors, together with recurrent food shortages and price rises, injured the artisans and small shopkeepers of the bazaars who formed a large part of the urban population, and also stimulated emigration, mainly to Caucasia. Only a small minority, consisting of intellectuals, most of whom were officials educated in the country's two modern colleges or in Europe, and of merchants with knowledge of the outside world, were aware of the fundamental defects of the governmental system and the laws. The Shi'ite clergy were the traditional spokesmen of the *bâzârîs*, but the merchants also were in touch with them and able to influence them.

Mîrzâ 'Alî Khan Amîn al-Dawla, Prime Minister for 14 months in 1897–8, obtained the Shah's approval for a council of high officials (*a'yân-i dawlatî*) to consider reforms, engaged Belgium experts to replace tax-farmers in the customs administration, and sought a foreign loan without political strings. He also set up an Education Council and helped Mîrzâ Hasan Rushdiyya and Mîrzâ Mahmûd Khan Ihtishâm al-Saltana to establish the first Iranian modern schools at Tabriz and Tehran. Opposition came not only from court reactionaries but also from clergy led by the then foremost *mujtahid* of Tehran, Hâjjî Mîrzâ Hasan Âshtiyânî, who in 1892 had played a big part in the agitation against the Tobacco Régie. The bankers of Belgium, Holland, and France would not offer a loan, and the London bankers insisted on hypothecation of the customs revenues, which in Amîn al-Dawla's view would have been derogatory to national sovereignty. Rather than seek a Russian loan, he resigned. His successor, the already unpopular Mîrzâ 'Alî Asghar Khan Atâbak-i A'zam (formerly Amîn al-Sultân) accepted two Russian loans on the security of the customs revenues, and made the Belgian expert Joseph Naus a minister with the task of planning reforms. Naus's main proposals were the creation of a central treasury, gradual transfer of tax collection from provincial governors and tax farmers to Finance Ministry officials, and gradual reassessment of the land taxes. Naus was also entrusted with the negotiation of higher tariffs than the capitulatory five per cent. Although his freedom was limited by the need for Russian consent, Mr Âdamiyyat notes that he followed as far as possible the sound principle of higher duties on luxuries than on necessities. There were rational grounds for objection to the Russian loans and the new tariffs, but the objections of the clergy were of a different order; in a telegram to the Shah, the senior *mujtahids* of Najaf complained about the employment of infidel Europeans and Armenians in the collection of taxes from Muslims and about the spread of abominations such as Babism and wine-drinking. (Numerous Bâbîs and alleged Bâbîs were killed in clerically instigated riots at Yazd and Isfahan in 1903.) The main reason for Atâbak's dismissal in September 1903 was the refusal of the other ministers to accept responsibility for Naus's reform plans.

Mr Âdamiyyat contests the view that the next Prime Minister, 'Abd al-Majîd Mîrzâ 'Ayn al-Dawla, was a mere reactionary. He was appointed because he was thought to be a strong man capable of forcing acceptance of Naus's proposals. He actually instituted a central treasury and imposed a ten per cent tax on official pensions and salaries. Moreover, he was a nationalist; he opposed further foreign loans and concessions, and placed the Cossack Brigade (at least nominally) under the War Ministry. In discussing British attitudes, Mr Âdamiyyat notes that the minister, Sir Arthur Hardinge, warned against the appointment of permanent inspectors in areas hereditarily ruled by semi-feudal vassals; he thinks that the motive was an imperialistic concern to protect British 'agents' such as Shaykh Khaz'al in Khuzistan and Hishmat al-Mulk in Sistan. On the other hand, the vassal ruler would have existed even if the British had not had dealings with some of them, and they survived until Rizâ Khan gathered enough strength to suppress them; meanwhile, their existence could not prudently be ignored. The significance of the matter is that the nationalism of 'Ayn al-Dawla, the constitutionalists, and Rizâ Khan alike presupposed a unitary, not a federal, Iranian state. Mr Âdamiyyât evidently agrees with this, though he approves of the attempt to set up a federal Caucasian state after the First World War.

'Ayn al-Dawla directed his repressive efforts against discontented *bâzârî*s rather than radical intellectuals. The indiscretion of Naus in letting himself be photographed in a *mujtahîd*'s garb at a fancy dress ball infuriated the clergy, and the action of 'Alâ' al-Dawla, the governor of Tehran, in bastinadoing two allegedly profiteering sugar traders without any proper trial united the *bâzârî*s, the merchants, and the intellectuals in opposition to the government. Although few of the provincial and not all of the Tehrani *'ulamâ'* joined in the wave of protestation, the support of the *mujtahid*s Sayyid 'Abdallâh Bihbihânî and Sayyid Muhammad Tabâtabâ'î and other respected clergy of the capital greatly added to its force. Their demands, however, were only for an undefined *'adâlatkhâna* (house of justice), for the dismissal of Naus and 'Alâ' al-Dawla, and for matters such as the vindication of a *mujtahid* of Kirman, Mîrzâ Muhammad Rizâ, who had been bastinadoed by the governor for his incitement of violence against the town's Shaykhî and Jewish communities.

According to Mr Âdamiyyât, the call for an objective parliament was first made at a meeting of court dignitaries on 5 May 1906 by the already-mentioned Ihtishâm al-Saltana, who was a former head of the Education Council and envoy to Germany. One of the counter-arguments was that a parliament would put state affairs under the control of 'corrupt' clergy. The intellectuals were able to take the lead because they were successful in influencing the *bâzârî*s through like-minded merchants and literate opinion through clubs (*anjuman*s) and through pamphlets and newspapers. With remarkable similarity to the previous year's events at St Petersburg, where a general strike had led to the Tsar's consent for the election of the First Duma, the bazaar closure and the great *bast* in the British legation at Tehran led to Muzaffar al-Dîn Shah's grant of the constitutional charter of 5 August 1906. Most of the 14,000 *bastî*s were members of bazaar guilds, but some were students of the modern colleges and schools. The expenses of the *bastî*s were paid by leading merchants such as Hâjjî Husayn Âqâ Amîn al-Zarb, and their demand for constitutional government was prompted by leading intellectuals such as the German-educated Murtazâ-Qulî Khan Sanî' al-Dawla. While recognising that the pro-constitutionalist *'ulamâ'* continued to play a very important role, Mr Âdamiyyat observes that they were not the driving force and that they were not motivated by approbation or understanding of constitutional principles. They shared the popular feelings of nationalism and desire for justice, and they also feared that the prestige of the clergy might decline if they stood aloof from the popular movement. Bihbihânî and Tabâtabâ'î certainly knew more about modern problems than other *'ulamâ'* did. Bihbihânî had long had a hand in high-level politics and, like his friend Atâbak, was temperamentally a conciliator. Tabâtabâ'î had founded a modern school (Dabistân-i Islâm) and was in touch with intellectual *anjuman*s; so too was the foremost pro-constitutionalist preacher, Sayyid Jamâl al-Dîn Isfahânî. Not even Bihbihânî and Tabâtabâ'î, however, understood the meaning of democracy. A retrospective comment by Tabâtabâ'î shows that he saw constitutionalism as a means, not an end: 'We had not experienced constitutional government, but had been told by those who had visited constitutional countries that it gave them security and prosperity. We therefore wished to establish a constitutional system here.' The same view appears in a remark of Muzaffar al-Dîn Shah also quoted by Mr Âdamiyyat: 'The kings of Europe all govern with the help of a parliament, and they are a great deal stronger than the Shah of Iran.'

The First Majlis was not in fact very democratic. The peasants and tribes, who had not taken part in the constitutionalist movement but formed eighty per cent of the population, were not represented in it at all, while Tehran, with 60 of the 156 seats, was overrepresented. The deputies were elected by six classes: Qajar princes, notables (*a'yân u ashrâf*), *'ulamâ'* and theology students, landowners and *fallâhîn* (i.e. small landowners and substantial tenants), merchants, and guilds. The reason for the choice of the class system and the discrimination in favour of Tehran was that these would produce a parliament in the shortest possible time. The deputies came from a wider urban social range than those in the second and later parliaments elected under universal suffrage, who were more representative of provincial and landowning interests. Mr Âdamiyyat points out that a deputy in the First Majlis did not have to belong to the class which elected him. Among the guild deputies were *mullâ*s and teachers as well as shopkeepers. About twenty well-informed intellectuals were elected by the *a'yân* and other classes. Many deputies owned land, but none of the big landowners held seats. Although there were no parties, Mr Âdamiyyat concludes from his study of the debates that there were four tendencies, which he defines as moderate, progressive, extreme right, and extreme left. The moderates, with deputies representing all the classes, were the most numerous. The progressives, who were intellectuals and enlightened merchants, initiated all the major measures. On the extreme right were a few anti-constitutionalist *mullâs*. On the extreme left were four deputies, Sayyid Hasan Taqîzâda and Hâjjî Mîrzâ Ibrâhîm Âqâ of Tabriz, Shaykh Husayn Falak al-Ma'âlî of Rasht, and Yahyâ Mîrzâ Iskandarî, a Qajar prince. Taqîzâda and Ibrâhîm Âqâ were members of the Ijtimâ'iyyûn-i 'Âmmiyyûn (Social Democrats), a semi-clandestine group affiliated to the Caucasian and Russian socialists, and Mr Âdamiyyat surmises that Falak al-Ma'âlî belonged to the group's Rasht branch. These deputies did not voice socialist doctrines and generally concurred with the progressives, but they used fiery language and were suspected of association with anarchists or nihilists. In fact, though this was not then known, the Ijtimâ'iyyûn-i 'Âmmiyyûn operated both overtly through *anjuman*s using the name *mujâhidîn* and covertly through secret committees and terror squads. Haydar Khan 'Ammûoghlî, the leader at Tehran, organised the assassination of Atâbak (again Prime Minister since May 1907) on 30 August 1907 and the attempted assassination of Muhammad 'Alî Shah on 27 February 1908. (He was arrested after the latter event and then released for lack of evidence.)

Mr Âdamiyyat examines the work of the First Majlis on the constitution, on its own procedures and powers, and on the country's financial, economic, and social problems. The first fundamental law was drafted by a committee in which the chief figures were Mîrzâ Husayn Khan Mu' tamin al-Mulk (Pirniyâ), a former ambassador to Russia, Mîrzâ Hasan Khan Mushîr al-Mulk (Pirniyâ), a teacher at the Political Science College, and Mîrzâ Rizâ Khan Mu'ayyid al-Saltana, a French-educated ex-minister; the first two were sons of the then Prime Minister, Mîrzâ Nasrallâh Khan Mushîr al-Dawla. The Majlis, then consisting almost solely of Tehran deputies, approved the draft after only three days of debate; but much wrangling with the court over important matters such as the composition of the future Senate and the immunity of the First Majlis from dissolution took place before the Shah and the Crown Prince signed the law on 30 December 1906. As regards procedure, only the progressive deputies knew how foreign parliaments worked; others wasted time through their fondness for digression, oratory, poetry recitation, ceremonial etiquette and late arrival. Non-members, from the *mujtahid*s Bihbihânî, Tabâtabâ'î and Fazlallâh Nûrî down to journalists and spectators, often joined in the debates. Mainly through the efforts of Ihtishâm al-Saltana, who became the second speaker (September 1907– April 1908), and of Mîrzâ Muhammad Khan Sadîq-i Hazrat, a deputy with a French law degree, the Majlis was ultimately persuaded to adopt timetables and agenda and to entrust matters of detail to special committees. Foreign diplomatists were often among the spectators, and the British oriental secretary Walter Smart reported that the Majlis in its last months had become as well ordered and efficient as the House of Commons. In the assertion of parliamentary authority, the protagonist was Mîrzâ Javâd Khan Sa'd al-Dawla, an *a'yân* deputy who had been minister at Brussels, where he engaged Naus, and Minister of Commerce under 'Ayn al-Dawla until he resigned in protest against the bastinadoing of the two sugar traders and was exiled to Yazd. His insistence on ministerial responsibility to parliament was partly, if not wholly, vindicated when the cabinet of Sultân 'Alî Khan Vazîr-i Afkham resigned in May 1907 after a vote of no confidence in the Majlis. It was Sa'd al-Dawla who first called for a supplementary fundamental law (*mutammim*) to define the functions of the legislature, executive, and judiciary. The Majlis, which had already put him in charge of a board of thirteen translators to translate foreign laws, appointed him head of a committee of seven to draft the *mutammim*. Among this committee's members were Sadîq-i Hazrat, Hâjjî Amîn al-Zarb, Taqîzâda and Sayyid Nasrallâh Taqavî, a constitutionalist clerical deputy. Before the committee finished its work, Sa'd al-Dawla resigned from the Majlis and the constitutionalist ranks, probably in the hope of high ministerial office. (He later became Foreign Minister, and in the last months of Muhammad 'Alî Shah's short autocracy he was acting Prime Minister.) The committee (like the Ottoman drafters in 1876) used the Belgian constitution of 1831 as a model and did not place any restriction on the legislative power of the parliament. The translation board produced the draft of a press law on the French model, and Mu'tamin al-Mulk produced the draft of a judiciary law.

Like the historian Kasravî, Mr Âdamiyyat recognises the irreconcilability of popular sovereignty exercised through parliament with supremacy of the *Sharî'a* interpreted by *mujtahid*s representing the infallible hidden Imâm. In the First Majlis, however, most of the deputies had the existing Iranian situation in mind. They thought that parliamentary legislation would not touch *shar'î* matters but would only deal with matters such as crime hitherto under the jurisdiction of *'urf* (custom) and financial and administrative matters. Sanî' al-Dawla, who was the first speaker, held this view. Mr Âdamiyyat quotes Mîrzâ Fazl 'Alî Âqâ, a clerical deputy and probably a Shaykhî, who said that matters which the *Sharî'a* treats as permissible or does not specifically regulate should be decided by the rational men (*'uqalâ'*) of every age in the light of its requirements; among such matters he mentioned taxes not specified in the *Sharî'a* but required for the community's defence and well-being, and treaties in circumstances where *shar'î* rules cannot be enforced. He thus endorsed parliamentary sovereignty in at least the determination of jurisdictional limits. This view was not acceptable to *'ulamâ'* and deputies who believed that the *Sharî'a* extends over all human activity. The draft of the *mutammim* gives rise to an agitation for either *hukûmat-i mashrû'a* (*shar'î* government) or *mashrûta-yi mashrû'a* (*shar'î* constitutional government, which in logic is a contradiction). The agitation was led by Shaykh Fazlallâh Nûrî, who had earlier supported the constitutional movement because of its nationalist content. Although the agitation was supported by court reactionaries and partly motivated by Nûrî's jealousy of Bihbihânî and Tabâtabâ'î, Mr Âdamiyyat does not wholly deny Nûrî's sincerity, and he also casts some doubt on Bihbihânî's intellectual honesty. Nûrî's attainments in *ijtihâd* were higher than those of Bihbihânî and Tabâtabâ'î, and he resented the Majlis's deference to the two *sayyid*s, who were consulted about almost everything. Nûrî is reported to have said, 'Sayyid 'Abdallâh and Sayyid Muhammad are not in favour of constitutionalism; they are against me.' Bihbihânî told the Majlis,

> I have a request to make. Never argue that in such and such a country they have done this or that, so let us do likewise! For the common people would not understand, and we would be offended. We now have laws (*qavânîn*), and we have the Qur'ân. I do not mean that you should not mention this; you certainly should. But if you analyse the matter, you will find that what they (the foreigners) have done is based on wisdom (*hikmat*) and derived from the laws (*qavânîn*) of the *Sharî'at*.

Asadallâh Mîrzâ Shihâb al-Dawla, a progressive English-educated prince deputy, endorsed Bihbihânî by saying, 'Foreign countries which have sound laws got them from our Qur'ân and *Sharî'at*.' Mr Âdamiyyat doubts whether the speakers and their hearers believed these words. While acknowledging the expediency of such casuistry at the time, he considers that the practice of concealing rational ideas under *shar'î* garbs had a detrimental effect on Iranian political thinking.

While deputies such as Ihtishâm al-Saltana did not hesitate to condemn clerical obstruction of the urgently needed passage of the *mutammim,* others insisted on supervision of legislation either by competent scholars (*hujaj al-Islâm*) among the clerical deputies, or by popularly elected *mujtahid*s, or by non-elected *mujtahid*s, or by the *marja' al-taqlîd,* i.e. senior *mujtahid* (at that time Âkhund Kâzim Khurâsânî, who lived outside Iran at Najaf). Under pressure from Bihbihânî for a compromise, the deputies finally voted, by an unrecorded majority, for article 2 of the *mutammim,* which Shaykh Fazlallâh Nûrî had drafted; and they then passed, without any major amendments, the rest of the *mutammim,* which received Muhammad 'Alî Shah's assent on 8 October 1907. Article 2, with its sanction for a veto on legislation by five unelected *mujtahid*s, was a potentially grave derogation of parliamentary sovereignty. Mr Âdamiyyat thinks that the progressive deputies accepted it in view of its probable unenforceability, and that most (though not all) of the clergy preferred acceptance of constitutional government with this restriction to a conflict with contemporary public opinion. Shaykh Fazlallâh Nûrî and other fundamentalist 'ulamâ' found grounds for continuing opposition in the rest of the *mutammim*. Article 8 granted equal rights before the law to all Iranian citizens, whereas the *Sharî'a* grants fewer rights to non-Muslims and women in matters such as taxation, evidence, retaliation, blood-money, family law and inheritance. Some of the deputies had wanted to refer the matter to Najaf, but the majority had voted for the article after hearing Sayyid Muhammad Tabâtabâ'î's endorsement of it and a petition from the Zoroastrian community. Article 20, granting freedom of expression and prohibiting censorship, excluded blasphemous and heretical writings, but placed such cases under the press law, thereby withdrawing them from *shar'î* jurisdiction. Feelings had been stirred by the case of Sayyid Jalâl al-Dîn Mu'ayyid al-Islâm, editor of the newspaper *Habl al-Matîn*, who had written, 'Arab laws of 1300 years ago may not be suitable for the Iranians of today.' Despite pressure for a *shar'î* trial, the Majlis had stood firm, and he had been punished by the civil authorities. Mîrzâ Hasan Khan Ahsan al-Dawla, a French-educated progressive, had remarked, 'The truth of a religion cannot be proved or disproved by a law.'

This remark implies acceptance of the concept that religion is voluntary. Mr Âdamiyyat mentions that some deputies criticised article 1 of the *mutammim*, which required the Shah and by extension the government to promote the state religion, and that they were severely rebuked; but he does not discuss the fact that under the constitution of 1906–7 religion continued to be a matter of inherited status and registration, not of voluntary belief and association. While a non-Muslim Iranian could legally become a Muslim, a Muslim Iranian could not legally become a non-Muslim, and neither could become a heretical Bâbî or Bahâ'î; and from 1945 to 1949 an Iranian could legally profess communism and therewith atheism but could not legally cease to be an adherent of his registered religion.

The most serious and lasting conflict between parliamentary and clerical authority was, in Mr Âdamiyyat's assessment, over the judiciary (articles 71–89 of the *mutammim*). He quotes an observation by Sayyid Muhammad Tabâtabâ'î as evidence of fear among the 'ulamâ' that the establishment of civil courts might deprive them of their function and social status as judges and lawyers. In spite of a letter from Âkhûnd Kâzim Khurâsânî demanding that procedures and penalties should be *shar'î* and unchangeable, the majority of the deputies had insisted that the judicial system should be determined by parliament and administered by the Justice Ministry.

In addition to the Majlis debates, Mr Âdamiyyat has studied contemporary clerical writings. The absolutist 'ulamâ' denied the competence of religiously ignorant laymen to legislate and decide policy, but took for granted the existence of a just ruler who would enforce the *Sharî'a* and defend the lives and properties of the Muslims. They either disregarded the risk of the ruler's unwillingness or inability to perform these functions, or thought that in such a case the believers could only pray to God to send them a better ruler. The alternative of a clerical assumption of political power was not entertained. The important pro-constitutionalist book *Tanbîh al-umma va tanzîh al-milla* by Mîrzâ Muhammad Husayn Nâ'inî has also been analysed in Dr 'Abd al-Hadi Hâ'irî's *Shi'ism and constitutionalism in Iran*.[6] Nâ'inî was the secretary and confidant of Âkhûnd Kâzim Khurâsânî and himself a *mujtahid* of high standing. The book was printed at Baghdad in March–April 1909 and reprinted in Tehran in 1910 and 1955. (It was cited by Engineer Mahdî Bâzargân in his trial after the religious riots of 5–8 June 1963.) Nâ'inî produced weighty arguments against despotism and for political freedom and representative parliamentary government subject to *shar'î* limitations (as laid down in article 2 of the *mutammim*). He approved of the parliamentary representation of religious minorities because they also are taxpayers, but did not discuss the problem of religious freedom. He approved of equality in the sense of legal equality of the strong and the weak, or the rich and the poor (an essential element of the *Sharî'a*), but did not discuss the *shar'î* inequality of non-Muslims and women. More forward-looking is another pro-constitutional book which Mr Âdamiyyat examined, namely Mullâ 'Abd al-Rasûl Kâshânî's *Risâla-yi insâfiyya dar usûl-i âzâdî*.[7] Keenly aware of the contemporary European advance and Eastern backwardness, Mullâ 'Abd al-Rasûl thought that this was because the Christians had abandoned monasticism while the Muslims had disregarded Islamic injunctions to seek knowledge and use reason. The Muslims must turn their minds to science and industry and to people's changing needs. A parliament representing the people must enact currently needed laws except in specifically *shar'î* fields. The head of state and the ministers and officials must be responsible to the parliament, and the legislative, executive and judicial powers must be separated to prevent tyranny. The most important task of government is to help the people to find work, because idle hands turn to evil deeds. The Iranians were being deprived of work by the importation of foreign goods. The government and the rich ought to build railways and factories, and the people ought to buy national goods. Setting up schools to teach people how to think and work is a religious duty. Taxation should be mainly direct and progressive, and sinecures should be abolished. There should be equality before the law (no doubt with *shar'î* limitations) and freedom of expression. The press could have a great educative value, though the abusive language of certain newspapers (in the time of the First Majlis) had done great harm. As regards religious freedom, it is for God alone to judge a person's belief. Mr Âdamiyyat finds traces of the social thinking of 'Abd al-Rahîm Tâlibov and Mîrzâ Âqâ Khan Kirmânî in this remarkable book by a *mullâ* of a small town. Having been written for the people of Kashan, it probably had few readers elsewhere.

Mr Âdamiyyat's conclusions about the struggle over the nature of the constitution give food for thought. The rational modernisers prevailed because they had the support of nationalist public opinion. In the circumstances, their prestige eclipsed the prestige of the clergy. Muhammad 'Alî Shah's justification of his Russian-backed coup d'état of 23 June 1908 as a move for *shar'î* government and Shaykh Fazlallâh Nûrî's endorsement of the coup did not carry much weight. Under the restored autocracy, however, the constitutionalists needed and sought clerical support. The stand of Âkhûnd Kâzim Khurâsânî and other eminent *'ulamâ'* against unjust despotism and foreign interference was one of the factors which made the overthrow of Muhammad 'Alî Shah possible. Thus the clergy regained much of their prestige after the restoration of constitutional government in July 1909. At the same time, the intelligentsia began to lose prestige because they failed to live up to their responsibilities. These findings prompt the question whether the ascendancy of the intelligentsia could have lasted for long if the constitutional régime had been secure and had survived. Mr Âdamiyyat thinks that the First Majlis might then have been able to set Iran on a broadly acceptable course of modernisation. On the other hand, it is possible that further rational reforms, particularly in economic and educational fields touching everyday life, might when operative have seemed alien and objectionable to large numbers of people. Even if all the intellectuals had been paragons of virtue and good sense, they might have incurred distrust as a *farangî-ma'âb* (Europeanised) minority, careless of Iranian culture and Islamic custom. The spokesmen of popular cultural and religious nationalism might well have been fundamentalist *'ulamâ'* of Shaykh Fazlallâh Nûrî's school. Nûrî's reputation was at least partly restored when he showed the same steadfastness before the special court which condemned him to death in July 1909 as the constitutionalist spokesmen Mîrzâ Jahângîr Khan Sûr-i Isrâfîl and Mîrzâ Nasrallâh Bihishtî Malik al-Mutakallimîn had shown before Muhammad 'Alî Shah's executioners in June 1908. Half a century later, the writer Jalâl Âl-i Ahmad declared in his pamphlet *Gharbzadagî* ('Infection by the West'),[8] 'Shaykh Fazlallâh Nûrî was hanged because he stood for the integrity of Islamic Shi'ism . . . To me the corpse of that great man hanging from the scaffold seems like a flag signalising the victory of *gharbzadagî* hoisted over this house (i.e. Iran).' Since the revolution of 1979, a street in Tehran has been renamed after Shaykh Fazlallâh Nûrî, but no streets have been renamed after Sayyid Muhammad Tabâtabâ'î and Sayyid 'Abd Allâh Bihbihânî.

On the subject of the First Majlis's attitudes to the country's financial and socio-economic problems, Mr Âdamiyyat notes that most of the deputies were conservative or cautious. Only the progressives made radical reform proposals, which the left-wing extremists criticised but supported. One of the first demands which the deputies put forward was for the dismissal of Naus, who resigned in February 1907, but the reforms which they enacted were on the lines of Naus's plans. Another early action of the Majlis was its refusal of a joint Russian and British loan offer which the Prime Minister, Mîrzâ Nasrallâh Khan Mushîr al-Dawla, considered necessary to meet the deficit – then so bad that payment of officials and troops was in arrear. Instead, the Majlis approved the plan of a merchant deputy, Hâjjî Muhammad Mu'în al-Tujjâr Bûshihrî, for a National Bank which would make loans to the government and receive monopolies of mining on state lands and pearl fishing; the initial capital would be subscribed by merchants and the rest by the public with no foreign participation, After the passage of the National Bank law on 28 December 1906, many patriots including women (among them, according to Kasravî, a poor washerwoman) subscribed, but few merchants and other rich men took the risk. Mr Âdamiyyat mentions that Atâbak during his last premiership strongly supported the National Bank scheme, and that the Majlis approved his Finance Minister Nâsir al-Mulk's recommendations to engage a foreign banking expert. This was obstructed by Russian and British insistence that the expert should be an adviser to the government, not just to the National Bank, and that he should be required to consult their two legations. The Majlis finally agreed to these terms, and the French adviser Bizot, who arrived in March 1908, found himself powerless. Mr Âdamiyyat attributes the rich men's chariness mainly to the political uncertainty but also to fear of embezzlement.

The First Majlis enacted important laws concerning land and taxation of land but did little to improve the status of peasants. Early in 1907, on the recommendation of the finance committee headed by Mîrzâ Hasan Vuthûq al-Dawla, the Majlis abolished fiefs (*tuyûl*), and therewith military duties attaching to certain fiefs and obligations of peasants such as corvées (*bîgârî*), but left the lands in the possession of the former fiefholders because resumption by the state was impracticable. On learning from the committee that the latest land tax assessments dated from 1886 and that the pricing of cash equivalents of taxes in kind (*tas'îr*) was based on old prices far below current levels, the Majlis abolished taxation in kind and legislated for future assessment on the basis of scientific surveys and censures. The Majlis also abolished tax farming and legislated for collection of all revenues by Finance Ministry officials, together with increased rates of land taxation to cover the costs of collection and of provincial administration. Time and adequate means were needed for implementation of these measures. Meanwhile, economies such as cuts in sinecures on which the Majlis insisted began to reduce the deficit.

In April 1908, proposals for both reform and development were put to the Majlis by the German-educated Sanî' al-Dawla, who was then Finance Minister. (He had resigned from the Majlis and the speakership in September 1907.) In a previously published essay entitled *Râh-i najât* he had cited statistics showing that on the average Iranians paid one *tûmân* per head annually to their government, while Germans paid 24 *tûmân*s and Ottoman subjects paid 14 *tûmân*s. He proposed that land taxes should be not only scientifically assessed but also reformed in ways to make the peasants and tribes more prosperous; that taxes should be levied on urban buildings and gardens, with half of the proceeds going to the government and half to municipalities for expenditure on schools; and that an extra excise should be imposed on sugar and tea to pay for the construction of paved roads and railways without recourse to foreign finance. (In Rizâ Shah's reign, taxation of sugar and tea provided much of the cost of the Trans-Iranian railway.) These proposals were welcomed by the great majority of the deputies, though criticised as premature by Taqîzâda. Russian and British approval was needed for an excise on sugar and tea, and the British minister told Sanî' al-Dawla that he ought to have consulted Bizot. A few weeks later, the Majlis was bombarded and dispersed.

Although the peasant problem was less immediate than others, the First Majlis was well aware of it. Fifty years earlier, Mîrzâ Malkam Khan and his father Mîrzâ Ya'qûb Khan, and more recently Âqâ Khan Kirmânî and Tâlibov, had written about the desirability of reforms such as transfer of land ownership to the cultivators. In the first Russian Duma of May– July 1906, the Constitutional Democrat (Cadet) majority as well as the socialists had demanded land reforms. Moreover, Gilan in 1906–7 was the scene of a peasant insurrection, which Mr Âdamiyyat discusses in detail. In that province, the main landowners were very rich while the peasants were subject to onerous burdens such as landlord's permission for marriage and were practically bound to the soil, though not legally serfs. The insurgents withheld landlord's crop shares, committed acts of violence, and began to leave the land. With guidance from the Anjuman-i 'Abbâsî, an artisans' association in touch with the Ijtimâ'iyyûn-i 'Ammiy- yûn branch at Rasht, the insurrection became organised, and it did not subside when the Anjuman's leaders, Mîrzâ Rahîm Shîshabur and Sayyid Jalâl al-Dîn Shahrâshûb, were bastinadoed and imprisoned. In the Majlis, the deputies, and also Sayyid Muhammad Tabâtabâ'î, maintained that the existence of constitutional government did not justify law-break- ing, though a few deputies also criticised the landowners and Asadallâh Mîrzâ Shihâb al-Dawla called for a progressive tax on landowners' in- comes. Mr Âdamiyyat found to his surprise that not a single deputy, not even Taqîzâda and the other leftists, ever spoke of distributing state lands to peasants or increasing peasants' crop shares. It could be argued that this was because peasants and tribes were not represented in the First Majlis. (The need for their representation was acknowledged, and in the second and later parliaments seats were reserved for tribes and also for religious minorities.) The speeches show, however, that the Majlis's main concern was the risk of Russian intervention in Gilan if the disorder continued. To pacify the province, the cabinet sent a new governor, 'Alî Khan Zahîr al-Dawla (well-known as a Sûfî of the Ni'matallâhî order), who set up an inquiry commission and brought about some alleviation of the peasants' burdens. A strike of 3,000 fishermen against the Lianozov caviar concession company in 1906 also caused anxiety. Mr Âdamiyyat regards this as the first strike in Iran (apart from bazaar closures). The Ijtimâ'iyyûn-i 'Âmmiyyûn of Enzeli were active in organising it. Finally, the company gave the fishermen better terms.

Foreign socialist ideas were bound to reach Iran, but on account of the lack of Iranian-owned capitalist industry, Marxist theories had little immediate relevance except in their antifeudal, i.e. anti-landlord, aspect. Nevertheless, the Ijtimâ'iyyûn-i 'Âmmiyyûn played an important part in Iranian history. For this reason, Mr Âdamiyyat's book *Fikr-i dimûkrâsî-yi ijtimâ'î* is of great interest; it is more balanced than another recent book, Schapour Ravasani's *Gilan: die sozialistische Bewegung in Iran seit Ende des 19. Jhdts. bis 1922.*[9]

Mr Âdamiyyat considers Âqâ Khan Kirmânî (1853–97) to have been the first Iranian socialist thinker. He was interested in contemporary European socialism as well as the Sâsânid Iranian Mazdakite movement, and he thought that Iran needed political and religious freedom, demo-cratic government and equalisation of wealth through limitation of pro-perty ownership, particularly land ownership. Despite censorship, his writings reached Iran and, according to Mr Âdamiyyat, were known to Mîrzâ Jahângîr Khan, the editor of the newspaper *Sûr-i Isrâfîl*. Iranian intellectuals were of course aware of European developments such as the Russian revolution of 1905 and the rise of the French socialist party under Jean Jaurès. They wanted Iran to have modern industries and knew that labour problems might result. Mr Âdamiyyat mentions the publication of a treatise on economics, *Usûl-i tharvat-i milal,* in 1323/1905 by Mîrzâ Muhammad 'Alî Furûghî Zukâ al-Mulk, who devoted fourteen pages to the need for factory inspection, working hours' limitation, and workers' rights to combine and strike. In a series of articles in *Sûr-i Isrâfîl,* the author 'A. A. D. ('Alî Akbar Dihkhudâ) expressed a socialist view when he wrote that the constitutional régime would make the rich richer by giving them the security of the rule of law and that anticipatory action on behalf of the poor was therefore needed. Iran's basic problem was peasant poverty and agricultural backwardness. Dihkhudâ feared (incorrectly) that the insurrection in Gilan would spread to the rest of the country. He proposed distribution of state lands to peasants and gradual transfer of private lands to the cultivators, and even though he thought that the landlords no longer performed a useful function, he recommended compensation for them to avoid political trouble. One of Dihkhudâ's beliefs was that Islam has more compassion than other religions for the poor and is therefore favourable to social reform – a belief held by Islamic socialists ever since.

From this account, it is clear that the Ijtimâ'iyyûn-i 'Âmmiyyûn did not contribute anything new and relevant to Iranian political thinking. Their importance lay in the sphere of organisation and action. In Caucasia there was a rapidly growing industrial sector centred on the oil of Baku, where Iranian emigrants constituted 22 per cent of the workforce. In 1904 a Muslim Caucasian socialist party called Himmat had been set up by Dr Narîmân (a doctor of medicine) under the auspices of the Russian Social Democrat Workers' Party. Its members held varying views and in the main were not only socialist but also nationalist. In 1904 the Himmat party set up the Ijtimâ'iyyûn-i 'Âmmiyyûn group with headquarters at Baku to work among the Iranian emigrants and in Iran. Branches were formed at Mashhad, Tehran, Rasht, Enzeli and Tabriz. The Mashhad and Tehran branches were started by Haydar Khan 'Ammûoghlî, a Maragha-born electrician who had returned to Iran to work in the country's first generating plants (the founder and owner of the Tehran plant was Hâjjî Amîn al-Zarb). As already mentioned, the branches had secret committees to which the public ('umûmî) committees were subordinate. The programme (marâm-nâma) of the Ijtimâ'iyyûn-i 'Âmmiyyûn drawn up at Mashhad on 10 September 1907 called for parliamentary government with universal suffrage (instead of class representation) without a second chamber, ministerial responsibility to parliament, freedom of expression, progressive direct taxation, compulsory military service (to replace the Cossacks and local levies), state provision of schools and hospitals, an eight-hour working day, free distribution of state lands to peasants and the compulsory sale of private lands to the cultivators through an agricultural bank with the permission for the landowners to keep only sufficient land for their own subsistence. Though obviously impracticable in the short term, this programme was scarcely revolutionary except as regards compulsory land expropriation; many of its points concurred with the long term aims of the progressive constitutionalists. For the secret leaders, the programme may have had only a preliminary or tactical significance. In any case, it was not made known to the general public. Mr Âdamiyyat indicates that the Enzeli and Rasht branches were more extreme, while the Tabriz branch started by Karbalâ'î 'Alî Musyû defended Islam. Complete unanimity would hardly have been possible and did not exist in the parent Himmat party either.

Haydar 'Ammûoghlî used his secret devotees (fidâ'îs) to assassinate Atâbak and to attempt to assassinate Muhammad 'Alî Shah, and after the

61

bombardment of the Majlis he arranged the recruitment of Caucasian volunteers to strengthen the resisters at Tabriz, who also used the name *mujâhidîn* but were independently organised and led by Sattâr Khan and Bâqir Khan. The *mujâhidîn* organised by Sardar Muhî Mu'izz al-Sultân of the Ijtimâ'iyyûn-i 'Âmmiyyûn of Rasht also received the help of Caucasian volunteers and were the most effective force in the march on Tehran which restored constitutional government in July 1909. After that victory, the Ijtimâ'iyyûn-i 'Âmmiyyûn took the lead in organising the Democrat Party of Iran to contest the elections for the Second Majlis. Haydar 'Ammûoghlî was on the Democrat party's central committee, and Taqî-zâda became its parliamentary leader. Its programme echoed the Mash-had programme of the Ijtimâ'iyyûn-i 'Âmmiyyûn, but was more radical with regard to the clergy in that it called for separation of state authority from religious authority, and less radical with regard to the landowners in that it only called for the cultivator's preemptive right of purchase, with loan assistance from an agricultural bank if the landlord should put the land up for sale. Other points were distribution of state land to peasants, a ten hour working day, prohibition of child labour under the age of 14 and health inspection of factories (both relevant to the carpet trade), and safety inspection of cabs, scaffolds, and *qanât*-tunnellers' ropes. After the establishment of the Democrat party, the Ijtimâ'iyyûn-i 'Âmmiyyûn ceased to operate in Iran but remained active at Baku; the Democrats took over the Iranian branches and formed their own network covering most Iranian towns.

Mr Âdamiyyat is censorious of the conduct of the Democrats in the Second Majlis. The elections under universal suffrage produced an unstable parliament in which the Moderates were the largest organised party and the Democrats had twenty seats. The Moderate party enjoyed the support of landowners, merchants and constitutionalist clergy, and had progressives among its deputies. Curiously enough, the Moderates added the word 'social' to their party's name (I'tidâliyyûn-i 'Âmmiyyûn), while the Democrats did not. The word 'revolutionary' was applied by adversaries to the Democrats, whose published programme was indeed alarming to *'ulamâ'* and scarcely reassuring to landowners, though this was not the only factor which made them suspect. Both parties were nationalist, but the Moderates inclined to caution and the Democrats to recklessness. Mr Âdamiyyat thinks that if the Democrats had adhered to their principles and had performed their proper parliamentary task of critical opposition, they could have won support among the artisans and the peasants and might have laid the foundation of a two-party system in Iran. Instead, they caused cabinet crises and entered into unprincipled compacts for the sole purpose of getting friends into important ministries and offices. Mr Âdamiyyat notes that in a debate on a plan to rent state lands on ten-year leases to Iranian-owned companies, a Moderate deputy made the criticism that it had no provision for greater rights for the peasants, while Taqîzâda recommended engagement of foreign experts to run the companies. Not a single deputy spoke of distribution of state lands to peasants, even though this was on the Democrat party's programme.

On the subject of the disbandment of the group of 300 *mujâhidîn*, Mr Âdamiyyat's account supplements Kasravî's. The government took on two-thirds of the *mujâhidîn* as police and troops, but had misgivings about the remainder, among whom were some Caucasian volunteers, and was under strong Russian pressure to disband them. The Democrats spoke out for the threatened *mujâhidîn*, while the Moderates spoke out for the government. A squad of Haydar 'Ammûoghlî's *fidâ'î*s who belonged to this group of *mujâhidîn* assassinated an influential Moderate politician, Mîrzâ Hasan Khan Amîn al-Mulk, in his house. Suspecting Taqîzâda of complicity, the Moderates asked Sayyid 'Abdallâh Bihbihânî to obtain a letter of excommunication (*takfîr-nâma*) against him from the *marja' al-taqlîd*, Âkhûnd Kâzim Khurâsânî. The letter arrived from Najaf and was discussed in secret session. Despite the *marja'*'s ruling that Taqîzâda was a corrupter of the earth (*mufsid al-ard*) and should therefore be expelled from the Majlis, the deputies preferred to offer him sick leave abroad. In the night of 14–15 July 1910, four of Haydar 'Ammûoghlî's *fidâ'î*'s assassinated Sayyid 'Abdallâh Bihbihânî in his house. The guilds closed the bazaars in protest. Retaliating gunmen shot a relative of Taqîzâda and another 'revolutionary' politician in a cab and later also killed a relative of Haydar 'Ammûoghlî. Mr Âdamiyyat is convinced that Taqîzâda, despite his later denials, must have been privy to the assassinations of Bihbihânî and Atâbak.

The rest of *Fikr-i dimûkrâsî-yi ijtimâ'î* is a study of the career and ideas of Muhammad Amîn Rasûlzâda (1884–1954) and of the rift between social democracy or parliamentary socialism and the dictatorial bureaucratic communism of Lenin and Stalin. Rasûlzâda was a Muslim Caucasian journalist and a member of the Himmat party. He began his career as editor of the Baku Azeri newspapers *Takâmul, Irshâd* and *Taraqqî*, which also circulated in Iran. (*Irshâd* had a Persian supplement written by the Iranian poet Muhammad Sâdiq Adîb al-Mamâlik Farâhânî). After arriving in Tehran by way of Rasht with the Caucasian volunteers in July 1909, Rasûlzâda became a member of the Democrat party's central committee and the principal writer of the Democrat newspaper *Îrân-i naw* (edited by Sayyid Mahmûd Shabistarî). He was the first writer to propound Marxist theories in Iran and to introduce Marxist terminology into Persian, but he was also a believer in parliamentarism. Forced to leave Iran in December 1911, he went to Istanbul where he helped to form a Muslim Caucasian Democrat party. After returning to his homeland under an amnesty for the 300th anniversary of the Romanov dynasty, he was one of the leaders of this party which was renamed Musâvât (Equality). After the fall of the Tsar, he consistently but unsuccessfully advocated Caucasian federation. The Musâvât party was the largest in the elected parliament of the Republic of Caucasian Azerbaijan, which lasted from 25 May 1918 to 26 April 1920 and, amongst other things, passed a law for compulsory sale of estates to the cultivators. In this parliament, the Musâvât party was opposed by the Himmat party, which remained under Dr Narîmânov's leadership and followed the revolutionary socialist line; so too did the Ijtimâ'iyyûn-i 'Âmmiyyûn at Baku, who changed their name to the 'Adâlat (Justice) party in 1916 and to the Communist Party of Iran in 1920. After the destruction of Caucasian Azerbaijani independence by the Russian Bolsheviks, Rasûlzâda went to Moscow, and in 1922 he escaped abroad. He lived in Germany, Poland, Rumania and Turkey until his death. His principal later works were published at Istanbul in 1926 and 1928. Mr Âdamiyyat discusses the development of Rasûlzâda's thought from his earlier writings in Iran to his later writings, which condemn bureaucratic socialism and call for genuine democracy representing the national ethos as well as the social aspirations of the people.

It is to be hoped the promised sequel to *Îdi'ûlûzhî-yi nahzat-i mashrûtiyyat* will come out. In the stormy months before the forcible dissolution of the Second Majlis and in the early part of the First World War, the Democrats regained prestige through their vigorous nationalism, but subsequently they became disunited and ineffective. A study of their vicissitudes and of later Iranian political thinking from Mr Âdamiyyat's pen would be of great value.

NOTES AND REFERENCES
1. New York 1955.
2. Tehran 1334/1955.
3. Tehran 1340/1961.
4. Tehran 2534 [1354]/1975, reprinted 2535 [1355]/1976.
5. Tehran 2535 [1355]/1976.
6. Leiden 1977.
7. Kashan 1327/1909.
8. Tehran 1962.
9. Berlin n.d.

5

The cultural implications of the Constitutional Revolution

In his essay entitled 'The Return of the Sacred', Daniel Bell, the famous Harvard sociologist, attacks the social scientists' common view of secularisation as a 'one way street'. Arguing that changes in culture arise in a very different way, and follow a different path, from changes in social structure, he distinguishes the term secularisation which deals with the institutional changes leading to the 'shrinking of ecclesiastical authority in temporal realms', from profanation which deals with changes in ideas.[1]

The autonomous tendencies of religion in the West, which undermined the cultural foundations of Western religious answers in the period of the seventeenth to nineteenth centuries, are not to be found in Iranian Islamic culture. However, this does not mean that there was no disenchantment with the given set of answers which had till then provided the Muslim with a coherent view of the world, nor decline in the belief in the doctrine as enforced by the orthodox religious establishment, nor challenge, nor attack, or even rejection of institutionalised religion.

If one is to accept Irving Howe's definition of the modern as 'an inclusive negative' a 'revolt against the prevalent style, an unyielding rage against the official order'[2] one would indeed find modernistic elements in nineteenth-century Iranian culture. A continuing adversary stance came from within the religious institution and was directed against its high-ranking leaders who were specialists of Islamic law and jurisprudence. The anti-*fuqahâ' 'ulamâ'* were eroding the ground of clerical authority in society and paving the way for secularisation. The discovery of Western knowledge and secular institutions added weight to the religious dissidents' traditional argument against the *fuqahâ'*'s social influence and cultural dominance, and caused a rapprochement between the former group and the lay reformers and political activists. While the religious dissidents had favoured doctrinal reforms, the lay activists were willing to undertake institutional changes curtailing clerical authority in the public domain (secularisation) without openly acknowledging the need for doctrinal change.

Cultural modernism was ushered in by way of a political revolution, namely the Constitutional Revolution of 1906–11. The literature of revolt of that period took the lead in raising questions and issues no longer tied to modalities of religious beliefs, and offering new views of the individual and society. This individualism was first introduced in Iran as a political, not an aesthetic or philosophical concept. Nevertheless, the movement was essentially aiming at social and cultural reforms. At first it did not necessarily arouse the hostility or suspicion of the religious establishment as to its ultimate significance and goal. The Âyatallâhs who joined the ranks of the revolutionaries supported the call for a constitution, in order to check the Qajar officials' abuse of power. The dissident *'ulamâ'* were hoping to accomplish publicly what they failed to achieve through doctrinal reforms. The merchants wished for a guarantee for freedom of trade. The lay men of letters desired structural changes in the socio-cultural institutions to establish freedom of expression. While constitutionalists like Tabâtabâ'î, Bihbihânî, Taqîzâda, Sa'd al-Dawla, to mention only a few of the lay and clerical leaders of the movement, carried the political struggle to its logical conclusion, the establishment of a majlis and the promulgation of a constitution, their important collaborators, Malik al-Mutakallimîn, Nizâm al-Islâm, Majd al-Islâm, Sayyid Jamâl al-Dîn Vâ'iz, Dihkhudâ, Mîrzâ Jahângîr Khan, clerical and lay men of the pen, took up the task of enlightening the public as to the significance and the goal of the movement. They lectured in mosques and public squares, set up anjumans and schools, wrote regular columns in newspapers, circulated pamphlets to disseminate their views, and arranged clandestine meetings in private homes to plan action together with the majlis deputies. Through them the public was informed almost daily on political issues and decisions made in the majlis, kept up to date with events and, when it became necessary, mobilised to fight back counter-revolutionaries. They were the intellectuals who were to dominate the cultural scene by imposing their novel ideas and formulating the nationalist ideology. Marked differences in temperament and in short term goals did not hamper their collaboration. Nor did the turban, which Malik al-Mutakallimîn, Nizâm al-Islâm, Majd al-Islâm, Jamâl al-Dîn Vâ'iz persisted in wearing, symbolically clash with the European hat or faux-col that their lay associates wore. A unity in ideological purpose overcame style and rhetoric.

Whereas the preachers' sermons in the mosques followed the traditional theological style, commenting on Quranic verses or traditions which they would use to demonstrate the religious validity of the modern ideas they would insert in their speech, the lay writers adopted a literary style with little or no reference to the holy texts. For instance, discussing *'ilm,* Jamâl would put forward the un-Islamic view that there exist two kinds of knowledge, worldly and other-worldly. Though insisting that the latter is the noblest, and its specialists, the high ranking *'ulamâ'*, are the noblest of all learned men, he would argue that human beings need to further their knowledge of this world too. He would lament the fact that science and technology have progressed in Europe but not in Iran because of *'ulamâ'* opposition. He would passionately proclaim that ignorance lies at the root of all national problems, and that it was of utmost importance that the educational system be reformed.[3] Dihkhudâ, writing on the same subject, would bluntly declare there can be no limit to knowledge men can acquire, that neither Socrates nor Aristotle, nor Spencer, nor Kant can set a limit. Man's knowledge is perfectible and ignorance can never succeed in obstructing his path to progress. Neither the temporal ruler's stick nor the religious leader's order can prevent him from seeking perfection in total freedom. There is and there can be no limit to individual liberty.[4] Such blunt profane views invariably attracted the wrath of conservative clerics who would then condemn the entire constitutional movement as heretical. Put on the defensive, preachers and men of letters would attempt to distinguish between true Islam and that of the *'ulamâ'*. Lecturing on human rights from the *minbar* of a mosque, Jamâl would explain that the masses have historically suffered two types of oppression, political and spiritual. Of the two, he would add, spiritual oppression is the worst to bear, since the religious leaders are believed to be the successors to the Prophet. And he would dramatically command his followers: 'O Muslims! Enough of the sleep of ignorance! . . . Do not worship your *'ulamâ'* instead of God. Open your eyes, broaden your mind!', before demonstrating to them with evidence from the holy texts the Islamic character of such concepts as liberty, equality and freedom of opinion.[5] He would audaciously assert that the majlis is the *valî 'l-amr* in the absence of the Imâm, since it protects Islam and applies its laws. The constitutionalists are therefore merely attempting to bring the Muslims back to the straight path. In his defence of human rights, Dihkhudâ would pronounce unequivocally that Iranians should no longer be blinded by the princes and *âkhûnd*s; nor should they wait for the angel Gabriel to descend from heaven once more, or for a *mujtahid* to grant permission, or the Shah to sign a decree, to obtain their human rights.[6] Though he would specifically mention Fadlallâh Nûrî and other anti-constitutionalist *'ulamâ'*, referring to them as *'ulamâ-yi sû'* (a term that appears in classical theological texts to mean the bad *'ulamâ'*), or *tujjâr-i dîn* (traders in religion),[7] his acerbic atack implied broader anti-clericalism. Iran is the only nation, he wrote, which, despite the spread of the light of Islam, continually produces false prophets. Widespread ignorance and the tradition of personality cult makes it easy for them to find gullible masses to convert. Iranians have not been properly taught; they were prevented from broadening their minds. The *'ulamâ'* are responsible for obscuring the real meaning of Islam. Their discursive theology and their philosophy is a diluted mixture of Greek, Indian, Chaldean, and Jewish nonsense. 'Those are our *awliyâ-yi amr,* the successors to the Prophet, the representatives of the Imâm, who still wish to remain the guardians of our life

67

and the trustees of our properties. . . . Those are the learned men of the community, who have no purpose other than the cult of self and love of leadership.'[8] At times he would adopt a classical religious dissidents' argument that the hidden truth of the Quran and the traditions have yet to be unveiled progressively, as men develop and mature. The Quran has to be continuously allegorically interpreted and the laws readjusted, and even abrogated if need be, to fit new conditions, as the Prophet himself had done. However, despite his feeble attempts to declare his views on human rights compatible with true Islam, he would never miss an opportunity to defiantly proclaim his freedom from *mullâ* and king and proudly predict that these principles would wipe out all superstition throughout the world, and the 'worshippers of the old' would be forced to accept them.[9]

Dihkhudâ's writings created a furore in Tehran both in anti-constitution circles and among moderate constitutionalists. In self-defence he would protest the Islamic purity of his views, arguing he was being declared infidel by those who stood to lose from his denunciation of oppression. His use of the term 'worshippers of the old' was political in intention, meaning conservative, or those in favour of the status quo. It did not mean those who profess belief in the old religions. In fact, the term had nothing to do with religion, and therefore could not be contrary to Islam. Similarly, 'superstitious beliefs' did not mean Islam or Islamic principles, but referred to what 99 per cent of the Tehran population believed in and practised even though it was not sanctioned by Islam. He would also deny that the principle of constitutional monarchy was incompatible with Islam. It was originally Islamic, he would argue, but an end was put to it with the last of the righteous caliphs and, since then, the Muslims had forgotten all about it. Now we find ourselves forced to borrow it from Europe and call it constitution.[10]

The majlis supported him and others like him. When it was forced by his opponents to discuss in a special session his alleged irreligiosity, the deputies absolved him from any anti-Islamic or blasphemous views.[11] They would even adopt his argument to silence some of the deputies' objections to the emulation of European laws. 'The Europeans had no laws of their own; they took them all from us, though they have improved them; we are only taking back what belongs to us in the first place.'[12]

Judging from the minutes of the First Majlis, these arguments did not arouse too much controversy. There was a general acceptance, open or tacit, of the fact that Iranian legislators, inexperienced as they were in their new task, had to study and accommodate European laws. Áyatallâh Bihbihânî himself, in the course of a debate on the law that would forbid government officials from holding two posts simultaneously, counselled the deputies not to mention by name the foreign government whose law was being considered as a model, because it is 'offensive'; they should merely state that their legal decisions were based on Quranic law.[13] Thus the legal foundation of modern Iran was being laid by lay and clerical politicians who blended or juxtaposed the profane and the sacred, the worldly and the holy, the Islamic and the European, without being fully aware of what such an experiment may entail for the traditional social order. The Âyatallâhs who sanctioned the constitution conceived the majlis as an 'assembly of wise men' that would institutionalise the traditional function of the individual '*ulamâ*' of 'setting limits to oppression, so it can be tolerated'; of insuring the protection and survival of the right religion and the application of its laws; of establishing reforms salutary to the nation's material life. They conceded to its deputies the right to legislate law pertaining to public affairs, following the traditional Islamic distinction of '*urf* from *shar*' jurisprudence. Thus in fact they viewed the majlis as the means to keep the government in conformity with the spirit of Islam, and as an instrument for the efficient application of '*urf* laws. As far as our research goes, there is no evidence that any of the grand Âyatallâhs who initially supported the constitution (with the possible exception of Tabâtabâ'î), were able or willing to fully appraise the significance of an institutionalised rule of '*urf* law inspired by profane models, which are not taken over by Muslim conquerors but imported from Europe.

On the other hand, clerical opposition to the constitution, led by Âyatallâh Fadlallâh Nûrî, was more perceptive and more farsighted in viewing its threatening implications to the Islamic socio-cultural order. Nûrî vehemently denounced three major articles: compulsory education to be brought under the jurisdiction of the ministry of education, including education for women in public schools; equality of all Iranians before the law irrespective of their religious affiliation; freedom of opinion. However, he mistook the key concepts that lay at the basis of these articles (spreading knowledge, equality and liberty) for Bâbî views. In fact, he saw the whole constitutional movement as a Bâbî conspiracy aiming at eradicating Islam and establishing the rule of *kufr* in Iran, rather than as a move to separate religion from public affairs.[14] Bâbism was the real concrete religious threat he and other '*ulamâ*' had experienced and confronted, unlike the European culture with which they were not familiar. He opposed compulsory education and freedom of opinion for fear of the spread of heresy and official tolerance of heretics. Thus this perception and farsightedness did not reflect a corresponding awareness of the modern European world, or an understanding of the social and individual consciousness entailed in the ideas being propagated by the constitutionalists.

It is important to note here, though, that the dispute that divided the ranks of the '*ulamâ*' into *mashrû'a*/*mashrûta* camps was not motivated by doctrinal considerations alone. In fact, doctrinal consideration was the least important cause for split in political opinion. Factionalism, rivalry, and personal interests, in short clerical power politics, lay behind the schism in official Shi'i circles. The intellectuals and clerical dissidents' denunciation of Nûrî and fellow anti-constitutionalists as *'ulamâ-yi sû'* or even enemies of Islam echoed the language of the traditional religious polemicists (*haydârî/ni'matî, usûlî/akhbârî, shaykhî/bâlâsarî*). The *mashrû'a/mashrûta* factionalism might have been just another such dispute, and each side might have survived entrenched in its own camp, were it not for the forcefulness of the lay revolutionaries determined to accomplish their goal.

The majlis deputies wished to push for reforms. They were debating not only the ways and means to make the cabinet ministers answerable to the legislative body, but also real social ills plaguing the nation: bribery, corruption, oppression by provincial officials which periodically forced the overburdened peasants to sell their women and children to tribesmen (and even grandees) to raise cash for the taxes extorted from them. Often the debates were hectic, allowing issues to overlap, picked and dropped as these issues were by zealous deputies so eager to accomplish miracles yet aware of the enormity of their task. Inexperienced, paralysed by their own feverish intensity to come up with immediate results, often driven by their emotions rather than their intellect, they would get lost in details and then, exhausted, end the session in tears and despair and, once the fever had burned out, would lapse into inaction or indifference to the plight of those people whose wretchedness had aroused their imagination in the first place. They struggled for the majlis' basic right to exist and to function as an autonomous legislative body, fighting against the relentless assault of the opposition. While attempting to remain afloat in the tide of counter-revolution, they were learning how to translate their ideal into pragmatic action. Thus they learned to tread slowly and with caution through the labyrinth of Iranian politics.

The intellectuals, no less than the politicians, were aiming at consolidating the authority of the majlis which would control the executive power of the Shah and his ministers, and enact the laws needed for social reforms. However, whereas the politicians were rapidly entangled in disputes and squabbles which necessitated not only caution but also a great deal of compromise for them to survive, the intellectuals concentrated on social and cultural issues which tolerated no such compromise or prudence, beyond mere asssurance of the religious respectability of their views. As avant-garde leaders of the movement, they were responsible for providing the radical tone which turned what began as a socio-cultural reform movement into a political revolution of such magnitude that it set Iran onto a new course of development.

By 1907 the united front of the constitutionalists was being eroded from within. Newspapers published daily articles addressing new problems and issues and taking to task the majlis and the leaders of the revolution. Thus they condemned the silence of the majlis over the recent news of the Anglo-Russian agreement that secretly divided Iran and Afghanistan into spheres of influence. They mocked the deputies' impotence in the face of such a national crisis. 'The whole world knows about it. Iranians read about it in the papers. Yet no one is crying out loud, no one is challenging them (the Russians and British), no one is defending Iran . . . Very few have the courage and ability to stand up and denounce the agreement. The rest are being their usual selves, the lackeys of grandees and *'ulamâ'* . . . The majlis is already being destroyed by its own incompetent representatives.'[15] It is remarkable that despite the magnitude of such foreign threat to national independence domestic social issues continued to be given priority in the burgeoning press and the minbar sermons. Articles were published denouncing the financial deals and the behaviour of the big merchants who controlled, directly or indirectly, the majlis and the economic life of the nation.

Toward the end of the nineteenth century, merchants of the big cities experimented with the formation of European-type companies dealing with trade and industry. They sold shares to other merchants, entrepreneurs, landowners, government officials, and members of the Qajar family, who invested their capital expecting lucrative returns. One such company, *Shirkat-i islâmî*, was founded by Hâjj Muhammad Husayn Kâzirûnî of Isfahan in 1898 with a capital of 150,000 tûmâns, and the full support of Zill al-Sultân the Qajar prince governor of the province. Kâzirûnî was a wealthy entrepreneur, who, among other things, owned a textile factory. He wished to expand the sale of his product and eliminate the severe competition of European textiles which had flooded the Iranian market since the beginning of the nineteenth century. He hired the services of Jamâl al-Dîn Vâ'iz and Malik al-Mutakallimîn, among others, to attract clerical support and advertise the company from the minbars of the mosques in Tabriz, Shiraz, and Isfahan, as a 'holy' endeavour set up to fight the economic penetration by the infidels, to save the honour of Islam, and to ensure national progress. Here, too, the profane and the sacred were blended for a worldly cause. In fiery speeches Jamâl and Malik al-Mutakallimîn would enjoin the faithful to boycott foreign textiles and buy the Iranian products of the company. They would also tell their audience to support the company by buying shares for which they would receive handsome returns. 'To serve this company is to serve Islam,' Jamâl would preach, 'and the gains of its trade constitute gains for Islam', adding that trade was good if it benefited all and not just a few, the whole nation sharing both risks and profits.[16] Some leading Âyatallâhs of the time were persuaded to pronounce *fatwâ*s in favour of the company, declaring it a holy cause incumbent upon all believers to support 'each according to his means' by buying shares.

Thus a religious aura was given to what in fact was an Iranian attempt to adopt a Western economic institution, a corporation of shareholders totally dominated by the big merchants and following increasingly the rules of international trade and capitalist financing rather than Islamic commercial code. In fact the *Shirkat-i Islâmî* and other similar companies, proved to be serving the interests of its wealthy founders. Perhaps the most notorious and least publicised merchants' deed was the National Bank.

The story of the first National Bank in Iran needs to be demystified. It is hailed by all standard historical accounts of the revolution and by contemporary historians as the best example of a national united effort to rescue the country from the clutches of foreign creditors. Though its establishment was officially announced in the very beginning of the revolution, and some funds were raised to help the government to meet its immediate need for cash, in fact it existed only in name. It did not function. The big merchants and wealthy individuals who were the original founders refused to advance loans promised to the government unless all concessions they demanded were granted. The concessions were no less demanding, no less exploitative than the notorious European ones which had aroused such national indignation. The terms were highly reminiscent of the Reuter concession which Nâsir al-Dîn Shah was forced to cancel in 1872 as a result of the mounting pressure from merchants, politicians and *'ulamâ'*. It demanded among other things, exclusive rights over the exploration of all mines, over pearl fishing in the Gulf, over the construction of railroads and roads, and a 9 per cent interest on loans to be guaranteed by customs, post, and telegraph receipts. Some clerical members of the majlis feebly attempted to object to it on the ground that it was un-Islamic to grant a few individuals access to all sources of national wealth which should instead benefit all. No discussion of its legality in Islamic terms took place. The majority of the deputies supported the *tujjâr*'s demands, and the debate was not carried further. It was the intellectuals and the clerical dissidents who took up the task of criticising them without, however, questioning the Islamic basis of the enterprise.

Jamâl, who had initially advertised the merchants' companies, turned against them, and claimed they had lost the nation's trust and loyalty. He declared the National Bank to be not national, since it did not safeguard national economic interests but the founders' commercial enterprises and interests.[17] He revealed to the public the cheating and embezzlement of company funds by one of the original founders of the *Shirkat-i Islâmî*, which damaged the reputation of the company and caused a decline in the value of its shares.[18] *Sûr-i Isrâfîl* carried an article on the need for a National Bank which would provide the capital necessary to undertake far-reaching socio-economic programmes. It complained that neither court officials, nor cabinet ministers, nor even the merchants (referred to as the Europeans' *dallâl* making fortunes with their trade) had worked to set up a capital for the Bank. They all agreed, it wrote, that a bank was the only means to national economic salvation, yet they would not sacrifice their interests or their money for the cause.[19] The same paper published a lengthy account of a company scandal involving its director, the Malik al-Tujjâr, his son who was a naturalised Russian, a Russian entrepreneur, the Russian Consulate in Tehran, and the Iranian Ministry of Justice. The affair was not reported in any other official paper in Iran, nor in the minutes of the majlis, since the deputies classified the debate. Therefore the whole matter was kept confidential until the editor of *Sûr-i Isrâfîl* had it translated from a Russian newspaper of St Petersburg.[20]

When Dihkhudâ, the most radical social critic of the time, began to increase his attacks on the social establishment, he, too, mixed the profane with the sacred to achieve his ends. Deploring the feudal (he used the French term in transliteration) system which kept the peasants at the mercy of the landlords, he called for land redistribution which would benefit the rural worker. The programme, he insisted, could be put into practice in no time. All that was needed were four daily newspapers to devote themselves to the cause; twenty preachers to propagate it in the mosques and religious gatherings; fifty *mujâhid*s (holy warriors) to work for six months at freeing peasants from their present wretchedness and at putting an end to landlord oppression.[21] But he did not attempt to discuss the issue of landownership in Islam, nor would he try to reconcile his views with Islamic practice. Instead he would publish several reports on the newly established Russian Duma and its struggle against conservative forces; the ideology of the Russian revolutionaries, their aims and projects, and, especially, their land reform programmes.[22] His opponents reacted by labelling him an anarchist and Khârijite who would not recognise the need for leaders and masters in society.[23]

Despite the vicious *takfîr* of the constitutionalists by Nûrî and fellow anti-constitutionalists, despite the obvious innovative interpretation of some aspects of Islamic law, despite the blunt nationalist and worldly messages of preachers' sermons, the constitutionalists were able to appeal to a large constituency in the mosques, madrasas and public squares. Their network could by-pass Nûrî's and spread among the urban classes. Traditionally the poet occupied an esteemed position in Iranian society, but he, like the philosopher, was subject to clerical censorship. With the revolution of 1906, as a result of the vital role he played and the fame he acquired through his pen, he was able to raise his social status and ensure the triumph of his word over that of the *'ulamâ'* in public matters. The poet, the man of letters, the intellectual displaced the *mujtahid* in influencing public opinion and becoming the new guide. But here too, he was not capable of consolidating his gains by affirming his opposition to, or even rejection of, the system of religious beliefs enforced by the Âyatallâhs. Nineteenth century attempts at doctrinal reform had failed, and the age of religious renewal had passed by. The secularisation of the social institutions in the first decade of the twentieth century dramatically marked the end of theological speculative ferment, and the beginning of a political era where religious doctrine and even men's relation to the ultimate conditions of his existence were no longer regarded as the crucial issues. Politics demanded caution in breaking loose the ties with the predominant religious culture. Hence, secularisation, or the institutional changes which the First Majlis inaugurated with the full support of the men of the pen, was not acknowledged as being accompanied by change in ideas. Nor was secularism officially adopted. The constitution specifically declared Twelver Shi'a Islam as the official religion of the state, and granted a council of five *mujtahids* the right to supervise majlis legislation. Moreover, religious studies were made compulsory in public schools. The official anti-clerical and modernising policies of subsequent governments did not enforce 'a shrinkage in the character and extent of beliefs', to use once more Bell's definition of profanation. Moreover, the intellectuals in the twentieth century, freed from the traditional clerical restraints, no longer tied to the modalities of the religious answers, did not offer alternative answers as their western counterparts did. In response to their own disenchantment with traditional culture, they searched in political nationalism, in modern scientific disciplines which they imported from the West, in new literary genres, the means of self-realisation, leaving untouched crucial existential issues. Metaphysics and philosophy in general were neglected, and thus remained, by default, the domain of the 'turbaned'.

NOTES AND REFERENCES

1. Daniel Bell, 'The Return of the Sacred', *The Winding Passage*, New York 1980, 324-54.
2. Irving Howe, *The Idea of the Modern*, New York 1967, 13.
3. *al-Jamal*, Tehran n.d., no.3, 12.
4. *Sûr-i Isrâfîl*, no.12.
5. *al-Jamal*, no.17, 18, 23.
6. *Sûr-i Isrâfîl*, no.2.
7. *Ibid.*, no.5.
8. *Ibid.*, no.4.
9. *Ibid.*, no.12, 13.
10. *Ibid.*, no.14.
11. *Muzâkarât-i Majlis*, vol.1, 331.
12. *Ibid.*, 128.
13. *Ibid.*
14. Ahmad Kasravî, *Târîkh-i mashrûtat-i Îrân*, Tehran 1974, 288-94.
15. *al-Jamal*, no.21.
16. *Libâs-i taqvâ*, Tehran n.d., 14, 19, 48-9.

17. *al-Jamal*, no.22.
18. *Ru'âyâ-yi sâdiqa*, St Petersburg n.d., 36-9.
19. *Sûr-i Isrâfïl*, no.17.
20. *Ibid.*, no.30.
21. *Ibid.*, no.18, 19, 20, 21, 24.
22. *Ibid.*, no.24, 25, 27.
23. See his self-defence article in *ibid.*, no.25.

6

Foreign powers' intervention in Iran during World War I

Iran's decline as an independent state, already advanced during the nineteenth century, became accelerated in the course of the last twenty-five years of Qajar rule (1900–25). This decline was particularly evident in the political and military sectors. Politically, Iran became first a pawn in the Anglo-Russian rivalry and then a victim of the zones of influence agreement of 1907. Most striking perhaps was Iran's decline in the military sector. Its only two military formations one could rely on were the Russian-officered Persian Cossack Brigade and the Swedish-led rural Gendarmerie. However, the Cossack Brigade could be regarded more as an instrument of Russian policy than as a dependable arm of the Iranian government.

These characteristics of Iran's weakness manifested themselves very emphatically during the First World War. Iran's territorial integrity was repeatedly violated by foreign powers and its sovereignty was reduced to a nominal level.

At the beginning of the war, Iran's government proclaimed its neutrality on 1 November 1914. Already before that date there were detachments of Russian and Turkish troops present on its territory. When war broke out, all four powers fighting on the eastern front – Russia, Turkey, Germany, and Britain – began to intervene in Iran on a substantial scale both politically and militarily. An account of these interventions and the problems encountered by the foreign powers will follow.

Iran in the strategy of the four powers

It is perhaps appropriate to begin with the position of the Ottoman Empire inasmuch as, of all the four powers in question, it was the one that, by its initiative to attack the Entente, caused the extension of the war to the Middle East. Turkey's motives in siding with the Central Powers were partly irredentist, partly anti-imperialist and partly ideological. This last objective was expressed by the proclamation of *jihâd* in the early days of the war. In the latter phase of the war, the Pan-Turanist programme emerged as a dominant ideology.

As for Germany, her alliance with Turkey presented new vistas in her wartime strategy. Germany hoped to relieve the pressure on the European fronts by diverting British and Russian attention to the Middle East. She also hoped to threaten Britain's position in India by encouraging Indian nationalism and combining it with the Islamic appeal addressed to India's Muslims.

Thus the Turkish and German strategies found a common denominator centring on their designs in India. The so-called Zimmermann Plan and Enver Pasha's proposal in the summer of 1914 to organise a joint Turkish-German expedition to Afghanistan via Iran were the formal expression of these strategies. In both plans, Iran had to play an important role as a transit area. Furthermore, the capture of the British-controlled oil installations in Khuzistan or their destruction through sabotage became an important strategic objective for Berlin and Constantinople.

As for Russia and Britain, their strategies had a more defensive character. They regarded Turkey's entry into the war as a strategic setback likely to complicate their operations in Europe. Consequently, Russia's strategy centred on defence on her Caucasian frontier. At the same time, in anticipation of a possible defeat of Turkey, Russia strove to secure possession of Constantinople, the Straits, and the eastern vilayets of Turkey. The inter-Allied Constantinople Agreement of 18 March 1915, and the Sazonov-Paléologue Agreement of 26 April 1916, pledged these areas to Russia. Moreover, according to the Constantinople Agreement, most of the 1907 neutral zone in Iran was to pass into the British zone, the easternmost part of the neutral zone into the Russian zone; the Russian zone was to extend into the districts adjoining Isfahan and Yazd; and Russia was to gain full freedom of action in her own zone, thus signifying its virtual annexation.

Similarly defensive in its essence was British strategy. With regard to Iran, Britain's objective was to keep it neutral and to dissuade it from being enticed into a Turko-German alliance. Another objective was to protect the oil installations in Khuzistan. And, last but not least, Britain strove to frustrate any attempt by Germany and Turkey to penetrate into Afghanistan and, through it, to endanger the security of India. Both military and diplomatic means were planned and used to accomplish these objectives.

The Turko-Russian front. The Turks initially directed their efforts at the Russian positions in Transcaucasia. In December 1914 they launched an offensive against the Russian stronghold of Kars. In their offensive, the Turks extended the front into Iranian Azerbaijan and, with the aid of Kurdish irregulars, captured Tabriz on 8 January 1915. On 30 January, however, the Russians recaptured Tabriz and in August launched a counteroffensive which led them, partly through Iranian territory, toward Van.

Even prior to this offensive, to reinforce their position in Iran and prevent a Turkish break-through toward Tehran, in May the Russians had landed their troops in Enzeli (later Pahlavi) and from there advanced to Qazvîn. In this sector, the Russian objective was to march toward the Turkish border on the historic Hamadan-Kirmanshah road. A Russian offensive in December 1915–January 1916 did not encounter serious Turkish resistance because the Turks did not venture in this sector deep within the Iranian territory. In early May 1916 Russian troops broke through the Paitaq Pass and via Qasr-i-Shîrîn entered Ottoman territory. This, however, coincided with Turkish successes on the southern Iraqi front against the British. Thus the Turks were in a position not only to stop Russian advances but also by the fall of 1916 to recapture Kirmanshah, which they held until late February 1917.

The Turko-British front in Mesopotamia. The campaign in Mesopotamia, as is clear from the preceding section, had its repercussions in Iran. In anticipation of the impending war with Turkey, a British expeditionary force from India had reached Bahrain already in the late summer of 1914. Thus Britain was in a position to land her troops at Fao on 6 November, only one day after her declaration of war on Turkey. By 23 November, the British took Basra and promptly proceeded to occupy Ahwaz on Iranian territory. Soon, British troops established a protective ring around the Abadan refinery and the adjoining oil installations. Soon afterwards, the British army began an offensive in Mesopotamia. It encountered stiff resistance from Ottoman troops commanded by Field Marshal Kolmar von der Goltz Pasha. After the inconclusive battle of Ctesiphon, 13,000 British troops, entrapped in Kut al-Amara, surrendered on 29 April 1916 to the Turks. Reinforcements sent from India permitted the British to renew their war effort, reconquer Kut on 17 February 1917, and then capture Baghdad on 11 March. This victory had a major impact on the situation in Iran.

The German expedition to Afghanistan

On 12 August 1914, ten days after the beginning of the war in Europe, but some eight weeks before Turkey's entry as a belligerent, an inter-agency conference at the German Foreign Office reached a decision that a special mission should be sent to Afghanistan in the hope of inducing it to take sides with the Central Powers.[1] According to this scheme, Afghanistan would have to play a diversionary role by interfering with Britain's war effort in India. German emissaries to Kabul would have to cross Iran. The plan dovetailed with a similar proposal presented by Enver Pasha, and once Turkey became a belligerent, the expedition was to have a bi-national, Turkish-German character.

To perform this task, the choice fell on three men who knew the area from previous service or travel in it: Wilhelm Wassmuss, a former consul in Bushire; Capt. Oskar von Niedermayer, an officer serving on the western front who had travelled extensively in the Iranian-Afghan-Central Asian region; and Professor Zugmayer, a naturalist familiar with the region from his pre-war scientific expeditions. They were to be accompanied by a number of officers and civilians. According to an agreement reached with the Ottoman authorities, the Turkish part of the mission was to be led by Rauf Bey, an officer renowned for his exploits in the Libyan campaign of 1912. Initially, in the fall of 1914, the leadership was to be entrusted to Wassmuss; but after the expedition had reached Baghdad, Wassmuss made ready for a separate action among the tribes of southern Iran. The command was then assumed by Niedermayer. Ultimately certain members, similarly to Wassmuss, were detailed to operate in Iran. Wassmuss left Baghdad for Iran as early as 28 January 1915, while Niedermayer was still busy making preparations in Mesopotamia.

It should be pointed out that, upon his arrival in Baghdad, Niedermayer had learned from Rauf Bey that the Turks had decided to cancel their own expedition to Afghanistan. Moreover, the Turks seized his arms (including machine guns) and equipment and blocked the exit road from Iraq to Kirmanshah. Due to interventions from Berlin, most of the seized equipment – minus the machine guns – was restored and, on 3 April 1915, after several months' delay, Niedermayer's expedition crossed into Iran. He was accompanied by the German and Austrian ministers to Iran who were returning to their posts in Tehran from their leaves of absence. The road to Tehran was clear inasmuch as the Russian troops, as noted earlier, did not appear in the Qazvîn-Karaj area until May and did not move toward the Hamadan-Kirmanshah area until several months later.

Having reached Tehran, Niedermayer undertook multifarious activities in Iran preparatory to his further march to Afghanistan. He established liaison with those German agents who were despatched to various centres in central-southern Iran to engage in anti-British sabotage actions, hired local help, acquired more pack animals necessary for crossing the deserts and set up a system of communications by couriers to serve him in the various stages of his expedition. British and Russian officials in Tehran were aware of these activities, but during that period – spring and early summer of 1915 – they had no adequate means of counteracting them. Niedermayer benefited from the diplomatic immunity of the German legation. He could also enlist the services of those Germans and Austrians who had escaped from the Russian prisoner-of-war camps in Central Asia. In fact, the German and Austrian legation compounds in Tehran became big armed camps teeming with people ready for action.

Initially, according to German plans, Afghanistan was to take precedence over Iran.[2] This was for three reasons: (a) Afghanistan was situated at the gates of India and had a long history of interest in Indian affairs; (b) the Afghan army constituted an effective military force estimated at between 20,000 and 90,000 men, in contrast to the weak Iranian army; and (c) although suffering from formal limitations on his sovereign status, the ruler of Afghanistan enjoyed a degree of independence which contrasted with the weakness and corruption of Iran's ruling group. Thus initially, Iran was conceived as playing a merely auxiliary role. In the course of 1915, however, this order of priorities was subjected to a gradual change. German diplomats and agents in Iran discovered enticing potentialities for swinging Iran from neutrality towards an anti-Entente stand. In fact, the network of German emissaries in southern Iran found the ground very receptive to their propaganda. Such agents as Consul Wüstrow in Shiraz, Klein in Kirmanshah, Dr Biach in Yazd and Baluchistan, Zugmayer and Friesinger in Kirman, and Seiler in Isfahan, in addition to Wassmuss in the southern area of Fars, were in a position to enlist the support of various local nationalists and to assume control of the cities and districts in which they operated. In a number of cases, British consular officials and bank managers were seized, murdered or wounded, and in some instances the entire British colonies in some of the cities were captured or had to be evacuated, mostly to the safer centres along the Gulf coast, where the presence of Anglo-Indian troops offered better security.[3]

In the course of his preparations for the entry into Afghanistan, Niedermayer became deeply involved in these activities in Iran and a feeling arose in Berlin that he was unduly delaying his departure.[4] Consequently, the German Foreign Office despatched their own representative, a legation secretary, Werner Otto von Hentig, to join him in Iran and hasten the march toward Afghanistan. Hentig's group was composed of Germans and certain Indian nationalists, some of whom hailed from Indian revolutionary committees initially formed in San Francisco and later transferred to Berlin. Among them were Prince Kumar Mahendra Pratap and Mawlawî Barakatallâh. Furthermore, Hentig carried with him a personal letter from Kaiser Wilhelm to Emir Habîballâh of Afghanistan. Niedermayer and Hentig gathered together their groups in Isfahan and from there began their journey to the east.[5]

On 19 August 1915, the main part of the caravan under Niedermayer and Hentig entered Afghanistan at the Iranian border locality of Yazdun, having crossed the main road parallel to the Afghan border north of Birjand. Crossing Iran was an achievement of heroic proportions requiring almost superhuman endurance and courage. Not only did the expedition have to cross waterless deserts, including the Dasht-i-Kavîr and various mountain ranges, but it also had to evade capture by the Russians and the British who had, since early 1915, established the so-called East Persia Cordon all along the Afghan boundary. The Birjand-Qâ'in area, a good way south of Mashhad, constituted the junction point for the

Russian and Anglo-Indian forces, the latter commanded by General R.E. Dyer, later replaced by General W.E.R. Dickson. The main German column succeeded in evading both forces, but another group was attacked by the Russians and barely managed to escape westward back into Iran. During these last nerve-racking stages the expedition either lost or abandoned much of its equipment and some precious gifts prepared for the Emir of Afghanistan. Moreover, a number of locally recruited escorts, apparently weaker than the German members of the mission, either defected or were left stranded in the desert, unable to move any further. The size of Niedermayer's own contingent (i.e. counted separately from Hentig's) and the losses sustained during the march from Isfahan to Herat were as follows: the total of men assembled in Isfahan and engaged on the way through Iran – 140; the total of pack and riding animals – 236. Of these only 37 men and 79 animals reached Herat. Further losses occurred on the way to Kabul.[6]

The account of Niedermayer's and Hentig's adventures in Afghanistan does not properly belong to our story. Briefly, the mission failed to attain its hoped-for objectives. Emir Habîballâh wanted independence from Britain and access to the sea. He made his alliance with Germany subject to two conditions: an anti-British uprising in India and the arrival in Afghanistan of a sizeable Turko-German force.[7] This Hentig and Niedermayer could not promise. After ten months in Afghanistan (end of August 1915 to end of June 1916), the mission left. Niedermayer chose to return to Mesopotamia through Iran, thus exposing himself to a new hazardous odyssey which led him in disguise through Russian Turkestan to Mashhad and then via Tehran to Turkish-occupied western Iran. He reported to the Turkish headquarters in Hamadan on 1 September 1916, and to the German legation in Kirmanshah a few days later. As for Hentig, he took the eastward trek via Vakhan, Afghanistan's panhandle, crossed China, and returned to Germany through Shanghai, San Francisco and New York.

The dissident government in Kirmanshah

While the German mission was engaged in the ultimately fruitless negotiations in Afghanistan, momentous events were taking place in the centre, west and south of Iran. Prince von Reuss, the German minister in Tehran, aided by a number of German agents throughout Iran, succeeded in enlisting the cooperation of various Iranian groups and individuals with the Central Powers. He concentrated on four highly diverse but strategic groups: the Democrats, religious clerics, tribal leaders and the Swedish-officered Gendarmerie. His military attaché, a Prussian nobleman, Count Kanitz, was particularly active in visiting tribal chiefs and provincial governors. To the Democrats and their proliferating committees, von Reuss's appeal was to their nationalism and hostility towards

Britain and Russia as the 'two partitioning powers' of the sad 1907 fame. Religious leaders were enticed by stories of German friendship toward Islam and a skilfully planted fable about Kaiser Wilhelm becoming a Muslim and a *hâjjî*. The tribal element was lured into collaboration by promises of ample pecuniary rewards. The Swedish Gendarmerie officers, already inclined toward Germany, were promised German army commissions with corresponding status and privileges if they joined the nationalist cause. In his work, von Reuss was greatly helped by the fact that the earlier-mentioned German agents in central and southern Iran succeeded in seizing control in many urban centres of the British zone. Generally, Iran's political scene became so feverish in the expectation of some anti-Entente revolt that a good number of cabinet ministers were ready to throw in their lot with the Central Powers. In August 1915 a nationalist leader sympathetic to the German cause, Mustawfî al-Mamâlik, became Prime Minister and promptly entered into secret talks with the German minister. On 10 September 1915, von Reuss made to him the following declaration: 'The Imperial [German] Government guarantees, after victorious war in the course of peace negotiations, to defend and confirm the territorial integrity as well as the political and economic independence of Persia, under the condition that Persia participates in the war against England and Russia'.[8]

Although gratified by this statement, the Iranian government made further demands upon Germany. These included the Kaiser's guarantee that, should the Shah be compelled to leave Iran, he would be assured of hospitality in Germany commensurate with his status. In response, von Reuss secured such a pledge from the Kaiser.

When on 7 November 1915, the Russian Grand Duke and commander-in-chief in the Caucasus, Nikolai Nikolayevich, issued orders to his troops to march from Qazvin toward Tehran, in an apparent move to intimidate the Persian Democrats and their allies, the Persian government decided to flee southward. As a result, in mid-November the Iranian capital witnessed a rapid exodus of Majlis deputies, officials, tribal warriors, gendarmes and the Central Powers' legations, all proceeding in hastily organised caravans. But, literally in the last minutes, when the young Shah Ahmad was about to join the exodus – his carriage was already waiting – the British and Russian ministers, assisted by the pro-Entente Prince Farmâ-Farmâyân, persuaded him to stay. Upon receiving this news, his cabinet ministers decided also to remain in Tehran and the few who had already left the city returned.

The fleeing Democrats and their allies first reached Qum, where they could count on a friendly reception in this *mujtahid*-dominated city. But, judging it too close to Tehran and the advancing Russians, the dissident group moved first to Hamadan and then to Kirmanshah. Although the Russians stopped short of occupying Tehran, they advanced in a western direction on the heels of the retreating dissidents and as noted earlier, occupied Hamadan (on 9 December 1915). Soon afterward, on 26 December, following protracted negotiations, Count Kanitz signed an agreement with the governor of Luristan, Nizâm al-Saltana. The latter undertook to assume leadership of Iran's liberation struggle (against Russia and Britain) and to mobilise for this purpose 40,000 armed men by mid-January 1916. In return, Kanitz pledged delivery of war matériel and money and the assistance of German instructors. Nizâm al-Saltana was promised a monthly subsidy of 20,000 tumans as well as a guarantee of 2 million tumans for his personal estate. The validity of this accord was later questioned by the German government, inasmuch as its concluding went beyond the competence of a military attaché.[9]

In due course, Nizâm al-Saltana formed a government largely composed of the Democrats, even though he himself did not belong to the Democrat Party. His pledge to provide 40,000 riders did not materialise. Instead, he managed to enlist no more than some 4,000 to 5,000 tribal warriors. These were supposed to block against the advancing Russians various high passes in the mountains on the Hamadan-Iraq road. But, in spite of their warlike appearance, the tribesmen showed a definite disinclination to face Russian machine guns, and thus stretch after stretch of the road was conceded to the enemy. To remedy this situation, a mission of a few dozen German officers headed by Colonel Bopp and assisted by three Turkish infantry battalions – some 1,000 men – was detailed to Iran to prop up Nizâm al-Saltana's flagging resistance. In January 1916, Field Marshal von der Goltz Pasha paid a visit to Nizâm al-Saltana's government. He was clearly disappointed by what he saw. Subsequently, in an oft-quoted statement, he said: 'Anarchy in Persia. Nothing to be done. Dust, cupidity and cowardice. Vast expenditure and no return'.[10]

In spite of the appearance of the Bopp mission on the scene, Nizâm al-Saltana's government and his forces withdrew from Kirmanshah and installed themselves in the last Iranian township next to the Ottoman Iraqi border, Qasr-i-Shîrîn. Nizâm al-Saltana was accompanied by Colonel Bopp, the remnants of the Gendarmerie under Swedish officers, and the German minister to Iran, Vassel, who in the meantime had replaced Prince von Reuss. Nizâm al-Saltana's tribal allies were not uniform in their loyalty to him. The Kurdish Sanjabis estimated at 1,000 to 2,000 riders remained faithful, but the Kalhurs, some 3,000 to 4,000 strong, proved unreliable and in some instances even treacherous. A German junior officer, Wipert von Blücher (later envoy to Iran in the 1930s), sent on a mission to the Kalhurs by Colonel Bopp, experienced all sorts of difficulties, especially the greed of the chiefs and thievery of ordinary tribesmen. 'The robbery-prone Kalhurs took advantage of stormy weather to pay nightly visits to our camp. They cut out holes in our tent walls and stole whatever they could get hold of.'[11] In fact, deciding in early April that it was futile to parley further with the Kalhurs, Blücher and his companions decided to return to their headquarters, but barely managed to escape from the violence-prone and hostile tribe. A month later, the Russians broke through the last obstacle, the Turkish defence position at Paitaq Pass, and forced Nizâm al-Saltana to seek asylum in Ottoman territory. On 6 May 1916, the whole dissident group, accompanied by their German diplomatic and military missions, settled down temporarily in Baghdad.

In the midst of these adversities, fortunes of war in Mesopotamia took a good turn for the Central Powers with the British surrender at Kut al-Amara on 29 April. Even though Turkish forces in Mesopotamia simultaneously lost an outstanding supreme commander through the death of Field Marshal von der Goltz, Turkish morale received a boost, and a new offensive toward Iran entered an active planning phase. This time, however, the combined German-Turkish action was to be based not on reliance on a loose coalition of tribal riders, Iranian Gendarmerie and local Democrat militants, but on regular Turkish troops with appropriate German support.

Linked with this was the issue of the Holy War. In launching a *jihâd* through a proclamation of the Shaykh al-Islâm in Constantinople at the beginning of the war, the Turks somewhat naively hoped for a positive response in other Islamic countries, including Iran. But, due to its particular beliefs, there was no question of a full adoption of the Holy War slogan by the Iranian Shi'ite hierarchy. Nevertheless, it was deemed useful by the German authorities at least to enlist support of the Shi'i divines in Najaf and Karbalâ'. A German officer, amply provided with Turkish gold currency, paid a visit to the *mujtahid*s in Karbalâ' and succeeded in eliciting from them a declaration of support for 'the national movement in Persia'.[12] (The holy man who negotiated with him subsequently burned his clothes, made unclean through contact with the unbeliever. He kept, however, the gold.) And furthermore, although an alliance with Iranian dissidents was still deemed important, it became subordinated to the main military objective, that of preventing a junction of Russian and British forces in Mesopotamia.

In Berlin there arose thus a feeling that, in the planning and execution of the Iranian operation, certain miscalculations had been made and that change was in order. And, indeed, changes were carried out. Not only Prince von Reuss but also his successor, Minister Vassel, were recalled. As Blücher put it in his memoirs: 'As in the military domain the time of tribal riders and nomads was over and regular troops had come into play, so in the political sphere the phase of dilettantes and adventurers came to an end and a professional diplomat had now the last word'.[13]

The professional diplomat was the Geheimrat (Secret Counsellor) Rudolph Nadolny who, in wartime, had initially been chief of the political section in the German General Staff. Appointed as Chargé d'Affaires to the government of Nizâm al-Saltana, Nadolny assumed his new post in July 1916. At about that time, with the supreme command in Mesopotamia having passed to Halil Pasha, General Gressman was appointed commander of all the German formations in Iraq and Iran. Simultaneously, orders were issued to the 13th Turkish Army Corps under 'Alî Ihsân Bey to mount an offensive against the Russians on the Khanaqin-Hamadan road. German artillery, machine-gun detachments, signal units and pilots were to aid the Turks in this new undertaking.

The offensive, carried out in August, was successful; with the Russians repulsed toward Qazvîn, the Nizâm al-Saltana government re-established itself in Kirmanshah[14] and the German Legation, this time under Nadolny, resumed its activities in September.

Nizâm al-Saltana's government functioned in the 'liberated areas' during the next six months. During this period, a number of contradictions were revealed between the German and Turkish policies toward Iran. It was clear that neither Pan-Islamism nor Pan-Turanism, both propagated by Turkey and not very subtly peddled in Kirmanshah by the Turkish military attaché Fevzi Bey, made any headway with Shi'i Iranians and that they were at odds with the German policy that stressed Iranian nationalism instead. Only the tact and perseverance of Nadolny spared the two allies major frictions.

In January 1917, the British launched a major offensive toward Baghdad and, recapturing Kut on 17 February, threatened to cut off Nizâm al-Saltana's government and the attached German missions from the main body of Turko-German troops in Iraq. Within nine days, General Gressman ordered the Germans in Kirmanshah to withdraw immediately to Turkish territory. Similar orders were given by Halil Pasha to the 13th Turkish Corps in Iran. By March, Nizâm al-Saltana and his German companions reached the safety of Kirkuk. The evacuation came in the nick of time because on 11 March the British took Baghdad, a move that ended by 2 April in a junction with the Russians at Qizil Ribât in Iraq.

In view of the Turkish retreats on both Iraqi and Iranian fronts, only two developments could alleviate the difficult situation of the Central Powers: reconquest of Baghdad with the aid of German troops or a collapse of Russia. The first could not and did not materialise. The second, by a twist of fate, did come about when, in March, following the abdication of Tsar Nicholas, Russia was plunged into revolution which was to culminate in the Bolshevik takeover in November.

When in April the remnants of Nizâm al-Saltana's establishment retreated to Mosul, there was no point in maintaining the fiction of an independent Iranian government. Accordingly, on 7 May 1917, the German Legation was abolished, and Nadolny returned to Berlin to resume his duties in the political division of the Auswärtiges Amt.

The collapse of German influence in the south. The year 1915 constituted the apogee of German influence in Iran: not only was Nizâm al-Saltana's dissident régime formed in the west under German protection, but as noted earlier, the British zone in the southeast also fell under German control. Moreover, by raising rebellion among the Bakhtiari, Qashqai and Tangistani tribes in the southwest, Wassmuss effectively blocked the line of communications between the British-controlled Gulf ports and Tehran while at the same time diverting British troops from the front in Mesopotamia to the protection of oil installations in Khuzistan. Wassmuss's almost-legendary exploits earned him the nickname of 'the German Lawrence'.[15] Both he and his colleagues further afield could probably qualify for the highest ratings of the 'cost-effectiveness' of their operations. With minimal investment of German and Austrian manpower (some 300 men) and only moderate outlay of gold, these resourceful men managed to remove British presence from most of the central-southern region of Iran.

Britain responded to this challenge by organising in India, in January 1916, an expedition under the command of General Sir Percy Sykes. Being as usual short on manpower, his mission which landed in Bandar Abbas was composed of a few officers and non-commissioned personnel, British and Indian. It recruited and trained local Iranian levies and, as the South Persia Rifles, began an arduous march to reconquer from the Germans and their allies various strategic strongpoints. It captured Kirman and Yazd in July-August and Isfahan on 11 September. There it met with the Russian forces. Finally, by November the force reached and occupied Shiraz. Then it began 'mopping up' operations in the tribal area between Shiraz and Bushire where Wassmuss and his nomadic allies were ensconced.[16]

Although the South Persia Rifles acted without prior permission of the Iranian government, the British legation in Tehran – represented by Sir Charles Marling – tried to legitimise its presence in Iran through a formal agreement. On 21 March 1917, Iran's prime minister, Vuthûq al-Dawla, granted the South Persia Rifles official recognition. But with the fall of his cabinet in June, the new cabinet formed by 'Alâ' al-Saltana refused to confirm this decision and, except for the prime minister – a man of pro-British orientation – adopted a hostile attitude toward the British force. By that time, thanks to reinforcements sent from India and Burma, the South Persia Rifles had grown to 8,000, organised into two brigades in the Fars and Kerman provinces and a regiment in Bandar Abbas.

The force's operations lasted until the autumn of 1918. While already by 1916–17 most German and Austrian agents in the south had fled or been captured (Zugmayer, Biach, etc.), local Iranian hostility toward the British persisted. During an uprising in Shiraz in mid-June 1918, troops of the South Persia Rifles were attacked while – in scenes similar to those witnessed sixty years later under Âyatallâh Khumaynî's instigation – the 'mullas issued written orders to kill everyone who had dealings with the British, and bands of men and boys paraded the streets with fanatical cries'.[17] By October 1918, however, the South Persia Rifles inflicted a final defeat on the Qashqais, thus concluding another chapter in Britain's wartime intervention in Iran. Even the indomitable Wassmuss was captured.

The shift in British policies following the Russian Revolution

Although by March-April 1917, thanks to their victorious campaign, the British were able to effect junction with the Russians in northeastern Iraq, their success was far from complete because of the simultaneously occurring Russian revolution. For some time, the Lvov and Kerensky cabinets in Russia continued their policy of participation in the war, but the advent of the Bolsheviks in November brought about a radical change. Under the slogan 'bread, peace and land', the Communist leaders sought an early end to the war. In Iran, the Russian revolution resulted in the mutinies of soldiers and, with a few exceptions, a disorderly withdrawal of troops from the fronts. These troops drifted toward the Caspian coast, abandoning or selling their arms and looking for an early repatriation to their homeland. Furthermore, Russian retreat in Transcaucasia spurred its three main components, Georgia, Armenia and Azerbaijan, to claim independence.

Thus a serious gap was opened in the long stretch of the front from Khanaqin in the south to the Caucasus in the north. Only a few Russian formations commanded by Generals Baratov and Bicherakov in northwestern Iran resisted disintegration. Should this thinly defended and porous front be penetrated by the enemy, a Turko-German breakthrough across the Caspian into Russian Central Asia was a distinct possibility. Thus, towards the end of 1917 and the beginning of 1918, many uncertainties faced the British in Iran. Much depended on two factors: the attitude of the emerging Transcaucasian nations and the course of events in Russian Central Asia, where some scores of thousands of Austro-Hungarian and German prisoners of war were being enticed into cooperation with the new Russian régime by Communist agitators.[18]

Under those difficult and entirely new circumstances, the British embarked upon two simultaneous policies: first, to close the gaps in the northwestern Iranian front and in the East Persia Cordon north of Birjand-Qa'in; second, to penetrate with special politico-military missions into Transcaucasia and Turkestan to see whether some native resistance against both the Central Powers and the Bolsheviks could be initiated and given assistance.

To carry out these plans, the British sent one major expedition through Iran toward Transcaucasia and several lesser ones to the East Persian-

Turkestan region. In the west, General L. C. Dunsterville left Baghdad in February 1918 at the head of a small motor caravan consisting of a limited number of officers and some token detachments of troops.[19] Almost recklessly he traversed a treacherous region between the Iraqi border and the Caspian. In Enzeli he found the city dominated by a local soviet composed mostly of hostile Russian soldiers and sailors. Deeming the situation too risky, he soon withdrew to Hamadan. When, in June, he received reinforcements from Baghdad (after a rather long wait caused partly by the jurisdictional struggle as to whether he should report to the Baghdad Command or directly to London),[20] he resumed his march north. This time, he encountered both collaboration and obstruction on his way. The Russian General Bicherakov offered him the assistance of his 1,200 still faithful Cossacks, but the Iranian rebel Kûchik Khan tried to obstruct his progress in the high Elburz passes and the jungles of Gilan. Finally, having reached Enzeli for the second time, Dunsterville sailed to Baku to organise defences against the expected offensive of the 9th Turkish Army Corps.

At the time of his arrival in the chief port city of Russian Azerbaijan (August 1918), Dunsterville found it under the control of the Central-Caspian Dictatorship, a mixed radical but anti-Bolshevik group, largely Armenian dominated, which was interested in protecting Baku against the Turks. Soon, however, Dunsterville found that his Centro-Caspian allies were unreliable and unwilling to take effective measures to defend the city. By 14 September, to avoid capture by the advancing Turkish army, he retreated by sea from Baku to Enzeli. The Turks captured Baku soon afterward. Although this was a low point in British war fortunes, soon afterward the armistice of Mudros of 29 October 1918, put an end to the Turko-British hostilities and the 11 November armistice at Compiègne marked the conclusion of the war with Germany. Britain's attention in the Iranian-Caspian region now shifted entirely to the Russian Communist menace, and before long another British force reoccupied Baku in a broader attempt to stem the Bolshevik advance in oil-rich Transcaucasia.

As for eastern Iran and Turkestan, in the summer of 1918 an expedition commanded by General Sir Wilfrid Malleson (originating in India) filled the gap in the East Persia Cordon caused by Russia's defection. Malleson established his headquarters in Mashhad and from there operated in Khurasan, Gurgan and Transcaspia to prevent any untoward events which might threaten the security of India. A Pan-Hindu revolutionary committee active in Soviet-controlled Tashkent was giving him cause for concern. Malleson found White Russian allies willing to collaborate with him along the railway west and east of Ashkhabad. To make sure that the southern reaches of the Caspian Sea would be free from trouble, a small British flotilla under Commodore Norris was formed in Krasnovodsk.

Simultaneously, a small British mission, composed of a few officers and men, was sent from India to Turkestan under the command of Lt.-Col. Etherton (later replaced by Colonel Sir George Macartney) to keep an eye on the volatile situation in Tashkent and the surrounding area. The mission reached Tashkent through Kashgar in Chinese Turkestan. The enterprise was certainly very risky, the Bolsheviks in Tashkent wondering whether to put the visitors before a firing squad. Even after most of the mission left Tashkent, one of its members, Lt.-Col. F. M. Bailey, remained in disguise and from there provided a flow of intelligence to the British command in Transcaspia and Iran.[21]

The British remained in Iran until 1920–1 when, on London's decision, they withdrew. At the end of the war they were in a dominant position not only in their traditional southern preserve but also in the north. But with the advent of peace and the cessation of Western intervention in the Russian civil war, military methods gradually gave way to political ones. A treaty with Iran negotiated on Britain's behalf in 1919 by Sir Percy Cox, the new minister to Tehran, was expected to ensure Britain's political and economic dominance. Cox, a man steeped in the imperial tradition – formerly Resident in the Persian Gulf and subsequently chief political officer in Mesopotamia – did not appreciate the depth of Iran's nationalist feeling. His treaty was rudely repudiated by the Majlis and soon – in early 1921 – a simple Iranian soldier who 'carried the marshal's baton in his knapsack', Rizâ Khan, seized power, inaugurating a new Pahlavi era of assertive nationalism, modernisation and reform.

Conclusion

The experience of foreign intervention in Iran during the First World War revealed a number of truths about that country. The first was that under the effete Qajar dynasty, Iran was so debilitated that it offered no effective resistance to the penetration of foreign powers. Secondly, it occupied too important a place on the map of the world to be ignored by the contending forces. In spite of its official neutrality it was sucked into the vortex of war operations. Thirdly, its ruling classes presented a picture of moral confusion, greed and poor credibility as to the pledges they gave to one or other belligerent power. In fact, despite all the outward gestures of respect toward their Iranian collaborators, the Germans and British held many of them in low esteem, sometimes bordering on contempt.[22] On the other hand, it is likely that as weaker partners in the intrigues mounted by stronger foreign powers, at least some Iranians viewed any evasive action as legitimate as long as it safeguarded their identity and carried the hope of ultimate liberation from foreign influence.

The wartime experience in Iran provided also some lessons regarding wartime alliances of the interventionist powers. Rather interestingly, in spite of the long record of rivalry in Asia, Anglo-Russian collaboration in wartime Iran appeared to be free from friction, and in their books and memoirs the British always referred to their Russian allies without rancour or condescension.

By contrast, there was much evidence of serious German-Turkish disagreements and frictions. German authors frequently used the word 'oriental' to describe the temperament and mentality of both Iranians and Turks. Niedermayer in his memoirs openly contrasted the German toughness, endurance and strong will in adversity with the absence of these qualities among the non-Germanic members of his expedition. The unexpected cancellation of the Turkish plan to send a joint mission to Afghanistan was implicitly taken by him as proof of shocking duplicity. He bemoaned the blocking of his expedition's way to Iran, the arrest of three members of his advance party, and the brutal seizure of his arms and equipment by the Turks. 'I cannot describe,' he wrote, 'with what joy we left the place of so many sufferings,' referring to his crossing of the Iranian border from Turkish territory.[23]

Similarly, Wipert von Blücher spoke contemptuously of the immaturity and incompetence of Halîl Pasha, the 30-year-old successor to von der Goltz as commander-in-chief in Iraq, and ridiculed the antics and tactlessness of prominent Turkish commanders in Kirmanshah.

Beyond these differences in temperament, one may observe major divergencies in policies, priorities and strategies of the two governments. The Turks clearly wanted to monopolise the conduct of eastern diplomacy on behalf of the Central Powers and aimed at a hegemony in western Asia. In their relations with Iran, aggravated by centuries of mutual distrust and hostility, they were oblivious to Iranian sensibilities. Whereas logic dictated that it should be Germany, a friendly and remote 'third power' whom the Iranians trusted, who should carry the main burden of negotiations with Iran, the Turks, by pushing themselves to the fore, always threatened to spoil the game. As noted earlier, their Pan-Islamism evoked only a conditional response from Shi'i Iran, and their Pan-Turanism, often brazenly proclaimed by their local representatives, filled their Iranian partners with suspicion and fear lest it lead to the ultimate dismemberment of Iran.

Finally, a few remarks may be in order regarding the mutual perceptions of the two adversaries, the Germans and the British. Generally, memoirs written by their respective nationals lack deep hostility or hatred toward the war enemy. The Germans refer to the British in terms of grudging respect and their accounts of British actions have a matter-of-fact tone, only occasionally betraying regret at the harsh treatment sometimes given the captured German agents. In British writings, the terrorist acts against British, Russian or Indian officials instigated by German agents are deplored and some authors refer to the Germans as 'Huns'.[24] But at the same time the British are not stingy in praising the valour, courage and heroism of men like Wassmuss and Niedermayer.

Interestingly also, the British invariably take their imperial system for granted. They do not apologise for their domination of India and appear to be morally certain that the preservation of this system is worth shedding British blood. By contrast, there are repeated evidences of a certain idealism in German writings, especially in those by former diplomats. Thus they refer to the principle of national self-determination as the proper one to be applied to Iran and Asia as a whole. How genuine this feeling is is open to question. Considering Germany's record of disregard for the nationalisms of her neighbours in Europe and her tradition of the 'Drang nach Osten' in the area between the Baltic and the Black Seas, this solicitude for Iranian, Afghan or Indian self-determination, in each case hurting Britain's position, may appear as self-serving.

NOTES AND REFERENCES

1. Wipert von Blücher, *Zeitenwende in Iran: Erlebnisse und Beobachtungen,* Biberach an der Riss 1949, 17.
2. *Ibid.,* 31.
3. Sir Percy Sykes, *A History of Persia,* London 1951, II, 446.
4. Blücher, 23.
5. For comprehensive accounts of this expedition, see W. O. von Hentig, *Ins verschlossene Land: ein Kampf mit Mensch und Meile,* Potsdam 1943; Oskar von Niedermayer, *Unter der Glutsonne Irans: Kriegserlebnisse der deutschen Expedition nach Persien und Afghanistan,* Dachau bei München n.d.; and for various references to the expedition, W. O. von Hentig, *Mein Leben eine Dienstreise,* Göttingen 1963.
6. Niedermayer, 129.
7. Ludwig W. Adamec, *Afghanistan's Foreign Affairs to the Mid-Twentieth Century,* Tucson, Arizona 1974, 40.
8. Blücher, 25.
9. *Ibid.,* 28.
10. Sykes, II, 544.
11. Blücher, 45.
12. *Ibid.,* 58.
13. *Ibid.,* 62.
14. Members of the government were: Nizâm al-Saltana, President; Muhammed 'Alî Khan Mâfî, Foreign Minister; Sayyid Hasan Mudarris, Minister of Jusice; Adîb al-Saltana, Minister of Interior; Muhammad 'Alî Khan Farzîna, Finance Minister; Qâsim Khan, Minister of Posts; and Hâjjî 'Izz al-Mamâlik, Minister of Public Works. Some of them subsequently served in high positions under Rizâ Shah.
15. There are three detailed accounts of his exploits: Christopher Sykes, *Wassmuss, 'The German Lawrence',* London 1936; Hans Lührs, *Gegenspieler des Obersten Lawrence,* Berlin 1936; and Dagobert von Mikusch, *Wassmuss der deutsche Lawrence* (partly based on Christopher Sykes' book, but not its translation), Berlin 1938.

16. Sir Percy Sykes' personal recollections of his service are incorporated in his *A History of Persia*, II, chs 87, 89.
17. *Ibid.*, II, 510.
18. L. V. S. Blacker, *On Secret Patrol in High Asia*, London 1922, 5.
19. For a comprehensive account, see Lionel C. Dunsterville, *The Adventures of Dunsterforce*, London 1920.
20. M. H. Donohoe, *With the Persian Expedition*, London 1919, 62.
21. Experiences of this mission were recorded in personal memoirs: Lt.-Col. P. T. Etherton, *In the Heart of Asia*, Boston and New York 1926; F. M. Bailey, *Mission to Tashkent*, London 1946; and Blacker, *op. cit.*
22. Thus Peter Avery, *Modern Iran*, London 1965, 192; Sir Percy Sykes: '. . . every governor is a robber and cares nothing whatever for the welfare of his subjects . . .', II, 484. Also Sykes, II, 449, 467, 475, 478, 519.
23. Niedermayer, 43.
24. Blacker, 5.

BRIAN SPOONER

7

Who are the Baluch? A preliminary investigation into the dynamics of an ethnic identity from Qajar Iran

1. The Baluch in time and space

Many of the distinctive patterns of modern Iranian life can be traced back through the Qajar period. Often it becomes difficult to follow the trail further because of a drop in the amount of social-historical information as one pushes back further. Where the trail does continue, it often supports the impression that many modern Iranian social patterns and cultural meanings were set in the eighteenth–nineteenth centuries, partly as a function of Qajar political practice and related events during the same period.

Baluch society as we know it ethnographically appears to be a product of the Qajar period. Although the Baluch arrived in what is now known as Baluchistan long before the Qajars came to power, many of the characteristic and distinctive forms of Baluch social life today can be traced to the effects of Qajar influence and, to some extent, of direct Qajar intervention. Because of the expansion of British interests northwestwards from India, the beginning of the Qajar period also coincides fairly closely with the beginning of European travel literature on the Baluch, which provides a much clearer window onto the area than had been available before and shows us a heterogeneous society significantly different from what the odd scattered references in earlier historical texts might lead us to expect. It is remarkable that although the Qajar period saw the formal division of Baluchistan among Iran, Afghanistan and India (much earlier than many other similar divisions of tribal societies among two or more states that have since occurred throughout the Middle East), the area remains culturally homogeneous today. That is, all Baluch – despite obvious differences in occupation and status – agree on what it means to be Baluch. In what follows I suggest reasons for this combination of social diversity and cultural homogeneity by reference to the peculiar natural conditions of Baluchistan and the political conditions of the Qajar period.

Let me state the problem in more detail. The majority of the present population in some 300,000 km² of western Pakistan, 200,000 km² of southeastern Iran and (at least until 1980) some 100,000 km² of southwestern Afghanistan call themselves Baluch and are so called by their neighbours and fellow countrymen. (There is also a significant Baluch diaspora: a further indeterminate number of Baluch are scattered in small groups through eastern and northeastern Iran, western and northern Afghanistan, Soviet Turkmenistan, and the former territories of the Muscadine Empire in Oman, the Persian Gulf and East Africa, apparently having left Baluchistan sometime during the last two hundred years or so in search of a better living, often as mercenaries. But although these groups are still known as Baluch, in most cases they have assimilated linguistically with their environment.) Attempts have been made, especially by Frye,[1] to explain how they arrived there by tentatively reconstructing a historical odyssey from northwest to southeast Iran over the early centuries of Islam on the basis of a combination of philological analysis and interpretation of sparse but tantalising textual and toponymic references. Today, despite variation within Baluchistan and similarity between the Baluch and many of their neighbours, such as the Pashtuns (Pathans), there is never any empirical confusion about who is and who is not Baluch. A Baluch is one who calls himself Baluch, and no one who is not Baluch will so call himself.

In earlier publications[2] I have simply left at that the question of Baluch ethnic identity, reserving for later investigation the question of how this identity as we know it ethnographically has evolved out of what can be reconstructed of its earlier history: how it came into being, how it became associated with the territory we now call Baluchistan, and how it has maintained itself into the present despite the lack of any unifying institutions or other centripetal forces. These questions have continued to occupy me, and I hope to publish a detailed investigation of them in the not too distant future. In the meantime, although I do not pretend to have definitive answers, it seems appropriate to offer here a preliminary review of the material and pursue some of its implications, in honour of Professor Elwell-Sutton, whose work has always evinced a special interest in the meaning of Iranian ideas for Iranians.

Although it would be interesting to pursue these questions with regard to any of the tribal societies of the Iranian world, the Baluch are especially interesting because of the frustrating nature of the scattered historical references to them, the great size and heterogeneity of Baluch society and territory, the confusing evidence for the history of the Baluchi language, and (in the context of this volume) the role of the Qajar regime in the social and political history of Baluchistan, particularly in the attempts of Muhammad Shah, after a period of relative neglect, to extend his government through it. Compared to most of the other tribal or ethnic minorities in Iran the Baluch (in Iran, Afghanistan and Pakistan) are probably more linguistically diverse, socially stratified, and numerous – they are estimated presently at four million) and constitute the majority population in over half a million square kilometres. Why, given their internal diversity in everything except ideology, which they anyway largely share with tribal neighbours, do they maintain such a marked ethnic identity?

The explanation I suggest below depends on a mixture of structural and historical components. Any one is Baluch who fits into the Baluch political structure, which, at the local level, survives independently of the Afghan, Iranian and Pakistani administrations. The Baluchi language is the medium of political communication. The structure is a product of the combination of two factors: (1) tribalism which may be glossed as the emphasis on kinship and descent as organising principles, in the absence of significant resources or other capital on which to base economic and political relationships; (2) small scattered agricultural settlements, that provided a relatively stable but local basis of power for political leaders. Most of the major agricultural populations of the area, although they speak of themselves in tribal terms, are in fact not tribally organised: they are concerned not with genealogies and group boundaries but with networks of kin and other personal relations which they extend as far as they can in all directions. Tribalism seems to have become the pervasive idiom of social organisation with the arrival of Baluch, whose leading families were able to take over some of the settlements and acquire a new basis of power (though they lost some of them to later immigrants). Before their arrival, both India and Iran had lost the ability to maintain governments in the area. The identity of Baluchistan developed in the eighteenth century as a result of the rise of a linguistic tribal minority to a status that was maintained only by outside powers. The geography and ecology are directly related to the settlement pattern, which places special constraints on political development and offers particular opportunities to outside influence. The structural factors are a function of both the settlement pattern and the cultural history of the populations that came to the area. The final result could not have come about if the history of Iran and India had not led to particular types of interference and withdrawal at particular times.

This interpretation is basically political and, although it draws heavily on the insights of two anthropologists as well as my own earlier work in southeastern Iran, has been inspired mainly by an appreciation of the total geo-political context of Baluch history which I have acquired only over the last few years. But first it is necessary to introduce briefly the geographical and historical context of the Baluch.

Baluchistan is defined by a semi-circle of historically important cities and agricultural areas that stretches from Bandar Abbas (the earlier Hormuz) on the Persian Gulf, through Kirman, the delta of the Helmand River in Sistan, Qandahar, and Sind. Within this semi-circle, whatever was not controlled on any permanent basis from the cities, at least from the seventeenth century until the middle of this century, was effectively

Baluchistan. Though the hinterland of the cities fluctuated, and the whole area has been subject to (often overlapping) claims by Iran, Delhi, and later, Afghanistan, most of it has been effectively independent and locally autonomous from at least the Mongol period down to the nineteenth and in some parts into the twentieth century. It is extremely arid, and is suited to extensive sheep, goat and camel husbandry and – in a certain number of well defined locations where cultivable soil and an accessible supply of water suitable for irrigation coincide – for small-scale irrigated agriculture. The topography is mostly extremely broken and mountainous, and varies in altitude from 1,500 m steppe on the edge of the Iranian plateau, at the base of mountains rising in one instance to over 4,000 m, to sea level on the coastal plain. In the part that is now southwestern Afghanistan, and here and there in the 500 km wide zone between the Afghan border and the coast, the land opens out into vast expanses of featureless semidesert and desert. The small agricultural settlements are situated on bends in river beds in the mountains or where the rivers issue onto the desert plains. Water is nowhere abundant or (with few exceptions) perennial, but in the mountains the limiting factor is soil. On the coastal plain the soil is often good but there is no water except from rain or runoff. Rainfall is irregular and unreliable, but owing to the overlapping of the Mediterranean and monsoon regimes may come at any season. Temperatures are continental in the highlands with bitter winters and extreme diurnal and seasonal ranges, and tropical on the lowlands.

Before the Baluch became the dominant ethnic group in the later Middle Ages the area was divided into two separate named districts: the higher, colder, northern and northwestern areas were called *sarhadd* ('the borderland', *sc.* of Sistan to the north) and the lower, warmer southern areas were Makran. Within Makran the coast was always somewhat distinct, populated by people known as Med, perhaps continuing the tradition of Arrian's Ichthyophagi, oriented towards the sea, and dependent on fishing and trading from small ports.

Throughout Baluchistan the nature of the topography makes communication difficult and the paucity and sparseness of natural resources limit the size of settlements – which traditionally has made it difficult for potential leaders to build up large confederacies or otherwise extend their authority beyond their immediate constituency. Typical nomadic populations of the Middle East migrate over vast distances in spring and autumn in order to be able to rotate or exploit the seasonality of the best available pastures, but in most of Baluchistan there is no such incentive to make long migrations and nomadic tribes are typically small, especially in the mountains that constitute the greatest proportion of the area, ranging from thousands (the Marri, on the eastern edge are an exception, quoted at 60,000) – to a few hundred. Their territorial boundaries often appear to be defined more by topographic limits to pastures than by social or political dynamics, or by any relationship to genealogically derived social boundaries.

Throughout Baluchistan the geographical factor places strict limits on both agricultural and pastoral potential. Given the available technologies, agriculture on any significant economic scale is limited to certain well-defined pockets. The limits to pastoralism are in terms of overall productivity. The Baluch have obviously pushed against those limits, and since at least the beginning of the last century there has been continual migration in search of more ample resources.

It is not possible to introduce Baluchistan adequately without referring to interactions and movements between populations inside and outside the area. Ethnographic and historical studies tend often to be too localised to catch the significance of exogenous influences. Given the geopolitical situation of Baluchistan as economically marginal country between the Iranian plateau and the Indus plains, it will be necessary to look to the political poles of those larger areas for influences that would explain local events, and to reconstruct the history of the relationship between local Baluch politics and economics and the larger political economy.

We must be careful to avoid biases that might be built into the available historical material. What we know about Baluchistan derives from studies that are essentially one-sided: Baluchistan has always been approached either from India or from Iran, and its history is implicitly reconstructed in terms of either one or the other of those cultural constructions of reality – never both. From the mid-first millennium onwards the area was divided into named provinces of the Persian empires. Little if any historical research has yet been focused on the area, and the relevant syntheses so far available derive from the pursuit of answers to questions that arise from primary interests in the civilisations to the east and west. These questions relate for example to the fall of the Indus civilisation, the administration of the Persian empires, the progress of the Islamic conquest from the Iranian plateau into northern India and the movement of tribes that appear tantalisingly in Iranian historical materials here and there before the Mongol invasions as Kuch and Baluch. The spread of Seljuq power into Kirman seems to have led to movements of population (including the Kuch and Baluch) that resulted in the lapse of the arterial route which until that time had passed through the area from the Iranian plateau into the subcontinent. After the Mongol invasion of the Iranian plateau in the early thirteenth century the area seems to have begun to take on the character of Baluchistan, firstly by becoming a refuge area – for which it is well suited geographically. But political and economic forces in both Iran (including the areas to the north of eastern Baluchistan which later became Afghanistan) and India continually affected events there, and Baluch leaders have generally looked in both directions for potential sources of external support in their internal conflicts.

Baluchistan seems to have come into being historically as a cultural borderland – as an indirect result of population movements and political upheaval in neighbouring areas during the mediaeval period. It appears to have absorbed a succession of immigrant groups, of which the Baluch were neither the first nor the last, and problems in the analysis of its composite society became soluble only when approached in historical perspective as a function not only of its internal social and cultural dynamics but also of the history of the more powerful and stable centres around it – Arab as well as Iranian and Indian. Most commentators have made this task more difficult either by ignoring the historical dimension or by seeing the area as an appendage of only one of the surrounding civilisations – as a backwater rather than a borderland. In what follows I attempt to show how the understanding of the interaction of internal processes and external influences in the Qajar period can form a bridge between what we know of the Kuch and Baluch and what we see in Baluchistan today. The aim behind this reconstruction is to understand better what it means today to be Baluch, and what might be the signific- ance of this meaning for the study of similar ethnic or other identities in the lands bordering the Sea of Oman and the Persian Gulf.

2. *Internal dynamics*

Ethnographic sources on Baluchistan are not abundant. The first profes- sional anthropologists to visit the area were the Pehrsons (mainly in what is now the Kohlu district of the province of Baluchistan in Pakistan in 1955). They were followed in the Pakistani province by Barth (in the same part in 1960, briefly), the Swidlers (in Kalât, Khuzdâr and Kacchi from 1963 to 1965), and the Pastners (Panjgur in 1969 and a Baluch coastal community in Sind in 1976–7); and across the border in Iran by Spooner (Sarâvân, Iranshahr, Châhbahâr, intermittently between 1963 and 1969), Salzman (Khâsh and Saravân, in 1967–8, 1972–3, and 1976) and Bestor (Khâsh in 1976). Though this may seem a lengthy list, the published material it has produced is not comprehensive. With the excep- tion perhaps of Robert Pehrson, whose particularly promising work was cut short by his tragic death in the field, each writer was pursuing a limited number of questions only, which in most cases were not derived from a study of the special conditions of the area.

This work does, however, include two significant insights which deserve attention. One of these relates the composition of camping groups among nomadic pastoralists to specific details of the technology of traditional pastoralism.[3] The other explains linguistic and cultural change in terms of specific properties of neighbouring social structures.[4] Neither Barth nor Swidler can be accounted area specialists, and I do not think their insights derive in any way directly from their reasons for choosing to work in Baluchistan, but Baluchistan does in fact provide particularly suitable conditions for the study of the processes that attracted their attention. The combination of their insights illuminates the political dimension of Baluch society and facilitates understanding of the historical relationship between the Baluch and their neighbours.

Warren W. Swidler studied the everyday life of pastoralists in a Brahui community near Kalât. The Brahui are a group of tribes concentrated in the south-central highlands of Pakistani Baluchistan. They are distinguished from the rest of the population of the area only by their language, Brahui, which is Dravidian and serves as the basis for arguments that relate them to pre-Indo-Iranian populations. Whether or not they are, or should be considered to be Baluch, or a separate ethnic group, has been a subject of debate among themselves and their neighbours in recent decades, but there is no doubt that from the point of view of the political history of Baluchistan, which is the focus of the present argument, they are Baluch. Among them Swidler found that the basic camping group was unstable as a social unit. The composition of camping groups was reshuffled frequently. Each group ran a flock which was composed by the combined holdings of the heads of household in the camp. The reshuffling correlated with changes in the size of the flock.

From these data Swidler developed a model which showed the size and structure of local camping groups of nomads as a function of their pastoral technology. In order to produce efficiently, sheep (the model works best with sheep, but with modification is also useful in the analysis of social processes among nomads who depend on other species) must be herded in flocks of a particular optimum size. This size depends on a number of factors which include the behavioural characteristics of the sheep and the logistics of shepherding and vary according to topography and pasture. Animals are owned individually and each man's holding is likely to vary independently year by year. Therefore, in order to keep the flock size close to the optimum, and also have the right number of hands for the various tasks of pastoral production, the composition of the group needs to be changed not infrequently. In order to facilitate this continual reshuffling within an overall ordered community, the nomads think of their society in terms of a larger tribal unit, large enough to include sufficient individuals (all inter-related in various ways by marriage as well as common descent) for the movement of personnel between camp groups to proceed smoothly with the minimum of conflict and insecurity.

This tribal unit – not the spatially segregated camping unit – turns out to be the structurally important grouping in most nomadic populations. Its actual size varies from one nomadic area to another, but two hundred seems to be a typical figure.[5] Structurally it corresponds with what has come to be known as the 'tertiary section' in the classic expositions of segmentary lineage theory in the literature of anthropology.[6] It is worth noting that tribalism generally implies an obsession with social cohesion based on kinship and descent – actual or presumed ties of blood – in the absence of the economic factors which are more conscious in the social and political organisation of more complex societies.

The principles underlying the formation of everyday camping groups among nomadic pastoralists in Baluchistan, therefore, are shown to be a function of certain technological requirements in a certain geographical situation. Because of their instability these day-to-day-living groups do not in themselves provide a basis for the development of larger political units or of well defined political roles – these evolve from the larger tribal structure which varies considerably from one situation to another according to the numbers of people that must be incorporated and the organising concepts that are at hand, which in the Middle East include patrilineal genealogy and endogamy. Swidler's work does, however, provide a basis for interesting comparisons with other tribal or lineage societies, many of which – especially within the Middle East – are also nomadic pastoralists. In the study of nomadic lineage societies elsewhere it has been noticed that there often appears to be a structural hiatus between the primary groups of everyday life and the political structure that incorporates them. The fact that the theory of complementary opposition that mediated this hiatus to some extent is now in dispute,[7] adds to the inherent interest of the Baluch situation.

Barth's work helps us to understand how this mediation is effected in the Baluch case. Taking a cue from Morgenstierne[8] concerning the relationship between linguistic and cultural change in the area, Barth adduces evidence[9] that the cultural border between Baluch and Pashtuns in northeast Baluchistan (Pakistan) has moved slowly and intermittently northward at the expense of the Pashtuns, without any associated movement of population. Groups known to have been formerly Pashtuns and Pashtu-speaking were, when he was there in 1960, Baluchi-speaking and fully accepted by themselves and others as Baluch. Barth argues that despite several factors that suggest that the border would move in the opposite direction, such as relative population growth rates and comparative affluence and aggressiveness, this Baluch assimilation of Pashtuns could have been predicted on the basis of a comparison of the ways their social and political relations are organised. He suggests that the socio-political structure of the Baluch is better adapted to the problems of incorporating disorganised personnel – refugees – than that of the Pashtuns.

'There can be no doubt about the anarchy that prevailed in the area', writes Barth[10] about the century or so prior to the intrusion of the British. This anarchy generated a complex history of local conquest and succession in which certain structural features of the tribal organisation of the competing groups became overwhelmingly significant.

Frequent wars and plundering forays inevitably tear numbers of people loose from their territorial and social contexts: splinter groups, fleeing survivors, and families and communities divested of their property, as well as nuclei of predators, are generated. From such processes of fragmentation and mobility, a vast pool of personnel results – persons and groups seeking social identity and membership in viable communities. The growth rates of such communities will then not depend so much on their natural fertility rates as on the capacity of their formal organisation to assimilate and organise such potential personnel.[11]

The structural difference between Pashtun and Baluch society that facilitates this one-way assimilation is the difference between egalitarianism and hierarchy. In both cultures the patrilineal principle determines political rights in the tribe and rights of access to resources; honour is defended obsessively against any person with whom equality is claimed; and honour involves obligation towards dependents – including clients and guests. However, Pashtun identity depends on membership in a council of equals – 'One might say that the model for the whole system is the group of brothers';[12] whereas

Baluch tribal organisation, though derived from the same concepts, is not based on the particular mechanism of the egalitarian council. Though defence of honour among equals is important, it thus does not become built into the *political* system as a major tactical consideration. A model for the Baluch political system is the relationship between a father and his sons.[13]

Though extremely brief and perhaps somewhat oversimplified, Barth's concise comparison of two neighbouring social structures is among the neatest in the literature. But it begs historical questions: why had the Baluch not assimilated all the Pashtuns long before? Why is the present border between the two identities where it is? Presumably the answer to these questions should be found in the history of the area (if sufficient historical information is available), and should provide even more valuable insights into a type of basic social process that anthropologists have tended to neglect – the formation of group identities. As an explanation of cultural change Barth's interpretation is attractive – if it is not contradicted by the available historical information.

In the same article Barth also helps us with the ideological aspect of our problem. Apart from reshuffling and seasonal movement in groups, nomads are always on the move as individuals. They need to travel widely to cultivate small plots of land, to find stray animals, to keep up visiting obligations, to purchase grain and other non-pastoral necessities, to make pilgrimages and to cultivate political connections. Besides structural flexibility, therefore, the nomadic round demands security for individual travellers. The Baluch ideology is especially evident in a code of honour, the most striking features of which safeguard the interests of the traveller and the refugee; e.g. in statements about marriage preferences and relations between the sexes, and in appeals to a genealogical idiom of social organisation. The tribal ideal is the essential underpinning of the cultural idiom that allows movement and communication throughout the otherwise heterogeneous society in the manner of a lingua franca. Its general pervasiveness and similarity to the ideologies of Pashtuns, Bedouin and many Iranian tribal groups may be explained functionally in that it provides security for interaction between individuals and groups in constant movement between autonomous polities scattered over an inhospitable terrain.

The Baluch version of this ideology is intimately bound up with the use of the Baluchi language. Barth has drawn attention to the institution of *hâl* – 'exchanges of information given in a peculiar intonation and stereotyped phrases as formal greetings whenever tribesmen meet'.[14] Baluch identity is also a linguistic identity. It appears that a social structure may be adaptive: in a particular situation it might spread as an idiom of interaction at the expense of a different structure. A linguistic idiom might similarly spread because it is the language in which a particular adaptive type of communication has developed. The spread of the linguistic idiom might facilitate the diffusion of the associated social forms.

The conditions of agriculture in Baluchistan are very different from pastoralism. The agricultural settlements seem to have had a long and continuous history – possibly, in some cases, since before the Persian empires.[15] Populations vary between a few hundred and a few thousand, but conform mostly to a recognisable pattern: the cultivation is done largely by serfs or helotised smallholders; in the centre is a fort – often high and imposing; in the fort there lived traditionally a chief, known variously as *sardâr, khân, hâkom* (Persian/Arabic *hâkim*), or *nawâb,* who by means of various forms of taxation or outright ownership effectively commanded the greater part of most of the agricultural production and operated from the settlement as a politico-economic base, building and rebuilding networks of alliances with similar chiefs in other agricultural settlements and with the nomads who covered the expanses of mountain and desert between the settlements. With few exceptions the alliances were ephemeral because no chief was economically capable of building a power base larger than those of his rivals.

The two types of social grouping (settled-agricultural and nomadic-pastoral) are closely interrelated and economically interdependent. They are in fact not thought of as two interdependent populations but rather as parts of a social whole which is stratified into four classes, *hâkomzât* (which I have elsewhere translated as dynastic family – they are in fact the families of *hâkom* or *nawâb*), *baluch* (mostly, but not all, nomads, whom the Baluch refer to as *baluch par excellence*, whose lives enshrine the values by which Baluch identify themselves; they may be descendants of the Kuch and Baluch), *shahrî* (cultivators, probably descendants of pre-Baluch landowners and peasants) and *ghulâm* (former black slaves; non-black slaves were able to change their status or leave the area when slavery was formally abolished). Each individual is identified by membership in a tribal group, and each tribal group belongs to one or other of these four classes. The ranking of *baluch* in relation to *shahrî* varies in practice from one place to another according to the experience of particular communities. The settlements produce grain and dates, and the nomads, milk and its products. The combination forms the staple diet of the area. The nomads come into the settlements in the late summer and autumn to help with the date harvest. The cultivators visit the nomad camps in the mountains in the spring to drink milk. The chiefs vie with each other for the allegiance of the nomads. In their forts in the agricultural settlements they are able to store grain, which they can then use to finance a militia. Such militias were used to impose a tithe and other contributions on the agricultural or pastoral populations they could control. The nomads are egalitarian, but they are encapsulated in a hierarchical system.

All social groups in Baluchistan describe themselves in tribal terms, using the word *zât* both for single lineages and for groups of affiliated lineages (though there are signs that many of the farming groups have not always thought of themselves in these terms). Many, though now accepted as Baluch, are of known recent alien origin – from Iran, Afghanistan, Muscat, or Sind. Each is categorised as chiefly family, nomad, cultivator, or slave and each individual has a place in a chain of allegiance or fealty relationships which crosscut the class categories. But the tribal ideology, which is implicitly associated with the *baluch*, pervades all communication. All these elements of the cultural idiom – language, ideology, code of honour, social structure – constitute identity in a large cultural community which does not have well defined boundaries.

The tribal ideology extends throughout Baluchistan and beyond. In contrast the individual political units are exclusive and competitive. Each family is a member of a primary social grouping which can be seen to develop from the conditions of pastoralism or agriculture. These primary groupings are strung together in chains of hierarchical relations. One of the more common words in Baluchi usage is *kamâsh* (from the Brahui) which denotes 'senior'. In any social situation someone is *kamâsh* – whether *inter pares* or not – and there is never any doubt about who it is (except in open conflict). The hierarchical chains of relations integrate the various types of grouping. Each is encapsulated in an asymmetrical model of the larger society. But within the groups there is often little or no interest in lineage or in extension of genealogy to provide a framework for social relations. In general, in Baluchi no terminological distinction is made between matrilateral and patrilateral kin; in many (though not most) groups men and women inherit land equally. The model of patrilineal genealogy is used to model links between groups and to represent political affiliation and legitimacy, and as a means of relating historical events to the present.

Within Baluchistan itself, although there is sufficient homogeneity for the development of some sense of cultural identity, there appears to be no basis for the development of a unifying political authority. In particular, the basic conditions of nomadic pastoralism throughout the area generate social flexibility and individual mobility to the extent that the existence of a general cultural identity, which facilitates easy communication between strangers over a large area, is not surprising. There are other technological and environmental factors that facilitate the diffusion of certain values and concepts over a much larger area and make for a great deal of cultural affinity between the nomads of Baluchistan and, for instance, the Pashtuns in the northeast and the Bedouin to the west and southwest. It is the combination of these features that is called Baluch, and is appealed to as Baluch. Paradoxically, these features do not distinguish the Baluch from their neighbours. What distinguishes them is the hierarchy generated by the economy of the settlements. However, each form – nomadic and settled – is dependent on the other, and the particular combination and distribution of settlement and pastoral activity is probably unique to Baluchistan.

3. The larger temporal and spatial context
While Muhammad Shah Qajar was seeking to reintegrate the Baluch into Iran, Baluchistan entered international history in an instalment of the Great Game in Asia. The failure of a British diplomatic mission to Kabul and the arrival there of a Russian envoy led to the viceroy's decision to invade Afghanistan. In order to ensure safe passage of the army to Qandahar, it was necessary to control Baluchistan. This need led in due course to a treaty with the State of Kalât in 1854 and the annexation and incorporation of the districts along the border with Afghanistan into the province of British Baluchistan in 1879. The boundaries of Iran, India and Afghanistan were demarcated through Baluchistan for the first time in the 1870s. There have been only minor revisions since. All of the Baluch territories that fell within India acceded to Pakistan and were finally integrated administratively into Pakistan in 1955. Baluchistan became a separate province within Pakistan in 1971. In Iran since the Qajar period most of the Baluch territories are incorporated into one province with Sistan to the north. In Afghanistan Baluch territory has not been accorded independent administrative status.

Historical information on the area begins to pick up at the beginning of the nineteenth century as its increasing strategic interest to the British in India leads first to the dispatch of spies, and then of open political agents, some of whom later along with *bona fide* travellers published accounts of their experiences. The accounts vary in detail, reliability and perception, but include a few of high quality and readability. Later, for the eastern part of the area these travellers' accounts were complemented by the decennial British Indian (from 1871) censuses, and consolidated in the District Gazetteers (1907). There is also a parallel increase in the amount of information published in Iran, but it is generally of less value for the present purpose.

The stage for the Qajar-period scenario in Baluchistan appears to have been set in the middle of the seventeenth century, when a significant political change occurred. The district southwest of Quetta, traditionally known as Sarâwân, 'highland', although located close to the centre of Baluchistan, is in fact unlike most of the rest of the area in that it constitutes a spur of the Iranian plateau reaching down towards the sea. It is therefore both the gateway into the area from the plateau to the north, and especially from Qandahar, and (when the powers are differently balanced) a gateway onto the plateau from India. Because of its altitude and the resulting severity of the winters, there is a distinct advantage to the pastoralists of the area if they can ensure access to winter grazing on the Kacchi plain, which lies over a thousand metres below and just to the east of them. It appears that a combination of circumstances, including population movements on the west and the weakening of Mughal power to the east, allowed the leader of a group of Brahui-speaking nomads from Jhalawân to oust the Mughal governor from Kalât and establish control of Sarâwân and the Kacchi plain, and so provide the basis for a new political development within the area. Control of the Kacchi plain must have been so desirable for Sarâwân nomads that it is surprising they had not managed to control it at earlier periods. But in the light of the arguments advanced above such control was probably not feasible in the long term unless it was facilitated by some felicitous combination of exogenous circumstances. On this particular occasion, the control of the highlands over the lowlands was later confirmed and legitimised in such a way that its effects continued to the present day. Nâdir Shah of Persia avenged the Afghan invasion (1722) of his country by capturing Qandahar in 1739. He appointed the Sarâwân leader Nasîr Khan as *beglerbegi* of Baluchistan. When Nâdir Shah was assassinated in northeastern Iran in 1747, Ahmad Shah Durrânî founded the Kingdom of Afghanistan based on Qandahar. Nasîr Khan at first acknowledged his suzerainty, but in 1758 he rebelled. Ahmad Shah defeated him in battle but could not take Kalât, and a treaty was negotiated.[16]

For a short period the Khans of Kalât were able to exploit this situation and extend their hegemony over most of what is now Pakistani Baluchistan and even into parts of what now lies on the Iranian side of the border. But the chiefs of the small agricultural settlements scattered throughout the area, and the nomadic groups, continually rebelled against any imposition of taxes or other feudal requirements, and even marriage alliances were not reliable for long. One chief was played off against another and Qandahar and Kalât competed for allegiance. Qandahar's record in this struggle provided the historical basis for Afghanistan's recent proposal to include Baluchistan in a new state of Pakhtunistan. On the Iranian side there was little interference until Muhammad Shah Qajar (1834–48) decided to reconquer the area and established a garrison at Bampur in the major agricultural area on the Persian side of the border, from which his officers made campaigns eastwards. This achieved little of any lasting significance, except insofar as they reasserted claims which affected the delineation of the border with the British in 1871, and familiarised the Baluch with Iranian administrative and military ways. This familiarity both increased their distrust of outsiders and reinforced their hierarchical tendencies. From then on, the Baluch called all Persians *'gajar'* Qajar, but (once the Qajars had seen fit to award a title here and there in return for loyalty) usurped the Qajar term *hâkim* ('governor', pronounced *hâkom*) as a general title for the occupants of their forts.

4. Historical and geographical significance

These structural and historical investigations into Baluch identity depend on an assessment of the territory of Baluchistan as a marginal area. That is, at a given level of technology Baluchistan supports fewer people per unit area in poorer circumstances than is the case in neighbouring areas where the Baluch identity has not spread. It is generally true of such marginal areas that their history is a function of the history of neighbouring areas which are more fertile and more densely settled; that political control of them is difficult except with the degree of force that only an external power can afford; but that unless the area is important for communications, mineral deposits or other strategic considerations, the investment required for an external power to achieve or maintain political control, or even provide significant support for a local leader, is not justified. Marginal areas are continually exposed to the indirect effects of exogenous factors which derive from processes of population movement, economic growth and decline, and cultural diffusion. These effects can lead to particularly interesting situations for study, because the social units are smaller and the cultural options are more obvious and easier to follow ethnographically (though perhaps not historically!) than in more fertile areas.

Historically, Baluchistan has been a no-man's land of over half a million square kilometres between the political poles of Afghanistan, Iran and India. Although diverse in terms of land forms and temperature, it is uniformly arid and low in productivity. As a result of these natural conditions settlement throughout the area is sparse and highly localised, and the vast distances between settlements are exploited by small groups of pastoral nomads. The Baluch became the dominant linguistic group in the area in the late Middle Ages, and their leaders took over some of the major agricultural settlements. Although they lost some of them again to later immigrant groups, the Baluch identity had by then become fixed and the later immigrants were subsumed into it. But no settlement provided a sufficient economic base for the development of a larger political centre. Neither did the conditions of nomadic pastoralism. From the combination of the two, however, together with the linguistic idiom of Baluchi as a lingua franca, a unique political structure evolved, based on the exchange of agricultural and pastoral products and the ability of the chiefs to store and redistribute and provide relatively stable leadership. This structure was particularly suited to the incorporation of refugees, individuals and groups who had lost their economic and political place in another society, and for this reason on the northeast edge of Baluchistan many Pashtuns became Baluch as a result of the insecurity that was endemic in the area. This did not happen to such an extent on other sides of Baluchistan because of the influence of more powerful polities such as Sind, Qandahar and Iran. It could happen on the northeastern edge only between the development of the Baluch structure and the establishment of the Pax Britannica, a period that is not likely to have lasted longer than 300 years.

The Baluch structure reached its final form in the eighteenth century. The decline of the Mughals had left a power vacuum in the area. In 1666–7 as part of the local manoeuvring to fill it, a group of Brahui tribesmen were able to expel their representatives from Kalât and establish themselves. In the 1740s, Nâdir Shah's treatment of the Brahui reinforced the idea of the political identity of the area. (It is important to note that this identity was always represented as Baluch, not Brahui.) The intervention of Muhammad Shah from the west and the British from the east towards the middle of the nineteenth century set the seal on the hierarchical model of society that had developed as a function of the interaction of the nomads and the settled communities.

Although there had been periodic intrusion and interference in Baluchistan throughout the mediaeval period – the most recent (before Nâdir Shah) had been from the Qizilbâsh under the Safavids in the early seventeenth century – there appears to have been no large-scale investment by foreign powers or establishment of long-term administration, or incorporation of the area into any larger political unit, from before the Seljuq period until the British began to interfere openly towards the middle of the nineteenth century. The intervention initiated by Nâdir Shah in the 1740s may have been unique in the Islamic period: it galvanised the balance of power in the area, giving the newly risen Brahui Khans of Kalât the ability to establish themselves. Later their position was stabilised and maintained by the British. The later status of the Khans of Kalât (which could not have evolved without outside non-Baluch intervention) was an important factor in the development of the idea that the Baluch were one people, despite the fact that they spoke Brahui and recruited their administration from among Persian-speaking 'Dehwâr' peasants. The idea of unity took on new significance as a result of the nationalist policies of the governments of Iran and Pakistan since the Second World War.

To arrive at this interpretation of Baluch identity it was necessary to begin by broadening the geographical and historical context of the problem. The historical boundaries of the study were extended back to the integration of the area into the early Persian empires, and the geographical boundaries are drawn to include Indian, Iranian, Afghan and Muscadine influences. Depending on how the universe of the study is defined, the range of obviously comparable cases in the historical and ethnographic literature varies. Baluchistan has been introduced as a refuge area. This type of area has been referred to elsewhere – Morocco – as 'lands of dissidence' to denote the continual problems caused to more fertile areas by its instability. Ibn Khaldûn was concerned to integrate such areas into the historiography of mediaeval Islam and emphasise the 'group feeling' or tribalism of their populations. Owen Lattimore has done the same for Central Asia in relation to China. Turner's treatment of the frontier in relation to modern American history belongs to the same pattern. But these conceptualisations address the problems of marginal lands only as they relate to the main currents of history – not in relation to the marginal areas themselves (though it is worth noting that Barth did squarely confront the problem from the point of view of the marginal lands themselves when he used the term 'shatter zone' to describe a similar situation among Kurds in the hills and mountains between the Iranian plateau and the Iraqi plains.[17]

In Baluchistan and neighbouring territories on all sides Islam and tribal custom – both from the west – have provided the conscious rationale for behaviour. The entire Gulf area was similar to Baluchistan in that it was dotted with small polities (based on various combinations of trade, piracy, pearling and agriculture) run by chiefs (khans, shaykhs, amirs), with mainly non-tribal populations of traders, helots, serfs or slaves, relating to a hinterland of nomadic pastoralists. The political structure was similar, though the identity was different and never became consciously unified. Baluchistan differed from the rest of the Persian Gulf/ Sea of Oman area primarily then in that it was oriented away from the water and developed a focus for a unified identity.

The name Baluch is of unknown etymology. As a tribal appellation it can be traced back into the pre-Islamic period, but the society to which it now applies appears to have formed mainly in the eighteenth century as a function of a number of historical factors in at least two different and relatively unrelated political histories. Seen in this perspective it provides interesting comparative material for the study of social and historical processes of broader significance.

In the last twenty years of course Baluchistan has undergone another significant change – again as a result of exogenous factors, this time in Tehran, Kabul, Islamabad, and perhaps most especially the Persian Gulf. The changing economic and political context has made the individual potentially independent of the tribal group and undermined the status of the chiefs. Though social change is not proceeding uniformly throughout the area, in many places people no longer know inherently where they stand socially and politically in relation to each other. As the economic opportunities and constraints have changed, so have the political relations. It is too soon to tell whether Baluch identity has built up enough momentum over the last two hundred years to survive this change or whether we are witnessing its disintegration. Perhaps the historical boundaries of the Baluch experience – as it has been decribed ethnographically – will appear in time to be comparable to its geographical boundaries: a function of geopolitical conditions that formed not long before the rise of the Qajars, were maintained and intensified by them, and faded away with other last traces of that pre-modern era in the second half of the twentieth century. This Baluch identity will then have been encapsulated historically in a two- or three-century period. If so, the answer to the question posed in the title of this article must be given in historical and geographical, rather than cultural terms. It will be interesting to look at some other tribal identities in the Iranian world in a similar light.

NOTES AND REFERENCES

1. R. N. Frye, 'Notes on a trip to the Biyabanak, Seistan and Baluchistan', *Indo-Iranica*, 6/2 (1952-3), 1-6; *idem*, EI², art. Balûcistân; *idem*, 'Remarks on Baluchi History', *Journal of the Central Asiatic Society*, 6 (1961), 44-50.

2. B. Spooner, 'Kuch u Baluch and Ichthyophagi', *Iran* (1964), 53-67; *idem*, *Religious and Secular Leadership in Persian Baluchistan*, unpublished DPhil thesis, Oxford 1967; *idem*, 'Politics, Kinship and Ecology in Southeast Iran', *Ethnology*, 8 (1969), 139-52; *idem*, 'Nomadism in Baluchistan', in *Pastoralists and Nomads in South Asia*, ed. L. S. Leshnik and E. D. Sontheimer, Wiesbaden 1975.

3. W. W. Swidler, *Technology and Social Structure in Baluchistan, West Pakistan*, PhD dissertation, Columbia 1968; *idem*, 'Some Demographic Factors Regulating the Formation of Flocks and Camps among the Brahui of Baluchistan', *Journal of Asian and African Studies*, 7 (1972), 69-75; N. B. Swidler, 'The Political

Context of Brahui Sedentarization', *Ethnology,* 12 (1973), 299-314.

4. F. Barth, 'Ethnic Processes on the Pathan-Baluch Boundary', in *Indo-Iranica: Mélanges Présentés à Georg Morgenstierne,* ed. G. Redard, Wiesbaden 1964, 13-20.

5. For a more detailed elaboration of Swidler's model, see B. Spooner, *The Cultural Ecology of Pastoral Nomads,* Reading, Mass. 1973.

6. See E. E. Evans-Pritchard, *The Nuer,* Oxford 1940; M. Fortes and E. E. Evans-Pritchard, *African Political Systems,* London 1940; J. Middleton and D. Tait (eds), *Tribes without Rulers,* London 1958; E. Peters, 'The Proliferation of Segments among the Bedouin of Northern Cyrenaica', *Journal of the Royal Anthropological Institute,* 90 (1960), 29-53.

7. Peters, *op. cit.* and *idem,* 'Some Structural Aspects of the Feud among the Camel-herding Bedouin of Cyrenaica', *Africa,* 37 (1967), 161-82; P. C. Salzman, 'Does Complementary Opposition Exist?', *American Anthropologist,* 80 (1978), 53-70.

8. G. Morgenstierne, *Report on a Linguistic Mission to North-Western India,* Oslo 1932.

9. *Op. cit.*

10. *Ibid.,* 15.

11. *Ibid.,* 15-16.

12. *Ibid.,* 16.

13. *Ibid.,* 17.

14. *Ibid.*

15. B. Spooner, 'Notes on the toponymy of the Persian Makran', in *Iran and Islam,* ed. C. E. Bosworth, Edinburgh 1971, 517-33.

16. For more details on this development and many other data and ideas relevant to this argument, see N. Swidler, *The Political Structure of a Tribal Federation: the Brahui of Baluchistan,* PhD dissertation, Columbia 1969, and *eadem,* 'The Development of the Kalat Khanate', *Journal of Asian and African Studies,* 7 (1972), 115-21; C. F. Minchin, 'Sarawan, Kachi and Jhalawan', *Baluchistan District Gazetteer,* VI, VIA, VIB (1907).

17. F. Barth, *Principles of Social Organization in Southern Kurdistan,* Oslo 1953.

PART

2

Social and Cultural History

8

Change and development in the judicial system
of Qajar Iran (1800–1925)

In Qajar Iran, a dual judicial system existed. On the one hand there were the religious or *shar'* courts presided over by the *'ulamâ'*. On the other hand there were the secular or *'urf* courts administered by government officials. The jurisdiction of both courts has always been a matter of dispute, and the point of preponderance has varied with the character of the Shah or provincial governor. In practice, there was a kind of division of labour. The *'urf* courts dealt primarily with offences against the state such as rebellion, embezzlement, theft and drunkenness. The *shar'* courts were mainly concerned with affairs of a civil nature, especially those of the personal status. There were of course areas which were claimed by both courts, and this led to conflicts between the state and the *'ulamâ'*.[1]

In order to have some degree of influence over the *shar'* courts, the Shah appointed in every principal town a mullah with the title of *Shaykh al-Islâm*. Although care was taken to respect the wishes of the population, and legal knowledge and reputation were also taken into account, the function of the *Shaykh al-Islâm*, like so many other religious and administrative functions, was hereditary. Although the *Shaykh al-Islâm* received a salary from the state, he went out of his way to avoid the impression that he was the Shah's man. In the larger towns there was also a *qâdî* or religious judge, who was subordinate to the *Shaykh al-Islâm*. In smaller towns there was only a *qâdî*, while in large villages there was only an *âkhund* (low-ranking *mullâ*). These *shar'* court judges in many instances referred to leading *'ulamâ'* or *mujtahids* for judgement by their superior knowledge of cases. At the beginning of the century there were only five *mujtahids* in Iran, while towards the end of the Qajar period there were five *mujtahids* in Tabriz alone and about 100 all over Iran. These *mujtahids*, like the *Shaykh al-Islâm*, were surrounded by a council of *mullâs* and *tullâb*, commonly referred to as *mahkama-yi shâgird* or court apprentices. They acted as the spokesmen of the disputing parties before the *mujtahid*.[2] Another group of court attendants were the professional witnesses or *'udûl,* who were indispensable in any lawsuit before a religious court. Disputing parties were free to choose their own religious judge, and the rivalry which existed between them forced them to acquire and to keep the reputation of being a just man in order not to lose their clientele.[3] Religious judges could only arbitrate between parties who consented to lay their case before him. When the parties could not agree on one religious judge, he was chosen by the local governor or by lot. Both parties then signed an *iltizâm* or undertaking to honour the judges' verdict. When this verdict had been given it was legal and enforceable, even when one or both parties disagreed with it. However, the principle of surannuation or limitation did not exist, so that a case could always be reopened before another judge. Moreover, if one or both of the parties decided to lay their case before a *mujtahid* of higher standing, his verdict overruled any other verdict. Although religious judges were not entitled to any fees, they nevertheless received considerable presents or just plain bribes to influence their judgement. Besides, the court attendants, such as the *mahkama-yi shâgirds* and the *'udûl,* fleeced both parties for as long as they could.

They were not above committing perjury in order to obtain an income. It is for this reason that the religious judges and their court attendants acquired a reputation for venality, which, according to Sykes, had increased considerably towards the end of the nineteenth century.[3]

The execution of the verdict of the religious judge was done by the state, which seldom contested these decisions. It was rare for the religious judge to carry out his decision by himself. This was only done in some cases by powerful *mujtahids*, who had at their disposal their own strong arm in the form of bands of *lûtîs* and *tullâb*.[5] The local governor, who had to execute the decisions of the *shar'* court, received a fee for this, which was known as *haqq al-ijrâ'* (execution fee). However, with the offer of a liberal payment, the governor was prepared to discuss the manner in which the court's decision was to be executed. Both plaintiff and defendant had to spend considerable time and bribes to bring this process to a satisfactory end.[6]

The *'urf* courts were administered by state officials. The highest *'urf* court was the *dîwân-i shâh,* which was the last court of appeal, against whose decision there was no appeal. Next in rank were the provincial governors, followed by the governors of smaller jurisdictions or towns. Within the cities, the governors had delegated part of their powers as *hâkim-i 'urf* to a few local officials.[7] These all functioned under the *kalântar* or mayor of the city, who dealt with more serious cases.[8] He was assisted in his task by the *kadkhudâs* or city wardens, who were each responsible for the security and public morality in their quarter. To this end the *kadkhudâs* employed servants like the *farrâsh bâshîs,* who were paid out of the fines and imposts collected from transgressors of the law.[9] In the bazaar area, this task was executed by the *dârûgha-yi bâzâr* or market police officer and the *muhtasib* or market overseer. Both these officials also checked weights, measures, quality and prices of products.

In all these cases trials were quick, summary and public, and were often concluded on the spot by the exaction of fines or by giving the bastinado.[10]

The *'urf* courts allowed confessions or *iqrâr*; enforced confession by use of torture was not uncommon in case of criminal cases. Documentary evidence also played an important role in *'urf* courts. Documents, however, had to be preserved by the disputing parties themselves, for neither court archives nor records were kept. If a judge was replaced, the whole case had to be examined and started from the beginning again. The taking of oaths hardly played a role in *'urf* courts, and when it happened, the oath taking had to be done by the *shar'* court.

The *'urf* judge acted on his own and according to his own views. He could rely on the *Sharî'a,* oral tradition, precedent, local customs and reason. Personal interest was another factor which influenced his judgement. Most cases in *'urf* courts resulted in a settlement or in arbitration, the more so if the judge stood to gain nothing by prolonging the case. This especially held true when the two disputing parties were not without influence, and the judge did not want to jeopardise his own position by his decision. Court costs, in case of civil cases, amounted to 10 per cent for Iranians and 5 per cent for foreigners of the total amount that was allotted by the court. In reality, however, these percentages were higher, because of the bribes that had to be paid.[11]

Criminal cases were the exclusive domain of the *'urf* courts. The use of torture to get confessions or money from suspects was quite common. So long as a prisoner or accused could pay, he would go free in case of petty offences. If the accused had no money and was found guilty, he received a sound thrashing. Serious offenders were fair game for the judicial authorities. According to Wills, 'while the prisoner's money lasts he is a guest; it is only when his means are exhausted that he becomes a criminal. His money gone, his clothes taken as the perquisite of his jailors, his feet in the stocks in a dark and stifling room crowded with other poor wretches in a similar plight, the position of a 'suspect' in Persia is a very bad one'.[12]

The standard punishment was the bastinado, fines or flogging for lesser offences. For serious crimes such as murder, highway robbery, rebellion and apostasy, the condemned men were 'crucified, blown from guns, buried alive, impaled, shod like horses, torn asunder, converted into human torches, and flayed while living' until the 1870s. After that period, 'the worst criminals are strangled, or decapitated, or have their throat cut. Robbery and thieving are expiated by mutilation, a finger or thumb, a hand or ear'.[13] In the case of murder, the legal heir of the victim could invoke the *lex talionis,* and if the suspect was found guilty, he was delivered into his hands to deal with as he chose. He could forgive him, demand blood money or kill him. In most cases, murderers sought sanctuary, from which secure place they negotiated with the victim's heir for the payment of blood money through the good offices of a *mullâ.*

Proper prisons did not exist in Iran nor was anything like a prison sentence, for life or a number of years, known in Qajar Iran. The same held for hard labour as a sentence. In the major towns, prisons existed, but their inmates were not confined there for any great length of time. Local political magnates also had room for prisoners in their private guard-houses. Female criminals hardly occurred; if they had to be detained they were kept in the house of a *mullâ*.[74]

In villages, most matters were taken care of by the *kadkhudâ* or village chief, or by the *mubâshir* or supervisor appointed by the *arbâb* or landlord, who had the authority to deal with petty cases. In villages of peasant proprietors (*khurda mâlik*), cases were tried and judged by the village elders. More serious cases were referred to the district officer, the *dâbit* or *kalântar*, while the worst cases had to be sent to the nearest town.[15]

In tribal areas, most cases were dealt with by the tribal authorities themselves without interference from the state. Customary tribal law differed materially from that of the rest of the population. Petty cases were dealt with by the *kadkhudâ* or tribal section chief, and more serious cases by the *kalântar* or *îlkhân,* the tribal leader assisted by a council of elders. Decisions were taken by a majority of votes, in which discussion the tribal *mullâ* also participated.[16]

Because the *'urf* judges were at the same time the chief local executive, they were above the law instead of being checked by it. Individuals could only therefore acquire some measure of judicial and political status by belonging to a corporate group (or groups). The prevailing political system was operated by patronage, which involved a wide system of contractual and personal loyalties based upon the bargaining power of the actors in the political arena. By virtue of their patron's *wâsita,* protection groups (or individuals) could improve their situation or see justice done. Whenever the government or its officials took oppressive measures, a powerful patron intervened on behalf of the oppressed group or individual. The principal bargainers in Qajar Iran, which can best be described as having a spoils system, were first the Qajar family, followed by the foremost tribal leaders and the bureaucratic families. Particularism, nepotism and inheritance of affairs were particular consequences of this state of affairs.[17] But it was not only the wealthy and powerful who shared in the spoils. A whole army of clients, relatives and other hangers-on also profited from their patron's position. They were often the executives of their patrons and/or the subtenants of offices. 'The lower classes are thus literally and strictly rayas – flocks – which are kept merely for their fleece; and they are usually shorn as often and closely as greatly to diminish their value and the profit of the owner', wrote Perkins.[18] There were of course traditional limits beyond which the élite could not go. This, according to Gordon, 'was the ability to pay; as measured by the patience of the sufferers'.[19] Apart from this physical limit, there were other checks and balances such as resistance, *'urf* and *shari'a* law, and the seeking of *bast* or sanctuary. The lower classes or *ra'âyâ* did not have much bargaining power and had no access to the government; they could only turn to a group of influential brokers (*wâsita*) who were accessible to all and had access to all levels of government, viz. the *'ulamâ'*. This was facilitated by the differences among the élite. For apart from personal rivalries among the élite (to whom the leading *'ulamâ'* also belonged) there was the congenital divergence of goals and functions between the secular and the religious élites, which undermined their stability and unity.[20] Although the *'ulamâ'*, through their role of social critics, served to blunt the oppression of the common people, they did not challenge the structure of society nor did they wish to reshape the norms of political life and the bases of the state.[21]

It was also for this reason that the population tried to avoid as much as possible having contacts with the authorities and to restrict these to as low a level as possible. According to Mustawfî, the judicial affairs (he was referring to civil cases) were completely taken care of by the population itself without state interference.[22] Although this is an exaggeration, there is some truth in it. Heads of families tried to settle disputes between members of their families, servants and retainers through bilateral contacts. This was facilitated by the fact that by custom they were allowed to give light punishments, e.g. the bastinado, to members of their family and their servants. Similarly, in the case of the guilds (*asnâf*), many petty offences were tried and punished by the guild head and the elders. The same held for differences between two or more guilds, which were also mostly dealt with by the guilds themselves. Similar practices existed among other corporate groups, while we have seen that village communities and tribal groups also preferred to exclude outsiders from interfering with their affairs. It was only when the negotiating process failed that *'urf* or *shar'* courts were appealed to, and then mostly to the *shar'* courts.[23]

The changes and development in the judicial system of Qajar Iran were part and parcel of the general changes which occurred in Iranian society, especially that of the bureaucratic structure and the body politic. On the one hand there was the need for military, administrative and financial reform to enable Iran better to cope with the increasing interference by Russia and Great Britain in its internal affairs. On the other hand, and closely bound up with it, was the struggle about who was to control the judiciary and to what extent. The manner in which the social-political system was to be changed became a third aspect of this struggle. Reformers like Mîrzâ Taqî Khan and Mîrzâ Husayn Khan believed that a new and better judicial system with codified laws would become the motor of change. For Nâsir al-Dîn Shah (1848–96), as has been aptly observed by Bakhash, these reformers, who advocated the establishment of a strong, central authority, were the instruments to attain his own goal, reassertion of royal authority and control. Although the paramount role of the *Sharî'a* was not challenged by the reformers, that of its traditional upholders, the *'ulamâ'*, was, and this led to conflicts.[24]

The changes in the judicial system were already begun early in the nineteenth century. Fath 'Alî Shah (1797–1834) had among his ministers a Minister of Justice, who, according to Mustawfî, was known as the *sadr*, short for *sadr-i dîwânkhâna*.[25] His son, the Crown Prince 'Abbâs Mîrzâ (died 1834), was the leading spirit of the small reform-minded group of Iranians. Among the many changes and modernisations which he initiated, we observe that 'Abbâs Mîrzâ in the judicial field tried to ensure that honest and capable judges were appointed to the *shar'* courts. He also established a new *dîwânkhâna* in Tabriz, his own seat of government, which supervised *qâdîs* who were appointed to the other towns in Azerbaijan.[26]

We do not know how effective the new system was, or whether it was able to improve the quality of the judicial process. Fath 'Alî Shah, at the instigation of Manûchihr Khan, created a central *dîwân* or court of justice in the 1830s which had four members (three secular and one religious member) and was chaired by Manûchihr Khan. It would appear that this court enjoyed the appreciation of the population and even of the *'ulamâ'*. However, due to the fact that the functioning of the court ran counter to the interests of influential members of the bureaucracy, the court was abolished.[27] Whether this court was copied from the one created by 'Abbâs Mîrzâ is not known, but no doubt the same circumstances led to its establishment. That 'Abbâs Mîrzâ was not working on his own is clear from the fact that one of his close collaborators, Mîrzâ Abu 'l-Qâsim, Qâ'im-Maqâm, when he was confirmed as chief minister by Muhammad Shah (1834–48), established a *dîwân-i 'adâlat* or court of justice. The president of this court was known as *amîr-i dîwânkhâna*. The other members of the court were the following: (1) the *sadr-i dîwân*, the representative of the *'ulamâ'*; (2) the *amîr-i dîwân*, a eunuch, chosen to deal with cases involving females; (3) *amîr-i nujabâ'*, a representative of the nobles or Qajar family; (4) the *amîr-i lashkar*, representative of the military; (5) *mustawfî-yi dîwân*, the comptroller of the fiscal affairs; (6) *nâzim-i 'adâlat*, the attorney general; and (7) the *munshî bâshî*, or secretary-general of the court.

Cases which were dealt with by the court were prepared by *munshîs* (secretaries) and *muharrirs* (clerks). It also had an executive branch; the *nâ'ib-i farrâsh* dealt with cases in Tehran, while the *nâ'ib-i ghulâm* was charged to deal with cases in the provinces. The *nâ'ib-i khalwat* was responsible for communicating the reports of the *dîwân* to the Shah, even when he had withdrawn to his private apartments (*khalwat*). He further had to finalise the minutes of the court. Because the Shah was the sole source of power, the centre of the universe, the *amîr-i dîwân* was granted royal honours whenever he went about. For he was the direct representative of the Shadow of God, the *zuhûr al-haqq* (manifestation of justice), Muhammad Shah, and was therefore entitled to royal treatment. During the first five years of its existence, it seems that the new *dîwân*, due to its novelty no doubt, acquired a reputation for dispensing justice. After this initial period, its influence diminished gradually under the new chief minister Mîrzâ Âqâsî. Towards the end of Muhammad Shah's reign, it no longer played any role, although the *dîwân* continued formally to exist.[28] The only development in the judicial field under Mîrzâ Âqâsî was the issue of a royal *firmân* relating to bankruptcies issued for the protection of British merchants in Jumâdâ I 1260 (May–June 1844). This *firmân* was issued at the insistence of the British government, and removed in effect cases of bankruptcies from the *shar'* courts. Moreover, in another way the influence of the *shar'* courts was also weakened, viz. through the abolishment of 'all places of asylum in the homes of individuals, except in certain mosques and sanctified places, such as the houses of well-known *'ulamâ'* and the Shah's palaces, which, from olden times, have been places of refuge' (art. 17). Although the *firmân* stated that the regulations were not incompatible with the religion of Islam, a few articles (such as arts 14 and 16, sub 3) deviated from or were in direct contradiction with religious law.[29]

The first attempts to change and improve the judicial process under Fath 'Alî Shah and Muhammad Shah had not aimed at a structural reform of the whole system. The new powerful chief minister of Nâsir al-Dîn Shah, Mîrzâ Taqî Khan, Amîr Kabîr, was the first, however, to attempt to bring about a structural reform of the judicial system. His reforms aimed at improving the quality of both *shar'* and *'urf* courts, and at the same time extending the control of the state over the courts. He at first tried to sit in judgement of cases himself, but he soon realised that he lacked the proper legal knowledge to do so. He therefore reorganised the *dîwânkhâna-yi 'adâlat*, which was also called *dîwânkhâna-yi buzurg-i pâdishâhî*, and extended its jurisdiction. Cases had first to be referred to the *dîwânkhâna-yi 'adâlat*, which selected the *shar'* court that would deal with the case. The decision taken by the *shar'* court, moreover, was only valid when it was confirmed by the *dîwânkhâna-yi 'adâlat*. Also, in another way the state tried to extend its influence over the *shar'* courts. Amîr Kabîr abolished the *nâsikh* judgements (i.e. reversing earlier decisions, which were often misused). Also, by giving precedence to a particular *shar'* court in Tehran, the decisions of which had force of precedence for all other *shar'* courts, he streamlined the functioning of the *shar'* courts and centralised government control over these courts. To enhance the prestige of this supreme *shar'* court, Amîr Kabîr appointed a famous jurist (*faqîh*), Shaykh Burujirdî, as president of this court. When differences arose between Shaykh Burujirdî and Amîr Kabîr, the latter appointed a new president of the *shar'* court, Shaykh 'Abd al-Husayn Tihrânî, another leading *faqîh*.

Amîr Kabîr also provided for the better treatment of suspects by abolishing the practice of torture. Non-Muslim Iranian subjects received better protection, and to prevent the misuse of authority to their detriment, he ordered that all cases involving non-Muslims had to be referred to the *dîwânkhâna-yi 'adâlat* in Tehran. This court also dealt with complaints by subjects against the state or against government officials, as well as with criminal cases. He also considerably restricted the number of places of asylum.[30] Colonel Sheil, the British Chargé d'Affaires, advised him against this measure, 'for sanctuary was natural as a protection against misrule and arbitrariness'.[31]

After Amîr Kabîr's downfall and execution in 1852, many of his reforms fell into disuse, but the spirit which had given rise to them remained, however, alive. The *dîwânkhâna-yi 'adliyya* continued to function as the highest court of justice, second only to the *dîwân-i shâhî*. Only with the Shah's consent could cases judged by the *dîwânkhâna-yi 'adliyya* be re-opened again, and then only by the same *dîwânkhâna* or by a special committee whose decisions had to be confirmed by the Shah.[32] Amîr Kabîr's successor, Mîrzâ Âqâ Khan Nûrî, even proposed in 1855 that in imitation of the Ottoman *Khatt-i sharîf-i Gulkhâna* and European laws, a code of laws for Iran be drawn up which would guarantee the security of life and property. The proposal, however, came to nought.[33] Attempts to generate ideas on judicial and other reforms and interest in them continued, however. In this respect the role of reformers such as Malkam Khan was of importance, for although his ideas were not implemented, he nevertheless influenced the attitude of the Shah and the leading politicians and bureaucrats vis-à-vis the need for judicial reforms.[34]

Not only did the interest for judicial reforms remain alive, but also one of its guiding principles, viz. the strengthening of the powers of the central authority. Amîr Kabîr had made the first step in that direction, and his successors followed suit. In 1275/1853, Nâsir al-Dîn Shah issued a decree in which the authority of the central *dîwân*, the *dîwânkhâna-yi 'adliyya*, would delegate a *dîwânbêgî* to each province, who would supervise the functioning of the local *shar'* and *'urf* courts. He had to report regularly to the Minister of Justice, and also acted as the intermediary between the central and the provincial *dîwân*s. The *dîwânbêgî* himself did not preside over the provincial courts, but apparently decided which court would deal with which cases and which cases had to be referred to Tehran. The decree, which also contained guidelines for court procedure, was soon suspended after criticisms from the provincial governors, who claimed that its implementation would lead to disorder and anarchy.[35]

In 1277/1860 Nâsir al-Dîn Shah, in order to show his concern for the lot of his subjects and to institute a check on government officials, issued a decree that everybody could personally present his or their petition(s) for his judgement. The Shah selected Sundays for that purpose, and he held court from sunrise till sunset, and refused to deal with other matters during that day. Although the court was not created to deal with criminal or civil lawsuits, but to hear complaints about the behaviour of government officials, the Minister of Justice and his deputy (*nâ'ib al-sadr*) acted as secretary to this court. The deputy had to record all petitions in a special register and add the Shah's decision on them on the opposite page. The plaintiffs had to appear in person before the Shah, one after the other. Petitions from the provinces had to be handed over to the *dâbit-i chappârkhâna* (supervisor of the postriders), who had orders to dispatch these petitions in a special bag to the Shah. The Shah soon discontinued this public court, however.[36]

In 1278/1861, he wished to revive the authoritative role of the central *dîwân* and issued a decree to re-establish the *dîwânkhâna-yi 'adâlat*. Those who hindered or neglected the implementation of its decisions were threatened with severe punishment.[37] One year later, in December 1862, a new decree reconfirmed the position of the *dîwânkhâna-yi 'adâlat* and laid down its purpose and competence.

The decree reiterated that the Shah was the sole source of judicial authority. Since all verdicts of the *dîwân-i 'adâlat* were prepared under the eyes of the Shah himself, they had to be executed by the government officials as if he had given these verdicts himself. Ignoring the *dîwân*'s decisions was tantamount to ignoring the Shah's wishes, who by applying the precepts of the *sharî'a* and using the *dîwân-i 'adâlat* as his instrument, wanted to combat oppression and injustice. The decree also established the paramount authority of the central *dîwân,* for everyone could refer his case to it. In that case, the ministry in whose jurisdiction the case normally fell could send an observer. Likewise, the central *dîwân* could send an observer to cases dealt with by a ministry, if one of the disputing parties requested this. Cases which were in the domain of two different ministries were henceforth the exclusive jurisdiction of the central *dîwân,* and the same held for those cases outside the normal domain of any ministry. The central *dîwân* could summon parties to any case from any ministry as well as all government officials, including governors and ministers.

To establish law and justice in the provinces, it was also considered necessary to create similar *dîwân*s in the provinces. However, because the provincial governors had raised objections against a sudden introduction of such *dîwân*s in their jurisdiction, fearing that it would lead to disorder in their administrative affairs, the decree stipulated that the central *dîwân* had to delegate trustworthy officials to the provincial towns. There they had to supervise the local judicial administration and to report to the central *dîwân* on the execution of its orders by these governors and how they dealt with cases in their own courts. They also were ordered to report on the manner of administration of the governors and to report in secret to the central *dîwân*, which would inform the Shah. Delegates who misused their position would be punished, dismissed and never be given a government function again. However, this part of the decree, like other parts, was never properly implemented. The provincial governors appointed members of their own staff as permanent delegates of the central *dîwân*. In this way, nothing was changed and the governors were able to act as formerly in total, unrestricted freedom.[38]

Despite the disappointing results of his experiment of 1860 with the court of complaints, Nâsir al-Dîn Shah in 1281/1864 issued a decree ordering the establishment of justice boxes (*sandûq-i 'adâlat*) once a month in the public places of larger towns. The boxes were sealed and the boxes were to be opened in his presence only. The effect of this measure was not very positive, for the governor 'ordered a watch to be kept on those boxes; and the bastinado was freely administered to any indiscreet person dropping in a petition'.[39] It would appear that Curzon is wrong in stating that therefore the boxes remained empty. For Âdamiyyat and Nâtiq, who studied a collection of such petitions, found that between 1300/1882 and 1303/1885 some 2,006 petitions reached the *dîwân-i tazallumât-i 'âmma* (court of public complaints), which had been ordered by the Shah to deal with these petitions. It would appear that this *dîwân*, which was also known as *majlis-i tahqîq-i mazâlim* (court for investigation of complaints), formed a part of the *dîwân-i 'adâlat*, which had been ordered by Nâsir al-Dîn Shah to deal with the petitions from the justice-boxes in 1285/1868.[40] Of the 2,006 petitions which were studied, more than two-thirds were from peasants (*ra'âya*) all over Iran, while the remainder were from artisans and labourers. From this study, it is also clear that this organisation did not have any effect at all on the well-being of the population.[41]

Early in 1287/1871 the Shah appointed Mîrzâ Husayn Khan[42] as the new Minister of Justice, who in his turn appointed his friend and fellow-reformer Yûsuf Khan as his chief adviser. The influence of Malkam Khan, Yûsuf Khan and Âkhundzâda, to name a few of the leading reformers, on Mîrzâ Husayn Khan's reforms is evident.[43] He created and made public in 1288/March 1871 by royal decree, six departments in the Ministry of Justice: a court of appeals to receive petitions (*majlis-i tahqîq-i du'âwî*), which was probably just the continuation of the *mazâlim* court. Further, a department to deal with criminal cases (*majlis-i khiyânat*); an executive department (*majlis-i ijrâ'*), and a legislative department to draw up regulations 'equally applicable to every case and to all classes' (*majlis-i tanzîm-i qânûn*). Shortly thereafter, two other departments were added: a commercial (*tijâratî*) and a real estate (*amlâk*) department. The decree also contained regulations, procedures and guidelines for the functioning of the courts, both for their administrative and judicial aspects. Better protection for suspects was also introduced; arrests without court orders were forbidden, restricted possibilities for bail (petty offences), and innocent people had to be released immediately.

The decree further forbade interference by officials if parties wanted to settle out of court, and it further upheld the rights of the *shar'* courts. The decisions of these courts had to be registered and enforced by the Ministry of Justice, while evidence presented before a *mujtahid* in conformity with the *sharî'a* was accepted.[44] Bakhash rightly remarks that Mîrzâ Husayn Khan had the intention to use the Ministry of Justice, with its legislative department, as an instrument to bring about reforms for the other branches of the administration. Its duty was to draw up regulations, and the provision of the monthly *Waqâyi'-yi 'adliyya* 'containing reports on administrative reforms, notices and miscellaneous intelligence' was also an indication of this intention.[45] Although Mîrzâ Husayn Khan failed in his objective (the monthly was soon discontinued and no regulations applicable to all classes were drawn up), the belief in the self-fulfilling and reforming character of law continued to be a driving force among Iranian reform-minded people, a belief culminating in the demand for an *'adâlat-khâna* or house of justice in 1905, an event which triggered off the Constitutional Revolution.

In 1288/July 1871, Nâsir al-Dîn Shah elaborated on the March decree, which also forbade the punishment of persons of lower ranks by their betters; it forbade governors to use unnecessary torture or to sentence suspects to punishments involving bodily harm. Moreover, they were only allowed to pronounce their verdict after the Ministry of Justice and the Shah had reviewed the case. Governors therefore had only to arrest suspects and to send all evidence to Tehran. However, at the same time provincial and district governors just ignored this order and continued to deal with suspects in the way they saw fit and according to their appreciation of the case.[46] But in Tehran, the reforms of Mîrzâ Husayn Khan had a temporary beneficial effect on the administration of justice and on the restriction of oppression and cruel modes of punishments.[47]

After his return from his first trip to Europe, Nâsir al-Dîn Shah not only introduced a police force along European lines in Tehran,[48] but he also ordered in 1279/September 1873 the establishment of provincial courts as had already been foreseen in the decree of 1862; the president of these provincial courts had to be appointed by the Ministry of Justice.[49] In 1280/1874 a new decree repeated this order, but it was rendered ineffective by the provincial governors who appointed their own men to these functions.[50]

Although Nâsir al-Dîn Shah was forced to dismiss his reforming chief minister Mîrzâ Husayn Khan, he nevertheless tried to profit from his expertise and capabilities by appointing him as Minister of Foreign Affairs. Although Mîrzâ Husayn Khan failed to regain his former influence, the Shah continued to show an interest in reforms of the judicial system. In 1294/1877 the Shah at the instigation of Mîrzâ 'Alî Khan Amîn al-Dawla established a committee which was charged with the codification of the provisions of the *Sharî'a*. The committee, chaired by Mîrzâ Sa'îd Khan Mu'tamin al-Mulk, was composed of leading *'ulamâ'* and high-ranking government officials and met twice a week in Tehran. However, the meetings of this committee produced no result and it was probably suspended, because nothing further was heard about it.[51]

In Rajab 1297/June 1880 Nâsir al-Dîn Shah in a new decree commented upon the dormant character of the *dîwânkhâna-yi 'adâlat*. The decree therefore once again confirmed the supreme authority of the central *dîwân* and stipulated that its decisions had to be executed without further ado by all government officials of whatever level. If the central *dîwân* met with any obstruction or negligence, it had to bring this immediately to the Shah's notice in order to put a stop to such untoward activities.[52] The Shah added to his own hand the following comments to this decree: the purpose of the establishment of the *dîwân* is the maintenance of justice, the abolition of oppression, and the execution of court decisions, and the Minister of Justice had to oversee this last with the greatest strictness.[53]

In Safar 1299/January 1882 the dominant position of the central *dîwân* was once again reiterated in a very forceful-sounding royal decree stating that all those who were summoned by the central *dîwân* had to report immediately and that no excuse would be accepted from anyone.[54]

The effect of this decree, as well as the role of the central *dîwân*, was negligible. This is not only brought out by the repetitive character of the various decrees and the independent behaviour of the governors and notables, but also by the unfinished judicial organisation which still had not acquired the form stipulated in the 1871 decree. In the 1880s there existed a court of appeals (*mazâlim*) for hearing petitions, and an investigative tribunal (*majlis-i makhsûs-i tahqîq*), while specialised courts outside the Ministry of Justice continued to exist, such as the commercial court in the Ministry of Trade. The reintroduction of the position of grand vizier, through the appointment of Mîrzâ 'Alî Asghar Amîn al-Sultân towards the end of the 1880s, reduced the influence of the Minister of Justice even further, and henceforth his jurisdiction totally depended on the leeway allowed by Amîn al-Sultân.[55]

In Ramadân 1305/May 1888 Nâsir al-Dîn Shah, undeterred by his previous failures as Curzon puts it, issued a decree to all provincial governors stating that 'our subjects are free and independent as regards their persons and property . . . no one has the right or power to interfere with, or to lay hands on, the property of Persian subjects, nor to molest their persons or property . . .'.[56] However, no measures were taken to supervise the implementation of the decree and it thus remained a dead letter. In 1307/1889 the Shah had given orders to form a committee for drawing up a code of laws based on a European model, and he appointed his brother Mulkârâ to chair the committee in the following year. Ottoman and European codes were translated; the British Muslim-Indian code and the French one for its Muslim territories were also studied by the committee. However, due to lack of commitment by the Shah to this project and because of opposition to it from Amîn al-Sultân, Mulkârâ, out of fear of the latter, resigned after a short time. The recommendations by the committee were not accepted by Nâsir al-Dîn Shah, acting on the advice of Amîn al-Sultân.[57] Despite this fresh abortive scheme, the Shah continued to show an interest in judicial matters. In 1310/1892 he asked his ministers for a proposal to improve the judicial administration. However, this idea also came to nought, just like the fancy which he entertained about a council which was to supervise the proper implementation of government decrees.[58] By that time, Nâsir al-Dîn Shah had more important problems to deal with (the opposition against the Tobacco Régie: monetary and revenue problems), while he also had lost interest in continuing the struggle with the bureaucracy. When he died in 1313/1896, all that had been achieved were cosmetic changes which were totally inadequate to meet the serious need for reform.[59]

Under his son Muzaffar al-Dîn Shah (1896–1907), the situation of Iran deteriorated. This was partly due to the Shah's unpopular economic measures, partly due to the increased foreign penetration of the Iranian economy. As a result of these developments, the commercial middle class, the bureaucracy and enlightened groups among the intelligentsia (the groups overlapped and included the 'ulamâ') made a common effort to exert more influence on government policy. Their purpose was to overthrow despotism and to establish the rule of law and justice. It was their combined efforts which made their struggle a successful one, by making use of the various demonstrations which were the expression of the discontent about the economic situation, the oppression and the prominent role of foreigners on the political and economic scene in Iran. Iran being a Muslim country, these problems were also ascribed to the neglect of the applications of the provisions of the *Sharî'a*. In December 1905, large-scale protests broke out in Tehran when some highly respected merchants were given the bastinado because of their alleged role in driving up the sugar prices. During these demonstrations the people demanded *inter alia* 'the enforcement of the *Sharî'a* and the establishment of a House of Justice (*'adâlat-khâna*)'. The concept of the House of

Justice was rather vague and was to be the subject of further negotiations with the government. When the Shah failed to do what he had promised, the people of Tehran again demonstrated in the summer of 1906. These events triggered off a series of protest demonstrations which finally led to the granting of a Constitution in August 1906. The formulation of the Constitution itself was the expression of the wish of the reformist forces to establish the rule of law and justice.[60]

Their concern about the importance of law and justice was also re-flected in the Supplementary Fundamental Laws of 29 Sha'bân 1325/7 October 1907 of which article two states that: 'At no time must any legal enactment of the sacred National Consultative Assembly . . . be at variance with the sacred principle of Islam'. Having established the supremacy of the *Sharî'a* as the origin of law and justice, the same law (art. 27) delineates the jurisdiction between the *shar'* and *'urf* courts. 'The judicial power . . . belongs exclusively to the *shar'* courts in matters connected with *shar'* law, and to the *'urf* courts connected with ordinary law'. A further article (art. 71) which confirms this division of jurisdiction also states that 'judgement in the *shar'* courts is vested solely in *mujtahids* possessing the necessary qualifications'.[61] In that same year of 1325/1907 four civil courts were created or revived: the court of property and financial claims; the criminal court; the court of appeals, and the *dîwân-i tamyîz* or the supreme court of appeals which had existed already before that time. Because as yet no civil codes of law existed, these courts applied *shar'* law. This led to difficulties with the *shar'* courts when parties appealed to these courts against the decisions given by the new civil courts, for the *shar'* courts gave different decisions. In 1326/1908, there-fore, a court was created to settle differences of opinion between *shar'* and *'urf* courts.[62] Attempts were also made to codify new laws, but the *'ulamâ'* were not willing to assist in this work. They even opposed the codification of *'urf* law, fearing that a systematised code of laws which also would rule their own behaviour would diminish their power.[63] In 1910 the office of *mudda'î al-'umûmî* or Attorney General was created, while finally in Hamal 1291 Sh./April 1911 the judicial system was totally reorganised. This was due to the suggestion made by the prime minister Mushîr al-Dawla that not only the judiciary be reorganised but that a civil code also be drawn up. A temporary judiciary was set up by the Majlis (Parliament), which with the assistance of the French jurist Adolphe Perni drew up the new civil code. In order not to antagonise the *'ulamâ'*, the code was allowed by the Majlis to be applied on an experimental and temporary basis from Mîzân 1291 Sh./November 1911. This proviso was necessary to circumvent a discussion on the compatibility of the new Civil Code with the *Sharî'a,* a discussion which would have made the swift introduction of the code impossible. In 1294 Sh./1915 a commercial code was adopted on the same experimental and temporary basis.[64]

The new codes had created separate courts for criminal (*jazâ'î*) and civil (*huqûqî*) cases.[65] The prosecution in both courts could be initiated both by a private individual (*khusûsî*) and by the state (*'umûmî*). In Tehran, the *mudda'î al-'umûmî* was appointed, who in some instances acted as public prosecutor and in others as public pleader in the *Tamyîz* court. He had representatives in the other courts and 'it is his duty to watch the conduct of all cases in which public interests are concerned, e.g. cases involving public money, religious endowments, orphans, bankruptcies, etc., and to assist unprotected persons to obtain justice'.[66] If he disagreed with a verdict, he could ask the Minister of Justice to order a retrial of the case.

Table of the 'adliyya courts[67]

---

(1) The supreme court of appeals (*Tamyîz*) existed in Tehran only. *Civil cases:* hears only cases from lower civil courts. *Criminal cases:* hears appeals from lower criminal courts. *Powers:* full powers.

(2) The court of appeals (*Istînâf*) existed in Tehran, Azerbaijan, Fars, Khurasan, Kirman, Gilan and Hamadan. *Civil cases:* hears appeals from lower civil courts. *Criminal cases:* sits with the *dîwân-i jinâyat-i khusûsî* and the *dîwân-i jinâyât-i 'umûmî*. It also hears appeals from lower criminal courts. *Powers:* full powers, including the death penalty.

(3) The court of first instance (*Bidâyat* or *Ibtidâ'î*). It is for both civil and commercial cases. This court was to be found in all principal towns and headed by a *ra'îs-i 'adliyya*. Its powers were unlimited, and the court could inflict a sentence of up to two years' imprisonment and a fine.

(3a) The criminal court (*Jazâ'î*) tries cases of petty offences (*junhâ-yi kûchik*) and serious offences (*junhâ-yi buzurg*) such as assault and murder. This court was established in Tehran; in the provinces it often still fell under the jurisdiction of the provincial governors or the military commanders. Cases in the provinces were also referred to Tehran or were referred to a special court. Its powers were unlimited, including the death penalty.

(4) The petty court (*Sulhiyya*). *Civil cases:* tries claims up to 400 tûmâns, and imprisonment up to one month. Trivial cases involving a fine or claim up to 20 tumans were dealt with by the police station. *Criminal:* deals with petty cases. *Powers:* it can inflict imprisonment up to one month and fines up to 250 tûmâns. The *Sulhiyya* courts were after 1920 established in some rural districts, especially around Tehran.

Although formally *'urf* courts, the *'adliyya* courts had religious judges on the bench as well as recourse to decisions by *shar'* courts which continued to exist, of course. The *Istînâf* court had an *'udw-i faqîh* (a *shar'* jurist member) as one of its members, while the *Sulhiyya* had an *âkhûnd* (lower rank *mullâ*) besides the *'urf* judge to settle cases within the jurisdiction of the *Sharî'a*. Moreover, many *mullâs* were normal members of the courts in their personal rather than their 'religious' capacity. This was due to the fact that formal training outside the madrasa (religious seminary) system was still restricted in scope, certainly where legal science was concerned, which in Iran after all was formally based on Islamic law. Many judges therefore had had a training as a *mullâ*.[68]

I. *Criminal cases* (Jazâ'î)

The civil code divided criminal cases into four classes: (a) *jinâyat* cases such as murder, rape, high treason, armed robbery. (b) *junhâ-yi buzurg,* cases such as theft, grievous hurt. (c) *junhâ-yi kûchik,* cases such as simple hurt, pilfering. (d) *khilâf,* cases such as abuse, committing public nuisance.

If a claim was made in cases (a), (b) and (c) by a private person, he addressed himself to the *mudda'î al-'umûmî-yi bidâyat*. The latter instructed the *mustantiq* (examining magistrate) to investigate the case and to report to him. If the *mustantiq* thought that he had a case against the accused, the latter was brought before the relevant court, where the complainant's pleader took over the prosecution. In regard to *'umûmî* cases, the same procedure was followed, but here the *mudda'î al-'umûmî* took over the prosecution of the cases in the proper court.

These courts were the following: (a) *Jinâyat* courts. (1) *'Umûmî* cases. A so-called *dîwân-i jinâyat-i 'umûmî* was formed consisting of the *ra'îs-i istînâf,* the three members of the *istînâf* court, and the *ra'îs-i mahkama-yi bidâyat*. The *mudda'î al-'umûmî-yi istînâf* prosecuted the case. The lawyers (*wakîl*) were nominated by the court for the defence of the accused, which choice he had to accept. (2) *Khusûsî* cases. A *dîwân-i jinâyat-i khusûsî* was formed consisting of one of the chief *mullâs* in town as president, and two junior *mullâs* with the *ra'îs-i istînâf* and the members of the *istînâf* court as members. Here the accused was allowed to appoint his own lawyer.

The law required that these courts (*dîwâns*) be constituted every six months, but in practice it happened often only once a year. Decisions by these courts were taken by a majority of votes. The *ra'îs-i istînâf* had no powers to overrule the other members of the court. The death sentence could be passed without having recourse to Tehran.

(b) Both *junhâ-yi buzurg* and *junhâ-yi kûchik* cases were tried by the *Bidâyat* court. The procedure for making a complaint, investigating the case and preparing it for the court as well as the prosecution were the same as in *jinâyat* cases.

(c) *Khilâf* cases, both *khusûsî* and *'umûmî*, were tried by the *Sulhiyya* courts. *'Umûmî* cases were prosecuted by the departments concerned.

II. *Civil cases* (Huqûqî)

The law distinguished three kinds of civil cases: (a) *shar'* or religious cases. (b) *'urf* or customary cases. (c) *mushtarik* or mixed cases.

(a) If a case was classified by the parties concerned as a *shar'* case, they had recourse to a *shar'* court, which gave a verdict. This decision had to be confirmed by the proper court concerned. There was no appeal against verdicts by *shar'* courts.[69]

(b) *'Urf* cases were tried in the *Sulhiyya*, *Bidâyat* or *Istînâf* courts. If the parties agreed, arbiters could be nominated whose decision was binding. These cases could also be referred to *shar'* courts, but only with a proper court order. However, it sometimes happened that parties had recourse to the *shar'* court without such an order, which caused irregularities and led not infrequently to injustice.

(c) *Mushtarik* cases were those about which the parties were uncertain as to their classification. If the parties could not agree upon a classification, the court took a decision with regard to the proper classification and referred it to either *shar'* or *'urf* courts, i.e. (a) or (b).

The decisions by the *'adliyya* courts were executed by the *Ijrâ'* or executive department which formed an integral part of the *'adliyya* court.

With the introduction of the *'adliyya* courts, the *shar'* courts were not of course abolished, but were adopted into the new judicial system. In fact the civil code of 1290 Sh./1911 delineated precisely the jurisdiction of the *shar'* courts and stipulated which cases had to be referred to them for arbitration.[70] From then onwards, the *shar'* courts became formally subordinate to and an instrument of the state. Henceforth, all *shar'* judges were appointed by the government, while the *'adliyya* courts referred cases to the *shar'* courts and also executed its decisions. Another formal weakening of the *'ulamâ'* class was the creation of the department for the registration of the copying of documents. Registration was not compulsory, and documents countersigned by a *mujtahid* were still valid. Nevertheless, people in Tehran started to make use of this new department.[71] It remained restricted to Tehran, however. For although in 1301 Sh./1922 the Majlis had passed a law ordering the establishment of such departments in all *'adliyya* courts, there still was not such a department in Shiraz in 1927, which the British consul considered to be a notable defect.[72] The civil code stipulated that seven branches of justice remained the sole domain of the *shar'* courts: *nikâh* (marriage), *talâq* (divorce), *iflâs* (admission of insolvency), *wasîhat* (probate), *ghasb* (misappropriation), and *waqf* (bequests), of which *iflâs*, *wasîhat*, and *ghasb* were fruitful sources of corruption and embezzlement.[73] Many cases, however, were not referred to the *'adliyya* courts but submitted to a *mujtahid* for arbitration, so that the *shar'* courts in practice had a larger scope than had been formally established.[74] Commercial cases also were seldom, if at all, heard in the *'adliyya* courts, for the merchants preferred to continue to refer their cases to courts of arbitration run by themselves or to reach a bilateral compromise. Their lack of trust and confidence was shared by, for example, the British consuls, who were of the opinion that since 'neither judges nor pleaders [in Fars] have any real business knowledge, and no acquaintance at all with the practice and usages of international trade', it was better to avoid them.[75]

Although Iranians and Europeans agreed that the *'adliyya* courts were easily the most corrupt and inefficient part of the Iranian administration, this was not due to the fact that the machinery for prosecuting cases and administering justice was problematic or objectionable; quite the contrary. For with properly-trained judges and court personnel who would have had a reasonable degree of honesty and efficiency, the system could have worked quite well. The problem, however, was that judges, lawyers, clerks, assistants and registrars were all corrupt. The degree of success in getting one's right depended on the length of one's purse and/or influence. Unless, of course, parties agreed to settle out of court, which British consuls, invariably suggested to British (protected) subjects. For it was better to take a 30 per cent loss on one's outstanding disputed debt than to take it to the *'adliyya* court, which would take much longer, and if finally a decision was taken, would result in bigger losses.[76]

The failure of the *'adliyya* courts was due to many factors, one of which was the socio-political system in which they had to function. This not only incapacitated the proper working and effectiveness of the courts but it also made them into despoilers rather than upholders of justice. A further handicap was the meagre resources available for the staffing of the courts, as well as for the extension of the number of courts throughout the country. Finally, the quality of the staff that was available, especially in the provinces, was often very low. It was therefore no surprise that the people had recourse to other courts and systems to get justice done.

The Ministry of Justice, which was responsible for the proper functioning of the *'adliyya* courts, was despite its modern trappings[77] run along the same lines as its pre-constitutional predecessor, namely as the personal fief of its holder.[78] The Minister therefore considered the Ministry as a means to improve his political and financial position by handing out favours and jobs. It was not so much the remuneration of the jobs themselves which drew candidates, but rather its *madâkhil* or money-making potential. For the Ministry itself had a very small budget only, namely 250,000 tûmâns, which was used to pay the salaries of the ministry staff and the personnel of the courts. However, this budget did not suffice to pay them all. To make up for the low salaries, the Ministry sent fiscal stamps to the various courts, out of the sale of which salaries could be paid and staff could be hired. This situation did not attract the best candidates, of course, for to sell stamps to obtain his salary was not a jurist's aim in life.[79] Although the *'adliyya* courts did not reach all towns of Iran, let alone the rural areas, where the old system remained in full force, by 1920 the main towns in Iran had an *'adliyya* court, i.e. up to the *Bidâyat* level. In Khuzistan, however, the first *'adliyya* court was opened only in 1922. It concerned a *Sulhiyya* and *Bidâyat* court (the nearest *Istînâf* court was in Shiraz) in Shushtar, which was transferred to Ahvaz in 1925.[80] Nevertheless, the budget did not even suffice for the existing courts, and the Ministry of Justice was obliged to close down a few courts each year. The courts to be closed down temporarily were rotated every year so as to bring some kind of evenhandedness to the system. The same held for the judges, of whom there were too many in the early 1920s according to Kasravî. These, more than 100 or so, spent part of their time in the ante-chamber of the Minister's assistant (*mu'âwin*) in order to apply and wait for a job. In order to accommodate these unemployed judges, the Ministry employed them in turns.[81]

Apart from the drawbacks of the socio-political system, there was the fact that there were no objective criteria for screening judges and other court personnel. At the beginning of the *'adliyya* courts, many people who had contacts with the royal court were employed as judges, while gradually droves of *mullâ*s joined the ranks of judges, registrars and lawyers. In fact, every unemployed person with a letter of recommendation from a *mujtahid* or a politician could get a job as judge, the more so if they had a madrasa training. In this way, a great many people were employed who knew neither civil law nor religious law.[82] Kasravî even mentions a *ra'îs-i 'adliyya* of Zanjan, a political nominee, who was illiterate.[83] Because *mujtahids* and other high-ranking *'ulamâ'* considered the function of judge to be below their standing, 'every ignoramus with some metres of black or white textile on his head could become a *qâdî* (judge)' commented Mustawfî.[84] The situation was even worse in the provinces, for it was difficult to find persons willing to serve there. The result was, that although the judicial system had been reorganised, the court personnel was not, and the majority of judges and lawyers were the same *âkhûnds* and *âkhûnd ma'âbs* (quasi-clergy) as before 1911. According to the British Minister in Tehran, Clive, 'Until now it may be said that the mullahs, who furnished 90 per cent of the judiciary, really controlled the administration of justice'.[85]

The result was that all court personnel, judges, prosecutors, investigators, lawyers, clerks and the *Ijrâ'* department were susceptible to corruption and formed the biggest problem of the judiciary. The *vakîls* often formed a ring to prevent the quick dispatch of cases, prolonging and complicating them in order to fill their pockets at the expense of their clients.[86] The further fact that the new judicial system had introduced a single, uniform system to the judiciary proved to be a disadvantage. For 'in the old days, the clerical courts were notorious for corruption, but there was generally in each town a *mullâ* of good repute, who could be trusted to intervene when affairs got too bad. Now there is no such control'.[87] Kasravî mentions various instances where he, being a new-comer, was offered a share in cases, if he would co-operate with the judge or lawyer. The judges classified cases according to the amount of money they could make out of them. The law officials also used their position to make money by trumping up cases.[88] The British consul in Kirman knew of at least one comparatively honest court official, 'as his opium smoking habits demand most of his energy'.[89] The officers in charge of the *Ijrâ'* department often only executed court decisions when bribed by the decree holder to do so, and they were not unwilling to delay doing so if the judgement debtor bribed him to delay execution. In this way, many court orders were lying unexecuted for years at a time.[90]

As result of these corrupt practices, which also had been characteristic of the pre-constitutional courts, many of the *'adliyya* court officials became well-off if not outright wealthy. In Kirman, the *ra'îs* of the *istînâf* court, Rukn al-Dawla, for example, came as a penniless man to Kirman in 1921, but in 1927 'he owned landed property worth 20,000 tomans, a motor car, etc., all of which money has been obtained by bribery'.[91] Many other cases were openly discussed in the Iranian local press and the *'adliyya* courts became popularly known as *zulmiyya* or courts of in-justice. Despite the complaints that groups of citizens regularly sent to the Ministry of Justice, nothing was done to correct the situation.[92] Kasrawî therefore noted that he was ashamed to apply for a job at the Ministry of Justice, because of the bad reputation of the *'adliyya* courts, although he had been invited to become a judge. He therefore, being unemployed at that time, first tried to get a job with the Ministry of Education, in which he was not successful.[93]

Because of the bad reputation of the *'adliyya* courts, the *shar'* courts and other rival procedures, such as the courts of arbitration, continued to dominate the judicial system. This was also caused by the fact that the *'adliyya* courts had not been extended to all parts of Iran, while existing courts regularly were temporarily closed down. During these interim periods, people took their cases to the local governor or to the military commander, which procedure gave them moreover more satisfaction than the *'adliyya* courts.[94] In civil cases especially, the *shar'* courts remained very important. In Bushire, all civil cases were in fact taken to the *shar'* courts because the people had no confidence in the *'adliyya* courts.[95] But in other towns also the *shar'* courts played an important role. However, British consuls had no very favourable opinion about the *shar'* courts either. This was due to the fact that they dealt mostly with them in cases of bankruptcy, where the *shar'* courts granted a certificate of bankruptcy without proper evidence or no evidence at all. Such a certificate made it impossible for a plaintiff to realise any claim from a judgement debtor, however just his claim was. Moreover, the *mullâs* in charge of these courts were corrupt also, while the system of allowing, without enquiry or cross-examination, friends and relatives as *shuhûd-i mu'tabar* (legally-sworn witnesses) on whose evidence decisions were given did not inspire confidence either.[96]

In those areas such as in Khuzistan, where the military were in charge of the local administration, the judicial situation became even more complex. Not only did the disputing parties try to influence the court's decision, but the local leading *mujtahid* was also in the habit of informing the *ra'îs-i 'adliyya* indirectly of his opinion about the case.[97] In military areas, the military commanders added their 'advice' as well. In Ahvaz, where the *'adliyya* court was opened on 7 Dalw 1304 Sh./26 January 1925, the military closed the court on 30 Hût 1303/20 March 1925, 'because of the general dissatisfaction with its corrupt methods, and incidentally because the military coveted the facilities enjoyed by the adliyah for extorting money from the populace'.[98]

When the *'adliyya* courts were suddenly abolished in Urdîbihisht 1307/April 1927 there was nobody in Iran, apart from the court officials, who lamented their demise.[99] Both Iranians and foreigners agreed on that issue, although they disagreed on what kind of system should replace the old one.

The position of foreigners

Foreigners had a special interest in the judicial system of Iran, because until 1928 they enjoyed special capitulary rights. Until the conclusion of the Treaty of Turkmanchay in 1828 between Russia and Iran, which formed the basis for the 'most favoured nation treatment' accorded to other states having treaty relations with Iran, the special legal position of foreigners (specifically Europeans) depended entirely on usage and custom. In Safavid, Afshârid, and Zand Iran, Europeans such as the English, French, Dutch and Russians had enjoyed capitulary rights which had been granted by subsequent Shahs. The nature and extent of these rights differed according to the period, but in general they accorded Europeans the right to be judged according to their own laws and practices by their own officials (in case of the East India Companies) or consuls. Although the Qajar Shahs had not granted similar rights to the Russians and British (the two nations had a considerable number of their subjects working and living in Iran), the Russian and British consuls were allowed the exercise of civil and criminal jurisdiction in case of their own subjects.[100]

It would appear that the nature and legal extent of the civil jurisdiction

133

was better defined than that of the criminal jurisdiction, and it amounted to the following: (a)) all cases between European subjects and protected persons; (b) all cases in which the same classes were defendants; (c) all cases between these classes and others (not being Iranian subjects), provided the parties consented; and (d) if an Iranian subject was defendant and a European subject plaintiff, the case was to be tried in the Iranian court, but a residency official might be deputed to watch the proceedings. This system preceded the Turkmanchay Treaty and thus was not dependent on it. Articles 7 and 8 of this treaty stipulated that all claims and disputes between Russian subjects were entirely reserved to the Russian legation or its consuls, and were to be decided according to the laws and practice of Russia. The same system was applied to disputes between Russian and other foreign subjects, provided the parties consented thereto. However, with regard to disputes between foreign and Iranian subjects, these had to be referred to the *hâkim* or governor for investigation and decision.[101]

However, the practice was that such cases were referred to the respective foreign legation or consulate if the foreign subject was the defendant, and to the Ministry of Foreign Affairs in Tehran or its representative in the provinces if the foreign subject was the plaintiff. Until the creation of the kârgudhârates in the 1850s as provincial representative of the Iranian Ministry of Foreign Affairs, this function was exercised by the *dabîr,* the provincial chief in charge of the department dealing with 'affairs of the Rayahs (sc. *ra'âyâ* or subjects), frontier traffic, and with resident or travelling foreigners'.[102] Both *Sharî'a* and *'urf* legal rules were hardly applied in these cases, because the cases had to be decided upon the principle of equity, a principle foreign to the Iranian judicial system. A foreigner could therefore protest against any ruling that was contrary to this principle. The (most favoured nation) clauses of treaties also did not allow the use of sworn witnesses, but admitted documentary evidence, which hardly played a role in e.g. the *Sharî'a* legal system. In that case, all documents which had been passed between foreigners and Iranians had to be previously authenticated by the *dabîr* (later *kârgudhâr*). In fact, documents played an overriding role in such legal disputes. In practice, the *kârgudhâr* and the consul tried to settle these disputes amicably and these therefore mostly ended with an agreement on a settlement or with a court of arbitration (*ijlâs*). If a satisfactory settlement was not reached, the case (if it came from the provinces) was referred to Tehran, where the matter was taken up between the foreign legation and the Iranian government. If this still did not lead to agreement, the foreign representative laid the case before his own government. Once a verdict had been given it could not be revised again, or the case reopened again, without the consent of the foreign legation or consulate. If this consent was given, the case could only be treated before a special court of appeals and in the presence of the consul.[102]

In the mid-1850s, an experiment was tried in Tabriz, namely to form mixed courts on the Turkish model. This meant that both parties would appoint a trusted person to the court, while the consul appointed the third person. This court would rule on the case and present its findings to the consul, who would pronounce the verdict. Although the system was successful in case of disputes between European subjects, the experiment failed in cases between European and Iranian subjects. According to Blau, the problem was that Muslim judges were unable to attach the same value to statements by non-Muslims as to those by Muslim witnesses. This meant that a non-Muslim party was in a disadvantageous position and would automatically lose, and the experiment was therefore stopped.[104]

The British government of India supported a proposal by Colonel Pelly in 1873 to establish mixed courts at Bushire for similar cases. However, the idea was given up when it became clear that this would require a new treaty, and the old-established system was retained. Finally, an Order in Council for consular courts in the Iranian coast and islands was issued which was based on the usage in existence, because that jurisdiction had never been questioned by the Iranian government. This was preferred to the reference to treaty stipulations, because usage gave the British consuls more jurisdiction. Moreover, there was the problem of deciding which of the nations having treaty relations with Iran was the most favoured nation, 'the German treaty of 1872 being in some respects more, in others less, favourable than the Russian treaty as to criminal cases'.[105]

Due to the increase of trade with Europe and the growth of the number of European subjects residing in Iran, the number of cases between foreigners and Iranians increased.[106] To deal with this situation, the Iranian government had created the kârgudhârates which had limited powers. Because the kârgudhâr had to steer a middle course, he was a conciliator rather than a judge; thus he tried to persuade creditors to accept payment of part of the debt or to agree to a court of arbitration. However, in the majority of these cases the same result would have been obtained anyway because the assessors aimed at reaching a compromise. It is not surprising that Europeans considered this to be an unsatisfactory situation which they tried to circumvent by doing business mostly on a cash basis. Nevertheless, however imperfect the kârgudhâr courts were, nobody wanted to exchange them for the regular Iranian courts.[107]

With the growth of nationalism in Iran, the demand for the abolition of the so-called capitulary rights of foreigners also increased. In 1910 in the Caspian provinces, the governors demanded that cases in which foreigners were involved should be transferred from the kârgudhâr courts to the ordinary courts. The kârgudhâr courts, moreover, also began to refuse to 'award sentences, inflicting fines, or punishments' on Iranians, while verdicts in favour of Russian subjects were not carried out.[108]

Russian intervention, the virtual status of a protectorate of Iran after 1911 and the violation of its neutrality in 1914, put an end to the attempts at the assertion of Iran's sovereignty in, *inter alia,* the judicial field. However, the sentiments in favour of asserting these rights were and remained strong.[109] In 1918 the government of Samsâm al-Saltana, which was anti-British, abolished all treaties with Russia and suppressed the Tribunal of the Ministry of Foreign Affairs and the kârgudhârates. However, when he fell from power on 9 August 1918, the old situation was restored.[110]

In 1921 the government of Diyâ' al-Dîn, who had come to power through a military coup, wanted to abolish the kârgudhârates as well and transfer their jurisdiction to ordinary courts. Although he soon fell from power, the Majlis later reduced the budget of the Ministry of Foreign affairs and decided that some kârgudhârates should be abolished. However, towards the end of January 1922, it was learnt that the kârgudhârates were not to be abolished but merely transferred to the local governors, as the British government had urged; then later, it was rumoured that all kârgudhârates had been abolished on 21 March 1922. After the dean of the diplomatic corps had made inquiries about this rumour, the foreign legations received an official note on 27 June 1922 which stated that the kârgudhârates of Fars, Isfahan, Iraq, Hamadan, Kurdistan, Qazvin, Khuy, Urumiyya, Birjand, Turbat-i Haydari, Enzeli, Lahijan, Zahidan and Bandar-i Nasiri had been abolished and that the local governors had been instructed to take over their functions. At the same time, the Iranian government informed the foreign legations that it intended to re-establish the kârgudhârates of Fars, Isfahan, Kurdistan and Enzeli. The heads of missions met in Tehran in September 1922, and it was found that there were no complaints about the new system. It was therefore decided to acquiesce in it.[111]

It is unclear whether, how many kârgudhârates were re-established in the provinces and when and where this took place. That some must have been re-established follows from the fact that in 1924 and 1925 the Iranian Ministry of Foreign Affairs instructed *kârgudhâr*s in the provinces to conform to the Iranian civil law. This development was considered by the British to be disadvantageous to suitors, because the *kârgudhâr*s had at least a certain amount of knowledge of international trade usages, while the presence of a consular representative prevented gross injustice and produced, in most cases, some settlement of the case.[112]

The disappearance of the *kârgudhâr* courts as part of the abolition of the capitulations was not mourned by the European states because it had been an imperfect system; British consuls with more than 20 years of experience had seen no improvement in these courts, nor did they see any possibility thereof.[113] What worried the European states was the question of whether the new Iranian judicial system would be worse than the *'adliyya* system. The discussion within, for example, the British government was not so much whether the capitulary rights should be maintained or not, but whether the new Iranian judicial system would be a fair one, one which would live up to certain standards of impartiality, equitability, capability and, as far as the carrying out of justice was concerned, to hygienic and modern modes of detention and the execution of sentences. Whether European fears were proved true or not lies outside the scope of this article, but when Rizâ Shah abolished the capitulations in 1928, not one European state protested.[113]

Conclusion

The struggle for the strengthening of the central authority which had begun timidly in the early part of the nineteenth century received considerable emphasis under Nâsir al-Dîn Shah, who dominated the political scene of Iran during the last half of the century. Despite the efforts of the various reforming ministers who received his support to reorganise the judiciary and to try to bring about a more just and less oppressive state of affairs, these proved to be abortive. The judiciary remained in the hands of the *mullâs*, whose courts continued to enjoy unrestricted jurisdiction. The *'urf* courts were not only subordinated to the Shah, Prime Minister and the other ministries, but in general played an insignificant role. In fact, Mustawfî observes that the *'urf* courts or what he called the *'adliyya Nâsir al-Dîn Shâhî* were but the *Mîr qalîj* or the 'executor' of the *shar'* courts. In the provinces it would appear that the judiciary situation had not changed at all, whilst the cosmetic changes had only touched the situation in Tehran.[115]

However, the need for *inter alia* judicial reforms was strongly felt among the population in general, and among the middle class in particular. The Constitution of 1906 represented the symbol of their victory, as did the re-organisation of the judiciary and the implementation of a civil code in 1911. However, the reformers' victory was a Pyrrhic one. Although they had given Iran a good judicial system on paper, Iranian society had not yet progressed to the point where it was able to digest these new ideas and concepts. The traditional idea of government, despite its modern form and organisation, had not given way to these new ideas, which were based on Western law. In the West, law had become the most effective agent of social control and the only reliable principle capable of moderating arbitrariness. However, law as it was practised in Iran was still the expression of social practice rather than a derivation from abstract principles. One of the reasons, apart from political and economic ones, was the fact that the government itself remained an instrument of injustice. Moreover, the reforms and the underlying ideas remained restricted to a very small group, mainly concentrated in Tehran. The judiciary therefore remained in the control of the 'old hands', the *mullâs*. The effect of the reorganisation of the judiciary in 1927 was that 'it deprived many of the minor clerics of their means of subsistence'.[116]

An interesting aspect of the *'urf* courts was the position of the Europeans in Iran, who enjoyed capitulary rights which were partly based on custom and usage and partly on treaty regulations. This special form of the *'urf* judiciary provided Europeans with a certain number of safeguards against arbitrariness and injustice. With the confirmation of the sovereignty of the people in 1906, the reformers also wished to end the special position of foreigners in Iran. Opposition against the abolishment of the capitulary rights in 1928 was almost non-existent, due to the fact that sufficient faith existed in the safeguards offered by the modernising new government of Iran.

I APPENDIX TO CHAPTER EIGHT

I. *Organogram of the Ministry of Justice in 1302/1923 (Tehran)*

Ministerial staff	91
Tamyîz court	18
Istînâf court	28
Mahkama-yi janâ'î-yi ikhtisâsî	3
Bidâyat court	32
Barka-yi bidâyat and *istînâf*	34
Tijârat court (commercial)	8
Sulhiyya Tehran	30
Sulhiyya outskirts (*nawâhî*)	12
Sulhiyya of the dependencies (*bulûkât*)	15
(Khvâr, Varâmîn, Sharyâr, Damâvand, Savjbulagh)	
Supporting staff	62
	333

II. *Provincial Judiciary (2nd class)*

Bidâyat court attached to the *istînâfiyya* of Tehran, each of 22 persons in: Rasht, Bârfurûsh, Hamadan, Isfahan	88
Bidâyat court 2nd category, each 7 persons, in Rasht, Isfahan, Hamadan	21
Tijârat court of Rasht	7
Sulhiyya, each 5 persons, in Rasht (2), Isfahan (2), Barfurûsh, Hamadan	30
Sulhiyya-yi nâhiya (Rasht, Hamadan, Isfahan)	3
Bidâyat 3rd class, mostly of 27 persons, in Qazvîn, Yazd, Shâhrûd, Zinjân, Âstârâbâd, Kurdistan, Kirmanshah, Iraq	156
Sulhiyya with restricted powers (*salâhiyyat-i mahdûd*) in Sârî, Kâshân, Mâlâyir, Burujird, Qum va Sâva, each 16 persons	80
Sulhiyya 3rd class, each of 7 persons, in: Enzeli, Lâhijân, Tunkabûn, Amul, Gulpâygân, Kamara va Khunsar, Nihâvand va Tûysarkân, Nâ'în, Simnân, Dâmghân, Natanz, Sâva	84
	366

III. Istînâfiyya *of Azerbaijan (Tabriz)*
Istînâf	9
Bidâyat	15
Tijârat court	3
Supporting staff	21
Sulhiyya (two)	10
Sulhiyya-yi nâhiya	1
	59

Attached to Azerbaijan *istînâfiyya:*
Bidâyat court 3rd class of Ardabîl, Âstârâ	27
Sulhiyya 3rd class, in Marâgha, Khûy, Urmiyya, Marand, Âstârâ, Mâkû, Savjbulagh, each 7 persons	49
	135

IV. Istînâfiyya *of Fars and 'Arabistan (Shiraz)*
Istînâf	9
Bidâyat	16
Supporting staff	20
Sulhiyya	5
Bidâyât 3rd class attached to Fars, each of 27 persons, in Bushire and 'Arabistan	54
Sulhiyya of Âbâda	7
	111

V. Istînâfiyya *of Khurasan (Mashhad)*
Istînâf	9
Bidâyat	16
Tijârat court	3
Supporting staff	21
Sulhiyya	11
Sulhiyya restricted, each of 16 persons in: Sabzivar, Qûchân	32
Sulhiyya 3rd class, each of 7 persons in: Turbat, Birjand, Nîshâpûr	21
	113

VI. Istînâfiyya *of Kirman (Kirman)*
Istînâf	9
Bidâyat	16
Supporting staff	20
Sulhiyya	5
Sulhiyya-hûza (district court) each of 7 persons, in: Bâm, Sîrjân	14
	64

The total amounts to 1,122 persons. Note that each attached *bidâyat* court of the third class consisted of 11 *bidâyat* personnel, 11 supporting staff and 5 *sulhiyya*; 27 persons in all.

The budget for the Ministry of Justice in this year amounted to 700,000 tûmâns of a total government budget of 22,592,44 tûmâns or slightly more than 3 per cent.

The judicial system

NOTES AND REFERENCES

1. Sir J. Malcolm, *A History of Persia*, London 1815, ii, 444; J. B. Fraser, *An Historical and Descriptive Account of Persia from the Earliest Ages to the Present Time*, Edinburgh 1834, 223; J. F. Polak, *Persien: Das Land und seine Bewohner*, Leipzig 1865, i, 328; the Hon. G. N. Curzon, *Persia and the Persian Question*, London 1892, i, 453.

2. Malcolm, ii, 444-6, who adds that there was also a *muftî* in the courts, whose duty was 'to prepare an exposition of the case before the court, and to aid with his advice'; Fraser, 223; Ahmad 'Alî Khan Vazîrî, *Jughrâfiyâ-yi Kirmân*, ed. Ibrâhîm Bâstânî-Pârîzî, Tehran 1346/1967, 53, gives an example of the function of *Shaykh al-Islâm* which was held by members of one family for more than 100 years; see also Public Record Office, FO 60/150, Stevens to Shiel, Tabriz, 11 June 1850, f.76, for another example; FO 416/80, Gilliat-Smith to Clive, Tabriz, 4 May 1927, f.113. 'Formerly there were only five mujtaheds, now there are many, sometimes several in one town, in Teheran for instance there are ten, but there are only a few whose decisions are accepted as final and without appeal', see FO 881/7364, Report on the Persian Army by Lt.-Col. H. P. Picot; for a brief overview of the most important *'ulamâ'* in Iran, see FO 881/7028, Biographical Notices, Tehran 1897, by Lt.-Col. H. P. Picot. (Crown-copyright material in the PRO appears with the permission of the Controller of Her Majesty's Stationery Office.)

3. Ahmad Kasravî, *Zindigânî-yi man*, Tehran 1323/1944, 155, with an example of a trumped-up case; Ahmad Majd al-Islâm Kirmânî, *Târîkh-i inqilâb-i mashrûtiyyat-i Îrân*, Isfahan 1350-51/1971-2, i, 194-5, states that the *mujtahids* had their informers among the people in order not to take too unpopular decisions.

4. See for a detailed discussion, J. Greenfield, *Das Handelsrecht, einschliesslich das Obligationen- und Pfandrechtes, das Ur-kundenrecht, Konkursrecht und das Fremdenrecht von Persien*, in *Die Handelsgesetze des Erdballs*, vi, Berlin 1906, 12-22; P. M. Sykes, *A History of Persia*, London 1969, ii, 385; H. Brugsch, *Im Lande der Sonne und des Löwen*, Freiburg 1892, 236. According to J. G. Lorimer, 'The religious authorities, who in some districts of the Persian [Gulf] Coast are respected and administer at least the semblance of civil justice, appear at Bandar 'Abbâs to be utterly venal and are not spontaneously resorted to by litigants even as an alternative to the court of the Deputy-Governor', see *Gazeteer of the Persian Gulf, Arabia, and 'Oman*, Calcutta 1915, repr. 1971, ii/A, 14.

5. See my 'The political role of the lutis in Iran', in *Modern Iran: The Dialectics of Continuity and Change*, ed. Michael Bonine and Nikki R. Keddie, Albany, NY 1981, 83-98.

6. 'Abdallâh Mustawfî, *Târîkh-i idârî va ijtimâ'î-yi dawra-yi Qâjâriyya yâ sharh-i zindigânî-yi man*, Tehran, 1343/1974, i, 100; Curzon, i, 453; Brugsch, 237. It was less favourable to have

recourse to the *shar'* court without the intermediary of the *Dîwânkhâna.*

7. Malcolm, ii, 448; Kasravî, 15.
8. See my 'The office of kalantar in Qajar Persia', in *JESHO,* xiv (1971), 253-68.
9. *Ibid.* ; Kasravî, 15.
10. See my 'The market police in Qajar Persia, the office of darughayi bazar and muhtasib', in *Die Welt des Islam,* xiii (1971), 212-39; and my 'Das Amt des Muhtasib im Iran – zur Kontrolle der "Öffentlichen Moral" in der Iranischen Geschichte', in *Revolution in Iran und Afghanistan,* ed. K. Greussung and J. H. Grevemeyer, Berlin 1980, 122-39.
11. Greenfield, *Das Handelsrecht,* 10-11; Curzon, i, 453.
12. C. J. Wills, *Persia as it is,* London 1886, 39; Mustawfî, i, 100; according to Malcolm, ii, 451, torture was seldom applied; see also Fraser, 224.
13. Curzon, i, 456-7; see also Malcolm, ii, 451-4; Fraser, 224. In case of the death sentence, a *fatwâ* from a *mujtahid* was obtained to make it legal. The Shah in general kept this prerogative to himself and seldom delegated this power.
14. Curzon, i, 458; Malcolm, ii, 455; Majd al-Islâm, ii, 74-5.
15. Mustawfî, i, 101; Malcolm, ii, 448.
16. *Op. cit.,* 458-60.
17. A. K. S. Lambton, 'Persian Society under the Qajars', in *JRCAS,* xlviii (1961), 131. The political and administrative situation was described as follows in 1844. 'You observe that this mode of administration resembles passably an organized banditism; it is the realisation of the principle of the right of the strongest to its largest extent. It is this spoils system that is adopted and put into practice everywhere', see 'De l'état administratif et politique de la Perse, *Revue de l'Orient,* iv (1844), 117; see also Fraser, 309.
18. J. A. Perkins, *Residence of Eight Years in Persia among the Nestorian Christians,* Andover, Mass. 1843, 282.
19. T. F. Gordon, *Persia Revisited,* London 1896, 38.
20. This difference between the secular and religious élite is not characteristic for Islam or for Shî'î Islam, but peculiar to all pre-industrial societies, see G. Sjöberg, *The Pre-industrial City,* Glencoe, Ill. 1965, 225.
21. H. Algar, *Religion and State in Iran 1785-1906,* Berkeley 1969, 260.
22. Mustawfî, i, 99.
23. *Op. cit.,* 100; for the situation of the guilds see my 'The guilds in Iran, an overview from the earliest beginnings till 1972', in *ZDMG,* cxxv (1975), 99-116, and art. 'Asnâf' in *Encyclopaedia Iranica;* for the situation among the merchants, see my 'The merchants (*tujjâr*) in Qajar Iran', *ZDMG,* cxxvi (1976), 101-35.
24. See on this subject, Sh. Bakhash, 'The evolution of Qajar bureaucracy: 1779-1879', *MES* (1970), 139-67, for an excellent analysis of this issue.
25. Mustawfî, i, 92. There was also a *nâ'ib-i sadr* or the minister's

deputy, a title which existed until the constitutional revolution according to the same source.

26. Nâsir Najmî, *Îrân dar miyân-i tûfân, ya sharh-i zindigânî-yi 'Abbâs Mîrzâ dar janghâ-yi Îrân va Rûs,* Tehran 1337/1958, 29, 198; Bâqir Qâ'im Maqâm, *Qâ'im Maqâm dar jahân-i adab va siyâsat.* Tehran 1320/1941, 19; see also Algar, 74.

27. J. Greenfield, *Die Verfassung des Persischen Staates,* Berlin 1904, 262.

28. M. A. Kazembeg, 'Note sur les progrès récents de la civilisation en Perse', *JA,* 5th ser., vol.9 (1857), 450-4.

29. Greenfield, *Das Handelsrecht,* 108-10.

30. Kazembeg, 454; F. Âdamiyyat, *Zindigânî-yi Mîrzâ Taqî Khân Amîr Kabîr,* Tehran 1327/1948, 300-5; Algar, 131.

31. FO 60/150, Sheil to Ameer Nizam, Tehran 5 June 1850, f.136.

32. Kazembeg, 453.

33. Lambton, 'The Persian ulama and the Constitutional Reform', in *Le Shî'isme imâmite,* ed. T. Fahd, Paris 1974, 253.

34. Âdamiyyat, *Andîsha-yi taraqqî va hukûmat-i qânûn-i 'asr-i sipâhsalâr,* Tehran 1351/1972, 173ff.

35. S. Bakhash, *Iran: Monarchy, Bureaucracy and Reform,* London 1978, 84; Farhâd Mu'tamid, *Sipâhsâlâr-i A'zam,* Tehran 1326/1947, 42.

36. Mustawfî, i, 92-3; J. Greenfield, 'Persien', in *Jahrbuch der Internationalen Vereinigung für Vergleichende Rechtswissenschaft und Volkswirtschaftslehre,* v (1899), Berlin 1902, 965.

37. I'timâd al-Saltana, Mîrzâ Muhammad Hasan Khan, *Mir'at al-buldân-i Nâsirî,* Tehran 1294-7/1877-80, ii, 284; the decree is dated Rajab 1278/December 1861.

38. Bakhash, *Iran,* 84-5; I'timâd al-Saltana, *Mir'at,* iii, 5; Greenfield, 'Persien', 962-4; Mustawfî, i, 99.

39. Mustawfî, i, 135-7, for the text of the decree; Curzon, i, 465.

40. Greenfield, 'Persien', 964.

41. Âdamiyyat and Humâ Nâtiq, *Afkâr-i ijtimâ'î va siyâsî va iqtisâdî dar âthâr-i muntashir nâshuda-yi dawra-yi Qâjâr,* Tehran 1356/1977, 376ff.

42. See on this reformer, Bakhash, *Iran,* and literature quoted there. Mîrzâ Husayn Khan's father, Mîrzâ Nabî Khan, had been *wazîr-i 'adlîyya* with the title *amîr-i dîwânkhâna,* see Mustawfî, i, 92.

43. For information on the ideas of these and other reformers, with special reference to their proposals for law and justice, see Manûchihr Kamâlî Tah, *Hukûmat-i qânûn,* Tehran 1352/1973; see also Bakhash, *Iran.*

44. *Ibid.,* 86-88; Kamâlî Tah, 333-5; Âdamiyyat, *Andîsha,* 173ff.

45. Bakhash, *Iran,* 88.

46. *Ibid.*; I'timâd al-Saltana, *Mir'at,* iii, 141.

47. Bakhash, *Iran,* 89; Curzon, i, 456.

48. See my 'The police in Qajar Iran', *ZDMG,* cxxiii (1973), 293-315.

49. I'timâd al-Saltana, *Mir'at,* iii, 188.

50. *Ibid.,* 194; see also Curzon, i, 460.

51. Greenfield, 'Persien', 959-69; Mîrzâ 'Alî Khan Amîn al-Dawla, *Khâtirât-i siyâsî*, ed. H. Farmânfarmâ'iyân, Tehran 1341/1962, 94.
52. I'timâd al-Saltana, *Târîkh-i muntazam-i Nâsirî*, Tehran 1300/1883, i, 243.
53. Greenfield, *op. cit.*, 964.
54. I'timâd al-Saltana, *Muntazam*, ii, 324.
55. Greenfield, *op. cit.*, 965; Bakhash, *Iran*, 89. The number of courts seems to have diminished in accordance with the influence of the ministry after 1890. In 1308/1890-1, there was one *majlis-i a'lâ*, one *majlis* which mostly dealt with *shar'î* and real estate cases, and four other courts, see I'timâd al-Saltana, *Kitâb-i durar al-tîjân*, i. appendix, 42. In 1309/1891-2, the situation was similar, as well as in 1310/1892-3, with this difference that there was also a *majlis-i dâr al-inshâ' wa thabt* (registration court), see *ibid.*, ii, appendix, 45, and iii, appendix, 16. In the years thereafter, the number of courts was reduced to three only, one of which was the *majlis-i ijrâ* (executive department). See I'timâd al-Saltana, *Târîkh-i salâtîn-i sâsânî*, Tehran 1314/1896-7, appendix, 45; *idem, Mustatâbnâma-yi dânishvarân-i Nâsirî*, Tehran 1323/1905, vi, appendix, 55; *ibid.*, vii, Tehran 1324/1906, appendix, 56. The *Sâlnâma* of 1318/1900, 45, mentions one general court, one registration department (*thabt*) and one execution department, and also the existence of representatives in Fars, Khurasan, and Isfahan and in other provinces, with the title *ra'îs-i nizâm va dîwânkâna va tijârat*.
56. For the text of this decree, see Curzon, i, 460-1.
57. Amîn al-Dawla, *Khâtirât*, 141-3; Curzon, i, 462; Bakhash, *Iran*, 281-2.
58. *Ibid.*
59. Bakhash, 'Bureaucracy'; F. Abrahamian, *Iran between Two Revolutions*, Princeton 1982, 9-49.
60. *Ibid.*, 50-81; Kasravî, 152, states that the people demanded the *'adâlat-khâna*, because they had lost patience with the *shar'* courts; see also Majd al-Islâm, i, 75, for similar sentiments.
61. E. G. Browne, *The Persian Revolution of 1905-1909*, Cambridge, 1910, 372-3, gives an English translation of these laws.
62. A. Banani, *The Modernisation of Iran*, Berkeley 1969, 69.
63. *Ibid.*, Mustawfî, ii, 374; see the remarks made by Sjöberg, 244, on this problem in pre-industrial societies in general.
64. Banani, 69-70; Mustawfî, ii, 374; Greenfield, 'Die geistlichen Schariegerichte in Persien und die moderne Gesetzgebung', in *Zeitschrift für Vergleichende Rechtswissenschaft*, xlviii (1933), 162.
65. The following description of the new judicial system is based on FO 410/80, Davies to Clive, Kirman, 4 May 1927, ff.124-6; and FO 248/1300, Capt. L. S. Fortescue, Military report on Tehran and some provinces in NW Persia, Tehran 1920, unfoliated.
66. *Ibid.*

67. According to FO 410/80, f.124 the staffing of the courts was as follows:

Istînâf

Ra'îs	1	175 tûmâns
'udw	2	111
'udw-i faqîh	1	111
public prosecutor	1	111
clerks	2	52
clerk	1	42
clerk		32

Bidâyat

ra'îs	1	111
'udw	2	70
public prosecutor	1	111
his clerk	1	42
clerk	1	42
clerk	2	32

Sulhiyya

ra'îs	1	60
head clerk	1	42
munshî		—

68. Mustawfî, ii, 374; FO 248/1300 Fortescue, unfoliated; see note 67; FO 416/80, Gilliat-Smith to Clive, Tabriz, 4 May 1927, f.113.

69. In 1301 Sh./1922 the *'adliyya* courts were given partial appellate jurisdiction over the *shar'* courts (Banani, 78).

70. *Loc. cit.*: '*Shar'* court jurisdiction is delineated and prescribed by the laws of Islam', which was a rather wide and vague stipulation. In *ibid.*, 77, a fairly detailed overview is given of the relevant articles of the civil code. Greenfield, 'Schariegerichte', 166, observes that the civil code accorded documentary evidence a larger role and significance than *shar'* law.

71. *Ibid.*, 162; FO 248/1300 Fortescue, unfoliated.

72. FO 416/80, Chick to Clive, Shiraz, 5 May 1927, f.116.

73. See Banani, 77; Greenfield, 'Schariegerechte', 162f.

74. *Ibid.*; despite the hold of the *shar'* court on the judiciary, the legislative branch of the government continued to make laws which formally weakened the position of the *shar'* courts. Under Rizâ Khan an experimental commercial code (1303 Sh./1924) and penal code (1306 Sh./1927) were introduced, which increasingly deviated moreover from the *shar'* provisions, see Banani, 79ff. and Greenfield, 'Schariegerichte', 160ff. The Majlis also permitted the government to continue to implement new laws on an experimental and temporary basis, see laws of 25 Dalw 1300/25 February 1922 and of 25 Thawr 1302 Sh./16 May 1923.

75. Reference given in n.72 above, f.115.

76. FO 416/80, Cowan to Clive, Kirmanshah, 2 May 1927, f.112; Kasravî, 134, observed that the *istînâf* court in Mazandaran was less corrupt than in Tabriz.

77. The ministry was divided into three main branches:
   (a) the minister's cabinet and personnel department, which dealt with the general administration of the department and personnel policy and appointments.
   (b) the department of judicial affairs which was charged with the supervision of the administration of justice, the investigation of complaints, etc.
   (c) the department of judicial accounts, which was charged with the administration of the finances of the ministry.
78. See on this matter, Bakhash, 'Bureaucracy', 143-7; and in general, Sjöberg, 238-44.
79. Mustawfî, ii, 374, 376; the *'adliyya* courts also acquired income through the collection of *'ushriyya* or 10 per cent impost, Kasravî, 151. Cf. also FO 248/1030, Kirman Diary, 27 April 1911: 'All the departments, viz. Adliyya, Nazmiyya, Amniyya are crying for arrears of their pay and are simply left to be called nominally'.
80. FO 248/1300 Fortescue; FO 416/81, Moneypenny to Clive, Ahvaz, 7 June 1927, f.20.
81. Kasravî, 138, 162-3; Mustawfî, ii, 376.
82. Kasravî, 145; Banani, 70.
83. Kasravî, 148.
84. Mustawfî, ii, 375.
85. FO 416/81, Clive to Chamberlain, Tehran, 21 October 1927, f.110; Mustawfî, ii, 375; the officials did not remain in the bad climatic areas long enough to gain useful experience of local conditions.
86. FO 416/80, Chick to Clive, Shiraz, 5 May 1927, f.000.
87. FO 416/80, Cowan to Clive, Kirmanshah, 2 May 1927, f.112.
88. Kasravî, 119.
89. FO 416/80, f.117.
90. FO 416/80, Davies to Clive, Kirman, 4 May 1927, f.130.
91. *Ibid.*, f.124.
92. FO 416/81, Moneypenny to Clive, Shiraz, 7 June 1927, f.21; FO 248/1300 Fortescue records already such petitions in 1920; FO 416/80, Davies to Clive, Kirman, 4 May 1937, f.124, 'a letter was sent by the public of Kerman to the Ministry of Justice . . . congratulating the minister on the closing of the courts and complaining of the great corruption and procrastination of the existing courts'. The Socialist party of Sulaymân Mîrzâ had as one of the objectives of its programme (article 4) 'the suppression of the Civil Courts and establishment of a system of arbitration of civil cases. Creation of an "independent" prosecutor-general. Election of district procurator-generals', FO 416/79, f.95, Programme of the 'Jammiat-i Ijtamaioun' or Persian Socialist Party, dated January 1923.
93. Kasravî, 117.
94. FO 416/80, Gilliat-Smith to Clive, 4 May 1927, f.113.
95. FO 416/80, Haworth to Clive, Bushire, 9 May 1927, f.123.
96. *Ibid.*, Davies to Clive, Kirman, 4 May 1927, ff.124, 126. This was

apart from the fact that it was extremely unlikely that the *shar‘* courts would ever give a decision in favour of a non-Muslim. Moreover, the *shar‘* courts were also notoriously corrupt; *ibid.,* f.126, states that 'In Kerman three out of the four leading mullahs concerned are reported as taking bribes, though definite instances have not been produced'. The significance of *shar‘* courts was, however, also recognised for certain areas, such as personal law; moreover, 'perjury in a civil court would be not only the rule, but a rule without an exception. The religious courts are not free from it, but a religious oath has some weight', see the reference in n.95, f.73.

97. Kasravî, 159; they also continued to oppose the *‘adliyya, ibid.,* 152, 162, 169-70; Mustawfî, ii, 375, n.1, relates that for two months during the cabinet of Qavâm al-Saltana, the *‘ulamâ’* co-operated with the judiciary and allowed themselves to become *qâdî-yi ‘urf* (a civil judge) using the *shar‘* law. However, there was so much work to be done that the *‘ulamâ’* themselves resigned. Towards the end of October 1923, in connection with the discussion of the Press Law in the Majlis and remarks made by Sulaymân Mîrzâ which were considered to be anti-Islamic by the *‘ulamâ’*, the latter presented the government with a list of demands which *inter alia* demanded the annulment of the Civil Code, for its 'having been inaugurated in the absence of a Medjliss, and never ratified by it, must be annulled, and a new Civil Code, in harmony with religious law, instituted and ratified by the Medjliss'. On 2 November a delegation of those *‘ulamâ’*, who had taken *bast* in a mosque, presented the government with their demands, which were accepted by the government with the exception of the demand for the annulment of the Civil Code. The government argued that 'as the Civil Code had never been ratified by the Medjliss, it could not be regarded as being in force, and, moreover that certain foreign States, such as Russia, whose subjects were amenable to local law, would probably demand consular jurisdiction if those subjects were now made liable to religious law'. After the Prime Minister had given the *‘ulamâ’* his government's promises in writing during his visit to them in the mosque they abandoned their action on 5 November 1923. FO 416/79, f.95, Loraine to Curzon, 9 November 1923.

98. FO 416/81, Moneypenny to Clive, Ahvaz, 7 June 1927, f.20; Kasravî, 228; FO 416/80, Chick to Clive, Shiraz, 5 May 1927, f.115-16.

99. On 24 April 1927 Rizâ Shah instructed the Minister of Justice, Dâvar, to abolish all capitulary rights. Dâvar informed all relevant Legations of this decision on 13 May 1927. In February 1927 the Majlis had already charged Dâvar to reorganise the Ministry of Justice.

100. See on these capitulary rights A. T. Wilson, *The Persian Gulf,* Oxford 1928, 136ff.; H. Dunlop, *Bronnen tot de Geschiedenis der Oostindische Compagnie,* The Hague 1930, 672-82; C. H. Alexandrowicz-Alexander, 'A Persian-Dutch treaty in the

seventeenth century', *The Indian Year Book of International Affairs,* vii, Madras 1958, 201-6.

101. O. Blau, *Commerzielle Zustände Persiens,* Berlin 1858, 55; Brugsch, *Im Land der Sonne und des Löwen,* 237; Greenfield, *Handelsrecht,* 23-5, 113-16.

102. Blau, 6; 'Abd 'Alî Adîb al-Mulk, *Dâfi' al-ghurûr,* ed. Îraj Afshâr, Tehran 1349/1970, 126, mentions the *dabîr-i mahâmm-i khârija* and says 'due to his benevolent behaviour, all merchants of whatever nation had no need to have recourse to the *muftî* or the *qâdî'.*

103. Greenfield, *Handelsrecht,* 23-5; FO 416/81, Haworth to Clive, Bushire, 6 August 1927, f.71; for a detailed analysis of such a case, see my 'Hotz versus Muhammad Shafî', a case study of commercial litigation 1888-1894', *IJMES,* xv (1982).

104. Blau, 55.

105. FO 416/81, Haworth to Clive, Bushire, 6 August 1927, f.71.

106. See my 'Bankruptcy in Qâjâr Iran', *ZDMG,* xccvii (1977), 61-76.

107. *Ibid.* ; see also n.105 above, f.74.

108. FO 371/966, O'Beirne to Grey, St Petersburg, 17 October 1910, f.2.

109. Abrahamian, 81ff.; see also Muhammad Musaddiq al-Saltana, *Kâpîtûlâsîyûn va Îrân,* Tehran 1332 Q/1914, repr. Tehran n.d. [1980]. Iran at that time also enjoyed capitulary rights in e.g. the Ottoman empire; see Kazemzadeh, *Âthâr va ahvâl-i Kâzimzâda Îrânshahr,* Tehran 1350/1971, 93.

110. FO 416/112 (Annual Report 1923), f.4.

111. *Ibid.,* f.12.

112. FO 416/80, Chick to Clive, 5 May 1927, f.116.

113. FO 416/81, Haworth to Clive, Bushire, 6 August 1927, f.73.

114. See all the FO 416/80 and 416/81 references quoted above, which also contain detailed information on trumped-up, corrupt, unjust and delayed cases.

115. Mustawfî, ii, 375, n.1; see also Greenfield, *Verfassung,* 263. Lorimer, *Gazetteer,* ii/B, 1790, states: 'Each hereditary local Shaikh at present . . . settles all civil disputes – except such as are of a religious or semi-religious character, for example matrimonial cases – according to his own idea of what is right and proper; he disposes of all criminal matters inflicting at his discretion imprisonment and the bastinado, but not the penalty of death'.

116. FO 416/113 (Annual Report 1928), f.34.

9

Changes in charismatic authority in Qajar Shi'ism

In the 1943 edition of the Khurâsân Yearbook, printed in Mashhad, there appeared what purported to be a Persian translation of a document entitled 'I'tirâfât-i siyâsî yâ yâd-dâshhâ-yi Kinyâz Dâlgorûki' ('Political confessions, or the memoirs of Count Dolgoruki'). These 'memoirs' were reprinted with various alterations in the following year at Tehran, published in some newspapers, and issued in several editions over the next few years. Now largely forgotten, they enjoyed considerable popularity and gained a certain notoriety at the time of their first appearance, providing (it was alleged) documentary evidence of a deliberate Russian plot to undermine the unity of Islam in Iran by initiating and fostering the growth of the heterodox Bâbî movement, through the agency of Prince Dmitrii Ivanovich Dolgorukov, Russian Minister in Tehran from 1845 to 1854. This supposed translation has long since been exposed as a rather clumsy forgery,[1] the main purpose of which was clearly to discredit the Bahâ'î religious minority. It is, however, primarily of interest as one of the earliest examples of what was to become a popular genre of Iranian writing in the post-war period: revelations of the secret machinations of the imperial powers during the nineteenth and twentieth centuries, designed to weaken and control Iran from within and to destroy the influence of Islam among the people.[2] This theme, which has been taken up with renewed vigour since the Islamic Revolution, is a particularly well-developed example of the conspiracy theory of history, resting as it does on circumstantial or misunderstood evidence and on a verificationist approach to the empirical data.[3] Such theories are of importance, less for the occasional truths they reveal about political intrigue (the reality of which can scarcely be denied) and more for what they tell the observer about the perspectives and preoccupations of those who originate or cling to them.

A marked feature of the Iranian perspective has been its continuing concern with Babism and, more particularly, its offshoot Baha'ism, as the favourite tools of first Russian, then British, and, eventually, American and Zionist policies within Iran. Exposure of the Dolgorukov memoirs has not prevented polemicists, even in recent years, from either retaining a residual faith in them[4] or looking for alternative evidence that the

Bâbî-Bahâ'î movement has been a central agency of foreign disruption in Iran.[5] More tragically, accusations, supported by excedingly flimsy evidence, of subversion on behalf of foreign powers, have been levelled at Bahâ'îs executed by the present régime.[6] It is undeniable that the British and Russians were seriously interested in the Bâbîs (as they were in any movement of potential significance in the Middle East at this period) and that later contacts between Bâhâ'îs and British and Russian government officials or missionaries were often cordial and of mutual benefit,[7] but the sort of evidence that would lead to the far-reaching conclusions of the polemical literature is lacking.

On a wider level, Ismâ'îl Râ'în has argued that the emergence of millenarian movements across the Islamic world in the nineteenth century was the result of deliberate British interference in religious affairs, with the intention of creating confusion and disunity among the Muslim populations under their political control.[8] If we leave aside the questions of deliberate plotting and collusion, this theory is not as implausible as it might at first appear. The work of Edward Said, Jacques Waardenburg and others[9] has, in recent years, provided us with sometimes profound insights into the ways in which Islam was reinterpreted and restructured in the European mind as part of the colonial process, before being returned in its reconstituted form to the Muslim world, there to be implanted in the Muslim mind. In direct and indirect ways, from the administration of the Oudh bequest by the British in Iraq[10] to Louis Rinn's plan to make the Tijâniyya Sûfî order the 'église nationale' of Algeria,[11] the imperial powers involved themselves deeply and not always impartially in Islamic religious affairs. The protection of religious minorities such as Druzes, Maronites, Jews, Armenians and Bahâ'is became a central prop for European politics in the Middle East; such groups were 'studied, planned for, designed upon by European Powers improvising as well as constructing their Oriental policy'.[12] More generally, external pressures have often led indirectly to changes of emphasis or direction in the religious sphere, as in the 'maraboutic crisis' of fifteenth- and sixteenth-century North Africa or in the effect of modern industrialisation and urbanisation in encouraging a possibly final shift towards a scriptural, puritanical form of Islam in some areas.[13] Nor should we forget the impact of European ideas and values on religious reformers in India, Turkey, Egypt and elsewhere.

Outside the Islamic world, the impact of western culture and religion, mediated through colonial agents, traders and missionaries, evoked significant mutations of indigenous religious forms and, in many cases, resulted in the emergence of revolutionist, millenarian, or modified thaumaturgical movements, such as the cargo cults of Melanesia, the Hau Hau movement of New Zealand, the Ghost Dances of North America, the numerous indigenous churches of sub-Saharan Africa, or the Taiping rebellion in China.[14] It would, therefore, seem not unreasonable to suppose that something of the same kind occurred in the Islamic world and that the numerous heterodox or extremist movements of the early modern period represent a similar, if culturally more sophisticated, response to foreign pressures. All the evidence, however, suggests that this was not the case and that the major movements of this type – the Wahhâbiyya, Tijâniyya, Sanûsiyya, Sudanese Mahdiyya and Bâbiyya – all emerged primarily in response to indigenous pressures and demands, whatever their later response to or involvement with foreign ideas and politics. There are, I think, numerous and complex reasons why the Islamic experience was, in fact, very different from that of peoples in less developed countries (the Taiping case requires separate analysis). A literate tradition, autonomous religious institutions such as the mosque, *madrasa, zâwiya, takiyya, hawza-yi ʻilmî, ʻataba,* or *imâmzâda,* the hierarchical establishments of the *'ulamâ',* a developed religio-legal system, and an abiding sense of cultural and spiritual superiority – these are undoubtedly among the factors that enabled the Muslim world to resist deep Western penetration in the religious sphere. Such resistance was virtualy impossible in the case of less developed societies lacking a reified and rationalised religious system or in whch the religious institution had not achieved any marked degree of autonomy within the overall social structure.

It is the contention of the present writer that Babism and, to a lesser extent, Baha'ism, apart from whatever intrinsic interest they may possess as sectarian movements, are significant, not as examples of foreign interference in religious affairs in Iran or mere reactions to less direct external pressures on Qajar society, but as indicators of a wider autochthonous development within Iranian Shiʻism during the nineteenth century. This development, which has continued through various phases down to the modern period (in which it has played a not inconsiderable role in the success of the Iranian Revolution) has several components, but it is, I think, best examined through two closely-related issues: the creation of a new orthodoxy and the regeneration of charismatic authority.

In a sense, there is a contradiction here. The establishment of an orthodoxy implies, even demands, an increase in charismatic routinisation rather than the reverse, while the emergence of fresh charismatic impulses in an already routinised situation would seem logically to lead to more heterodox developments. Babism is, of course, an excellent example of the latter process, with its achievement of a major charismatic breakthrough around 1848, but even here the situation is confused by the existence of what Peter Berger has called a 'charismatic field',[15] whereby both original and semi-routinised charisma was spread unusually widely through the movement, linking it even in its later stages with wider developments in orthodox Shiʻism. Not only that, but Babism is clearly the extreme example of charismatic change in the period and can only be well understood against a background of less thoroughgoing, original charismatic authority throughout the Shi'i establishment.

The contradiction is, however, more apparent than real, since it presupposes a rather more rigid demarcation between the three types of Weberian authority – rational-legal, traditional, and charismatic – than is actually present in most empirical situations. The idea that charismatic leaders emerge only outside existing institutional structures, whether by breaking entirely free of them or by appearing in a context external to them, has been questioned.[16] Michael Hill has referred to the concept of charismatic 'latency' as a means of explaining the continuation and even revival of charisma within ostensibly routinised institutions: 'Although the process of routinization is concerned with the development of more formalized roles and ideological definitions, and thus depicts a movement towards traditional or rational-legal types of legitimation, we still hold open the possibility that any institution that claims a charismatic pedigree will retain in its structure of roles a latent form of charisma which is always available as a source of legitimacy for office-holders who are involved in the process of innovation.'[17]

Rather, therefore, than try to resolve the apparent contradiction inherent in the pattern of orthodox/charismatic developments within modern Shi'ism by judicious juggling of theory or historical data, I prefer to argue that the various paradoxes involved are of the essence of the Shi'i experience in the past two centuries and that the latter provides an important example of charismatic latency. The search for a new form of Shi'i orthodoxy since the late eighteenth century has been largely, if not exclusively, centred on the question of authority, while traditional methods of clerical organisation have necessitated the resolution of this question within a charismatic rather than a strict rational-legal or traditional context.

Ernest Gellner, basing his argument on an important but neglected sentence in Hume's *Natural History of Religion,* argues that Weber's routinisation formula does not distinguish between non-scripturalist, mediatory, pluralistic religion on the one hand and monistic, puritan, scripturalist ('enthusiastic') religion on the other. Routinisation of charisma, he maintains, is 'specially characteristic of monistic faiths', whereas 'in pluralistic religion, charisma is *born* routinized, so to speak, and does not *decline* into such a condition'.[18] Although Gellner may be thinking primarily of popular Sufism in North Africa, this theory can be applied, albeit with qualifications, to Shi'ism from, if not the very earliest period, one very close to it.

That routinisation of some sort is present in the very concept of the Imâm as successor to the original charismatic authority of the Prophet is evident, but it is, I think, also clear that this does not preclude further routinisation or, perhaps more importantly, revitalisation of charisma within a context of routinisation less thoroughgoing than that experienced in the case of monistic religions. It would, for example, be misleading to speak in terms of a strictly Weberian charisma of office in early Shi'ism, even though subsequent rationalisations and regularisations appear to create such a picture. Rather than an easy passage of routinised charismatic authority from father to son in a basically primogenital line, as is suggested by retrospective definitions of a chain of twelve 'legitimist' Imâms,[19] the evidence suggests a much more flexible situation, in which allegiances shifted, often radically, between numerous contenders for the Imamate. Not only that, but the ever-present possibility that any one of these Imâms might be the *Qâ'im* who would lead the final *khurûj* against injustice, coupled with the fact that so many did, in fact, advance such claims,[20] kept a form of original charisma on the boiling point, as it were, for along time. There might be no prophets after Muhammad, but a would-be *Qâ'im* could advance charismatic claims every bit as influential as those of a prophet and in many ways more intense.

Even when some degree of routinisation has been achieved, mediatory movements have a tendency to reassert the force of original charisma (preserved in its latent form) without necessarily destroying the framework of routinised authority. This can be achieved by means of enhancing the link between the bearer of routinised charisma and the original charismatic figure, as happened in the genesis of new Prophet-centred Sûfî orders, such as the Tijâniyya, Sanûsiyya, or Khatmiyya (Mîrghaniyya), in the late eighteenth and early nineteenth centuries.[21] Or it can come about through a radical change in the political or economic power of the holder of the charismatic office, as in the case of the Ismâ'îliyya following the move to India of the Âghâ Khan in the 1840s.[22] Berger has pointed to a similar process involving the Israelite prophets from the eighth century BC, emphasising the radicalisation of the basic message of the institutionalised *Nabî* movement.[23] Similar developments in modern Shi'ism, however, appear to be the result of a much longer and more complex process.

The first major charismatic crisis for Imâmî Shi'ism was the death in 260/872 of the eleventh Imâm, al-Hasan al-'Askarî, at the early age of twenty-seven. As had occurred on similar occasions in the past, Hasan's death precipitated a large number of schisms among his followers, including one centred on his brother Ja'far that seems to have already been brewing during the Imâm's lifetime.[24] The present situation was particularly critical, however, in that Hasan was widely assumed to have died without offspring, thus threatening to put an end to the direct line of the Imamate. From the point of view of the present discussion, it is more or less irrelevant whether or not a son actually survived Hasan. What is significant is that the most successful resolution of the crisis was that achieved by a section of the Qat'iyya faction, which clung to the belief that a son existed but was at present in concealment from all but an élite handful of his followers – a belief that preserved the locus of authority in a living Imâm while facilitating a routinisation of his charisma in the persons of the four successive intermediaries who claimed to act on his behalf between 872 and 940. Discussions that centre on the existence or non-existence of the twelfth Imâm in empirical terms miss the point, at least as far as the question of authority is concerned. It is sufficient that the four *abwâb* succeeded in convincing a majority of the Imâmî Shi'a of the reality of his occultation and the legitimacy of their vicegerency.[25]

Since the time of the sixth Imâm, an organised system of representation (*wikâla*) had existed in the main Shi'i centres, and this had been considerably expanded under the seventh and eighth Imâms.[26] The seclusion of the Imâms Hâdî and al-Hasan al-'Askarî in Sâmarrâ under 'Abbâsid supervision had led to an increase in the religious and political roles of their agents,[27] but there seems to be no evidence that this resulted in any very marked transfer of charisma to the latter. Nevertheless, there had been a tendency towards routinisation of the *wikâla* system itself, with a number of families in Baghdad, Hamadân, al-Ahwâz, and elsewhere coming to monopolise the function of *wakîl*,[28] and on al-'Askarî's death this facilitated the move to routinise the Imâm's charisma in the person of the principal *bâb* or *safîr,* through whom alone access to the source of authority was possible. Such routinisation as took place, however, although considerable, was far from total. During the seventy-year period of what was later termed the 'lesser occultation', charisma remained 'wild'. The four *abwâb* had to combat not only competing theories concerning the method of continuation of the Imamate, but also rival *wukalâ'* in various Shi'i centres,[29] some of whom, like Abû Ja'far Muhammad al-Shalmaghânî, are said to have advanced 'extremist' claims to prophethood or divine incarnation. What is significant in the present context – it is a point to which we shall return – is the way in which the *abwâb* used excommunication as a means of defending not merely doctrinal orthodoxy but, primarily, their own authority. Nevertheless, it is evident that, by the time of the fourth *bâb*, Abu 'l-Hasan 'Alî b. Muhammad al-Sammarî (d. 329/940), the charismatic authority of the agent, on the one hand, had been increased to the point where his utterances came to be regarded as statements of the Imâm himself,[30] while the systematisation of the representative system, on the other, had been much advanced by the establishment of a *dâr al-wikâla* in Baghdad and by a formalisation of the method of appointment to the position of *bâb al-imâm.*

Al-Sammarî's death threw this as yet undeveloped system into confusion. Whatever the reasons for his failure to appoint a successor or for the subsequent non-appearance of plausible claimants to that rank, the trauma of total occultation demanded radical initiatives on the part of the Imâmî leadership. What is, on the face of it, extraordinary is the fact that the *wikâla* organisation did not seek to link in some way the new theory of complete occultation with its obviously well-developed base for a continuing charismatic leadership system. The most likely solution to this somewhat curious historical problem – and I offer it only tentatively here – seems to lie in the increased authority of the Imâmî *'ulamâ'* from as early as the time of the second *bâb*.[31] The authority of the *'ulamâ'* was originally legal-traditional rather than charismatic, being based on their role as jurisprudents and transmitters of the *akhbâr* of the Imâms, and it had been much overshadowed from the beginning by the charismatic authority of the latter.[32] Following the occultation of the Imâm, therefore, the *'ulamâ'* – who functioned as individuals rather than as a corporate body – were no obvious threat to the authority of the *abwâb* and were, presumably, relatively free to extend their own influence without coming into direct conflict with the principal bearers of charisma. This influence was obviously sufficient to carry the community over the obstacle presented by total occultation, while the greater freedom of action now available to the *'ulamâ'* permitted the relocation of charismatic authority, not only in them as individuals and as a group, but in several other related loci of continuing significance, such as the collections of traditions transmitted from the Imâms and the major books of Shî'î *fiqh*.

It is of the very essence of Shî'îsm that knowledge of God cannot be obtained without knowledge of the Prophet and that this, in turn, is unattainable without knowledge of a living Imâm: 'he who dies without an Imâm, it is as if he has died in the days of barbarism before Islam'.[33] It was essential, therefore, to the very continuation of Shi'ism that the Imâm himself be perceived as an abiding presence, an ultimate source of authority, not only in the logical but also in an existential sense. Living in an interworld spiritually connected to this world, the Imâm could continue to exercise his function as maintainer of the equilibrium of the universe and object of the active faith of the Shî'a, with whom he remained in contact through dreams, visions and revelatory intuition (*kashf*).[34] Remarkably little of the theoretical authority of the Imâm can be said to have been dissipated by his entry into occultation: he was (and is) alive, not only in the heart of the believer, and not merely in a supernatural realm accessible to the saint or mystic, but, potentially at least, in real places, where he has been seen by real people. At the same time, he *is* in occultation, and it is this that strengthens his symbolic function by making him a source of legitimation for authority, rather of authority *per se*. The sense – one might better say 'the experience' – of the Imâm's continuing presence confers upon all other loci of charisma within Shi'ism a special status, simultaneously slowing down the process of routinisation and legitimating or sanctifying it in all its aspects. There is an important parallel here with the New Testament resurrection story, which, it has been argued, facilitated the transmission of charisma to the apostles, thus overcoming the 'blocking' effect of a cult based on the founder's actual death.[35]

One of the most effective means of avoiding premature routinisation of charisma is the introduction of eschatological and chiliastic themes into the overall charismatic perspective. By identifying the hidden Imâm as the promised Mahdî and al-Qâ'im bi 'l-Sayf, the one who would arise with the sword to restitute the rights of the Shî'a,[36] the very act of postponing the moment of his return itself served as a further brake on the routinisation process. At the same time, it left open the possibility of a fully-fledged reassertion of charismatic authority legitimated by messianic claims. That no major Twelver messianic movement appeared until the nineteenth century indicates how successfully routinising strategies were balanced up to that point by a sense of the Imâm's presence and expectation of his imminent advent.

Within this context, the shift from a strictly legal-rational to a charismatic authority among the 'ulamâ' was necessarily hesitant and prolonged, whatever retrospective lists of marâji' al-taqlîd from the time of al-Kulaynî to the present may seek to suggest.[37] Such a shift was, however, implicit in the theory of the necessity for a living 'proof' of God on earth, which, in its extended form, could be applied to those outstanding scholars and saints who would protect the true faith from corruption and act as guides to the truth: 'In every generation of my people', the Prophet is recorded as saying, 'there shall be an upright man who shall cast out from this religion the corruption of the extremists, the arrogation of the false, and the interpretation of the ignorant'.[38] In their most charismatically developed form, such traditions centred on the existence within the Shi'i community of individuals known as nuqabâ' and nujabâ'.[39] A tradition ascribed to the eleventh Imâm, for example, states that 'we shall send unto them the best of our shî'a, such as Salmân, al-Miqdâd, Abû Dharr, 'Ammâr and their like in the age following them, in every age until the day of resurrection'.[40]

Except for these early examples, however, there is a certain reserve about naming these supreme 'nobles' and 'directors' of the Shi'a, whereas no such reservations apply to the major Shi'i 'ulamâ', seen (particularly by later generations) as renewers (mujaddidûn) or propagators (murawwijûn) of the faith in each century, or simply as inheritors (wurathâ') of the authority of the Prophet and the Imâms. Through such actual figures, the 'polar motif' of Shi'ism[41] could be continued much as it was in the Sûfî orders. It was not, however, until the thirteenth/nineteenth century that the role of the individual scholar began to take on in practice something of the charismatic significance with which it had been endowed in theory from the time of the lesser occultation. In the meantime, attention was focussed more generally on the *'ulamâ'* as a body: 'Were it not for those of the *'ulamâ'* who will remain after the occultation of your Imâm, calling [men] unto him, producing evidences on his behalf, and striving for his faith with the proofs of God, delivering the weak among the servants of God from the snares and demons of Satan and from the traps of the wicked, there would be no-one but would abandon the faith of God'.[42]

The coincidence of freedom from charismatic restraint following the death of the last *bâb* with relative political tolerance under dynasties such as the Sâmânids, Hamdânids and Bûyids gave powerful impetus to the development of Shi'i scholarship but, in the absence of any fully-fledged, centralised, and stable Twelver state, the religious authority of the *'ulamâ'* was not unduly routinised in the service of a secular system in which ultimate power resided. The very fact that the *'ulamâ'* remained scattered in the various centres of Shi'i activity throughout the Middle East meant that they preserved a high degree of independence from the demands of functioning within a wholly Shi'i context in a single state system as well as from the hierarchical imperatives of a church-like structure which would be imposed by a centralised body of *'ulamâ'*.

This situation changed radically following the rapid emergence and consolidation of the Safavid state in the early sixteenth century. From this time on, it became possible to think and act in terms of a centralised body of Twelver Shi'i *'ulamâ'*, a development which had two major consequences. On the one hand, there occurred the routinisation of the inherited charismatic authority of the *'ulamâ'* in something resembling an ecclesiastical system in the context of a church-state symbiosis; on the other, as the dynasty declined in power, the very large numbers of *'ulamâ'* who did not accept positions as state-appointed ecclesiastical functionaries and who refused to recognise the ultimate legitimacy of the Safavid or any other secular state became highly influential over the Shi'i masses, particularly in rural areas. It was their ability to claim charismatic authority inherited from and wielded on behalf of the Imâm over against the secular, illegitimate state that gave and still gives the Shi'i *'ulamâ'* so much of their popular appeal and, hence, their effective power base. Ironically, therefore, the very existence of the Safavid, Qajar and Pahlavi states did much to enhance the charismatic authority of the *'ulamâ'*, providing them with a political role which was clear throughout the nineteenth century and which is, perhaps, best exemplified in the part played by them in the recent revolution.

It is probably this factor, together with the availability of the Ishrâqî school of thought as a tolerably respectable form of quasi-heterodoxy (but not of overt social deviation), that explains the absence of important sectarian movements in the later Safavid period. The Shi'i position provides an unusual and significant exception to Werner Stark's thesis that 'in general terms it can be said that sects arise above all where there is an 'established' religion, a state church'.[43] The reason for this may become clear if, bearing in mind what we know of the opposition of the Shi'i *'ulamâ'* in general to secular government, we continue with our quotation from Stark: 'As this state church is, by nature, by definition, an adjunct of the conservative forces in the country, any and every movement of social dissatisfaction must condemn it as it condemns the existing property or power relations. And as it is easier to contract out of a church than out of an economic or political system, revolutionary sentiment may work itself out, by preference, in the abandonment of the official form of religion and the formation of, and the joining in, sectarian efforts'.[44] Stark's thesis may, in fact, need much qualification, since it applies only to certain types of sect, but it does serve to point up the curious situation that pertained in Safavid Iran, where the orthodox religious leadership itself provided an alternative to the state system that had established the faith in the first place. What is, perhaps, more significant, however, is the possible relevance of Stark's comments to the nineteenth-century situation, where a radical sectarian movement provided precisely that kind of revolutionary alternative both to the state and to the established church, despite the fact that a large body of the *'ulamâ'* remained, if only *in potentia*, opposed to secular rule. How can this be explained?

Several strands come together in the first half of the nineteenth century. The *'ulamâ'*, first properly developed under the Safavids, find themselves regrouped, protected, and increasingly powerful. The position of the *mujtahid* had been, as we shall note, defined and stressed, and the way was now open for the appearance of outstanding clerical figures with unprecedented charismatic authority; legal authority, in the form of jurisprudence, had reached the peak of its development,[45] but its expression was closely linked to charismatic figures such as Shaykh Muhammad Hasan al-Najafî (d. 1266/1850), whose *Jawâhir al-kalâm* is the most outstanding work of *fiqh* in the post-Safavid period; messianic expectation was on the increase with the approach of the year 1260, the one thousandth lunar year after the first disappearance of the Imâm. By this time, however, it is obvious that there was growing tension between these elements. The authority implicit in the exercise of independent *ijtihâd* did not mesh well with that contained in the definitive volumes of *fiqh*, nor did the charismatic role of *marja' al-taqlîd* as developed during the nineteenth century harmonise readily with the chiliastic hope of the Imâm's return, although it clearly represented a major development of the authority inherent in the concepts of an outstanding scholar in each generation and the continued presence of *nuqabâ'* and *nujabâ'* in the community. The extreme veneration accorded the most outstanding *'ulamâ'* conflicted to some extent with the charismatic role of the *'ulamâ'* as a body, and also with the more diffuse concept of *nuqabâ'* and *nujabâ'* within the more widely charismatic Shî'î ecclesia. The early nineteenth century can, then, be described as a period for Shi'ism in which several related issues came to a head at once and in which potential charismatic tensions which had remained unresolved from the time of the lesser occultation rose to the surface and shrilly demanded attention.

The beginnings of this process are to be found in the revolution in Shî'î thinking that occurred towards the end of the eighteenth century in the shrine centres of Iraq. The collapse of the Safavid dynasty in 1722 had left Twelver Shi'ism peculiarly vulnerable to the fluctuations of political fortune, but it had, at the same time, temporarily freed the *'ulamâ'* from the constraints under which they had functioned, even in the later period of Safavid rule. Sequestered in the comparative safety of the *'atabât* or in the various enclaves in an Iran deprived of effective central or, at times, even local government, the *'ulamâ'* could well regard themselves as the remaining representatives of the vanished Shî'î state and could now give free rein to speculation on the role of the *mujtahid* class, continuing and extending a debate which had begun within the context of that state.[46]

This debate reached its climax in the clash between the Akhbârî and Usûlî (or Mujtahidî) theological schools, which ended in the victory of the latter party on the eve of the Qajar restoration. For our present purposes, the most significant thing about this doctrinal struggle is the fact that it seems to represent a process exactly the reverse of that which it has come to typify in subsequent Shi'i writing, in which the Akhbârîs are portrayed as innovators first appearing in the seventeenth century under the inspiration of Mullâ Muhammad Amîn Âstârâbâdî (d.1033/1623-4). The truth of the matter would appear to be that the emergence of a definable 'Akhbârî' school at this date is more a reflection of the growing power of the *mujtahids* and the early development of what came to be identified as the Usûlî position.[47] Âstârâbâdî himself regarded his views as representative of a 'purer', more primitive line of Shî'î thought, and held the Usûlî school to be an innovation which had not existed before the time of al-Kulaynî (d. 329/940-1), that is to say, the later period of the lesser occultation.[48] He saw his own role as that of restoring the Akhbârî teachings to their former position of dominance within Shi'ism, emphasising traditional and rational-legal bases of authority (primarily the Qur'ân and *sunna*) as against the routinised charisma of the *mujtahids*. Not only was Âstârâbâdî opposed to the practise of *ijtihâd* as current in his own day, but he criticised retrospectively several of the leading figures of Shî'î theology in the period following the occultation of the Imâm.

Central to the Akhbârî-Usûlî dispute as it developed through the eighteenth century was the question of the legitimacy of *ijtihâd*. The Akhbârî stance here echoes a phenomenon to which we have referred above – the inhibition of independent theological thought or discussion by the presence of the Imâm or the sheer pressure of his charismatic authority rooted in a view of him as the sole infallible source of guidance. Whereas Akhbârî thinking rejected *ijtihâd* uncompromisingly, limiting *fiqh* to the extrapolation of rulings from the Qur'ân and canonical works of *hadîth*, the Usûlîs employed the additional principles of consensus (*ijmâ'*) and reason (*'aql*) applied through *ijtihâd*.[49] Usûlî rationalism provided the basis for a more flexible response to unaccustomed situations (which multiplied in the nineteenth century), particularly since it was possible for *mujtahids* to recommend action on the basis of presumption (*zann*), in contrast to Akhbârî scholars, who were committed to acting only on matters of absolute certainty (*yaqîn*) or positive knowledge (*'ilm*), these latter being derived only from the Qur'an or traditions related from the Imâms.[50]

Theological considerations apart, the practical consequences of the Usûlî stance were considerable. For the Akhbârîs, all men, the *'ulamâ'* included, were directly subject to the decisions of the Imâms, whom they were obliged to imitate in all their affairs. But the Usûlî school proposed a division of mankind into two groups: those required to practice imitation (*taqlîd*) in religious and legal matters, and those entitled to exercise their own judgment (*ijtihâd*).[51] The former, known as *muqallidûn*, must imitate, not the Imâms, but the *mujtahidûn* or, to be more precise, each *muqallid* must choose a single *mujtahid*, whose decisions he will follow in all matters. Since the Usûlîs regard the exercise of *ijtihâd* as obligatory during the period of *ghayba* and prohibit *taqlîd* to a deceased *mujtahid*,[52] the actual prestige and authority of living scholars of that rank were necessarily raised to an unprecedented level. Not only that, but the criteria of learning and intellectual ability became paramount among the factors (which also included piety, asceticism, and so on) contributing to a scholar's prestige. A perfect *mujtahid* (*mujtahid mutlaq*) was one versed in all the religious ordinances and sciences (especially *usûl al-fiqh*) – a quality the Akhbârîs restricted to the Imâms.[53] This being so, it is evident that the success of Usûlî thinking would lead, not only to an increase in the prestige of individual *'ulamâ'*, but also to a heightened importance for the Shi'i theological school complexes (*hawzât-i 'ilmî*), especially those at the shrine centres, as the sole locations where comprehensive learning of this kind could easily be acquired. This, in its turn, necessarily gave a considerable impetus to the creation of a more centralised ecclesiastical network and to the greater systematisation of the methods of role and status ascription within it.

Despite the advances made by the Usûlî party during the latter part of the Safavid period, the collapse of the dynasty led initially to an increase in the influence of their rivals. It was only gradually that the Usûlî position, redefined in the context of the absence of a Shi'i state, was reasserted at the *'atabât* during the interregnum, reaching its climax towards the end of the eighteenth century in the work of Âqâ Muhammad Bâqir Bihbahânî (d. 1208/1793), generally regarded as the *mujaddid* of the thirteenth-century *hijrî* and as the man responsible for the final victory of Usûlî Shi'ism. Bihbahânî succeeded in reformulating the nature of *ijtihâd*, in establishing on a firm foundation the role of the *mujtahid*, and in laying the basis for a system of jurisprudence which has been in use in Twelver circles ever since.[54]

Bihbahânî's influence was paramount in the effective centralisation of Shi'i scholarship at the *'atabât* by the beginning of the Qajar period and in the weaving of a complex web of master-pupil relationships, in which generations and individuals repeatedly overlapped. Where the Safavid and earlier periods had seen a scattering of Shi'i learning through Iran, Arab Iraq, and the Bahrayn and Jabal 'Amil regions, the second half of the eighteenth century witnessed a high degree of concentration of scholars in a central location to which students headed in growing numbers, and from which some left as well-qualified *'ulamâ'* to teach in Iran, India and elsewhere. A noticeable proportion of those *'ulamâ'* trained by Usûlî teachers in Iraq during this period were Iranians, which has led one recent writer to argue that 'the Usûlîs may perhaps be regarded as the Persian element against the Arabs, or at least against the Arab element, which predominated in the intellectual and social background of the Akhbârî leaders'.[55] While there are, I think, good reasons for regarding this as an exaggerated or oversimplified picture of the situation – it fails, for instance, to take into account many leading Iranian Akhbârîs, such as Astarâbâdî himself, Mullâ Muhammad Fayd Kâshânî, Qâdî Sa'îd Qummî or Mîrzâ Muhammad b. 'Abd al-Nabî Nîshâpûrî – it does, nevertheless, bring to light what is certainly a factor worth considering in any study of the development of Usûlism, linked as the movement became to the revival of organised Shi'ism in Iran and the rapid spread of Usûlî *'ulamâ'* there in the early Qajar period.

The reformation inspired by Bihbahânî was fraught with serious consequences for Twelver Shi'ism. Before his offensive against the fundamentalism of Akhbârî thought, relations between the two parties had not been unduly embittered and neither side seems to have attempted outright condemnation of the other on the grounds of heresy. Bihbahânî's *takfîr* against the Akhbârîs set a dangerous precedent to be followed in the case of the Ni'mat Allâhî Sûfîs and the Shaykhîs. From Bihbahânî onwards, Twelver Shi'i orthodoxy becomes increasingly well-defined and the threat of outright *takfîr* emerges as an ultimate sanction against ideas, groups, and individuals likely to challenge the orthodox system, its doctrines, or its exponents.

A further consequence of the Usûlî victory was the rapid growth in the power of the small *mujtahid* class throughout the nineteenth century, leading to the emergence of outstanding individuals as 'sources of imitation' (*marâji' al-taqlîd*; sing. *marja' al-taqlîd*), whose importance lay not only in their role as centres of charismatic authority, but increasingly in their notional and actual value as focal points for the unity of the Shi'i population. The current practice of identifying certain leading *'ulamâ'* from Kulaynî to individuals in the modern period as principal *marâji'*[56] is, I think, little more than an attempt to rationalise an unsystematic historical development. The concept of *marja'iyyat* seems to have been clearly defined in the sense that it now bears only around the middle of the nineteenth century, with the general recognition as *marja'* of Shaykh Muhammad Hasan al-Najafî, referred to previously as the author of the *Jawâhir al-kalâm*. It was a pupil of al-Najafî, Shaykh Murtadâ Dizfûlî Ansârî, Shaykh al-Tâ'ifa (d. 1281/1864–5), who carried the role of *mujtahid* and *marja'* to its highest point. Having succeeded al-Najafî as the leading *'âlim* at the shrine centres, Ansârî was soon acknowledged as *marja'*, not only in Iraq and Iran, but also in Turkey, Arabia and India, thus becoming the first of that rank to be universally recognised throughout virtually the entire Shi'i world.[57]

The sense of unity achieved under Ansârî was ruptured for a short time by various claims to leadership on his death, but it was continued in the end by Mîrzâ Muhammad Hasan Shîrâzî (d. 1312/1895), the Mîrzâ-yi Shîrâzî who issued a *fatwâ* against the Tobacco Régie in 1892. In many respects, Shîrâzî's influence exceeded that of his predecessor. He is described by his own pupil, Hasan al-Sadr, as 'the leader of Islam, the vicegerent of the Imâm, the renewer (*mujaddid*) of the divine laws (sc. at the beginning of the fourteenth century). . . . The leadership of the Ja'farî sect throughout the world was centred in [him] towards the end of his life'.[58] The lack of any real, hierarchically-organised ecclesiastical system meant, however, that the situation was again destabilised on Shîrâzî's death, with general disagreement as to which individual might qualify for the title of 'most learned' (*a'lam*) and thereby be deemed acceptable as sole *marja'*.

Although it is obvious that, by the end of the nineteenth century, there was considerable pressure in the direction of full-scale routinisation of charismatic authority in the person of a single *marja'*, it is equally apparent that the religious establishment as a whole was not then sufficiently organised to act as a suitable framework within which supreme *marja'iyyat* could operate to full advantage or, more importantly, perpetuate itself by means of a rational system of succession. In the years following the death of Shîrâzî, a succession of scholars emerged to foster the role of *marja'*, whether on an absolute or restricted basis, thus keeping alive the possibility of a living charismatic authority in the Shi'i world.[59] Âyat Allâh Husayn Burûjirdî (d. 1961) was particularly successful in consolidating the position of the sole *marja'*, but even in his case there were many who tended to look on him as the head of the body of *'ulamâ'* in a primarily organisational rather than a charismatic sense. In spite of his efforts to centralise the religious establishment by emphasising the organisational and educational roles of the *hawza-yi 'ilmî* at Qum and to rationalise the system of *marja'*-based leadership,[60] Burûjirdî was still unable to resolve the problem of succession. Nevertheless, his reforms had touched a responsive chord among many *'ulamâ'* faced with the need to re-evaluate and restructure their role in the light of changing conditions, and, in 1962, a group of Shi'i thinkers met to discuss changes in the curricula of the theological colleges and in the function of the religious leadership. Their recommendations for reform in these areas apart, the deliberations of this group (published in the same year) are significant for the proposal that a form of collective *marja'iyyat* would be more suitable for present conditions,[61] a proposal that has effectively been implemented by the recent election of a *majlis-i khibrigân* to deliberate on the succession to Khumaynî or, perhaps, to succeed him as a body. Routinising and rationalising tendencies, encouraged by new social and economic demands and by the example of modern bureaucratic techniques and systems then being developed in Iran, were clearly becoming vigorous by the early 1960s.

It is, therefore, all the more significant for our present argument to note that, in spite of this, the appeal of undiluted charismatic authority has continued with unabated strength among the masses, that it proved a basic factor in the success of the revolution in 1978, and that it continues to act as a central rallying-point without which the present régime would almost certainly have collapsed long since. Âyat Allâh Khumaynî's direct appeal to straightforward charismatic authority, combined with his unprecedented personal popularity (the latter much enhanced by his exposure in the media and reinforced by the emotional upsurge generated by the revolution of which he has been the figurehead) has successfully withstood new pressures towards the wholesale routinisation of the religious institution. At the same time, Khumaynî provides an excellent illustration of an obvious but acknowledged problem inherent in the traditional system of *marja'* selection. The insistence on *a'lamiyyat* necessarily results in the incumbency of aged men of greatly limited life expectancy, whose opportunities for developing the institution are thus circumscribed. By comparison with the system of transmitting charismatic office by direct descent, the more open Shi'i method reveals here a central weakness.

This increased concentration on individual charismatic authority is further indicated by the growing use in the present century of the title *âyat allâh* for *mujtahids* of the rank of *marja'*. The title seems to have been first applied to two leading *'ulamâ'* of the constitutional period, Sayyid 'Abd Allâh Bihbahânî and Sayyid Muhammad Tabâtabâ'î, after which its use was extended and normalised.[62] Recently, there has been a tendency to institutionalise the title, particularly and significantly in the form *âyat allâh al-'uzmâ*, used of the chief *marja'*, as in the case of both Burûjirdî and Khumaynî.

In thus seeking to identify individual *'ulamâ'* as centres of supreme or nearly-supreme authority, Shi'ism since the last century has taken its most far-reaching step since the end of the lesser occultation in the projection of the Imâm's charisma into fresh loci. The implications of such a development are clear. The supreme *marja'* or *âyat allâh* is the living deputy of the Imâm in a distinct and active sense: '. . . public deputies who have a thorough knowledge from the proper sources are, during the long absence, like an Imâm, and following them is comparable to following an Imâm. Since Shi'a depends (*sic*) upon the one who is the most learned and accepts him as the public deputy, in every epoch the person who is the most learned and pious is regarded as the public deputy, and the people follow his ideas and his decisions concerning religious affairs.'[63] This link with the Imâm is vividly illustrated by Hâjjî Mîrzâ Yahyâ Dawlatâbâdî, who writes that among the factors inducing Mîrzâ Muhammad Hasan Shîrâzî to live in Sâmarrâ was the existence there of the cellar in which the hidden Imâm had first entered occultation, a connection which increased the stature of his *nâ'ib*.[64] According to Binder, 'Burûjirdî's supporters came close to representing him as the sole spokesman for the hidden Imâm',[65] and it has recently become common to refer openly to Âyat Allâh Khumaynî as the *nâ'ib-i Imâm*.[66] The Islamic revolution, by transforming radically the role of the *'ulamâ'* in Iranian society and by laying the foundations for a full-scale institutionalisation of the religious establishment, has already created a new context within which the question of charismatic leadership (expressed as *vilâyat-i faqîh*) can be further explored. Whether or not the present régime remains in power, the religious institution in Iran can never return to its position prior to 1978.

I have referred briefly to the contemporary situation in order to draw attention to the continuity that has characterised developments in the sphere of charismatic leadership over the past two centuries, in spite of frequent hiatuses and fresh initiatives. The picture I have drawn, however, is defective in several respects, not least in its neglect of the general development of the *'ulamâ'* as a class during this period. The emergence of outstanding *marâji'* must be set against the wider background of the appearance of large numbers of important scholars, many of them wealthy and politically powerful in their own right. We can detect, moreover, a growing tendency to supplement the links provided by *ijâza* or shared discipleship by those of physical descent and marriage. Not only was the power of the individual *mujtahid* increasing, but that of certain clerical families, such as the Bihbahânîs, Tabâtabâ'îs or Najafîs, was growing in proportion, to the extent that entry into the highest ranks of the *'ulamâ'* class became increasingly difficult (though not impossible) for someone outside the circle of this power structure. Of equal significance, although rather less straightforward, are the links established by intermarriage between the upper echelons of the religious class and the political and economic élites of pre-revolutionary Iran.[67]

In the modern period a new development has occurred, the implications of which have yet to be fully appreciated. This is the emergence of 'lay' scholars like 'Alî Sharî'atî or Mahdî Bâzargân, whose manifestly non-clerical training and position served to point up the clerical characteristics of the traditional *'ulamâ'*. For the first time in Shi'i history, religious scholarship has ceased to be the prerogative of a *madrasa*-trained élite (except in its more specialised aspects), but this in itself can only encourage an emphasis on the institutional characteristics of the latter – their role as *fuqahâ'*, their mosque- and *madrasa*-related functions, their control of *awqâf* and other endowments (particularly the stipends paid to *tullâb*) and, above all else, the charismatic base of their authority.

Of considerably greater interest for the topic under discussion, however, are the heterodox developments referred to at the beginning of this article. It is, I think, axiomatic that attempts to redefine orthodoxy will lead to the identification or emergence of heterodoxy, particularly in the context of an established church system like that which began to reappear in Iran under the Qajars. I have suggested above that the Safavid experience provides an exception to Stark's thesis that sects are more likely to emerge where there is a state church. That the opposite is true of the nineteenth century tells us much, I think, about the nature of the Qajar establishment and the development of the religious institution under it.

The earliest crisis faced by the newly-triumphant Usûlî school was the excommunication around 1822 of Shaykh Ahmad al-Ahsâ'î (d. 1241/1826), from whom the later Shaykhî school took its name and inspiration.[68] The attempt to condemn al-Ahsâ'î as a heretic (initiated in Qazvîn by Mullâ Muhammad Taqî Baraghânî, d. 1263/1847) is significant because of its contemporary unpopularity. Al-Ahsâ'î, an Arab *'âlim* long resident in Iran, was one of the best-known and most admired Shi'i scholars of his day and had attracted the attention of Fath 'Alî Shah and his son Muhammad 'Alî Mîrzâ, the Governor of Kirmânshâh, under whose patronage the Shaykh had lived for several years. Although doctrinal issues were made the formal basis for the *takfîr*, these were of a nature which might not have attracted undue attention during the Safavid period, nor does al-Ahsâî's basic orthodoxy seem to have been in doubt to many leading *'ulamâ'* who refused to sanction the excommunication. It is hard to avoid the conclusion that al-Ahsâ'î and his more recondite theories simply provided suitable targets which helped crystallise the position of the 'orthodox' school.

There is, however, another aspect to the problem. Al-Ahsâ'î was the outstanding representative of a continuing theme within the Usûlî tradition, namely the placing of emphasis on non-rational modes of understanding and perception in religious matters.[69] This emphasis is particularly clear in the case of Sayyid Muhammad Mahdî Bahr al-'Ulûm (d. 1212/1797), the leading contemporary of Bihbahânî, who attempted to combine intuitive revelation (*kashf*) with reason ('*aql*), the latter being the mainstay of the Usûlî method. Tunakâbunî refers to mystical encounters between Bahr al-'Ulûm and the hidden Imâm, in the course of which various mysteries were revealed to him.[70] Many other scholars of the period, such as Sayyid Ja'far Dârâbî Kashfî (d. 1267/1850) and Mullâ Asad Allâh Burûjirdî Hujjat al-Islâm (d. 1271/1854), claimed to have been granted revelations of hidden truths.[71]

Al-Ahsâ'î himself believed that his knowledge was directly granted him by the Prophet and the Imâms (the latter in particular). Speaking of his knowledge of various sciences, his successor, Sayyid Kâzim Rashtî (d. 1260/1844), states that they 'came to that distinguished one in true and veracious dreams from the Imâms of guidance.'[72] The role of the Imâms as spiritual guides has always been emphasised in Shi'ism, and Akhbârî reliance on intuition before reason brought it to the forefront of religious practice, but al-Ahsâ'î seems to have gone further than most in his claims to such guidance. 'The '*ulamâ*',' he wrote, 'derive their knowledge one from the other, but I have never followed in their way. I have derived what I know from the Imâms of guidance, and error cannot find its way into my words, since all that I confirm in my books is from them and they are preserved from sin and ignorance and error. Whosoever derives [his knowledge] from them shall not err, inasmuch as he encountered the Imâms.'[73] In one place, al-Ahsâ'î speaks of his dreams, in which he encountered the Imâms, as *ilhâm*,[74] but more usually he speaks of *kashf* or *mukâshafa*, the 'unveiling' of inner meanings by means of these visions. The importance of *kashf* as a means of attaining knowledge supplementary or complementary to either reason (as emphasised by the Usûlîs) or tradition (as stressed by the Akhbârîs) is reflected in the alternative name of 'Kashfiyya' applied to the Shaykhî school.

Yet al-Ahsâ'î did not seek to dissociate himself or his teachings from the Usûlî tradition. There is no reason to believe that he ever wished to divorce his inward inspirations obtained from the Imâms (who, he claimed, had given him spiritual *ijâzât*) from the more conventional guidance to be gained from a teacher who provided, through a physical *ijâza*, a living link with a chain of *mujtahids* going back to the Imâms and the Prophet and, in a sense, transmitting their *baraka* as well as their knowledge to men. The relationship between al-Ahsâ'î's direct visionary experiences of the Prophet and the Imâms, on the one hand, and his formal links with the '*ulamâ*' (through reading and writing books and letters, studying and teaching, receiving and granting *ijâzât*) on the other, is a particularly compelling example of the complex functioning of charisma and authority in Shi'ism. We have already observed how routinised and direct forms of charismatic authority could co-exist fairly easily within a single system of Shi'i orthodoxy, and, from this point of view, there is no reason why al-Ahsâ'î would not have been able to continue as a leading representative of the intuitive end of the spectrum of authority, had it not been for the insistence of a relatively tiny group of *'ulamâ'* who wished to press the issue of orthodoxy in his case.

The Shaykhî school that crystallised round Sayyid Kâzim Rashtî in Karbalâ' between 1826 and 1844 emphasised the charismatic role of al-Ahsâ'î and his successor. Rashtî's appointment as head of the body of al-Ahsâ'î's disciples is noteworthy for several reasons. It is the earliest example of an attempt to regularise the method of authority transmission, preceding by several decades the efforts of al-Najafî and al-Ansârî to appoint successors to the rank of supreme *marja'*. It was, moreover, unorthodox in content, for Rashtî was seen, not merely as a *mujtahid* inheriting the authority of his teacher, but as the direct recipient of a body of knowledge derived by means of *kashf* through al-Ahsâ'î from the Imâms and, through them, from God Himself: 'he (Rashtî) has learnt what he knows orally from me (al-Ahsâ'î), and I have learnt [what I know] orally from the Imâms, and they have learnt from God without the mediation of anyone.'[75] Karîm Khan Kirmânî explicitly makes a comparison between al-Ahsâ'î's appointment of Rashtî with the *nass* of Muhammad designating 'Alî or that of each Imâm in respect of his successor.[76] This system of appointment became further routinised in the Kirmânî branch of Shaykhism, in which a line of descendants of the above Karîm Khan succeeded one another as heads of the school.[77]

The crisis that followed the death of Sayyid Kâzim Rashtî at the beginning of 1844 led to the emergence of Babism,[78] a short-lived but tremendously influential millenarian movement that carried the role of charismatic leader to its greatest lengths. The founder of the movement, Sayyid 'Alî Muhammad Shîrâzî, the Bâb (d. 1266/1850) was profoundly influenced by the Shaykhî doctrine of the 'Fourth support'(*al-rukn al-râbî'*), according to which the faith was based on four 'supports': God, the Prophet, the Imâms, and the Shi'a.[79] An extreme development of this doctine tended towards the identification of the fourth of these supports with the *'ulamâ'* or with one individual from among them. Shîrâzî urged this latter version of the doctrine in terms which illustrate with extreme clarity the central argument of the present article, that a renewed emphasis on charismatic authority among the *'ulamâ'* as a whole tended to result in an increased focussing on individuals. In his *Tafsîr sûrat al-kawthar,* Shîrâzî writes: 'Just as you stand in need of an individual sent from God who may transmit unto you what your Lord has willed, so you stand in need of an ambassador (*safîr*) from your Imâm'.[80] If it should be objected that the *'ulamâ'* as a whole fulfill this function, he would reply that the latter differ in rank and that they are not always in agreement. Having accepted this argument, he goes on, we are compelled to abandon an *'âlim* of inferior rank for one of higher standing, a process which must, in the end, lead to recognition of a single individual superior to all others.[81] 'It is impossible,' he concludes, 'that the bearer of universal grace from the Imâm should be other than a single individual.'[82] This is not, in essence, markedly different to the principle from the single *marja'*, but the application of the theory in a Bâbî context had much more radical consequences.

In the first phase of his prophetic activity, Shîrâzî claimed to be a bearer of divine knowledge like Rashtî and al-Ahsâ'î, but also proclaimed himself to be a new 'gate' sent by the hidden Imâm to prepare men for his imminent advent. As gate and representative of the Imâm, the Bâb is, in a sense, identified with him: 'there is none who has followed this remembrance (i.e. the Bâb) but that he has followed me (the twelfth Imâm); whoever loves the remembrance for the sake of God loves me; whoever seeks to behold me, let him behold his face; and whoever seeks to listen to my words, let him give ear to the novelties of wisdom and the keys of mercy from the tongue of God'.[83] Identification with the Imâm passed at times beyond the limits of simple representation. Thus, the Imâm declares that 'we are he and he is we, save that he is himself and is our servant'[84] or that God has made him (the Bâb) my own self in the worlds of command and creation. I am, by God's permission, never absent from him for the least period that your Lord, the Merciful, can calculate, nor is he ever absent from me.'[85]

The early Bâbî preaching mission, directed towards the advent of the Imâm in 1845, collapsed for a variety of reasons, including the Bâb's own failure to appear in Karbalâ' in Muharram 1261 to initiate the *zuhûr,* his subsequent recantation of his claims in Shîrâz in the same year, and his adoption for a period after that of a policy of *taqiyya.* In late 1847, however, while in prison in Azerbaijan, the Bâb announced himself as the Imâm in person, returned as the *Qâ'im* to abrogate the laws of Islam and to usher in the millennium. This claim itself led imperceptibly to the promulgation in the later works of the Bâb, such as the *Bayân-i fârsî,* of a new doctrine, based on a theory of successive theophanies, of which the Bâb himself was the latest.[86] Whereas in the earlier stages of his short career, the Bâb's authority was derived latently from the overriding charismatic image of the Imâm, in this final stage he assumed an independent authority that cancelled all previous notions of charismatic relationship, transforming latent into original, 'prophetic' charisma. This is significant enough in itself, providing in one sequence almost the entire spectrum of nineteenth-century Shi'i charismatic modes, but Babism exhibited yet another curious feature in its later stages: a multiplicity of claims to charismatic 'stations' within the movement, including a rash of theophanies following the death of the Bâb.[87]

Out of the theophanic chaos of Babism in the 1850s there emerged two main successor groups: the Azalîs, led by Mîrzâ Yahyâ Nûrî Subh-i Azal (d.1333/1912), and the Bahâ'î's, led by the latter's half-brother, Mîrzâ Husayn 'Alî Nûrî Bahâ' Allâh (d. 1309/1892).[88] The former group, which based its legitimacy on Azal's appointment as successor to the Bâb, remained committed to conservative policies and rapidly exhausted the charismatic dynamism of the original movement. On Azal's death in 1912, leadership of the movement passed in little more than theory to Hâjjî Mîrzâ Yahyâ Dawlatâbâdî (d.1359/1939), and since then the Azalî group has lacked any very clear principle of organisation or leadership.[89] By way of extreme contrast, Baha'ism from the beginning stressed the original charismatic role of Bahâ' Allâh, revered, not as a successor to the Bâb, but as the next in the sequence of theophanies, identified with a messianic figure mentioned in the later Bâbî scriptures. This is in itself an extremely interesting development, involving as it did the immediate invocation of prophecies whose obvious reference was to the distant future, a device which clearly became essential as a means of avoiding the premature routinisation of charisma within the movement.

Although official Bahâ'î doctrine emphasises Bahâ' Allâh's claim to be a 'divine manifestation' (*mazhar ilâhî*), and rejects any notion of incarnationism,[90] numerous passages in the prophet's own writings express unequivocal claims to divinity. He is 'the creator of all things'[91] who taught all the names to Adam[92] and sent Moses to Pharaoh.[93] He explicitly writes 'verily, I am God' (*innanî anâ 'llâh*),[94] declares that 'the essence of the pre-existent (*dhât al-qidam*) has appeared' (evidently in his person),[95] and claims (again in reference to himself) that 'he has been born who begets not nor is begotten'.[96] Several passages, indeed, refer to the undesirability of making public his claims to divinity (*ulûhiyya*) and lordship (*rubûbiyya*)[97] as well as to the permissibility of regarding him equally as the direct appearance of the unseen or as an indirect manifestation of the divinity.[98] Even the more moderate Bahâ'î doctrine that knowledge of God can only be obtained in any age through His manfestation (and, hence, today, only through Bahâ' Allâh)[99] provides an extreme example of charismatic development, in which all other intermediaries between man and the deity have been removed.

In the later stages of its development, Baha'ism provides an almost ideal model of charismatic routinisation, a process much facilitated by the spread of the movement in the West and the incorporation into it of rational methods and elaborate, increasingly baroque bureaucratic mechanisms.[100] But it is precisely here that we are confronted by an interesting and significant paradox. The absence of a recognised successor to Shoghi Effendi (d. 1957), a great-grandson of Bahâ' Allâh who had been intended as the first in a line of 'guardians of the faith' (*awliyâ-yi amr Allâh*), left the movement without a major charismatic focus, and subsequent developments accelerated the routinisation process to the point where the running of affairs was almost exclusively in the hands of bureaucratic institutions. Perhaps more significantly, attempts to continue the guardianship in another line or to find an alternative charismatic base were effectively blocked by the remarkably well-developed coercive powers of the routinised institutions. In the late 1960s, however, steps were taken by those same institutions to introduce what is, in effect, a clerical hierarchy whose power is based increasingly on charisma of office, their principal legitimation being that of continuation of the guardianship in a collective sense. Theological problems aside, Baha'ism presents us with the most extreme case of charismatic renewal in nineteenth-century Shi'ism and, in the modern period, with an extraordinary example of the endurance of charisma in a highly routinised system and its muted resurgence under unfavourable conditions.

The link between charismatically-based authority claims and concern with doctrinal purity and a sense of orthodoxy is well illustrated in Babism and Baha'ism. In the former case, early attempts to organise the religious community involved the excommunication of individuals who challenged the authority of the Bâb or his leading followers,[101] while, in the later phase of the movement, an extreme exclusiveness was combined with marked intolerance towards non-believers.[102] Baha'ism reversed the Bâbî doctrine of intolerance to preach a message of universal brotherhood and inter-religious harmony, but this was paralleled by an increased emphasis on internal unity and doctrinal purity, with frequent resort to excommunication in the case of dissidence. Several of the movements we have referred to as examples of revived charismatic authority share this feature of heightened exclusiveness and internal rigidity, the Tijâniyya, Sanûsiyya, and Khatmiyya Sûfî orders being cases in point.

Babism and Baha'ism by no means exhaust the range of charismatic options available within the context of Qajar Shi'ism. A more extended study would need to examine the revival of Ni'mat Allâhî Sufism from the late eighteenth century,[103] the charismatic element in popular religion of the period,[104] the Indian and Iranian Ismâ'îlî revivals centred on Hibat Allâh b. Ismâ'îl, Shah Khalîl Allâh, and Âghâ Khan Husayn 'Alî Shah,[105] the career of Mullâ Sâdiq Urdûbâdî in the Caucasus in the late 1830s,[106] the revolt of Sayyid Husayn Kalârdashtî (Sayyid 'Âlamgîr) in 1891[107] and other similar developments. It is a period of extremist claims, with charismatic and millenarian themes to the fore, but such movements are in themselves meaningless unless interpreted as part of a broader pattern, just as the more moderate developments of the age are given context and depth when set beside the growth of heterodoxy.

NOTES AND REFERENCES

1. See 'Abbâs Iqbâl Âshtiyânî, *Yâdgâr*, VIII-IX (1328 sh./1949), 148 ('. . . it (the tract) is absolutely fictitious and is the work of impostors'); Mujtabâ Mînuvî, *Râhnamâ-yi kitâb*, I-II (1342 sh./ 1963), 22 ('I have confirmed that these memoirs have been forged'); Ahmad Kasravî, *Bahâ'îgarî*, Tehran 1327/1948, 88-9 ('Without doubt, it is a forgery and, as I have recently learnt, an extremely ambitious man who lives in obscurity but has for years been trying to make himself famous, wrote it and spread it secretly among the people'). For a more detailed analysis of the contents, see Anon, *Bahthî dar radd-i yâd-dâshthâ-yi maj'ûl*, Tehran 1973.

2. Among the best-known examples of this literature, we may note: M. Mahmûd, *Târîkh-i ravâbit-i siyâsî-yi Îrân va Inglîs dar qarn-i nuzdahum*, 4 vols., Tehran 1949-50; M. Mujtahidî, *Îrân va Inglîs*, Tabriz 1947; Ismâ'îl Râ'în, *Huqûqbigîrân-i Inglîs dar Îrân*, Tehran 1968.

3. On conspiracy theories of ignorance and society, see Karl Popper, *Conjectures and Refutations*, London 1972, 7-8, 123, 341-2; idem, *The Open Society and its Enemies*, 2 vols., London 1962, II, 94-5, 101, 133, 330. On the verificationist approach, see idem, *Conjectures*, 35ff., 39ff., 228ff.

4. Sayyid Hasan Kîyâ'î. *Bahâ'î, az kujâ va chigûna paydâ shuda ast?*, Tehran 1349/1970.

5. See, for example, Ismâ'îl Râ'în, *Inshi'âb dar Bahâ'iyyat pas az marg-i Shawqî Rabbânî*, Tehran n.d., chs 1, 3; Sayyid Muhammad Bâqir Najafî, *Bahâ'îyân*, Tehran 1979, Book 2, Section 2. Some Western writers have seen Babism as a response to foreign pressures during the 1840s: see, for example, N. R. Keddie, 'Religion and Irreligion in Early Iranian Nationalism', *Comparative Studies in Society and History*, IV, 3 (1962), 268.

6. See Roger Cooper, *The Baha'is of Iran*, Minority Rights Group Report, no. 51, London 1982, 10-11, 13.

7. For examples, see M. Momen, *The Bâbî and Bahâ'î Religions, 1844-1944: Some contemporary Western Accounts*, Oxford 1981, which provides numerous materials from diplomatic and missionary records.

8. *Inshi'âb dar Bahâ'iyyat*, 128-32.

9. Edward Said, *Orientalism*, New York 1978; Jacques Waardenburg *L'Islam dans le miroir de l'Occident*, The Hague 1963.

10. This was a *waqf* fund established by the Shi'i ruler of Oudh and Lucknow, Sultân Ghâzî al-Dîn Haydar (1814-27), originally administered directly by two Shi'i *mujtahids*, one in Karbalâ' and one in Najaf. The fund came under British control following the annexation of Oudh in 1856.

11. See Jamil Abun-Nasr, *The Tijâniyya – a Sufi Order in the Modern World*, Oxford 1965, 58-9.

12. Said, *Orientalism*, 191.

13. See Ernest Gellner, *Muslim Society*, Cambridge 1981, 56-69.

14. The most comprehensive study of this subject is Bryan Wilson's

D.M.MACEOIN

Magic and the Millenium, London 1973. On the Taiping, see
Guenter Lewy, *Religion and Revolution*, New York 1974, ch. 7
(with bibliographical references in notes) and, in the present
context, E. P. Boardman, *Christian Influence upon the Ideology
of the Taiping Rebellion 1851-1864*, Madison, Wisc. 1952. Nikkie
Keddie has drawn parallels between Babism and the Taiping
movement ('Religion and Irreligion', 268-70) and speaks of
western influences on similar developments elsewhere (*ibid.*,
270).

15. *From Sect to Church: A Sociological Interpretation of the Baha'i
    Movement*, unpublished Ph D dissertation, New School for Social
    Research, New York 1954, 161-2.

16. See Michael Hill, *A Sociology of Religion*, London 1973, 151-2,
    165-9.

17. *Ibid.*, 172.

18. *Muslim Society*, 14.

19. On the concept of a 'legitimist' line of Imâms, see S. H. M. Jafri,
    The Origins and Early Development of Shi'a Islam, London and
    New York 1979, chs 9, 10, 11. On the rationalisation of a line
    limited to twelve Imams, see E. Kohlberg, 'From Imâmiyya to
    Ithnâ'-'Ashariyya', *BSOAS*, xxxix/3 (1976), 521-34.

20. See, for example, J. M. Hussain, *The Occultation of the Twelfth
    Imam*, London 1982, 12-15.

21. See J. S. Trimingham, *The Sufi Orders in Islam*, Oxford 1971, ch.
    4. For further details, see Abun-Nasr, *Tijâniyya*, N. Ziadeh
    Sanûsîyah, London 1958, and J. Voll, *A History of the Khatmiyya
    Tariqah in the Sudan*, unpublished Ph D dissertation, Harvard
    University 1967.

22. For a short but perceptive discussion of this point, see Gellner,
    Muslim Society, 104-9.

23. Peter Berger, 'Charisma and religious innovation: the social
    location of Israelite prophecy', *American Sociological Review*,
    xxviii/6 (1963), 940-50.

24. Hussain, *Occultation*, 57-65.

25. I do not wish to suggest that the matter is entirely irrelevant, even
    in terms of the present question. If, for example, the four *abwâb*
    were, as the present writer is inclined to believe, perpetuating a
    pious fraud, even for the best of motives, that alone would tell us
    much about perceptions of authority within the Shi'i community
    and the degree (in such a case minimal) of routinised charisma
    'invested' in the leading agents of the Imâms before the death of
    al-'Askarî.

26. Hussain, *Occultation*, 79-84.

27. *Ibid.*, 81.

28. *Ibid.*, 82.

29. See *ibid.*, 9, 99-104, 126-31; Muhammad Jawâd Mashkûr,
    Târîkh-i Shi'a wa firqahâ-yi Islâm tâ qarn-i chahârdahum,
    Tehran 1976, 138 and n.2, 142-6.

30. Hussain, *Occultation*, 156.

31. *Ibid.*, 117.

32. See 'Abbâs Iqbâl, *Khândân-i Nawbakhtî*, Tehran 1386/1966, 69: 'the Imâmiyya differed from other Islamic sects in that they always had recourse to the infallible Imâms in matters of Quranic commentary, interpretation of revealed verses, and the *sunna* of the Prophet'. Many early Shi'i theologians were 'corrected' in their views by the Imâms or their close companions (*ibid.*, 74).

33. *Hadîth* of Muhammad transmitted by Ja'far al-Sâdiq in Abû Ja'far Muhammad b. Ya'qûb al-Kulaynî, *Rawdat al-Kâfî*, Najaf 1385/1965-6, 129.

34. On the question of visions of the Imâm, see Hâjj Zayn al-'Âbidîn Khan Kirmânî, 'Risâla dar jawâb-i Âqâ-yi Nizâm al-Islâm Isfahânî', in *Majma' al-rasâ'il fârsî*, VIII, Kirman 1352/1973, 72-103.

35. See Hill, *Sociology of Religion*, 173-4.

36. On Shi'i millenarianism, see A. A. Sachedina, *Islamic Messianism*, Ithaca, NY 1979.

37. For a more radical discussion of this theme, see J. Eliash, 'Misconceptions regarding the juridical status of the Iranian 'Ulama', *IJMES*, X, 1 (1979). J. Eliash's view that the *'ulamâ'* had no real authority in terms of actual Shi'i doctrine is, in a sense, irrelevant to our present concern with perceptions of authority rather than the genuineness or otherwise of its declared sources.

38. *Hadîth* in Hâjj Muhammad Khan Kirmânî (ed.), *al-Kitâb al-mubîn*, Kirman 1354 sh./1975-6, I, 434.

39. On this theme, see *idem, Irshâd al-'awâmm*, Kirman 1380/1960-1, IV, 142-449.

40. *Hadîth* in *idem* (ed.), *Fasl al-khitâb*, Kirman 1392/1972, 95.

41. The 'polar' concept is derived from that of the *qutb* or *aqtâb* as human centres of religious authority.

42. *Hadîth* transmitted from Imâm Hasan al-'Askarî, from the *Tafsîr al-imâm*, in Kirmani, *Fasl al-khitâb*, 95.

43. *The Sociology of Religion: A Study of Christendom*, London 1966-7, II, 60.

44. *Ibid.*

45. Cf. Hâjj Muhammad Karîm Khan Kirmânî: 'In these days . . . the knowledge of *fiqh* and the outward form of the religious law . . . has reached the state of perfection . . . the beginning of the appearance and spread of the jurisprudence and traditions of the Shi'a was at the end of the eleventh century, that is, one thousand one hundred; now (1268/1851-2), it is less than two hundred years that these manifest Shi'i sciences have been spread in the world. The truth of the matter is that the outward stages of the holy law reached perfection in the twelfth century, that is, one thousand two hundred' ('Risâla-yi tîr-i shihâb', in *Majma' al-rasâ'il fârsî*, I, Kerman 1386/1966-7, 175).

46. For a contemporary account of this earlier debate, see Jean Chardin, *Voyages de Monsieur le Chevalier Chardin en Perse*, Amsterdam 1711, II, 207-8, 337.

47. Sayyid Kâzim Rashtî (d.1260-1844) confirms this view in the course of a defence of the Usûlî position, where he indicates

D.M.MACEOIN

that, although the practice of *ijtihâd* dates back as far as the time of the Imâms, the written presentation of Usûlî theory is a modern phenomenon ('Risâla dar jawâb-î ba'd-i ahl-i Isfahân', in *Majma' al-rasâ'il fârsî*, XVI, Kirman n.d., 303-4). Watt has suggested that the appearance of Akhbarism may have been due to 'the forcible incorporation of men of Hanbalite sympathies into the Imamite state' (W. M. Watt, *Islamic Philosophy and Theology*, Edinburgh 1962, 170).

48. Muhammad Amîn Astarâbâdî, 'Dânish-nâma-yi Shâhî', quoted in Mîrzâ Muhammad Bâqir al-Mûsawî al-Isbahânî (Khwânsarî), *Kitâb rawdât al-jannât fî ahwâl al-'ulamâ wa 'l-sâdât*, n.p. 1367/1947-8, 33.

49. *Ibid.*, 35, no. 2; Rashtî, 'Risâla . . . ahl-i Isfahân', 301-2.

50. Isbihânî, *Rawdât*, 35, no. 3.

51. *Ibid.*, no. 6. Âqâ Muhammad Bâqir Bihbahânî deals with this point at length in his *Risâla dar inhisâr-i mardum bi-mujtahid wa muqallad*.

52. Ibid., 35-6, nos 7, 14.

53. *Ibid.*, 36, nos p, 10. On the qualifications of a *mujtahid jâmi' al-sharâ'it*, see Rashtî, 'Risâla . . . ahl-i Isfahân', 306-39.

54. See Hamid Algar, *Religion and State in Iran 1785-1906*, Berkeley and Los Angeles 1969, 34.

55. Vahid Rafati, *The Development of Shaykhî Thought in Shî'î Islam*, unpublished PhD dissertation, UCLA 1979, 30.

56. For examples, see 'Abd al-Hâdî Hairi, *Shi'ism and Constitutionalism in Iran*, Leiden 1977, 62-3 (citing 'mimeographed research' entitled *Tashkîlât-i Madhhab-i Shî'a* by Âqâ Muhammad Vakîlî Qummî); (Husayn) Khurâsânî, *Maktab-i tashayyu' dar sayr-i târîkh*, Tehran 1341 sh./1962-3, 194-6; M. J. Fischer, *Iran: From Religious Dispute to Revolution* Cambridge, Mass., and London 1980), 252-4 (referring to Sayyid Ahmad al-Husaynî Ashkvarî Âsaf-âqâ, *al-Imâm al-hakîm*, Najaf 1384/1966).

57. See Hairi, *EI²* art. 'Shaykh Murtadâ Ansârî' (with a good bibliography).

58. Quoted in Muhammad Muhsin Shaykh Âghâ Buzurg al-Tihrânî, *Tabaqât a'lâm al-Shî'a*, Najaf 1954-6, I, 440.

59. We may note the following as particularly important: Shaykh Muhammad Kâzim Khurâsânî (d.1329/1911), Hujjat al-Islâm Sayyid Muhammad Kâzim Tabâtabâ'î Yazdî (d.1337/1919), Mîrzâ Muhammad Taqî Hâ'irî Shîrâzî (d.1338/1920), Shaykh Fath Allâh Sharî'at-i Isfahânî (d.1338/1920), Hâjj Sayyid Abu 'l-Hasan Isfahânî (d.1365/1946), Hâjj Âqâ Husayn Qummî (d.1366/1946), Shaykh Muhammad Kâzim Shîrâzî (d.1367/1947), Hâjj Âqâ Husayn Burûjirdî (d.1380/1961), Âyat Allâh Kâzim Sharî'atmadârî Qummî, Âyat Allâh Muhammad Hâdî Mîlânî and Shaykh Muhsin al-Hakîm (d.1970).

60. See Algar, 'The oppositional role of the Ulama in twentieth-century Iran', in N. R. Keddie (ed.) *Scholars, Saints and Sufis*, Berkeley and Los Angeles 1972, 243-4; on the early re-establish

173

ment of the *hawza* at Qum, see Fischer, *Iran*, 109-12.

61. *Bahthî dar bâra-yi marja'iyyat wa rûhâniyyat* Tehran 1341/1962; for an analysis, see A. K. S. Lambton, 'A reconsideration of the position of the *Marja' al-Taqlîd* and the religious institution', *SI*, x (1964), 115-35.
62. J. Calmard, *EI²* Suppl. art. 'Âyat Allâh'.
63. Mahmoud Shehabi, 'Shi'a', in K. W. Morgan (ed.), *Islam, the Straight Path*, New York 1958, 202.
64. *Târîkh-i mu'âsir ya hayât-i Yahyâ*, Tehran n.d., I, 27.
65. L. Binder, 'The proofs of Islam: religion and politics in Iran', in G. Makdisi (ed.), *Arabic and Islamic Studies in Honor of Hamilton A. R. Gibb*, Leiden 1965, 132.
66. See Fischer, *Iran*, 6.
67. For modern examples of both developments, see *ibid.*, 89-95.
68. See D. M. MacEoin, art. 'Shaykh al-Ahsâ'î', in *Encyclopaedia Iranica* (forthcoming). For further details of the development of early Shaykhism, see *idem, From Shaykhism to Babism: a study in charismatic renewal in Shî'î Islam*, unpublished PhD dissertation, Cambridge University 1979, chs 2, 3; Rafati, 'Development'; H. Corbin, 'L'École Shaykhie en théologie shi'ite', *Annuaire de l'École Pratique des Hautes études, Section des sciences religieuses* (1960-1), 1-59. I have recently been notified of a new work dealing with nineteenth-century heterodox developments in Iran: Mangol Bayat, *Mysticism and Dissent*, Syracuse 1982.
69. Attention has been drawn to this theme by Abbas Amanat, *The Early Years of the Babi Movement*, unpublished PhD dissertation, Oxford University 1981, 23-9.
70. *Ibid.*, 24, quoting *Qisas al-'ulamâ'*.
71. *Ibid.*, 25-9.
72. *Dalîl al-mutahayyirîn*, n.p. 1276/1859-60, 11.
73. *Sharh al-Fawâ'id*, n.p. 1272/1856, 4 (the original text was completed in 1233/1818).
74. *Kuntu fî tilka 'l-hâl dâ'iman arî manâmât wa-hiya ilhâmât:* autobiography in Abu 'l-Qâsim b. Zayn al-'Âbidîn (Ibrâhîmî), *Fihrist-i kutub-i Shaykh Ahmad Ahsâ'î wa sâ'ir-i mashâyikh-i 'izâm*, Kirman 1977, 141.
75. al-Ahsâ'î, quoted in Karîm Khan Kirmânî, *Hidâyat al-tâlibîn*, Kirman 1380/1960-1, 71. For a later Shaykhî attempt to interpret this passage conformably to orthodox Shi'i thought, see Hâjj Zayn al-'Abidin Khan Kirmânî, 'Risâla . . . Nizâm al-Islâm Isfahânî', 49-72.
76. Kirmânî, *Hidâyat*, 71-2. The later Shaykhî schools of Tabriz and Kerman (the latter enduring to the present) became somewhat routinised and attempted to reintegrate themselves within the main stream of orthodox Shi'ism.
77. On Kirmânî Shaykhism, see Corbin, 'L'école shaykhie'. Following the assassination in 1979 of 'Abd al-Ridâ Khan, leadership of the school passed out of the family to a Shaykhî scholar in Iraq, Hâjj Sayyid 'Alî Mûsawî, who is regarded as *a'lam*.

78. For a bibliography of Babism, see D. M. MacEoin, 'Babism', in L. P. Elwell-Sutton (ed.), *Bibliographical Guide to Iran*, London 1982; for details, see *idem*, arts. 'Bâb', 'Babism', 'Bayân', in *Encyclopaedia Iranica* (forthcoming); *idem, From Shaykhism to Babism*; Amanat, *Early Years*.

79. On this doctrine as developed by the Shaykhîs of Kirmân, see MacEoin, *From Shaykhism to Babism*, 168-70; Hajj Muhammad Karîm Khan Kirmânî, *Rukn-i râbi'*, Kirman 1368/1949.

80. *Tafsîr sûrat al-kawthar*, Cambridge University Library, Browne Or. Ms., f.10, f.36b (cf. f.68a).

81. *Ibid.*

82. *Ibid.*, f.37a.

83. 'Alî Muhammad Shîrâzî, *Qayyûm al-asmâ'*, Cambridge University Library, Browne Or. Ms., f.11, f.76a.

84. *Ibid.*, f.73b.

85. *Ibid.*, f.76b.

86. On this theory, see E. G. Browne (ed.), *Kitâb-i Nuqtatu'l-Kâf* Leyden and London 1910, introd. xxvi-xxix.

87. See, for example, MacEoin, 'The Bâbî concept of holy war', *Religion*, XII (1982), 114-15; *Nuqtatu'l-Kâf*, 252-61. Berger's reference to this as a 'charismatic field' is relevant (*From Sect to Church*, 161-2).

88. For a brief bibliography of the latter group, see MacEoin, 'Baha'ism', in Elwell-Sutton (ed.), *Bibliographical Guide*.

89. On the contrast between Babism and Baha'ism in this respect, see Peter Berger, 'Motif messianique et processus social dans le Baha'isme', *Archives de Sociologie des Religions*, IV (1957), 93-107.

90. See, for example, Shoghi Effendi, 'The Dispensation of Baha'u'llah', in *idem, The World Order of Baha'u'llah*, rev. ed. Wilmette, Ill. 1969, 112-14.

91. Bahâ' Allâh, letter in *Âthâr-i qalam-i a'lâ*, II, Tehran n.d. (= a repaginated reprint of texts originally published with *al-Kitâb al-aqdas*, Bombay 1314/1896), 177.

92. Letter in *ibid.*, 194.

93. Letter (*sahîfat Allâh*) in *idem, Alwâh-i mubâraka-yi hadrat-i Bahâ' Allâh . . .shâmil-i ishrâqât . . .*, Tehran n.d., 195.

94. Letter in 'Abd al-Hamîd Ishrâq Khâvarî (ed.), *Mâ'ida-yi âsmânî*, Tehran 1971-3, IV, 208.

95. Letter to Hâjjî Muhammad Ibrâhîm Qazvînî, in *ibid.*, VIII, 113. The passage continues: 'the spirits of the prophets circle around him, together with the lote-tree of the extremity. Say, Muhammad ascended for seventy thousand years before he reached the porch of this gate'.

96. 'Lawh-i mîlâd-i ism-i a'zam', in *ibid.*, IV, 344 (the reference is to the Qur'an, sura 112). Other statements of interest in this context include his claim that the sun was created from 'a spark of his radiance' ('Sûrat al-hajj' in *idem, Âthâr-i qalam-i a'lâ*, IV, Tehran 1976-7, 77) and his curious assertion that, in exiling him from Iran, the Ottomans had 'expelled God from His house' (*ibid.*, 68).

97. See, for example, passages in Ishrâq Khâvarî (ed.), *Mâ'ida*, VIII, 123, 155, 162.

98. See Bahâ' Allâh, 'Lawh-i Jamâl', in *idem, Alwâh-i Bahâ' Allâh,* ?Bombay 1893, 219.

99. See *idem, al-Kitâb al-aqdas,* text printed in 'Abd al-Razzâq al-Hasanî, *al-Bâbiyûn wa 'l-Bahâ'iyyûn fî hâdirihim wa-mâdîhim,* Sidon 1962, 109; *idem,* 'Lawh-i tajallîyât', in *Ishrâqât,* 201; *idem,* letter in *ibid.,* 293-4; *idem,* 'Lawh-i Salmân', in *Majmû'a-yi alwâh-i mubâraka,* Cairo 1920, 144-5; *idem,* 'Lawh-i Salmân', in *Majmû'a-yi alwâh-i mubâraka,* Cairo 1920, 144-5; *idem,* 'Lawh-i tawhîd', in *ibid.,* 311; *idem, Kitâb-i mustatâb-i îqân,* Cairo n.d., 110.

100. On developments up to 1957, just before the death of Shoghi Effendi, see Berger, 'Motif messianique', and *idem, From Sect to Church*; on these and subsequent developments, see Vernon E. Johnson, *An Historical Analysis of Critical Transformations in the Evolution of the Baha'i World Faith,* unpublished PhD dissertation, Baylor University 1974.

101. See MacEoin, *From Shaykhism to Babism,* 199-207.

102. See *idem,* 'Babi concept of Holy War', 108-9.

103. On this, see W. R. Royce, *Mîr Ma'sûm 'Alî Shâh and the Ni'mat Allâhî Revival 1776-77 to 1796-97,* unpublished PhD dissertation, Princeton University 1979.

104. See Amanat, *Early Years,* ch.2, 'Sufism and popular religion'.

105. See *ibid.,* 91-2; Algar, 'The revolt of Âghâ Khan Mahallâtî and the Transference of the Ismâ'îlî Imâmate to India', *SI,* XXIX (1969), 55-81.

106. See Ishrâq Khâvarî, *Rahîq-i makhtûm,* Tehran 1973-5, II, 309-10.

107. See N. R. Keddie, *Religion and Rebellion in Iran,* London 1966, 136-40.

10

The Metaphysics of Sadr al-Dîn Shîrazî and Islamic Philosophy in Qajar Iran

Despite the flood of literature in recent years on Qajar Persia and its religious and even intellectual history, little systematic study has been carried out in European languages on the very active tradition of Islamic philosophy during this era which is closely tied to the more manifest religious and social movements of the period.[1] While most scholars of this era simply ignore this tradition as if it did not exist, a few who have read a work or two on the later tradition of Islamic philosophy believe that because of the predominance of the teachings of Sadr al-Dîn Shîrazî, Islamic philosophy during the Qajar period was simply a continuation or repetition of his teachings. In reality, however, the Islamic philosophy of this period, far from being homogeneous, displayed a rich variety ranging from those who defended Avicennan metaphysics to the Shaykhîs who rejected all the schools of *hikmat-i ilâhî* in the name of their own *hikma* based only on the teachings of the Shi'ite Imams. Even Sabziwârî, the most illustrious defender of Mullâ Sadrâ during this period, had to defend Sadrian metaphysics constantly against its opponents.[2]

Yet there is no doubt that the metaphysical teachings of Sadr al-Dîn were central to the intellectual life of Qajar Persia and were of great importance not only for those who considered themselves as his followers, but even by those who opposed him, as is seen in the writings of Shaykh Ahmad Ahsâ'î, the founder of the Shaykhî movement and Sayyid Muhammad the Bâb, founder of Babism. To understand the main current of religious philosophy during this period, it is necessary to comprehend the central tenets of the incomparable metaphysical edifice of Mullâ Sadrâ, along with its influence among both those who accepted it fervently or partially and those who opposed it for one reason or another.

Many of the traditional masters of Islamic philosophy in Persia to this day consider Mullâ Sadrâ as the foremost among Islamic metaphysicians, and indeed this view has been expressed by numerous authorities since the writings of Mullâ Sadrâ first became disseminated in the Safavid period. It would not be an exaggeration to say that within the annals of Islamic philosophy no single figure has dealt with metaphysics in such a detailed, systematic and at the same time profound manner.[3] Compared to Ibn Sînâ, Mullâ Sadrâ's treatment of *ilâhiyyât* is at once more inward and gnostic and more extensive, although Ibn Sînâ's treatment of *tabî'iyyât* is more complete than that of Mullâ Sadrâ. And compared to Ibn 'Arabî, Mullâ Sadrâ's exposition of metaphysics is more systematic and 'continuous', in many instances incorporating those 'discontinuous' flashes of inspiration, which characterise the gnostic doctrines of the master from Murcia, into a closely woven pattern.

Mullâ Sadrâ, in his metaphysics, is concerned essentially with Being, although he was fully aware of the supra-ontological nature of the Supreme Principle and its state above all limitations, including even the condition of standing above limitations. His discussion of the Absolute in its completely undetermined and supra-ontological aspect reveals the completeness of his metaphysical doctrines, which do not remain bound to the ontological level in the Aristotelian sense, even while making use of the language of ontology. When Mullâ Sadrâ speaks of Absolute Being as the 'Hidden Ipseity' (*al-huwiyyat al-ghaybiyya*) transcending all limitations, he is in fact speaking of the supreme Principle in its completely unmanifested state, even above the ontological principle which is its first determination. Yet he uses the term *wujûd* in connection with it, so that at a superficial glance it might seem that he is not discussing anything above ontology. In actuality, however, the metaphysics of Mullâ Sadrâ begin with the Absolute Principle which transcends all limitations, then leads to Being which is its first determination and the creative Principle, and finally concerns itself with existence, in both its universal and particular aspects.[4]

To understand the metaphysics of Mullâ Sadrâ, it is necessary to be thoroughly familiar with Islamic philosophy before him. Only then can one understand the transformation that was brought about by Mullâ Sadrâ in this philosophy.[5] The earlier Islamic philosophers, especially of the Peripatetic school, were concerned with existents, *mawjûd* (*ens*, or *das Seinende*) following Aristotle, who defined metaphysics as the science of the 'existent *qua* existent' (*to on ê on*). Although later Islamic philosophers interpret *mawjûd* and *wujûd* to be the same,[6] there is no doubt that Fârâbian and Avicennan ontology was concerned primarily with *mawjûd*. It was in fact this interpretation of metaphysics that the West adopted from Islamic sources and which remained alive in Western philosophy until modern times. For Mullâ Sadrâ, however, the proper subject of metaphysics is the very act of being, *wujûd* (*esse, actus essendi* or *das Sein*).[7] Long before M. Heidegger pointed out the difference between *das Sein* and *das Seinende*, Mullâ Sadrâ had elevated true metaphysics to the level of the study of the very act of being, that mysterious *fiat lux* which causes things to leave the ocean of non-existence and become endowed with the gift of existence.[8] For Mullâ Sadrâ, metaphysics must be concerned not with things that exist, or existents, but with the very act of existence which is a ray cast from Pure Being Itself in the direction of nothingness.[9] Through this major transformation Mullâ Sadrâ resuscitated Islamic philosophy and made of it a bridge between exoteric religion and pure esotericism, of which in fact his theosophy is a particular version.

The metaphysics of Mullâ Sadrâ are based, like that of other Islamic philosophers and going back to al-Kindî and al-Fârâbî, upon the distinction between existence (*wujûd*) and quiddity (*mâhiyya*) or essence.[10] This distinction is one of the most profound in metaphysics and stands along with such distinctions as principle and manifestation, essence and form, substance and accident, etc., as basic to an exposition in human language of the nature of Reality in its source and various levels of manifestation. It is in fact so deeply ingrained in the structure of Islamic philosophy that no school has left it out of its consideration and doctrinal language. It has also left its indelible mark upon Latin scholasticism where the very term quiddity (from *quid est* in Latin) is a literal translation of *mâhiyya*.[11]

In traditional courses on Islamic philosophy, long sessions are usually devoted to infusing the mind of the student with the habit of being able to distinguish clearly between existence and quiddity, and only after these two concepts are clear in his mind is he allowed to proceed with the study of the general principles of metaphysics (*al-umûr al-'âmma*). In the works of Mullâ Sadrâ, however, usually the discussion of existence comes at the beginning – with only a reference to the distinction between existence and quiddity – and only after elucidating the 'principles concerning quiddity' (*ahkâm al-mâhiyya*).[12]

The order in which Mullâ Sadrâ sets out to expound the 'principles' of existence and quiddity can be best understood by turning to the contents of the first *safar* of the *Asfâr* in which his most extensive discussion of ontology is to be found, with a more condensed version of the ideas appearing in some of his other works such as *al-Shawâhid al-rubûbiyya* and *al-Mashâ'ir*.

In his *magnum opus*, the *Asfâr*, the first three stages (*marâhil*) of the first *safar* deal with *wujûd*, the fourth with *mâhiyya*, and the fifth once again with *wujûd* in the light of the relation between the one and the many.

The first three stages, which contain the heart of Mullâ Sadrâ's metaphysics, proceed in the following order:

The first stage (*marhala*)

The first 'way' (*minhaj*)

Chapter (*fasl*) one: That *wujûd* is the subject of metaphysics.

Chapter two: That the concept of existence is shared in meaning by various existents.

Chapter three: That the concept of existence is not among the

179

constituent differentia of individual existents.

Chapter four: On the principiality of existence.

Chapter five: On what is the cause of the individuation of existence.

Chapter six: That ontological realities are simple entities.

Chapter seven: That the reality of existence has no cause.

Chapter eight: On the connection of existence with the substantiality of things (*shay'iyya*).

Chapter nine: On the various meanings of 'inhering existence' (*al-wujûd al-râbitî*).

The second 'way' – On the tripartite division of being (*al-mawâdd al-thalâth*).

The 'way' consists of twenty-two chapters, of which the first twenty-one deal with the Necessary Being (*wâjib al-wujûd*), contingent (or possible) being (*mumkin al-wujûd*) and impossible being (*mumtani' al-wujûd*) and the last with the unity of existence and quiddity objectively, that is, outside the mind. As for the third 'way', it consists of five chapters dealing with mental existence (*al-wujûd al-dhihnî*), which involves the question of knowledge.

The second stage, 'Supplements to the principles concerning existence and non-existence', is not divided into separate 'ways'. It consists directly of fourteen chapters dealing first with *wujûd*, then *'adam*, and finally *imkân* in the various meanings it possesses in Islamic philosophy.

Finally, the third stage deals with *ja'l*, the effect of the agent or cause upon the caused, which plays an important role in Mullâ Sadrâ's theosophy and complements his discussion of causality. The first three chapters of this stage deal with *ja'l* proper and the last two with the gradation of being.

With an awareness of the order in which Mullâ Sadrâ expounds his metaphysics we can now embark upon an analysis of the basic aspects of his doctrines by returning to the primary distinction between existence and quiddity.

The explanation of the distinction between existence and quiddity in the theosophy of Mullâ Sadrâ begins with an analysis of man's experience of the external world. In ordinary perception, man becomes aware of concrete things which exist in the objective world. But once man analyses this perception within his mind he realises that the concrete objects perceived can be analysed into two components: one which bestows reality upon the object, which is existence, and the other which determines the object to be what it is, which is its quiddity. Of course in the external world there is but one reality perceived, but within the mind the two components are clearly distinguishable. In fact, the mind can conceive clearly of a quiddity completely independently of whether it exists or not. Existence is an element added from the 'outside' to the quiddity. It is not part of the essential character of any quiddity in question save the

Necessary Being, whose Being is none other than Its Quiddity. Existence and quiddity unite and through their union form objects which at the same time exist and are also a particular thing.

Existence and quiddity can never be found separately in the external world. But in the analysis carried out by the mind the two elements are in fact totally different. They provide the key with which the mind can seek to understand the structure of reality.[13]

It is in the nature of the intellect (*al-'aql*) to unify (the word *'aql* itself in Arabic being related to the root meaning 'to bind' or 'unite') and to guide man from multiplicity to Unity. Sensory experience places man before the world of multiplicity, of objects that seem to be distinct and separate. It is the intellect which pierces through this veil of multiplicity and is able to distinguish between the permanent and the transient, substance and accidents, the Absolute and the relative, the Principle and its manifestation, the One and the many, and through this distinction to integrate multiplicity into Unity. The distinction between existence and quiddity is of such a nature. The intellect distinguishes between these two elements within each existent. This is the first stage in guiding man to the awareness of a reality which binds and also transcends individual objects, for the distinction between existence and quiddity leads in turn, in the theosophy of Mullâ Sadrâ, to the awareness of the interrelatedness of existents and finally to the gradation, principiality and unity of being.

Before embarking upon his exposition of metaphysics, Mullâ Sadrâ seeks to show first of all that existence cannot be defined, that it is the most spontaneous, evident (*badîhî*) and basic of all realities and also concepts. He discusses this idea under the heading of *badâhat al-wujûd,* the 'spontaneity' or 'self-evidence of *wujûd*'. All things are known by it and so it cannot possess definition (*ta'rîf*) in terms of anything else. The logical definition which requires genus and specific difference is in fact impossible to apply in the case of *wujûd*, which is beyond every genus and specific difference, beyond internal division or composition upon which logical definition is based. The concept of existence is the most evident and primary concept in the mind, with the aid of which all other concepts are understood, and the reality of existence is the most immediate and primary experience of reality, an experience which is the foundation of all our knowledge of the external world. Hence how could one seek to define existence? Man's awareness of existence is immediate and intuitive. He is immersed in it and can gain an awareness of it only in an immediate, experiential manner which no mental analysis can hope to reach. Both the mental or subjective world and the external or objective one are encompassed by and plunged in the ocean of being and therefore cannot encompass or comprehend it. Existence in its purity can become neither an external object on the physical plane to be perceived nor a finite and bound concept in the mind to be logically defined, although it is the basis of every external object and the most evident and clear of all mental concepts.[14]

Having made the distinction between existence and quiddity and having pointed to the impossibility of defining existence in the usual sense of the word definition, Mullâ Sadrâ takes the first step towards an intellectual comprehension of the unity of things by proving that the term *wujûd* as used in the case of various things such as A, B and C refers to the same concept and reality and is not just based on verbal resemblance, as for example in the case of the word 'date' as used in the phrases 'the date of an event' and 'the date picked from a tree' which refers to completely different meanings but is verbally the same. According to Mullâ Sadrâ, when we say A exists and B exists, the word 'exist' is shared in meaning (*ishtirâk-i ma'nawî*) by A and B and not only in verbal form (*ishtirâk-i lafzî* 'homonymy'), in contrast to what is claimed by so many of the *mutakallimûn* and earlier philosophers, who as far as the term *wujûd* is concerned do not pass beyond the level of homonymy. Mullâ Sadrâ offers many arguments in favour of the nature of 'existence' as possessing *ishtirâk-i ma'nawî*. This includes his reference to direct perception by the intellect according to which the difference between 'man exists' and 'an animal exists' is not the same as between, let us say, the sun and the moon. 'Exists' in the first sentence conveys a common and related meaning in the case of man and animal which is most direct and undeniable, so that even if in poetic rhyme the term *wujûd* is repeated, we naturally understand a similar meaning to be conveyed in each stanza, not as if several words with completely different meaning but only verbal resemblance were placed at the end of each verse. Moreover, the whole discussion of causality would become meaningless, were the term 'exists' in the phrase 'A exists' to have no relation in meaning to the term 'exists' in the phrase 'B exists', where A and B are causality related.[15]

Having established the reality of existence as reflected in human language, Mullâ Sadrâ turns to a distinction which is fundamental to his ontology and which characterises much of later Islamic philosophy in Persia, namely the distinction between the notion or concept (*mafhûm*) and the reality (*haqîqa*) of existence.[16] When a general discussion concerning existence takes place, people are not usually aware that they are in fact dealing with something on two very different planes of reality, reflecting the object-subject distinction of discursive knowledge itself. Transcendent theosophy insists on clarifying this primary distinction before embarking any further upon the difficult road of metaphysical exposition. It speaks of the notion of existence and the reality of existence. When a person says 'this house exists', he has an immediate notion of 'exists' at a pre-conceptual stage. The 'existence' of the house implied by the sentence is self-evident (*badîhî*). It is a notion that the mind knows directly and immediately. It is in fact the most evident of all notions, that which is known better and more directly, than anything else.[17] Its knowledge is so evident that everyone has an intuitive awareness of what it means before conceptualising it in his mind. All discursive and conceptualised knowledge concerning 'existence' follows later and is based upon that immediate 'understanding of existence' which is in fact implied by the term *mafhûm* itself in Arabic (*mafhûm*) meaning 'that which is understood'.

In contrast to this notion of existence in the mind, the reality of existence is the most difficult of all things to know in depth, for it requires a spiritual preparation which not all people possess, to say the least. Everyone with a sane mind has an intuitive grasp of the reality of existence, but only in its most outward mode. Everyone at the stage of immediate perception knows that when he perceives that a house exists, the existence of the house is not only a notion in his mind but also a reality independent of him.[18] If he is a contemplative, he becomes aware of this profound mystery of existence itself or of being in its virginal purity, which is like the Divine Breath that animates all things from within or like the Divine Ocean into which all things are plunged. He becomes conscious of Universal Existence which is itself the effusion of Pure Being and ultimately of the Divine Essence.[19] If he is not a contemplative he is nevertheless aware of the presence of the reality of existence, even if the remarkable mystery of existence becomes veiled before his dulled vision. Moreover, because being possesses various stages and grades, as we shall discuss soon, the higher realms remain inaccessible to the untrained mind and eye, and its root or *kunh* to which Sabziwârî refers in the poem already cited remains the most hidden of all things, for this root is none other than Pure Being Itself, which none can know except those who have lost their separative existence and become 'united' with it.

The reality of existence in its deepest aspect is, therefore, at the antipode of the notion of existence as far as man's approach through the usual channels of knowledge is concerned, the first being the most inaccessible and the second the most evident of all things. But this rapport is true only from the point of view of discursive knowledge and the modes of perception of 'fallen man'. For the spiritual man whose eye of the heart (*'ayn al-qalb* or *chishm-i dil*) has opened through spiritual discipline and Divine Succour, the most certain and evident of all things is precisely that root of the reality of existence which is the Source and Origin of all things and before which the self-evidence of all mental notions pales into insignificance. Mullâ Sadrâ is fully aware of this reversal of relationships in the case of spiritual vision and alludes to it in many parts of his work. But because his *hikmat al-muta'âliya* has the function of guiding the perceptive mind to the doors of spiritual vision and the experience of the reality of existence, he begins with the distinction between the notion and the reality of existence and the self-evidence of the first in contrast to the hiddenness of the second. But his final goal is to lead man to the stage in which he can have that vision of the reality of existence which transforms the most hidden to the most manifest and the manifest to a pale shadow of that which first appeared as the most hidden and unknown.

One of the cardinal doctrines of Mullâ Sadrâ is the gradation of being (*tashkîk al-wujûd*) according to which being possesses various levels of reality which encompass ultimately not only the reality of existence but even its notion, which belongs in fact to a particular form of existence called mental existence (*wujûd-i dhihnî*). The doctrine of the gradation of being, stretching from Pure Being to *materia prima,* in the form expounded by Mullâ Sadrâ marks a major transformation in Islamic philosophy, although it is related to the universal doctrine of the 'great chain of being' found in various traditions both ancient and medieval[20] and more particularly to the concept of the gradation of light found in Suhrawardî.[21] Mullâ Sadrâ took this universal doctrine and made of it a cornerstone of his transcendent theosophy, interpreting it in the light of his particular version of the *philosophia perennis.*

Analogical gradation or analogicity (*tashkîk*) is interpreted in the school of Mullâ Sadrâ to mean that a single universal is predicable in different degrees and grades of its particulars.[22] The example often cited is that of light which is predicable of the 'light of the sun', 'the light of the lamp' and the 'light of the candle'. In each case one is dealing with light, but in each case in a different degree of intensity. If we ponder the concept of analogical gradation we will discover, however, that there is not one but two kinds of gradation: the first is one in which what causes the difference (*mâ bihi'l-ikhtilâf*) in various degrees of something partaking of gradation is the same as that which these degrees or grades share in common (*mâ bihi'l-ishtirâk*), for example, numbers or light. Both the number two and three are grades of the 'universal' number. Moreover, what they have in common is numerality and what separates them is also numerality. The same holds true of light. This type of gradation is called *tashkîk-i khâssî* or particular gradation. The second is one in which what various grades share in common is not what separates them from each other, such as the existence of Abraham and Moses. What these two prophets share in common is existence but what separates them is their separation in time as well as other factors. This second type of analogical gradation is called *tashkîk-i 'âmmî* or general gradation.

When this analysis is applied to existence, it becomes clear that the notion of existence partakes of general gradation but the reality of existence partakes of particular gradation. When we think of the existence of A and existence of B in our mind, the notion of the existence of A and the notion of the existence of B share the notion of existence in common, but are separated by other factors. But the reality of existence is a single reality partaking of grades, so that which distinguishes the existence of A from the existence of B is the reality of existence and what unites them is also the reality of existence. This is the basis of the doctrine of the 'transcendent unity of being' (*wahdat al-wujûd*) which crowns Mullâ Sadrâ's metaphysics and to which we shall turn shortly.

Of major importance for an understanding of Mullâ Sadrâ's metaphysics is his exposition of the relation between existence and quiddity. This problem, which was of major concern to the Latin Scholastics as well as to the Muslim Peripatetics, as already mentioned, goes back to al-Fârâbî and Ibn Sînâ who wrote extensively about it.[23] Both men realised that when we say A exists, existence is from the linguistic and logical point of view an accident (*'arad*) added to the particular quiddity in question, and that it is unlike other predicates in that it does not tell anything additional about the subject. In the *Tahâfut al-tahâfut*[24] in his criticism of Ibn Sînâ, Ibn Rushd misconstrued the Avicennan position, interpreting existence to be an accident in the ordinary sense. Ibn Rushd in fact contributed in a major way to the misunderstanding of this aspect of Avicennan ontology in the West, and this fact in turn led indirectly to the inability of later Western philosophers to formulate an ontology of the depth and dimensions of a Mullâ Sadrâ.

Ibn Sînâ was in fact also misinterpreted on this account by certain Eastern philosophers and theologians such as Fakhr al-Dîn al-Râzî, who interpreted Ibn Sînâ's reference to existence as a category to mean that it was a category like other categories such as quality and quantity. The true reviver of Ibn Sînâ's school in the East, Nasîr al-Dîn al-Tûsî, was forced in fact to reject the Fakhrian interpretation of existence as an accident explicitly in his *Sharh al-ishârât*.[25] Ibn Sînâ himself clarified his own words in his *Ta'lîqât*, which unfortunately never became known in the West but which were well-known to Mullâ Sadrâ, who in fact cites them when he wishes to discuss the question of the accidentality of existence.[26] By returning to this basic text of Ibn Sînâ whose very words he quotes[27] Mullâ Sadrâ is able to draw support from the master of Islamic Peripatetics for his own position concerning the reality of existence and in fact its principiality (*asâlat*) as well, which follows from his doctrine concerning the reality of existence.

Mullâ Sadrâ's metaphysics is based on the thesis that although outwardly we see in the world objects that exist and for which existence is an accident added from the outside – as moreover human languages seem to imply – in reality there is but one Being with grades of existence issuing from It and stretching from Being Itself to the level of matter. With respect to this reality, it is not existence but the quiddities which are accidents. It *appears* that things exist; in reality, universal existence takes on the accidentality of things while remaining for ever within its primordial oneness and virginity. Using the language of Sufism, Mullâ Sadrâ calls this creative and expansive aspect of Universal Existence the 'Breath of the Compassionate' (*nafas al-rahmân*) or the sacred effusion (*al-fayd al-muqaddas*) of which all things are but cosmic coagulations on various levels of cosmic reality. According to Mullâ Sadrâ, even Suhrawardî, the master of *ishrâq,* was not able to interpret this point in its true sense and so remained content with an 'essentialistic' metaphysics. It was for Mullâ Sadrâ to bring about this major transformation of metaphysics by realising the true relation between existence and quiddity and becoming aware of the 'principiality of existence' (*asâlat al-wujûd*), which is a major pillar of his metaphysics.

If one were to study *hikmat* with a traditional master in Persia until recently, one would be introduced early in one's studies to the distinction between the 'principiality of existence' (*asâlat al-wujûd*) and the 'principiality of quiddity' (*asâlat al-mâhiyya*). Moreover, it is usually said that not only Mullâ Sadrâ but also Ibn Sînâ was a follower of *asâlat al-wujûd* and that Suhrawardî and Mîr Dâmâd belonged to the school of *asâlat al-mâhiyya*. In fact, the whole of Islamic philosophy would be viewed from this perspective and divided accordingly. Among contemporary *hakîm*s also the same classification is made, most being followers of *asâlat al-wujûd,* and a few such as 'Allâma Hâ'irî Mâzandarânî, the famous commentator of Ibn Sînâ who died fairly recently, belonging to the school of *asâlat al-mâhiyya.*[28]

When we study the actual texts of earlier Islamic philosophy, however, we find that no such idea is ever expressed in them explicitly. A historical study will show that the very idea of the principiality of either existence or quiddity came to the fore in the writings of Mîr Dâmâd and became a major problem of Islamic philosophy only from the Safavid period onwards. The Safavid and later Islamic philosophers read this distinction back into the history of Islamic philosophy because of its central importance, and re-interpreted Islamic philosophy accordingly. The major question underlying this way of looking at ontology is whether the reality of an existent comes from its existence or from its quiddity; in other words, whether 'existence' as used for various existents is merely a mental construct (*i'tibârî*) and the quiddity possesses reality, or existence possesses reality and the quiddity is nothing but the limitations of a particular mode of existence abstracted by the mind. Suhrawardî was a keen defender of the *i'tibârî* nature of 'existence' and the reality of the quiddities, although he spoke of light in terms similar to those Mullâ Sadrâ used for *wujûd.* Mîr Dâmâd, likewise, believed that quiddity and not existence, possessed reality. Both masters therefore created an 'essentialistic metaphysics' and became known as *asâlat-i mâhiyyatî,* the Persian term for those who uphold the principiality of quiddity.

In his youth Mullâ Sadrâ also belonged to this school. In fact he did not become *asâlat-i wujûdî,* or a defender of the principiality of existence, simply through reasoning or mental reflection. The change came through a divine inspiration and with the aid of Heaven. It seems that Mullâ Sadrâ underwent a spiritual experience which enabled him to have a new vision of reality and to carry out that profound transformation of Surawardian metaphysics from an essentialistic doctrine to an 'existentialistic' (*wujûdî*) one, a transformation which is a veritable turning point in the history of Islamic thought.[29] In his *Kitâb al-mashâ'ir*, Mullâ Sadrâ describes his 'conversion' in these terms:

> In earlier days I was a passionate defender of the thesis of the principiality of quiddity and the *i'tibârî* nature of existence, until God provided me with guidance and permitted me to witness His demonstration. All of a sudden my spiritual eyes were opened and I was able to see that the truth of the matter was contrary to what the philosophers in general had held. Praise be to God who by means of the light of illumination guided me out of the darkness of the baseless idea (of the principiality of quiddity) and established the thesis (of the principiality of existence) firmly within me, a thesis which will never change in this world or the next.
>
> As a result (of this experience), (I now believe that) the existences are realities, while the quiddities are the permanent archetypes (*al-a'yân al-thâbita*) which have never smelt the fragrance of existence.[30] The existences are nothing but rays of light, radiated by the true Light which is the absolutely self-subsistent Being, except that each existence is characterised by a number of essential properties and intelligible qualities. It is these latter aspects which are known as quiddities.[31]

In these words, Mullâ Sadrâ expresses clearly the inspired origin of his belief in the principiality of existence, but in nearly all his discussions of the 'general principles' of the Transcendent Theosophy (*al-umûr al-'âmma*), in such works as the *Asfâr, al-Shawâhid al-rubûbiyya, al-Mashâ'ir* and *al-Mabda' wa'l-ma'âd,* he offers numerous proofs for this view, rejecting all the arguments of Suhrawardî and others in favour of the principiality of quiddity.[32] These arguments relate to the problem of *ja'l,* or the effect of the agent or cause upon the caused, priority and posterity in cause and effect, existence as the source of goodness, etc. As an example one can mention the argument of priority and posteriority within one quiddity which is repeated often by Sadr al-Dîn. If a quiddity called (A) such as a fire causes another quiddity called (B) which is also a fire, both (A) and (B) must be said to be the same quiddity, both being fire. If we accept the principiality of quiddity, then reality resides in the quiddity, and at the same time we would have to concede that the cause precedes the effect. Therefore, the self-same quiddity fire is prior as cause (A) and posterior as effect (B). There must as a result exist an analogical gradation in one and the same quiddity which is impossible as proven by all Islamic philosophers. Therefore, the reality of a thing must belong to existence, which partaking of gradation, can be both prior and posterior, both cause and effect, united in both instances to the same quiddity, which happens to be fire in this case.

The importance of the doctrine of the 'principiality of existence' in Transcendent Theosophy can hardly be over-emphasised. Based upon a new inspired vision of reality, this doctrine became in turn a major pillar of Mullâ Sadrâ's metaphysics, one which he sought to demonstrate logically and one which itself became the basis for the demonstration of so many other aspects of his teachings. This doctrine transformed the 'Aristotelian mould' of earlier Islamic philosophy, making the subject of metaphysics not the existent (*ens*) but the act of existence itself (*esse*), and provided a new vision of the profoundest order of reality in which everything is viewed as the 'presence' (*hudûr* or *shuhûd*) of the act of *wujûd* or the Divine Command (*al-amr*) itself. Moreover, it was through this doctrine that Mullâ Sadrâ was able to display the link that connects all the levels of reality together[38] and finally to bring to light the doctrine of the 'transcendent unity of being' (*wahdat al-wujûd*) which crowns his whole metaphysics and in fact all of Islamic gnosis.[34]

The doctrine of the 'transcendent unity of being', contained implicitly in numerous Quranic verses and in the *Shahâda, Lâ ilâha illâ'llâh*, itself, was not formulated in an explicit manner until the sixth/twelfth and seventh/thirteenth centuries when it appeared in the writings of Ibn 'Arabî and other masters of Islamic gnosis. Based upon the ineffable experience of annihilation (*al-fanâ'*) and of unity (*al-tawhîd*) at its highest level, the doctrine of *wahdat al-wujûd* nevertheless gave rise to an even more refined intellectual formulation based on Ibn 'Arabî's didactic expositions. Various interpretations and ever more detailed analyses of its meaning appeared in the writings of Sadr al-Dîn al-Qûnawî, 'Abd al-Karîm al-Jîlî and many other sages of later centuries, including figures in Muslim India who developed particular formulations of this doctrine in the light of the challenges of Vedantic teachings.

Mullâ Sadrâ consummates his metaphysics based upon the principiality and gradation of being with the unity of being which lies at the heart of his doctrinal teachings. He elaborates upon various views concerning *wahdat al-wujûd*, finally providing his own understanding of the doctrine which regards this Unity in the light of the gradation of being and of this gradation in the light of that Unity which not only unites all the levels of being but also transcends all that exists.[35]

The basis of Mullâ Sadrâ's metaphysics is thus the unity (*wahdat*), principiality (*asâlat*) and gradation (*tashkîk*) of being. The Universe issues from Pure Being through states which are all grades and levels of being separated from each other through the intensity or weakness of the light of being itself. Quiddities or what appear to be 'real things' are no more than abstractions made by the mind of the limits of various levels of being, limits which do not in any way prevent all these levels from being united together and in fact to Pure Being Itself. The vast expanses of universal manifestation are so many 'presences' or acts of existence which at once veil and reveal the One Being who alone *is*.

It should not be strange, therefore, to see Mullâ Sadrâ treating theology and theodicy (*ilâhiyyât bi ma'na'l-khâss* or *rubûbiyyât*) in nearly all of his works after having dealt with the general principles of metaphysics (*al-umûr al-'âmma*). In reality 'the general principles' already contain the principles of theology and theodicy and are therefore treated before the sections which deal with God's Names and Attributes, His Unity and the like. Mullâ Sadrâ himself was a remarkable theologian as well as an outstanding *hakîm*, and separate works need to be devoted to his theological views. In fact, he was of the view that *kalâm* is unfit to discuss the questions with which it concerned itself and that these questions are the proper domain of *hikmat* rather than *kalâm*. But he was fully aware that the 'general principles' which form the heart of his metaphysical doctrines apply to all levels of reality, from Pure Being to the lowest level of existence, and to all realms of knowledge, from the knowledge of God and His Qualities and Attributes to the knowledge of the physical world. That is why he sought to provide with their help a key for an understanding of all branches of knowledge and to establish with their aid the basis of his transcendent theosophy. These principles apply to theology and theodicy as well as to cosmology, to ethics as well as to spiritual psychology and eschatology. All branches of transcendent theosophy, like those of any other traditional doctrine, are united to the trunk of a tree which is rooted in Being Itself and which is ultimately identifiable with the cosmic reverberations of Being, the tree to which the Holy Quran refers in the verse, 'a good tree, its roots set firm and its branches in heaven, giving its fruit at every season by the leave of its Lord' (Quran xiv: 24–5).

The metaphysical synthesis which has been briefly outlined here did not become philosophically dominant immediately, despite the fact that Mullâ Sadrâ had such illustrious students as Mullâ Muhsin Fayd Kâshânî and 'Abd al-Razzâq Lâhîjî and that his teachings spread rapidly to India. An examination of the writings of Mullâ Sadrâ's own students reveals in fact that, probably because of political considerations, they dissimulated their attachment to their master's teachings and wrote mostly about either religious sciences such as Quranic commentary, *hadîth* and *kalâm* or Sufism and gnosis primarily in the form of poetry.[36] Lâhîjî in fact expressly refuted such characteristic teachings of Mullâ Sadra as transsubstantial motion. Nevertheless, these figures must have continued to study and teach Mullâ Sadrâ's doctrines, some of which at least are reflected in such a work as Lâhîjî's *Shawâriq*. Through them and their own students such as Qâdî Sa'îd Qummî, the 'transcendent theosophy' of

Mullâ Sadrâ must have been kept alive to the end of the Safavid period, despite the change in the religious climate which became more unfavourable towards such teachings during the years preceding the fall of the Safavids. It is said in fact that the golden chain of transmission of this school through the traditional master-disciple relationship became narrowed down to one or two figures, the most important being Mullâ Muhammad Sâdiq Ardistânî who was banished from Isfahan just before the Afghan invasion.[37]

In any case, the school of Mullâ Sadrâ did not come to the fore in Persia until the early Qajar period when Mullâ 'Alî Nûrî began to teach his works in Isfahan, the old capital which became once again the centre for the study of Mullâ Sadrâ, although the capital had now been moved to Tehran. Nûrî, who hailed originally from Mazandaran, was a most respected religious scholar, possessing sufficient stature to teach the works of Mullâ Sadrâ without facing any opposition from excessively exoteric religious scholars.[38] He taught the *Asfâr* and other works of Sadr al-Dîn for over fifty years and by the time he had died in 1246 AH (lunar), he had not only written important works in the line of the school of Mullâ Sadrâ but had also trained a whole new generation of philosophers who followed the Sadrian school. His commentaries upon Mullâ Sadrâ include glosses upon the *Asfâr,* the *Mashâ'ir* and the *Sharh usûl al-kâfî*.[39] Of those works, the elucidation of the difficult passages of the *Asfâr* is particularly important.

The most important contribution of Nûrî is, however, the training of such outstanding masters of Islamic philosophy as Mullâ Muhammad Ismâ'îl Isfahânî, Mullâ 'Abdallâh Zunûzî, Mullâ Muhammad Ja'far Langarûdî, Mullâ Ismâ'îl Khâjû'î, and through them and other direct disciples the most famous of Qajar philosophers, that is, Hâjji Mullâ Hâdî Sabziwârî, Mullâ 'Alî Mudarris Zunûzî and Âqâ Muhammad Ridâ Qumsha'î. These figures made Sadrian metaphysics central to the teaching of Islamic philosophy in Qajar Persia, although it was not the only school, as is seen in the works of such figures as the Narâqîs and Mîrzâ Abu'l-Hasan Jilwih. Even in the case of such 'non-Sadrian' philosophers and theologians of note, however, the influence of Mullâ Sadrâ can be felt.

Among the most important exponents of Sadrian metaphysics after Nûrî, namely Sabziwârî, Zunûzî and Qumsha'î, Sabziwârî was the only one not to migrate finally to Tehran which, following the death of Mullâ 'Alî Nûrî, became the centre for the study of Islamic philosophy and remained so until the Pahlavi period and in fact throughout this century until recent times. Yet Sabziwârî is also the best known *hakîm* of the Qajar period and the only one about whom there are a few works in European languages.[40] The very popular philosophical poem of Sabziwârî, the *Sharh al-manzûma,* which summarises the teachings of Mullâ Sadrâ, soon became a favourite work on Islamic philosophy in traditional schools (*madrasas*) throughout Persia, and remains to this day perhaps the most popular introduction to Islamic philosophy in that land. His commentary upon Mullâ Sadrâ's *al-Shawâhid al-rubûbiyya* made this masterpiece of 'Transcendent Theosophy' much better known,[41] while Sabziwârî's Persian work, the *Asrâr al-hikam,* helped to make Mullâ Sadrâ's teachings more accessible to those who could not master philosophical Arabic.[42] Through his radiant sanctity, intellectual rigour and poetic gifts Sabziwârî became one of the major intellectual and spiritual figures of Qajar Persia, a master whose teachings were simply the resuscitation of the doctrines of Mullâ Sadrâ.

Mullâ 'Alî Zunûzî, a contemporary of Sabziwârî, who studied under his own father Mullâ 'Abdallâh Zunûzî,[43] was the foremost exponent of Mullâ Sadrâ's teachings in Tehran during the later Qajar period and is considered as the most intellectually original figure of the Sadrian school during this period. Not only did he compose important glosses on major Islamic philosophical works such as the *Asfâr* and the *Shifâ',* but he also wrote the *Badâyi' al-hikam* as an answer to questions posed to him by a Qajar prince, Badî' al-Mulk Mîrzâ 'Imâd al-Dawla, who had learned about Kantian philosophy while travelling to Europe. This work represents the first confrontation between the school of Mullâ Sadrâ and modern European philosophy and deserves much greater attention than it has received until now. Âqâ 'Alî Mudarris, as he was usually known, was also a Sufi initiate and occasionally composed poetry similar to his famous contemporary, Sabziwârî.[44]

As for Âqâ Muhammad Ridâ Qumsha'î, he too migrated from Isfahan to Tehran, where he became known as the leading expositor of the gnosis of the school of Ibn 'Arabî while also teaching Mullâ Sadrâ and expounding his metaphysics. Many consider him in fact to be the greatest exponent of Ibn 'Arabî's school in Persia during the Qajar period, and he is best known for his commentary upon the *Fusûs al-hikam* of Ibn 'Arabî as well as some of the works of Ibn 'Arabî's well-known commentator, Dâ'ûd al-Qaysarî.[45] At once an accomplished poet and a Sufi of the Dhahabiyya order, Qumsha'î represents the integral expression of Ibn 'Arabian gnosis in conjunction with Sadrian metaphysics and displays yet another facet of Islamic philosophy in Qajar Persia as it was influenced by Mullâ Sadrâ's metaphysics.

The famous philosophical figures of the late Qajar and early Pahlavi periods, such as Mîrzâ Tâhir Tunakâbunî and Mîrzâ Mahdî Âshtiyânî, were students of these three great masters of Sadrian metaphysics and transmitted the teachings of Mullâ Sadrâ to the *hakîms* of the last two generations who have kept the flame of this school burning to the present day. Moreover, the most important intellectual and religious questions of the Qajar period such as the rise of new religious sects and schools, confrontation with Western thought and new educational experiments

191

which were closely tied to the major social and political transformations of the late Qajar period and the Constitutional Revolution were related to the revival of Mullâ Sadrâ's school during the Qajar period, when in fact it became more central and powerful than in the late Safavid period. No full understanding of the intellectual and religious life of Qajar Persia and in fact of post-Safavid Iran as a whole is possible without a better knowledge of the teachings and especially the metaphysics of Mullâ Sadrâ and their impact during the period of over three centuries which has passed since their first exposition by the sage from Shiraz. Besides their innate sapiential value, these teachings hold the key to the understanding of many facets of the intellectual life of Persians during that turbulent period when they were confronted for the first time with the full impact of Western civilisation and its challenge to the foundations of their own traditional culture and way of life.

NOTES AND REFERENCES

1. The only serious studies on Islamic philosophy during the Qajar period in European languages are those of H. Corbin who, besides writing many essays, prepared in conjunction with S. J. Âshtiyânî the *Anthologie des philosophes iraniens,* Tehran-Paris, from 1972 onwards. Four of seven projected volumes of this anthology were completed before Corbin's death. Volume IV is of particular importance for the Qajar period although this volume lacks the analysis in French which Corbin had provided for the other volumes which set the background for the Qajar period. The French prolegomena have been assembled in his posthumous work *La Philosophie iranienne islamique aux XVIIe et XVIIIe siècles,* Paris 1981.

    The work of T. Izutsu and M. Mohaghegh on Sabziwârî is also of great importance for an understanding of the philosophical thought of this period. See T. Izutsu, *The Concept and Reality of Existence,* Tokyo 1971; Mohaghegh and Izutsu, *The Metaphysics of Sabzavârî,* Delmar (N.Y.) 1977; and their edition of *Sharh-i manzûma,* Part 1, *Metaphysics,* Tehran 1969.

    See also S. H. Nasr, 'Sabziwârî', in M. M. Sharif (ed.), *A History of Muslim Philosophy,* Wiesbaden 1966, II 1543-56.

2. For example in his *Sharh-i manzûma* he writes, while providing a proof for the gradation of existence according to Mullâ Sadrâ, 'All that we hear from our contemporaries is nothing but sophistry based on a confusion between concepts and the objects to which they apply.' Mohaghegh and Izutsu, *The Metaphysics of Sabzavârî,* 41-2.

3. On Mullâ Sadrâ see Nasr, *Sadr al-Din Shirazi and His Transcendent Theosophy,* London 1978; Corbin, *En Islam iranien,* IV, 1972, 54-122; Corbin, *La Philosophie iranienne islamique,* 49-82; and J. W. Morris, trans., *The Wisdom of the Throne – An Introduction to the Philosophy of Mulla Sadra,* Princeton 1981.

4. We must draw attention to the importance of terms used in this

connection, considering the vast confusion that has arisen in European languages since the end of the Middle Ages as a result of different ways in which 'being' and 'existence' have been used. In this exposition whenever we used 'Being' capitalised we mean the Absolute and Pure Being transcending the created order or particular existents. When we use 'Existence' capitalised we refer to that universal 'emanation' from Pure Being which forms the indifferentiated primordial substance of cosmic reality. Finally when we use 'existence' with a small 'e' we refer to particular things or to the principle of existence *vis-à-vis* quiddity, as for example the existence of a table or chair or the existence of an object in contrast to its quiddity. However, since Mullâ Sadrâ's whole metaphysics is based upon the unity and gradation of *wujûd* we shall also use 'being' in the lower case to refer to this graded aspect of reality which stretches from Being to individual extents. We hope to evoke through the use of this language the rapport of particular existents to Being Itself. In this latter sense, being is closely related in meaning to existence in that it implies separation from Primordial Being; but it also implies union with the source and reflects the metaphysical principle that although the grades of being or existents are separated from Being Itself, they are also united with the Source. It must be remembered that existence (*ex-sistere*) means, as the Scholastics knew so well, subsistence by or through something else, namely through Being (*ex alio sistere*). Our separation of the meaning of existence and Being in the sense that the first is based upon the second which is its Principle has nothing to do the modern existentialist separation of the two terms. See Corbin's introduction to Mullâ Sadrâ, *Le Livre des pénétrations métaphysiques*, 77.

5. Corbin goes so far as to call Mullâ Sadrâ's transformation of earlier Islamic philosophy a 'revolution'. He writes 'Mollâ Sadrâ opère une révolution qui détrône la véritable métaphysique de l'essence, dont le règne durait depuis des siècles, depuis Fârâbî, Avicenne et Sohrawardî.' *Le livre des pénétrations métaphysiques*, 62.

6. Masters of the school of Mullâ Sadrâ always mention the principle that in *hikmat-i ilâhî* the active participle, the verb or infinitive and the passive participle of root forms are ultimately the same, for example, lover (*'âshiq*), love (*'ishq*) and the beloved (*ma'shûq*); he in whom intellection takes place (*'âqil*), the intellect (*'aql*) and the intelligible (*ma'qûl*); and He who gives existence (*wâjid*), existence (*wujûd*) and the existent (*mawjûd*). But this is a later synthesising and unifying perspective characteristic of the school of Mullâ Sadrâ which cannot in any way obliterate the difference in perspective between the metaphysics of Ibn Sînâ, at least the Peripatetic Ibn Sînâ, and that of Mullâ Sadrâ.

7. See Izutsu, *The Concept and Reality of Existence*, Tokyo 1971, 68ff. This study contains a profound analysis of the ontology of

Mullâ Sadrâ as seen in the writings of his great commentator Sabziwârî. We are fully in accord with the theses of this study, save for certain comparisons made by the author between the school of Mullâ Sadrâ and Western existentialism.

8. One must be very careful in making any comparisons between the ontology of Mullâ Sadrâ and modern existentialism despite some superficial resemblance concerning certain points. The metaphysics of Mullâ Sadrâ are based on the inner vision of Universal Existence before all of its cosmic coagulations, a vision that is made possible only through tradition and the spiritual means contained within it. Western existentialism cannot but be a parody and caricature of traditional metaphysics since its exponents such as Sartre or even Heidegger are totally cut off from those spiritual means which alone make that vision possible. The experience described by J-P. Sartre in *La nausée,* Paris 1938, 161ff., cannot but be of the reflection of the *materia prima* at the lower boundary of cosmic manifestation and at the very antipode of Universal Existence. It is, therefore, an error of a most dangerous kind to confuse the two. On the basic differences between the school of Mullâ Sadrâ and modern existentialism see Corbin, *Le Livre des pénétrations métaphysiques,* ch.IV, 62ff.

9. See F. Schuon, 'Atmâ-Mâyâ', *Studies in Comparative Religion,* Summer 1973, 130ff.

10. Mullâ Sadrâ, like earlier Islamic philosophers, distinguishes between *mâhiyya* 'in its most particular sense' (*bi'l-ma'na'l-akhass*), which is in answer to the question 'what is it?' or *mâ huwa* in Arabic, hence the word *mâhiyya* itself, and the meaning of *mâhiyya* 'in its most general sense' (*bi'l-ma'na 'l-a'amm*), which is in answer to 'what is the reality (*haqîqa*) by which a thing is what it is?' (*mâ bihi huwa huwa* in Arabic). See Mullâ Sadrâ, *Asfâr,* first *Safar,* vol. II, 2ff. See also Izutsu, *op. cit.,* 101. Izutsu translates *mâhiyya* in its first sense as 'quiddity' and in its second sense as 'essence'.

11. For an excellent account of this subject in Western philosophy see E. Gilson, *L'Être et l'Essence,* Paris 1948. Unfortunately, a similar treatment cannot be found for Islamic philosophy. For Ibn Sînâ's views on the subject see A. M. Goichon, *La Distinction de l'essence et de l'existence d'après Ibn Sina (Avicenna),* Paris 1937.

12. For example in the *Mashâ'ir,* which is devoted to ontology, the first four chapters (*mash'ars*) of Book One (*al-minhaj al-awwal*) are devoted to *wujûd* and only the fifth *mash'ar* to the relation between *wujûd* and *mâhiyya.* In the *Asfâr,* however, the first *fasl* of the second *maqâla* of the first *safar* is devoted to the distinction between existence and quiddity, and then after extensive discussion of existence and its *ahkâm,* in the fifth *maqâla,* he turns to the detailed analysis of quiddity and questions pertaining to it.

13. The discussion of *wujûd* and *mâhiyya* is so vast that no elementary discussion such as this can do justice to it. In fact, in as much

as the understanding of the theosophy of Mullâ Sadrâ presumes a knowledge of Avicennan philosphy, concerning the question of *wujûd* and *mâhiyya* also we expect the reader to have some acquaintance with the discussions of the earlier Islamic philosophers on the subject in order to grasp the discussion at hand.

14. On the impossibility of defining *wujûd* see *Asfâr*, first *safar*, vol.I, 83ff.; *al-Mashâ'ir*, 6ff. In *al-Shawâhid al-rubûbiyya* he says,

* الوجود لا يمكن تصوّره بالحدّ ولا بالرسم ولا بصورة مساوية له ، اذ تصوّر

العيني عبارة عن حصول معناه وانتقاله من حدّ العين الى حدّ الذهن · فهذا

يجري في غير الوجود · وأمّا في الوجود فلا يمكن ذلك إلا بصريح المشاهدة

وعين العيان دون اشارة الحدّ والبرهان وتفهيم العبارة والبيان ··

15. On the discussion of *ishtirâk-i ma'nawî* and reasons brought forward in its support, see *Asfâr* first *safar*, vol.I, 35-6.

16. This theme runs throughout the first *safar* of the *Asfâr* and is especially emphasised in Sabziwarî's summary of Mullâ Sadrâ's doctrines in *Sharh al-manzûma*. For a detailed analysis of this distinction in reference to both Mullâ Sadrâ and Sabziwarî see Izutsu, *op. cit.*, 68ff.

17. That is why Sabziwarî, summarising the teachings of Mullâ Sadrâ, says in his *Sharh al-manzûma* edited by Izutsu and Mohaghegh, Tehran 1969, 4,

مفهومه من أعرف الأشياه ، وكنهه في غاية الخفاء ·

18. Of course, Mullâ Sadrâ was aware of the argument of the sollipsist and the subjectivist, which he refutes through various arguments. But in making this distinction between the notion and reality of existence he is appealing precisely to our immediate perception of reality and not to whatever conceptual schemes certain philosophical minds of other tendencies may have imposed upon that immediate perception.

19. On 'sacred effusion' (*fayd-i muqaddas*) and 'most sacred effusion' (*fayd-i aqdas*) used by Sûfîs of the school of Ibn 'Arabî as well as Mullâ Sadrâ, see Ibn 'Arabî, *La Sagesse des prophètes*, trans. by T. Burckhardt, Paris 1955, 23-4.

20. For an exposition of this doctrine in ancient philosophy and the West see A. Lovejoy, *The Great Chain of Being*, Cambridge (USA) 1936; see also S. H. Nasr, *Knowledge and the Sacred*, Edinburgh 1981, ch.4.

21. Suhrawardî in his ontology bestowed all reality upon the *mâhiyyât* and believed existence to be a mere accident, but as already mentioned by many scholars, spoke of light (*al-nûr*) in terms that make it synonymous with being. As far as light is concerned, he spoke explicitly of its gradation and is in fact the first Islamic philosopher to have given a rational demonstration of the possibility of *tashkîk*, answering the criticisms Ibn Sînâ and other Peripatetics had given against it. Mullâ Sadrâ took Suhrawardî's concept of *tashkîk* as applied to light and applied it

to *wujûd*. See Suhrawardî, *Hikmat al-ishrâq,* ed. by Corbin,
Tehran-Paris 1952, 119-20. That is why in his *Sharh al-manzûma*
Sabziwârî attributes *tashkîk* to the ancient Persian sages' (the
fahlawiyyûn) saying, Izutsu and Mohaghegh edition, 5,

الفهلويّون الوجود عندهم   حقيقة ذات تشكّك تعم

22. On *tashkîk*, see *Asfâr*, first *safar*, vol.ɪ, 423ff.; also Izutsu, *The
    Concept and Reality of Existence*, 138ff. In his fine discussion on
    tashkîk, M. Ilâhî Qumsha'î says, 'The meaning of *tashkîk* is
    realised whenever a single "truth" (*haqîqa*) is predictable of its
    particulars in different degrees', معنى تشكيك آنگاه محقق

    شود که حقيقت واحدى برافراد كثير بتغاوت صدق کند

    M. Ilâhî Qumshâ'î, *Hikmat-i ilâhî khâss wa 'âmm*, Tehran 1335
    (A. H. solar), 9.
23. Al-Fârâbî discusses it in his *Risâla li'l-mu'allim al-thânî fî jawâb
    masâ'il su'ila 'anhu,* and Ibn Sînâ in several of his works includ-
    ing *al-Ishârât wa'l-tanbîhât*. See Izutsu, *op. cit.,* chapters 3-6
    where this whole question is thoroughly analysed.
24. See *Tahâfut al-tahâfut,* ed. by S. van Den Bergh, London 1954,
    1, 237; also Izutsu, *op. cit.,* 81.
25. The appropriate passage has been translated into English by
    Izutsu in his *The Concept and Reality of Existence,* 121-2.
26. The *Ta'lîqât,* which is a major work of Ibn Sînâ and necessary for
    an understanding of many facets of his thought, has been neg-
    lected in contemporary research on him and only recently
    appeared in its first printing, ed. by A. Badawî, Cairo 1973.
27. See Mullâ Sadrâ, *Kitâb al-mashâ'ir,* ed. by Corbin, 34, 83 and 84
    where he quotes the words of Ibn Sînâ to show that the particular
    'accident' we call existence is such that 'its existence in a sub-
    stratum is the very existence of that substratum' (وجوده فى
    موضوع نفس وجود موضوع)‚ unlike other accidents which
    need a substratum that already possesses existence in order to
    become existent. It is of interest to note that immediately follow-
    ing the quotation from the *Ta'lîqât,* Mullâ Sadrâ describes his
    conversion to the school of the 'principiality of existence'.
28. All the *hakîms* of Persia have been followers of either one school
    or the other except Shaykh Ahmad Ahsâ'î, the founder of the
    Shaykhî School, who thought one could uphold the principiality
    of both existence and quiddity at the same time. The impossi-
    bility of such a view has been demonstrated by followers of both
    schools.
29. See note 5 above for Corbin's description of this transformation
    as a revolution in Islamic philosophy.
30. This is in reference to the famous words of Ibn 'Arabî,
    " الأعيان الثابتة ما شمّت رائحة الوجوه "
    see *La Sagesse des prophètes,* 67.
31. *Mashâ'ir,* ed. by Corbin, p.35 of the Arabic text. Corbin's trans-
    lation of this passage into French appears on p.152 of the French

part of the book. There is an English translation of this passage in Izutsu, *The Concept and Reality of Existence*, 104, which we have followed closely with certain changes.

It is of great interest to note, as Corbin has already pointed out in the above source, that Suhrawardî uses nearly the same terms in his *Hikmat al-ishrâq*, 156-7, to show how he was awakened from the limited confines of Peripatetic philosophy to become aware of the luminous world to which *ishrâqî* theosophy is devoted.

32. For arguments in defence of *asâlat al-wujûd* see especially the *Asfâr*, first *safar*, 38ff. These arguments have been summarised by Mullâ Sadrâ in the *Mashâ'ir*, 37ff. The arguments given by Sabziwârî in his *Sharh al-manzûma*, 4 and 43-6, are also taken from Mullâ Sadrâ's demonstrations. The arguments of Mullâ Sadrâ have been likewise analysed and summarised by S. J. Âshtiyânî in his *Hastî az nazar-i falsafa wa 'irfân*, Mashhad 1379 (A. H. lunar), 205ff.

33. In a sense the two schools of the principiality of existence and principiality of quiddity in later Islamic philosophy correspond to the views based on the continuity and discontinuity of cosmic reality, or the substance and the essence. The first school emphasises more the gradation and stages of being of the one Divine Substance from whose matrix all multiplicity flows forth while preserving its primordial unity (although in terms of Islamic philosophy *wujûd* is considered to be above the category of *jawhar* or substance as usually understood). The second school emphasises the discontinuity of things, their separate essences which reflect the divine possibilities on the cosmic plane.

34. On the centrality of the doctrine of *wahdat al-wujûd* in Islamic gnosis see Nasr, *Science and Civilisation in Islam*, Cambridge (USA) 1968, New York 1970, ch.13.

35. We have dealt extensively with Mullâ Sadrâ's doctrine of the 'transcendent unity of being' in Nasr, *Islamic Life and Thought*, London 1981, ch.16, 'Mullâ Sadrâ and the doctrine of the unity of being.'

36. See the Persian introductions of Âshtiyânî to vols I and II of the *Anthologie des philosophes iraniens*; and Corbin, *La Philosophie iranienne islamique*, 96ff. and 179ff.

37. On Ardistânî and his role in the transmission of the teachings of Mullâ Sadrâ to the Zand and Qajar periods, see Âshtiyânî, *Anthologie...*, vol.IV, 2ff.

38. On Nûrî, see M. Sadûghî Suhâ, *A Bio-Bibliography of Post-Sadr-ul-Muti'allihîn Mystics and Philosophers*, Tehran 1980, 33-40; and Ashtiyânî, *Anthologie...*, vol.IV, 139ff.

39. On these works of Mullâ Sadrâ, see Nasr, *The Transcendent Theosophy of Sadr al-Dîn Shîrâzî*, 40ff.

40. See the works of Izutsu, Mohaghegh and Nasr already cited as well as the English preface of Nasr and the Persian introduction of S. J. Âshtiyânî to his edition of Sabziwârî, *Rasâ'il*, Mashhad

1970; and the introduction of Izutsu to the Mohaghegh and Falâtûrî edition of M. M. Âshtiyânî's *Commentary on Sabza-wârî's Sharh-i manzûma*, Tehran 1973.

41. See the English preface of Nasr to S. J. Âshtiyânî's edition of *al-Shawâhid al-rubûbiyya* with the complete glosses of Sabzi-wârî, Mashhad 1967.

42. A notable feature of Islamic philosophy during the Qajar period is the revival of Persian as a vehicle for philosophical writings going back in a sense to the pre-Safavid period from the time of Nâsir-i Khusraw and Suhrawardî onwards, when Persian prose witnessed its golden age and when most of the philosophical masterpieces of Persian prose were produced. Many Persian philosophical texts of the Qajar period remain to be edited and studied including some of the translations of the works of Mullâ Sadrâ from Arabic into Persian.

43. Mullâ 'Abdallâh was himself a notable Sadrian philosopher especially interested in questions of eschatology. See the intro-duction of Nasr to Âshtiyânî's edition of *Lama'ât-i ilâhiyya*, Tehran 1976.

44. On Mullâ 'Alî, see Sadûghî Suhâ, *op. cit.*, 155ff.

45. See the introduction of S. J. Âshtiyânî to his edition of *Rasâ'il-i Qaysarî*, Tehran 1357 (A. H. solar), which includes Âqâ Muhammad Ridâ's important treatise on *walâya*.

11

Patterns in urban development;
the growth of Tehran (1852–1903)

When Tehran was chosen by Âghâ Muhammad Khan in 1200/1785–6 as his capital, it was a very small and insignificant town and remained so during the reigns of the next two monarchs. All foreign travellers who visited Tehran described it as small, poor and uninteresting; many even believed it was doomed to decay. It was surrounded by mud walls built in the sixteenth century, and had a deep ditch and five gates.[1] The streets were narrow, dirty and deserted and the houses were surrounded by mud walls. There were no public monuments before 1222/1806, except the *Masjid-i Shâh*. Slowly however, Tehran began to expand; its population grew and economic life intensified and developed.

No reliable statistics of the population of Tehran exist before 1286/1869;[2] but Bémont has compiled the following list based on foreign travellers' accounts and estimates, and he calculates that the population increased threefold in a century, between 1807 and 1910.[3] These are his figures:

1807	45 to 50,000
1816	67,000
1860	less than 100,000
1865	85,000[4]
1890	100,000
1910	150,000

In 1286/1869 Hâjji Najm al-Mulk, a graduate of the *Dâr al-Funûn* was ordered by the government to prepare a census of the population of Tehran, which as he records was accomplished with great difficulty, as people were reluctant to cooperate or suspicious of his undertaking.[5] Nonetheless he was successful and prepared the following account. He first gives the total number of the population, men, women, children, non-Tehranis, black slaves and so on. He then gives the same information regarding each district of the town, and he also gives the number of houses, *hammâm*s, *masjid*s, *takâyâ* and so on. In the list below the population in 1286/1869 is given, according to his account,

Ark	3,014
Châlmaydân	34,547

199

Sangilaj	29,673
Bâzâr	6,673
'Awdlâjân	36,495
Outside the town	16,853

The total population was 155,766, of whom 8,480 were soldiers. The date of Najm al-Mulk's census does not correspond to the dates of the two census reports of the buildings of Tehran which we are discussing here; nonetheless it helps to give an idea of the population of Tehran at a date more or less mid-way between the other two.

The oldest and the most detailed of these census reports[6] was compiled in 1269/1852 by an anonymous person at the command of the Shah.[7] The second, prepared by Akhzar 'Alî Shah, was begun in 1317/1900 and completed in 1320/1902–3.[8]

The 1269 census is in several parts,[9] and we shall deal with each part separately. It begins by giving the complete number of the buildings inside the walls of Tehran and then divides them into: (1) houses, (2) *takâyâ*, etc. (mostly public buildings), (3) shops.

Each house is calculated according to the number of doors or *bâb* it had leading outside. For instance, the houses are recorded as having 8,697 units or *dast*, and 12,772 *bâb*.[10] In the case of the shops or other buildings, only the number of doors are given.

1. Houses

(a) Those houses whose owners were *nawkar*.[11] (i) those houses with four or five *hayât*s, (ii) those houses with one, two or three *hayât*s.

(b) Those houses whose owners are *ra'âyâ* (non-government officials in this context). (i) the houses of the ordinary people and the *kasaba*, (ii) the houses of the minorities.

2. *Takâyâ*, etc.

In this section the number of public buildings are enumerated as *takâyâ, juba-khâna, dâr al-sanâ'a, maktab-khâna, qur-khâna, hammâm,*[12] *châp-khâna,*[13] *anbâr-i dawlat, kârvânsarâ va timcha, zarrâb-khâna, tavîla-yi khârij az khâna.*

3. Shops

(a) Those shops which were open and functioning.

(b) Those shops which were closed or abandoned.

Several shops were classed together without connection from the point of view of trade or the kind of articles made or sold.[14]

Having given the total number of houses, *takâyâ*, etc. and shops, the census subdivides into districts and follows the same pattern. There were five districts in Tehran, the Ark,[15] Awdlâjân, Sangilaj, Bâzâr,[16] and Châlmaydân. First the total number of houses, *takâyâ*, etc., and shops in each district is given, then each *mahalla* is divided into *pâtuq* and *guzâr* giving the names of these, the name of the owners of the houses, the names of the *takâyâ*, etc., and the kind of shops.

As mentioned, the houses whose owners were *nawkar* and those who were *ra'âyâ* are given separately. If a house was rented or if part of it was rented, the name of the owner is mentioned. For instance, we read that Âghâ Muhammad-i Chamidân-furûsh in Awdlâjân in the *Mahalla-yi Shâhî va 'Arabhâ* lived in one part of his house, whilst the other part was rented to five families. We also notice that often the servants of the wealthy lived in the same district as their masters; thus for instance five of the servants[17] of Mu'ayyir al-Mamâlik who lived in the Ark and their houses were classed amongst those with one, two or three courtyards. Another lived in Awdlâjân. Mu'ayyir's house had four or five courtyards, and had two baths and a small and a large stable.

In the case of the shops, a distinction is made when the shop was owned by someone else other than the shopkeeper. For instance we read that Mashhad-i 'Alî Shaypurshî owned a *baqqâlî*, a *mâst-bandî*, an *allâfî* and a *najjârî* in the Ark. Presumably when such a distinction is not made the shopkeeper was the owner of the shop. The census further indicates if a shop was a *vaqf* and sometimes the name of the person who made the *vaqf*, and its purpose are also mentioned.

Following the section on the shops in each district, the number of baths not attached to a house and the number of common stables are given. Another section deals with the areas outside the five city gates,[18] which were as yet undeveloped and deserted.

After 1269/1852, Tehran grew and developed, as the figures given by Najm al-Mulk corroborate. Nâsir al-Dîn Shah decided to modernise his capital and have new walls built to encompass the areas which had grown outside the old walls and which paid no taxes on their merchandise. Some travellers who visited Tehran thereafter describe these improvements. The new walls were built on the French model in 1284/1867–8, encompassed an area 19 kilometres square and included much open ground.[19]

The second census was made in 1320/1902–3. By then many of the open spaces inside the confines of the city walls had been used, and the city had begun to expand once more outside the walls, particularly to the north. According to some foreign observers, the quality of life had improved in these years, but there was little social change. For instance, there were few hospitals and schools in Tehran by the beginning of the twentieth century.[20]

This second census was completed by Akhzar 'Alî Shah. It is much shorter and not as detailed as the first and follows different divisions and criteria.[21] For instance, whereas the older enumerates such buildings as *zarrâb-khâna*, *matabb va jarrâhî* and *tup-khâna*, the latter gives the number of churches, Jewish synagogues, *yakhchâl*, *maydân* and *sarbâz khâna* and so on. Thus a full and complete comparison[22] is not possible. We shall therefore compare the houses, baths, shops, *masâjid va madâris*,

201

takâyâ and *kârvânsarâ*s which are common to both censuses.

As in the earlier census, Akhzar 'Alî Shah gives the total number of buildings first, then deals with each district separately.[23] It is noteworthy generally in this census that the city had been growing to the north and west rather than the south and east, a phenomenon which was to remain one of the characteristics of Tehran in the next half century.

In this census, first the buildings in each *mahalla* are enumerated, then it is subdivided into the number of *pâtuq* and *guzâr,* and the number of the buildings in each is then given. It is interesting to note that each *pâtuq* and *guzâr* is named after the policeman responsible for it,[24] and not by its actual name.

Tables 1 and 2 have been prepared to show the total number of buildings in Tehran. In tables 3–8 a comparison is drawn between the number of houses, shops, baths, *kârvânsarâ, takâyâ* and *masâjid va madâris* and the percentage of change in each case is also given. Table 9 shows the total changes in the number of these buildings which occurred between these two dates, and the percentage of the change is also recorded. Tables 10 and 11 include figures given by Najm al-Mulk in 1286/1869–70. Table 10 lists the changes in the number of houses in each district, whilst table 11 enumerates the changes in the numbers of *takâyâ, hammâm, kârvânsarâ, masâjid va madâris* and houses. Table 12 records the percentage of change in each district and table 13 shows the percentage of total change. Finally, table 14 records the number of houses per unit of bath, shop, *madâris va masâjid* and *takâyâ.*

As seen from these tables, Tehran had obviously expanded and developed but the patterns of development varied in each district due to socio-economic and political factors. The Bâzâr district shows a steady growth in the number of houses, baths and shops. Mahalla-yi Dawlat was, as mentioned, a new district and we cannot make any comparison with the past. However, we may note that by 1320/1902–3, it had grown into a large district. The number of houses surpassed those of Awdlâjân and the Bâzâr, and the number of baths those of Sangilaj and Châlmaydân, and the number of shops was greater than those of all the other districts (see tables 3, 4 and 5). It also included large gardens and vacant lands.

In Awdlâjân on the other hand, the number of houses had been decreasing since 1286/1869–70, and continued to do so up until 1320/1902–3 (see table 10), but the number of baths and shops had increased, the reason probably being that many of the more wealthy were leaving it and it was becoming more of a commercial district. In fact a map made by 'Abd al-Ghaffâr Najm al-Mulk in 1891 shows that the area of Awdlâjân had not grown and was hemmed in to the north and east by Dawlat. Sangilaj and Châlmaydân had, on the other hand, grown considerably (see tables 3 and 5). But the interesting fact here is the decrease in the number of baths. It is possible that a large number of those who worked in these two districts did not live there (see table 12). There were also large open tracts of land and many gardens, particularly in Sangilaj.

Another phenomenon which must now be discussed is the marked drop in the number of *madâris va masâjid*, and *takâyâ* (except in Sangilaj where the number of *takâyâ* increased considerably). The growth of a secular trend and the fact that from 1305/1887–8, modern schools were being opened in Tehran, might explain the drop in the number of the more traditional *madâris va masâjid* in which the new trend in secular education was not followed, and the *takâyâ* where religious ceremonies were held. It is interesting to speculate on the growth of religious buildings in Sangilaj. There was also a remarkable number of *takâyâ* built in the Mahalla-yi Dawlat, an area which had grown recently.

Were these *takâyâ* used for religious purposes only or had they other uses, such as for instance political meetings? Or were they built in order to counteract radical trends amongst the population? We must not forget that we are on the eve of the Constitutional Revolution and the people of Sangilaj and Dawlat were very active in the aftermath of the Revolution.[25]

These two census reports have certain inaccuracies and are vague on some points so that we do not obtain a complete picture of Tehran as it was in the 50 years they encompass. However, they do give us a general view of the city's steady growth and its patterns of development. The growth of Tehran was due to political, geographical and environmental factors, and though at the time none could foretell its later expansion, we can see, however, that by the early twentieth century it was a different city from its modest beginnings.

Patterns in urban development

Table 1. 1269/1852-3

	Mahalla-yi Ark	Mahalla-yi Bâzâr	Mahalla-yi Sangilaj	Mahalla-yi Châlmaydân	Mahalla-yi Awdlâjân
Takâyâ	3	17	12	10	12
Dakâkîn	128	538	516	512	1,016
Imâmzâda	2	3	—	2	1
Buyûtât	232	1,524	1,695	1,802	2,619
Masâjid	3	17	24	20	34
Madrasa	2	6	6	—	4
Juba-khâna va Dâr al-sanâ'a	1	—	—	—	—
Tup-khâna va qûr-khâna	2	—	—	—	—
Hammâm-i' umûmî	14	30	33	16	53
Matabb va jarrâhî	1	—	—	—	—
Maktab-khâna	—	—	—	—	—
Châp-khâna	1	—	2	—	—
Anbâr	2	—	—	—	—
Kârvânsarâ	27	2	—	—	—
Timcha	—	—	—	—	—
Zarrâb-khâna	—	1	—	—	—
Tavîla-yi-'umûmî	22	45	53	12	33
Âb anbâr	20	—	19	—	—

Table 2. 1320/1902-3

	Mahalla-yi Dawlat	Mahalla-yi Bâzâr	Mahalla-yi Sangilaj	Mahalla-yi Châlmaydân	Mahalla-yi Awdlâjân
Khâna	2,705	2,625	4,448	3,372	2,125
Dakâkîn	2,546	2,333	1,824	1,403	1,314
Kârvânsarâ	52	60	24	23	27
Hammâm-i 'umûmî	38	27	59	28	30
Masâjid va madâris	23	20	14	6	16
Bâq va bâqcha	40	9	155	3	8
Takya	7	14	9	5	8
Yakhchâl	8	2	10	4	—
Kâr-khâna	3	2	1	—	—
Sarbâz-khâna	4	—	1	2	—
Kalîsâ	2	1	—	—	—
Maydân	2	1	—	2	—
Marîz-khâna	2	—	—	—	—
Ma'bad-i Yahûd	—	—	—	—	2
Madrasa-yi-dawlatî	2	—	—	—	—
Tavîla	70	37	117	—	52
Navvâb	10	5	9	60	4

Table 3. Changes in the number of houses (*buyûtât*) between
1269-1320/1852-3–1902-3

Mahalla	1269	1320	Change	% of change
Awdlâjân	2,907	2,125	−782	−26%
Châlmaydân	1,802	3,372	+1,570	+87%
Dawlat	—	2,705	+2,705	+100%
Sangilaj	2,028	4,448	+2,420	+119%
Bâzâr	1,524	2,625	+1,101	+72%
Ark	232	—	—	—

Table 4. Changes in the number of baths (*hammâm*) between
1269-1320/1852-3–1902-3

Mahalla	1269	1320	Change	% of change
Awdlâjân	30	53	+23	+76%
Châlmaydân	28	16	−12	−42%
Dawlat	—	38	+38	+100%
Sangilaj	59	33	−26	−44%
Bâzâr	27	30	+3	+11%
Ark	14	—	—	—

Table 5. Changes in the number of shops (*dakâkîn*) between
1269-1320/1852-3–1902-3

Mahalla	1269		1320	Change	% of change
Awdlâjân	1,016		1,314	+298	+29%
Châlmaydân	512		1,403	+891	+174%
Dawlat	—		2,546	+2,546	+100%
Sangilaj	516		1,824	+1,308	+253%
Bâzâr	538	1,774	2,333	+559	+31%
Râsta bâzâr	1,236				
Ark	128		—	—	—

Table 6. Changes in the number of *takâyâ* between
1269-1320/1852-3–1902-3

Mahalla	1269	1320	Change	% of change
Awdlâjân	12	8	−4	−33%
Châlmaydân	10	3	−7	−70%
Dawlat	—	7	+7	+100%
Sangilaj	2	9	+7	+350%
Bâzâr	17	14	−3	−17%
Ark	3	—	—	—

Patterns in urban development

Table 7. Changes in the number of *kârvânsarâ*s between
1269-1320/1852-3–1902-3

Mahalla	1269	1320	Change	% of change
Awdlâjân	12	27	+15	+125%
Châlmaydân	10	23	+13	+130%
Dawlat	—	52	+52	+100%
Sangilaj	12	24	+12	+100%
Bâzâr	27 } 44	60	+16	+36%
Râsta bâzâr	17			
Ark	—	—	—	—

Table 8. Changes in the number of mosques and *madrasa*s between
1269-1320/1852-3–1902-3

Mahalla	1269/1852-3	1320/1902-3	Change	% of change
Awdlâjân	38	16	−22	−57%
Châlmaydân	20	6	−14	−70%
Dawlat	—	23	+23	+100%
Sangilaj	30	14	−16	−53%
Bâzâr	23	20	−3	−13%
Ark	5	—	—	—

Table 9. A summary of the changes in the number of buildings between the
years1269-1320/1852-3–1902-3

Buildings	1269/1852-3	1320/1902-3	Change	% of change
Houses (*buyûtât*)	7,872	16,275	+8,403	+106%
Baths (*hammâm*)	153	182	+29	+18%
Shops (*dakâkîn*)	3,791	9,420	+5,629	+148%
Takâyâ	54	43	−11	−20%
Kârvânsarâs	78	186	+108	—
Mosques and *madrasa*s	116	80	−36	−31%

Table 10. The gradual growth of the number of houses in each district, taking into consideration the census of 1286*/1869-70

Mahalla	1269/1852-3	1286/1869-70	1320/1902-3
Awdlâjân	2,614	2,508	2,125
Châlmaydân	1,802	2,347	3,372
Dawlat	—	—	2,705
Sangilaj	1,695	1,964	4,448
Bâzâr	1,524	1,480	2,625
Ark	232	195	—
Outside the city	115	1,024	—
Total	7,872	9,523	16,275

* The census of the population of Tehran taken by Najm al-Mulk.

Table 11. The general growth of Tehran, taking into consideration the 1286 census

Buildings	1269/1852-3	1286/1869-70	1320/1902-3
Takâyâ	54	34	43
Buyûtât	7,872	9,523	16,275
Dakâkîn	3,791	—*	9,420
Hammâm	53	90	182
Masâjid va madâris	116	82	80
Karvânsarâ	47	130	186

* Najm al-Mulk does not give the number of shops except for bakeries.

Table 12. Percentage of change in buildings in each mahalla between the years 1269/1852-3 and 1320/1902-3

Mahalla	Buyûtât	Hammâm	Dakâkîn	Takâyâ	Masâjid va madâris
Awdlâjân	−26%	+76%	+29%	−34%	−57%
Châlmaydân	+87%	−42%	+174%	−70%	−70%
Sangilaj	+119%	−44%	+253%	+350%	−53%
Bâzâr	+72%	+11%	+31%	−17%	−13%

Table 13. Percentage of change in buildings
in the whole of Tehran between 1269/1852-3
and 1320/1902-3

Buyûtât	+106%
Hammân	+18%
Dakâkîn	+148%
Takâyâ	−21%
Masâjid va madâris	−32%

Table 14. The number of houses per unit of bath, shop, masâjid va madâris
and takâyâ

Building type	1269/1852-3	1286/1869-70	1320/1902-3
One bath per	148 houses	105 houses	89 houses
One shop per	21 houses	—	1.72 houses
One masjid va madrasa per	65 houses	116 houses	203 houses
One takya per	140 houses	280 houses	378 houses

NOTES AND REFERENCES

1. These were: Darvâza-yi Mahmûdiyya. Shah 'Abd al-A'zam, Qazvîn, Dulâb, Shamîrân and Dawlat.
2. Karîmân also compiled a list of the population of Tehran, but he does not give his sources. Cf. H. Karîmân, Tihrân dar guzashta va hâl, Tehran 1355, 256.

    H. Bahrambeygui gives the population of Tehran at the turn of the century as 350,000: Tehran: an Urban Analysis, Tehran 1977, 23.
3. F. Bémont, Les Villes de L'Iran, Paris 1969, 1, 104.
4. There was a severe cholera epidemic and later a famine in these years which decimated the population and probably accounts for the fall in the numbers we see in 1865.
5. Hâjj 'Abd al-Ghaffâr Najm al-Mulk, Târîkh-i nufûs-i dâr al-khilâfa, 1286/1869-70; N. Pâkdaman, Farhang-i Îrân Zamîn, 20 (1353), 351-91.
6. The figures of these two reports are in siyâq and were read by Mr S. Sa'dvandian who helped to prepare this article. It is hoped to produce these two censuses in book form in the near future. In the present essay these reports are introduced in general outline and a comparison is made to show the growth or in some cases the decay of Tehran in the fifty years they encompass.
7. This manuscript is in the E. G. Browne Collection in the University of Cambridge and is probably the original text. It is listed with the following comment: 'Complete account of all the houses in the Persian capital street by street, quarter by quarter, with no connected text except a few introductory lines at the

beginning'. A copy of this manuscript exists in the Tehran University Central Library and is registered under the number 844F.

8. This manuscript is in the Central Library of the University of Tehran. Its full title is: *ta 'yîn-i abniya-yi muhât-i khandaq-i shahr-i dâr al-khilâfa-yi Tihrân,* and is registered under the following number: *Adabiyyât* 20B.

9. In *siyâq,* divisions and subdivisions are shown with a *madd* which is a vertical line of varying length. For instance the total number of *takâyâ, imâmzâdas* and *masâjid* come under a long *madd,* then it is subdivided under shorter *madds,* giving the number of *takâyâ, imâmzâdas,* and *masâjid;* or for instance in the case of the minorities, a long *madd* indicates the total number of their houses, and shorter *madds* show the number of houses of the Jews, Turcomans, and Armenians. In order to make explanation easier each section has been numbered in this paper.

10. Persian buildings, and particularly houses, consisted of several parts, comprising courtyards, stores, stables, water reservoirs, bath houses, women and men's quarters etc. In these censuses each house is treated as a unit, *dast,* but is calculated according to the number of its doors, *bâb.*

11. It is interesting to note the official class distinction made between *nawkar* (government officials) and *ra'âyâ* (non-government officials and the ordinary people).

12. These are public baths. The richer people had private baths attached to their houses.

13. This could also be read as *chây-khâna.*

14. It must be remembered that the shops were often the place where goods were made and sold, and that the shopkeeper often lived on the premises.

15. The Ark or citadel was surrounded by walls and a ditch. In this census the government buildings and the houses of the Sadr A'zam situated in the Ark are omitted. Moreover, when the larger houses of this district are enumerated, a distinction is made between those houses which belonged to the *umarâ'* and *khavânîn* and those of the *nawkar.* The houses of the *ulamâ'* are mentioned separately.

16. The Bâzâr district is treated separately from the *bâzâr* proper and from the Râsta Bâzâr which is given under a different subsection, where all the shops, *kârvânsarâs, timchas* etc. in the Râsta Bâzâr are enumerated.

17. In the text the word for servant is given as *âdam,* but it could also mean a public servant who worked with Mu'ayyir.

18. In all, there were 115 houses, 204 shops (of which 152 were open and functioning), 11 *kârvânsarâs,* 5 gardens, 33 *gach-pazîs,* and *kûza-garîs.*

19. There was no important industry at the time, and economic activity was mostly commercial. The little industrial activity which existed was concentrated in the south of the city around the Darvâza-yi Shâh 'Abd al A'zam and Darvâzeh-yi Gumruk and Khurâsân in the east and south of the city.

20. In the introduction he wrote that in 1317 he decided to work a year in the government and offered his services to Mukhtâr al-Mulk who was the head of the *nazmiyya* at the time, and who had decided to prepare a census of all the buildings of Tehran. It was agreed that he should be paid 30 tumans a month, but in reality he only received 10. The census was complete by 1320, and was presented to 'Ayn al-Dawla, who was the governor of Tehran.

21. As mentioned, a comparison is made between these two censuses only from the point of view of the growth of Tehran. When both censuses are published, many more aspects of life can be studied.

22. He omits the Ark, but it is possible that he calculated it with one of the other districts, possibly the Bâzâr. The walls of the Ark had now disappeared and the ditch had been filled. The Râsta Bâzâr is also omitted. It must be noted also that despite the growth of Tehran the same divisions into five districts was kept as before, though each *mahalla* had grown much larger. Dawlat of course was a new district.

23. This is probably due to the fact that he was preparing this census for the police.

24. According to Bahrambeygui, many foreigners and foreign embassies moved to the north, followed by Tehranis. It was for a long time a first class residential district and enjoyed a better climate and purer water. Bahrambeygui, *op. cit.,* 19.

25. When elections were held for the Majlis, 32 members of the *asnâf* were elected, but these deputies who in fact represented the lowest social class in the Majlis did not play a significant role politically. On the other hand, political activity of a radical and revolutionary nature was concentrated outside the Majlis, in the *anjumans,* which were organised to support the Majlis against the Shah who was suspected of plotting its overthrow. Other revolutionary *anjumans* were the *Anjuman-i barâdarân-i Darvâza Qazvîn* and the *Anjuman-i Barâdarân-i Darvâza Dawlat,* situated one in Sangilaj, the other in Dawlat. Other radical *anjumans* of repute were the *Anjuman-i Âzarbayjân, Shâhâbâd,* and *Muzaffarî,* all located in Dawlat. We do not, however, hear of an *anjuman* of the *bâzârîs* for instance. Thus we can surmise that perhaps these districts which were more populated, or perhaps poorer, were more prone to new ideas, whereas the *bâzâr* functioned under stricter rules and customs and a fixed hierarchy. We can also speculate that perhaps the *asnâf* deputies were from the *bâzâr* and that the members of the *anjumans* were from these other districts, or worked at different trades. Of course, this problem needs further study to establish the connections between the development and growth of Tehran and the political implications of such growth.

26. The maps are taken from Bahrambeygui, *op. cit.,* 18-22.

GLOSSARY

Âb-anbâr	water reservoir
Âdam	servant, in this context
Anbâr	store
Anbâr-i dawlat	government store
Anjuman	society
Asnâf	guilds
Bâb	door
Bâgh	garden
Bâghcha	small garden
Bahârband	large stable
Baqqâlî	grocery
Bâzâr	market
Buyûtât	houses
Chamidân-furûsh	suitcase vendor
Châp-khâna	printing-house
Chây-khâna	tea-house
Dakâkîn	shops
Dâr al-funûn	college founded in 1852
Dâr al-sanâ'a	work shop
Darvâza	gate
Dast	unit, in this context
Dukkân	shop
Gach-Pazî	lime burning/plaster making works
Gumruk	customs
Guzâr	passage
Hammâm-i' umûmî	public bath
Hayât	courtyard
Imâmzâda	shrine
Jarrâhî	surgery
Jûba-khâna	arsenal
Kalîsâ	church
Kâr-khâna	factory
Kârvânsarâ	caravanserai
Kasaba	tradespeople
Khâna	house
Khavânîn	tribal nobility
Kûza-garî	potter's shop
Ma'bad-i Yahûd	Jewish temple
Madd	vertical line used in *siyâq*
Madrasa (plural: madâris)	school
Mahalla	district
Maktab-khâna	school
Marîz-khâna	hospital
Masjid (plural: masâjid)	mosque
Mâstbandî	yoghourt maker's shop
Matabb	dispensary
Maydân	square
Najjârî	carpenter's shop
Navvâb	guard house

211

Nawkar	government servant
Nazmiyya	police
Pâtuq	square
Qur-khâna	arsenal
Ra'âyâ	subjects, in this context particularly non-government people
Râsta Bâzâr	in this context, the term means the actual *bâzâr* with covered passages
Sarbâz-khâna	barracks
Siyâq	special accounting in the Arabic alphabet
Shaypurchî	bugler
Takya (plural: takâyâ)	a place or places where religious ceremonies were held, especially in the month of Muharram
Tanbâkû-furûshî	tobacco shop
Taryâk-furûshî	opium shop
Tavîla	stables
Tavîla-yi dawlat	government stables
Tavîla-yi khârij az khâna	stables outside the house
Tavîla-yi 'umûmî	public stables
Tîmcha	small caravanserai inside the bâzâr
Tûp-khâna	artillery
Umarâ	nobility
'Umûmî	public
Vaqf	pious bequest
Yakhchâl	a place where ice was made and kept for summer use
Zarrâb-khâna	mint

12

Muharram ceremonies and diplomacy (a preliminary study)

The first and – to my knowledge – the only international symposium on *ta'ziya-khânî* (Persian mystery plays) was held at Shiraz in August 1976. The fact that Professor Elwell-Sutton could not attend this meeting was all the more regretted, as a discussion on his interesting paper on literary aspects of the *ta'ziya*, prepared for this occasion, would have enhanced the debate on this and other topics.[1] By the time of the symposium, I had prepared a study on *ta'ziya* patronage under Nâsir al-Dîn Shah (1848–96).[2] Along with my research on various aspects of Shi'ite rituals, I also prepared a detailed study on Muharram ceremonies and diplomacy, a preliminary draft of which is given here in homage to Professor Elwell-Sutton. Particular attention is paid in this study to problems raised by the invitation of diplomats to Muharram ceremonies and to 'Christian themes' in *ta'ziya* rituals. Diplomats' attitudes regarding the patronage of these ceremonies are also outlined here.

1. The Safavid precedent
The commemoration of the drama of Karbalâ (Imâm Husayn's martyrdom, 61 AH/680 AD) had a lengthy background both in Iraq and Iran before the Safavids (1501–1722) declared Twelver Shi'ism as the state religion of Iran.[3] Shi'ite commemorations, including pilgrimages, were not limited to the Shi'ite community. Early in Iraq and at least from the Seljuq period (eleventh–twelfth centuries) in Iran one can see Muslims of various creeds participating in these mourning rites (*a'zâ-dârî*) and in the reciting and writing of elegies (sing. *marthiya*) and, later, more specific 'books of murder' (*maqtal-nâma/maqâtil*).[4] Even the *Rawzat-al-shuhadâ'*, the text-book of Shi'ite preachers (hence called *rawza-khân*) was written by a Naqshbandî Sûfî in 908/1502–3.[5]

Since the Safavids experienced difficulties in imposing the Shi'ite faith

---

* The idea of writing this study sprang from research on Ambassador C. A. Murray's case with the Persian government about inviting diplomats to official *ta'ziya-khânî* performances (see p.220). In my efforts to retrace C. A. Murray's correspondence in this respect, I received advice from Miss A. K. S. Lambton (in London, 1978) and unpublished private documents from Mrs E. Murray (in Edinburgh, 1979), whom I beg to accept my gratitude.

in their dominions, it seems that great efforts were exerted by Shah 'Abbâs I (1588–1629) to encourage the development of traditional mourning customs and particularly those focused on the commemoration of the tragedy of Karbalâ. Although information regarding the socio-religious status of the various participants in Shi'ite rituals at this juncture is both scanty and rather late, it seems that individuals from non-Muslim minorities may have been admitted in some way to popular commemorations such as Muharram ceremonies.[6] This may have influenced the admission of European Christians to these commemorations. However, due to the paucity of our information, it is difficult to know where and when invitations were first extended to them.

In 1637, under Shah Safî (1629–42), Adam Olearius together with the other members of the mission of Frederick, Duke of Holstein, were invited at Ardabil by the governor to the celebration of the 'Aschur' (*'âshûrâ*) on the tenth day of Muharram; mournful ceremonies were (exceptionally) followed by fireworks in honour of the ambassadors.[7] In 1667, under Shah Safî II (1666–94, crowned by the name of Sulaymân), J. B. Tavernier was invited to watch the celebration of 'la fête célèbre de Hossein et de Hussein, fils d'Ali' (i.e. Hasan and Husayn, whose names are constantly proclaimed together by the mourners in their dirges sung in processions). This invitation of Tavernier – together with a party of Dutchmen probably belonging to the Dutch East India Company – had been made through the favour of the 'Nazar' (*nâzir*) or 'Grand Maître de la Maison du Roi'.[8] These Europeans were seated in a good place over-looking the royal *maydân,* opposite the huge ceremonial balcony of the palace where the Shah was sitting surrounded by his retinue (i.e. Âlî Qâpu).

From Tavernier's account, it appears that Dutchmen were more easily invited to these ceremonies than other foreign residents. This confirms the economic influence which the Dutch East India Company enjoyed in Persia in the mid-seventeenth century. According to Melton, a member of that Company, a party of Dutchmen was invited through the Nazar, 'Great Master of the King's House', in 1673, to watch the same cere-monies, apparently from the same place.[9]

There were, of course, many other travellers, diplomats and residents who could watch Muharram and other religious ceremonies in Safavid Persia. Although they provide us with precious (and generally reliable) accounts of what they actually saw, they very seldom let us know whether or not a formal invitation had been extended to them. Typical in this respect is the account of the well-informed French traveller, Jean Chardin, who says in his description of *rawza-khânî*, without further detail: 'Je me suis trouvé à ces sermons . . .', which roughly means: I happened to be present at these (elegy-singing) sermons.[10]

2. Later developments of some 'Christian' themes in ta'ziya rituals

Considerable improvements in the dramatic aspects of these ceremonies were made in the seventeenth and eighteenth centuries. Some particulars of 'Safavid' Shi'ite rituals spread to Iranian-controlled areas (mostly to the Caucasus) and to the Indian sub-continent and farther east; in these faraway countries, their most dramatic developments were not, however, retained. Some old themes of the commemoration could promote feelings of sympathy towards followers of pre-Islamic monotheism, i.e. Jews and Christians.[11] These themes are generally centred on the miracles performed by Imâm Husayn's severed (and speaking) head, brought by his enemies to Kufa and Damascus together with other martyrs' heads and the survivors of Husayn's family. Among these old themes, one can find the story of a prior of a Christian monastery who 'bought' (for one night) Imâm Husayn's head from the soldiers on their way to Damascus. After seeing and hearing the proofs about Imâm Husayn's martyrdom, he converted to Islam. The gold he had given to the soldiers turned later on into dust.[12] In later compilations of accounts related to Imâm Husayn's martyrdom and its revenge, the above story seems to have split in two. We have, on the one hand, the prior of the monastery who converts to Islam together with all his monks[13] and, on the other hand, an envoy of the Byzantine Emperor (Qaysar-i Rûm) to Yazîd's court in Damascus; this envoy cursed the caliph for having ordered the killing of Hasan and Husayn.[14] In further accounts, which found their way into marthiya-khânî (elegy-singing) and ta'ziya-khânî, this ambassador converted to Islam and was slaughtered by Yazîd's men, thus becoming a martyr.[15] In further developments in ta'ziya-khânî, there is a story of a Christian king who converts to Husayn's cause in even more fictitious circumstances.[16]

Whatever may have been the original spring or link between these stories, the theme of the 'Elci Farangi' (i.e. the Frankish envoy or ambassador) was well spread in the commemoration. It was represented with pageantry in Muharram processions.[17] The presence of this 'Elci Farangi' in ta'ziya-khânî – sometimes shown as sacrificing his life in interceding with Yazîd to spare the lives of Imâm Husayn's family – undoubtedly favoured the admission of foreign diplomats to these ceremonies. From the late Safavid period, one can see persons in charge of organising pageants and mystery plays, borrowing from foreign residents some props to present the play of the Elci Farangi at Yazîd's court. These consisted mostly of clothes for the ambassador and his attendant, among which were the indispensable hats. Early in the eighteenth century, these props were borrowed from English or Dutch visitors or residents to represent pageants on chariots.[18] This practice was to be widespread in Qajar Persia.

3. Diplomats and 'Christian' themes in ta'ziya-khânî *under the early Qajars*
Invitations of European envoys to *ta'ziya-khânî* representations are well
documented in the first half of the nineteenth century. Available evidence starts from the very beginning of the rivalry between French and
English missions. Among the diplomats and scientists who accompanied
the French military mission of General Gardane, there are two who left
detailed accounts in this respect. In 1808, A. Dupré saw at Shiraz the
representation of Imâm Husayn's martyrdom in the Prince Governor's
palace.[19] At the same time, the rest of the French mission could attend the
ceremonies patronised by Fath 'Alî Shah (1797–1834) in Tehran. A vivid
description of them is provided by J. M. Tancoigne.[20] The French mission
was not invited for the last day of the commemoration. According to
Tancoigne's report, the Shah wanted to spare the legation the sight of the
murder of a 'Greek ambassador' whom Yazîd ordered to be put to death
for having interceded in favour of 'Husayn's brother'.[21]

After the temporary removal of the French from the diplomatic scene
in Iran, English diplomats were invited to Muharram ceremonies. One
year after Tancoigne's account, in 1809, James Morier could attend these
ceremonies in different places in Tehran. He could even see the Elci
Farangi's *majlis* (representation, literally 'sitting') in the house of Amîn
al-Dawla, Hâjjî Muhammad Husayn Khan Isfahânî, in the presence of
the 'Prime Minister' (Mîrzâ Safî Mâzandarânî), the British Envoy, Sir
Harford Jones, and others.[22] This *majlis* tended to become in a way
compulsory in the *ta'ziya-khânî* 'répertoire'. It moved considerably the
Muharram celebrants, including Qajar dignitaries.[23] In 1811, Morier
returned to Persia as secretary to the embassy of Sir Gore Ouseley,
'Ambassador Extraordinary and Plenipotentiary' to the Persian court.
He remarked on the influence of the story of the European ambassador
on the Persians, saying that 'the population was in consequence inclined
to look favourably upon us'. On the eighth night of 'the Muharram', 'The
great vizier invited the whole of the Embassy to attend his takieh'. Official
ceremonies of the tenth of Muharram (*'Âshûrâ, Rûz-i qatl,* etc.) were
organised on the *maydân,* in front of the palace. British diplomats were
invited to see the representation of Husayn's martyrdom. They were
accommodated in a small tent 'over an arched gateway, which was
situated close to the room in which His Majesty was to be seated'. At that
time, negotiations on an Anglo-Persian treaty were in progress. Important British support (military and financial) was expected by Fath 'Alî
Shah. British diplomats were therefore lavishly entertained. Magnificent
pageants were displayed on the *maydân,* the most conspicuous items in
the processions being 'four led horses caparisoned in the richest
manner'.[24] Jewels from the royal treasury were used on these occasions.
According to Ouseley, who describes the same ceremonies for the next

year (1812), the various decorations (jewels, carpets, tapestries etc.)
exhibited on the *maydân* were probably more valuable than any props
ever displayed in a European theatre.[25] Apart for the Qajar treasury (the
richest part of which came from Nâdir Shah's booty in Delhi), valuable
presents, including jewels, had been offered by Jones and Malcolm to the
Shah and his ministers. The heavy cost of these gifts had been borne by
the East India Company. Sir Gore Ouseley's expenditure on presents was
less impressive.[26] Battle scenes were represented with large quantities of
horsemen in full array.[27]

In the years following Persia's defeat against Russia and the humiliat-
ing treaties of Gulistân (1813) and Turkmânchây (1828), a climate of
xenophobia – kindled by some religious elements – apparently prevented
Iranian officials from inviting foreigners to Muharram ceremonies. However, after these troubled years, diplomats (at first, mostly Russian
envoys or agents) regained some favour and managed to attend or to be
invited to these ceremonies. The Polish orientalist Alexandre Chodzko,
who arrived in Tehran in 1831 and acted as Russian consul at Rasht, in
Gîlân, provides us with the first collection of *ta'ziya-khânî* dramas.[28]
These probably represent the 'official répertoire' under Fath 'Alî Shah in
the late years of his reign. The Elci Farangi's *majlis* is significantly absent
from this collection. During Chodzko's stay in Iran (from the end of Fath
'Alî Shah's reign until the beginning of that of Muhammad Shah), the
most popular theme was 'Un monastère de moines européens'.[29]
Chodzko probably attended the 'célèbre représentation' given by Mîrzâ
Abu'l-Hasan Khan 'Elci' Shîrâzî at Tehran in 1833, as an ex-voto for the
recovering of his son from illness. This representation lasted fourteen
days and was lavishly given; magnificent cashmere shawls were displayed
together with jewels borrowed from the royal *haram*, the value of which
was estimated to about three million francs.[30] Mîrzâ Abu'l-Hasan Khan
was himself a diplomat since he was the first Qajar envoy to London. He
was also pensioned by the East India Company.[31] His *takya* built near his
residence was then probably the most famous in Tehran and its fame
remained in the 1840s.[32]

Under Muhammad Shah (1834–48), while diplomatic friction between
Russia and Great Britain was centred on the Herat question, France
played again the part of a possible third power able to provide military aid
to Persia. After the elimination of Mîrzâ Abu'l-Qâsim Qâ'im Maqâm
(1835), this period was dominated by the government of Hâjjî Mîrzâ
Âqâsî (1835–48). Although British diplomats and residents were less in
favour, some of them at least were still invited to Muharram ceremonies.
Captain Richard Wilbraham arrived in Iran in the middle of 1836. He was
invited in Tehran to a local *takya* and lent chairs and uniform to help
represent the Elci Farangi's *majlis*.[33]. This became a common practice in
the following years. 'Actors' from one of these 'theatres' borrowed the

'tricorne' hat and other elements of the costume from the French mission.[34] Lady Sheil tells us that in Sarâb (Mâzandarân), Persians borrowed her husband's hat and the jacket of the 'Elchee Fering' now called 'Elchee Inglees' there. In Tehran, horses and chairs from the English mission were requisitioned for private representations in town.[35] French diplomats and other French residents who held more or less official missions were then invited to Muharram ceremonies, even occasionally by provincial governors.[36]

Ta'ziya-khânî performances then underwent a great development. To meet the need of accommodating large crowds, there followed the construction or transformation of many permanent or temporary Muharram gathering places (*takya, husayniyya, kârvânsarâ,* palaces or bourgeois houses provided with balconies, terraces and gardens and so on. The *takya* of Mîrzâ Abu'l-Hasan Khan was still one of the best in Tehran.[37] But the most influential and impressive *takya* was the one built by the great vizier Hâjjî Mîrzâ Âqâsî.[38] It seems that the only foreign diplomats invited to this *takya* under his mandate were his neighbours from the Russian mission.[39] The Elci Farangi's theme was increasingly popular. It moved Muharram audiences and enhanced the diplomats' prestige, particularly amongst women.[40]

Ta'ziya-khânî performances had then become such a common feature of Persian social life that even Russian and British missions had a (temporary) *takya* set up on their premises.[41] Foreign diplomats and residents thus contributed to the patronage of Muharram ceremonies. This contribution went even further, for there is evidence that Russian agents or diplomats acted as customary patrons of these ceremonies. Chodzko himself may well have been a kind of initiator in this matter. Amidst the pathos of his first article on Persian theatre (intermingled with translations of Persian official and literary figures of rhetoric), he clearly states that he had spectacles of a tragic and comic kind performed at his own expense.[42] Another diplomat, Count Simonitsch – the Russian Minister Plenipotentiary (*vazîr mukhtâr*) who backed Persian efforts to reconquer Herat in the years 1837–8 and enjoyed good relations with prominent *'ulamâ'* – appointed 'a hundred ducats per annum for the expenses of the month of Muharram'. Italian born, Count Simonitsch fought in Napoleon's army. He was made prisoner at Moscow and ultimately sent to Persia after the tragic murder of Griboëdov and the Russian legation in 1829. According to the fashion of the *'ulamâ'*, he used to wear a black *'abâ* (given to him as a robe of honour) when visiting high ranking 'mullahs' of Tehran during religious festivals.[43]

4. The exclusion of diplomats from Muharram ceremonies

At the beginning of Nâsir al-Dîn Shah's reign (1848–96), the status of official Muharram ceremonies remained more or less the same. In fact, during the first ten years, following the example set up by his father, he left the care of organising these celebrations to his ministers.[44] The inviting of diplomats to such festivities had been restricted so far to welcoming at one time limited groups of people connected with foreign missions. A great improvement in this respect was made by Mîrzâ Taqî Khan 'Amîr Kabîr' (whose government lasted from 1848 until 1851). This minister invited the whole British and Russian missions to official Muharram ceremonies in Tehran, probably in his predecessor's *takya*. Diplomats came with their wives. The Queen mother, Mahd-i Awliyâ' and ladies from the Shah's *andarûn* were also present.[45] In spite of the great amount of studies published on Amîr Kabîr – generally reckoned as the initiator of important reforms in Persia – his attitude towards *ta'ziya-khânî* remains unclear. The above initiative does not tally with what is generally said of his dealings in this respect.[46]

Amîr Kabîr's invitation was probably not renewed and remained unique in Qajar Persia. Inviting foreign diplomats or residents to these ceremonies tended to be left to the initiative of Persian individuals ranking from the Shah to dignitaries or private persons. This tendency resulted from a rivalry of influence between civil and religious power; in this struggle, not only the invitation of non-Muslims was at stake but also the religious legality of performing such dramas. Whether or not Amîr Kabîr took measures against *ta'ziya-khânî* performances, one learns that under his mandate a French diplomat was invited by the governor of Isfahan to watch Muharram ceremonies and *ta'ziya-khânî* organised on the Maydân-i Shah from the terrace of the 'Âlî Qâpu – 'the very place whence Shah 'Abbâs attended public festivals'.[47]

The most precise threat to these invitations came under the vizirate of Mîrzâ Âqâ Khan Nûrî (1851–8). As soon as he could gain control over Muharram ceremonies, this *sadr-i a'zam* went beyond Hâjjî Mîrzâ Âqâsî's own initiatives in this respect. He and officials under his control widely promoted Muharram ceremonies and particularly *ta'ziya-khânî* performances in Tehran. Since there is no clear mention of the construction of any important new *takya* in the capital in the first years of his mandate, one may well suppose that he used Hâjjî Mîrzâ Âqâsî's *takya* which he styled 'Takya Dawlat' or 'Takya Dawlatî'.[48] However, there is no evidence that he invited any diplomats or foreign residents there.[49]

Although Mîrzâ Âqâ Khan Nûrî had been formerly employed by the British legation, the most serious diplomatic friction and even armed conflict between Persia and Britain occurred under his vizirate.[50] While the question of Herat remained unsettled, most of the troubles arose from British protected subjects. The case of Hâjjî 'Abd al-Karîm led to a brief suspension of diplomatic relations in 1853.[51] But real difficulties came with the arrival of the Minister Plenipotentiary, C. A. Murray, in Tehran in April 1855. It was then announced that Murray intended to make the Persian government respect its unilateral engagement of January 1853 on Herat. Although Murray inherited his predecessors' errors regarding British protection rights, his stubborn championship of Mîrzâ Hâshim Khan and his wife irritated the Persian court and government. His insistence on obtaining for the British legation an invitation to official Muharram ceremonies and the obvious lack of support from the French ambassador, Prosper Bourée, in his demand for redress about the Shah's and his *sadr-i a'zam*'s allegations with respect to Mîrzâ Hâshim's wife (a Qajar lady related to the Shah) were too much to bear. In November 1855, he hauled down his flag and went to Tabriz and then to Baghdad.[52]

An edict excluding diplomats from Muharram ceremonies appeared before Murray's final troubles, in Zu'l-Hijja 1271/September 1855. This was made by the *sadr-i a'zam* who alleged that he was complying with the injunctions of the *'ulamâ'* in this respect.[53] Murray in his turn retorted that, prior to his arrival, diplomats had been repeatedly invited to these ceremonies which, he said, were placed under the entire control of the Persian government. As he could obviously not obtain redress, he went as far as to declare that he could well advise his government and the governor-general of India to take measures against Muharram ceremonies in India, the performance of which was placed under government protection there. The only effect of this and other threats was that Mîrzâ Âqâ Khan reluctantly granted him (through the 'Master of the Mint') a vague promise of an invitation to a government-sponsored *ta'ziya* in the citadel for the next Muharram.[54]

In this same year, Muharram ceremonies were celebrated with fervour in Tehran well beyond the first ten days of the month (Muharram 1272/September–October 1855). The next year, official celebrations, both religious and civil, were enhanced by Persian military success at Herat. The new 'Takya Dawlatî' was then inaugurated near the Shah's summer palace at Niyâvarân (Muharram 1273/September 1856). After the Anglo-Persian war, Murray left Baghdad for Tehran where he arrived in July 1857. Together with other recriminations, he soon renewed his demand to obtain, as promised, an invitation for the British mission to attend official Muharram ceremonies (Muharram 1274/August 1857). In his correspondence in this respect, Mîrzâ Âqâ Khan included, in his turn, various matters regarding unsettled problems of the Anglo-Persian conflict. This wore out Murray's patience and he eventually refused an invitation granted *in extremis* with much reluctance.[55]

5. Diplomats and 'Christian' themes in ta'ziya-khânî *after the exclusion measure*

Among the various questions which were raised by the *sadr-i a'zam* and even by the Shah in the correspondence related to these invitations (both in 1855 and 1857), there was a repeated concern about the lack of available space in the existing *takya*s to accommodate an increasing number of diplomats in Tehran. Inviting them would have meant excluding Persians from these celebrations.[56] It has been wrongly stated that Nâsir al-Dîn Shah then endeavoured to build or repair *takya*s in the capital.[57] In fact, there is still some doubt about the viability of the newly built *takya* at Niyâvarân in the first years of its existence.[58]

One thing remains certain: the measure of excluding diplomats from the official celebrations, which occurred after the arrival of the ill-starred Murray, was to influence the subsequent evolution of *ta'ziya-khânî*. Whether the original idea came from the *'ulamâ'* or whether it was enforced to comply with their injunctions, there were increasing attacks on officially sponsored *ta'ziya-khânî*; these came both from *'ulamâ'* and from members of the Persian élite, ranging from various intellectual opponents to reformist and even conservative elements. It remains also certain that diplomats experienced greater difficulties in obtaining invitations to official *ta'ziya-khânî* performances. This was probably the case with Gobineau who was then in Tehran (1855–8: French Chargé d'affaires from October 1856). Although he ridiculed Murray's fruitless efforts to get an invitation, he probably never attended these ceremonies in presence of the Shah, even during his second stay at Tehran as French Minister in 1862–3.[59]

Although Gobineau remains a precious source of information, he does not indicate the relative importance of each *majlis* of the 'répertoire' in the early 1860s. The theme of the Elci Farangi – which was to become the most theatrical pageant in Nâsir al-Dîn Shah's *Takya Dawlat* – was apparently eclipsed by new Christian themes such as the *majlis* of 'La fille chrétienne' which was 'composed' and represented then.[60]

In spite of the increase in the number of fixed *takya*s in Tehran in the 1860s, there is no evidence of diplomats being invited to royal or government sponsored *ta'ziya-khânî*. Even after the construction of the huge circular *Takya Dawlat* in Tehran (which became operational in the 1870s), one can see diplomats deploring these circumstances. Such is the case with A. H. Mounsey, second secretary in the British legation in Vienna, who says that in spite of the borrowing from Europeans of articles required for the clothes of foreign ambassadors, 'Christians are now as absolutely excluded from these performances, as they are from all the mosques and the baths used by Mussulmans'. He had to content himself with witnessing some acts performed in a private 'bourgeois' *takya* belonging to a personal friend.[61] Whenever Europeans (diplomats or others) could attend *ta'ziya-khânî* performances in *Takya Dawlat* this was possible through personal invitations from officials entitled to occupy their particular lodges or boxes; this included ladies from the *andarûn*, Qajar princes and (seldom) the Shah himself. Among the beneficiaries of such invitations one can find Madame Carla Serena who could attend a performance in the lodge of the Shah's favourite 'Aniseh-ed-Dowleh'.[62] She says that Europeans admitted to these performances had to wear on their heads the Turkish 'fez' or the Persian 'bonnet' to avoid offending the public.[63]

Despite continued opposition by clerics and other elements against *ta'ziya-khânî*,[64] individual Europeans managed to get invited not only in Tehran but also in provincial *takya*s. Among them, S. G. W. Benjamin, the first American ambassador in Persia, deserves a special mention for his admirable and lengthy description of *ta'ziya-khânî* performances in *Takya Dawlat* in the mid-1880s. He speaks of the difficulty for non-Shi'ites of gaining access to the royal *takya*. He was himself invited there by the 'Zahir-i Dowlêh', 'Grand Master of Ceremonies' (a son-in-law of the Shah), into his box. Like others, he had to disguise his nationality and religion and make 'a concession to popular feeling by wearing a Persian kulâh'.[65]

As time went on, access to Muharram ceremonies became apparently easier for some diplomats and foreign residents. Some of these observers were more critical about the dramatic aspects of these commemorations which were on the verge of decadence. In 1888, the eminent British scholar and orientalist E. G. Browne could 'watch' a *rawza-khânî* (he then says *'rawza-khwân'*) given 'on a splendid scale' by the prime minister Amîn al-Sultân in his house. The next evening, he accompanied several members of the British Embassy to the 'Royal *tekyé*'. Although he was impressed by the playing of the actors, he noticed the intrusion of Qajar bad taste in the *mise-en-scène*.[66] He also fancied that 'the Persians are, as a rule, not very willing to admit Europeans or Sunnite Muhammadans' to these ceremonies. On another evening, he could 'visit some of the smaller *ta'ziyas* and *rawza-khwâns*' with his servant in disguise.[67] Dr C. J. Wills – who spent some years in Persia with the Indo-European telegraph department – was invited to attend a *ta'ziya-khânî* at Shiraz by the prince governor.[68] He had the same opportunity at Isfahan.[69] Wills described more the material and social aspects of the commemoration (stage, 'actors', public, women, etc.) than the inner feelings of the mourners. He was interested in the biblical stories incorporated into the *ta'ziya* repertory. He also remarked on the disapproval of the 'higher class of the priesthood'.[70] Dr Feuvrier, one of the last medical doctors of Nâsir al-Dîn Shah, was invited in 1889 by the monarch himself (in a lodge next to his) at Takya Dawlat. He was, to say the least, not impressed at all by 'cette insipide représentation' of Husayn's martyrdom.[71] One of the last lengthy descriptions of Takya Dawlat is provided by E. Aubin. He gives a detailed account of *ta'ziya-khânî* as they were represented there in 1907, together with a repertoire of the ten days' performances. The *majlis* of Bâzâr-i Shâm (which included the Elci Farangi's scene) was still represented on the ninth day, before Imâm Husayn's martyrdom on the tenth day of 'Âshûrâ.[72] Even after the decline of Takya Dawlat, Christian themes continued to evolve in *ta'ziya-khânî*s, as is shown by the *majlis* entitled 'Kânyâ, King of Farang'.[73]

6. *Prospective research and remarks*

There are, of course, many other accounts and various aspects of the relationship between Muharram ceremonies and diplomacy which could not be mentioned in this limited survey. Among the questions requiring further investigation are:

(1) To determine the exact role played by the *'ulamâ'* with respect to *ta'ziya-khânî* in general (some were favourable, some were opposed to their 'theatrical' developments as well as to other 'fanatical' or even degrading aspects of the commemoration) and to the exclusion of diplomats or other unwanted persons from Shi'ite ceremonies.

(2) To investigate the intrusion of diplomats or other foreign residents in the socio-economic system of the Shi'ite community in matters of patronage of these ceremonies. Apart from isolated cases such as the setting up of *takya*s on the premises of the British and Russian legations or direct sponsoring by Russian diplomats (see above), there seem to have been some other similar initiatives.[74]

(3) To study the impact of diplomats or other foreigners' presence on Muharram ceremonies. In some instances, there was even direct participation of non-Muslims in the performance (willingly or otherwise, such as in the case of Russian prisoners who played the enemies). The efforts of foreign scholars to investigate the remnants of these ceremonies in remote places which contributed, together with more recent initiatives from Iranian intellectuals, to bringing about a revival of *ta'ziya-khânî* in the 1960s (on television, at festivals, etc.) should also be taken into consideration, for they enlarged the possibilities of contact between Muharram celebrants and foreign guests. A study of *ta'ziya-khânî*'s audiences (one can hardly say 'spectators') including these elements might well be undertaken with the help of new methods of investigation, such as semeiology, the use of which was inaugurated by Professor A. Wirth.[75]

As a concluding remark, I would like to point out that – due to the lack of substantial indigenous information – it remains obvious that very little would be known about Muharram ceremonies and *ta'ziya-khânî* without the precious observations of diplomats and European residents in Persia. They also provided drawings, photographs and, most of all, texts of elegies and *ta'ziya-khânî* which would have been otherwise irretrievably lost. These extend from Chodzko's collection (33 dramas, 1833) to that of the Italian ambassador in Tehran, Enrico Cerulli (1,055 dramas, collected in the 1950s, see *Elenco*). Between these two important collections, one can find those of Sir Lewis Pelly (37 dramas, in English translation)[76] and Wilhelm Litten (15 dramas). Both Pelly and Litten were diplomats.[77]

ABBREVIATIONS

Le culte:	J. Calmard, *Le culte de l'Imâm Husayn, Etude sur la commémoration due Drame de Karbalâ dans l'Iran pré-safavide,* thesis, University of Paris III (Sorbonne), March 1975.
Elenco:	E. Rossi and A. Bombaci, *Elenco di drammi religiosi persiani* (fondo mss. Vaticani Cerulli), Vatican City 1961.
Jung:	A. Chodzko, 33 dramas, Bibliothèque Nationale, Paris, Catalogue Blochet, Supplément persan, no. 993 (*Jung-i shahâdat* is the name given by Chodzko to this collection: see n.28).
Kâshifî:	Husayn Vâ'iz Kâshifî, *Rawzat-al-shuhadâ' (Garden of Martyrs),* ed. Ramazânî, Tehran 1341s.
Litten:	W. Litten, *Das Drama in Persien,* Berlin and Leipzig 1929.
Mécénat I:	J. Calmard, 'Le mécénat des représentations de ta'ziye, I. Les précurseurs de Nâseroddin Châh', in *Le monde iranien et l'Islam,* II, Paris-Geneva 1974, 73-126.
Mécénat II:	J. Calmard, 'Le mécénat des représentations de ta'ziye, II. Les débuts du règne de Nâseroddin Châh', in *idem,* IV, Paris 1976-7, 133-62.
Pelly:	Sir Lewis Pelly, *The Miracle Play of Hasan and Husain,* 2 vols, London 1879 (reprinted in England in 1970).
Ta'ziyeh:	P. J. Chelkowski, ed., *Ta'ziyeh: Ritual and Drama in Iran,* New York 1979 (based on the proceedings of the international symposium on *ta'ziya,* at Shiraz in August 1976).
Le Théâtre en Perse:	A. Chodzko, 'Le Théâtre en Perse', in *La Revue indépendante,* XV, Paris 1844, 161-208.
Théâtre persan:	A. Chodzko, *Théâtre persan, choix de téaziés ou drames traduits pour la première fois du persan,* Paris 1878.

NOTES AND REFERENCES

1. L. P. Elwell-Sutton, 'The literary sources of the ta'ziyeh', in *Ta'ziyeh* (1979), 167-81.
2. As I stayed in Tehran only for a few weeks, I could not go through all available sources kept there. I had no opportunity to resume my research on the spot and only parts of the documents which I saw then have been exploited in my second article on *ta'ziya* patronage. To this day (Jan. 1983), I have published only three articles on *ta'ziya* patronage: *Mécénat I* (1974); *Mécénat II*

(1976-7); 'Le patronage des ta'ziyeh: Eléments pour une étude globale', in *Ta'ziyeh*, 121-30.

3. See Calmard, *Le culte*.

4. *Idem*, 'Le chiisme imamite en Iran à l'époque seldjoukide d'après le *Kitâb al naqd*', in *Le monde iranien et l'Islam*, I, Genève-Paris 1971, 43-67 (see 63-7). This subject is studied at length in *Le culte*, 84ff. I am preparing a study on the first available *maqtal-nâma* in Persian (of the late Timurid period?).

5. Husayn Vâ'iz Kâshifî, *Rawzat-al-shuhadâ'*. On the author and his book, see Calmard, *Le culte*, 286-418, 519-70, and index.

6. At the beginning of this century, votive offerings (*nazr*) from non-Muslims were accepted at each Muharram in regions near Baku (see I. Lassy, *The Muharram mysteries among the Azerbaijan Turks of Caucasia*, Helsingfors 1916, 62. See also *Mécénat II*, 138, n.20).

7. *Vermehrte Newe Beschreibung Der Muscowitischen und Persischen Reyse*, Schleswig 1656 (reprint, Tübingen 1971, 457).

8. *Suite des voyages . . .*, Rouen 1724, II, 84. The 'Nazar' was probably the *Nâzir-i Buyûtât*, on which see V. Minorsky, *Tadhkirat al-Mulûk*, London 1943, 118f.

9. Eduward Melton, *Zeldzaame en Gedenkwaardige Zee en Land Reizen*, Amsterdam 1681, 312. There is still, however, some doubt about the genuineness of Melton's account. The date he gives (3 July 1673) does not correspond to the month of Muharram. The nearest 10th of Muharram ('*Âshûrâ*' day) to fall in July would be in 1077/1666 or 1078/1667, the latter date corresponding with Tavernier's account!

10. *Voyages . . .*, éd. Langlès, Paris 1811, IX, 54.

11. It seems that most of these themes originally sprang from legendary accounts of miracles accomplished by Husayn's blood or by his (speaking) head. See Kâshifî, 359ff. (study and translations in *Le culte*, 402-9, 543-7). Direct Christian influence on the early development of Husayn's legend and cult is not analysed here.

12. For an early account of this story in Persian, see *Târîkh-i Sîstân*, ed. M. Bahar, Tehran 1935, 99f.

13. Kâshifî, 372-5; cf. *Le culte*, 405.

14. Kâshifî, 382f.; cf. *Le culte*, 409, 545-7.

15. This became the famous play generally entitled *Bâzâr-i Shâm* (see *Elenco*, Indice, 358). In Kâshifî's account, the Byzantine envoy's conversion to Islam had taken place before and he kept his faith secret in Rûm.

16. See Charles Virolleaud, *Le théâtre persan ou le drame de Kerbéla*, Paris 1950, 115ff. ('Le roi Kania', from Litten, no. 12); see also *infra*, n.73.

17. The first substantial account is provided by William Francklin, *Observations made on a Tour from Bengal to Persia in the Years 1786-1787*, London 1790 (in his chapter entitled 'Pageants and Ceremonies during Mohurrum', 246ff.).

18. *Lettres édifiantes et curieuses écrites des missions étrangères*, Paris 1780, IV, 212f.

19. *Voyage en Perse*, ii, 314-17. On this account see *Mécénat I*, 80f.
20. *Lettres sur la Perse et la Turquie d'Asie*, Paris 1819, ii, 3-10; cf. *Mécénat I*, 81.
21. Tancoigne, *op. cit.*, 8-9.
22. *A Journey through Persia . . .*, London 1812, 194-7.
23. 'The prime minister cried incessantly' said Morier (see *Mécénat I*, 82, n.23).
24. J. Morier, *Second Journey through Persia . . .*, London 1818, 175-84. Morier provides drawings of certain elements in procession, including Husayn's horse being led (see *Mécénat I*, 85, n.31).
25. W. Ouseley, *Travels . . .*, London 1823, iii, 162ff. (165, see *Mécénat I*, 86f.).
26. Sir Denis Wright, *The English amongst the Persians*, London 1977, 35.
27. Ouseley, *op. cit.*, iii, 168. On this we have the concomitant testimony of Gaspard Drouville (see *Mécénat I*, 87).
28. *Jung* (33 dramas acquired at Tehran in 1833: see *idem, Djungui Chehâdet*, Paris 1852, Preface).
29. *Jung*, no.30, translated by Chodzko in *Le Théâtre en Perse* (1844), 190-208, reprinted in his *Théâtre persan* (1878), 179-219.
30. *Idem, Le Théâtre en Perse*, 165 (see *Mécénat I*, 88).
31. Wright, *op. cit.*, 7.
32. *Mécénat I*, 89ff.
33. R. Wilbraham, *Travels in the Transcaucasian Provinces of Russia*, London 1839, 421.
34. *Mécénat I*, 94, n.61 (quoting E. Flandin).
35. *Ibid.*, 121, n.157 (after Lady Sheil, *Glimpses of Life and Manners in Persia*, London 1856, 126).
36. In 1839, C. Texier was invited by the governor of Gulpâygân to attend *ta'ziya-khânî* in the courtyard of his palace (see *Mécénat I*, 92ff.).
37. *Mécénat I*, 89f. and map 124f.
38. A lengthy account of this *takya* is provided by the Russian orientalist I. N. Berezin, *Puteshestvie po severnoj Persii* (Travels in Northern Persia), Kazan 1852. A critical analysis of Berezin's testimony on *ta'ziya-khânî* (*op. cit.*, 297-347) is provided in *Mécénat I*: 94ff.; on Hâjjî Mîrzâ Âqâsî's *takya*, 100ff. (and drawings, 108-9).
39. *Mécénat I*, 196f. (after Berezin).
40. *Ibid.*, 121, n.157 (after Berezin who notes: 'During the representation, women often looked towards our lodge, when the Elci was speaking').
41. *Ibid.*, 95 (after Berezin).
42. Chodzko, *Le Théâtre en Perse*, 162.
43. See 'Confidential print', FO 881/4135 (Public Record Office at Kew Gardens), 26 (this report is in French).
44. This has been studied in my *Mécénat II*.
45. *Mécénat I*, 111f. (after Sheil, *op. cit.*, 126); *Mécénat II*, 145.

46. The position of F. Adamiyat on this matter is criticised in *Mécénat II*, 145ff.
47. On Muharram 1267/November 1850. This diplomat was Amédée Querry, 'drogman' (secretary-interpreter), then 'chancelier' of the French legation in Tehran (see *Mécénat II*, 146, n.48).
48. *Mécénat II*, 154ff.
49. Contrary to what H. Algar asserts in his *Religion and State in Iran 1785-1906*, Berkeley and Los Angeles 1969, 158 (see *Mécénat II*, 160, n.95; see also below, n.53).
50. *Mécénat II*, 147ff. See also my forthcoming article 'The Anglo-Persian war 1856-7' in *Encyclopaedia Iranica*.
51. This has been studied in detail by A. K. S. Lambton, 'The Case of Hâjjî 'Abd al-Karîm . . .', in *Iran and Islam*, Edinburgh 1971, 331-60.
52. *Mécénat II*, 157f.
53. According to Hidâyat (*Rawzat al-safâ-yi Nâsirî*, Tehran 1339s., x, 788), the presence of diplomats at *ta'ziya-khânî* (he does not say when they could attend them for the last time) was too much to bear for the *'ulamâ'*. In consequence, the *sadr-i a'zam* decided to exclude them from these ceremonies, an exception being made for His Excellency Haydar Efendi, 'Chargé d'affaires' of the Ottoman State. The dating of this measure is provided by an extensive correspondence preserved in London (Public Record Office, FO 60/203, copies at the India Office Library and Records, PS/9/156).
54. A very concise summary of this correspondence is given in *Mécénat II*, 158.
55. *Ibid.*, 159. In spite of thorough research in London and Edinburgh, I could not find any trace of this correspondence either in official or in Murray's private papers. Most of the letters between Murray and the *sadr-i a'zam* on this matter have been fortunately preserved in Persian in the archives of Farrukh Khan Amîn al-Dawla, edited by Karîm Isfahâniyân and Qudratallâh Rawshanî (see vol. II, Tehran 1347s.; documents nos 114, 115, 117, 120, 123, 134, 136, 137; I have prepared translations and commentaries on these documents which are not put in chronological order).
56. *Mécénat II*, 159 (both the Shah and his *sadr-i a'zam* expressed their concern about this lack of space in the existing *takya*s).
57. By Algar, *op. cit.*, 158, n.37 (see *Mécénat II*, 159, n.91; the *Mir'ât al-buldân-i nâsirî*, II, 195 quoted by Algar refers to *takya*s in Shiraz, not in Tehran).
58. See *Mécénat II*, 160f.
59. On the caution with which Gobineau's statements should be viewed, see *Mécénat II*, 135ff. (142f. on the *'takya* du roi' and others).
60. On this drama, see A. Gobineau, *Religions et philosophies dans l'Asie centrale*, Paris 1957, 395ff. (and *Mécénat II*, 137f.). For the text, see *Elenco*, 363 (with references to Pelly and Litten).

61. *A Journey through the Caucasus and the Interior of Persia,* London 1872, 312.

62. *Hommes et choses en Perse,* Paris 1883, 187. She says she was invited by His Majesty (i.e. the Shah) to watch a *ta'ziya* in the favourite's lodge.

63. *Ibid.,* 181.

64. Attacks against these commemorations (theatrical performances, ceremonial mortifications and street fightings causing many casualties etc.) and other aspects of religiosity under Nâsir al-Dîn Shah went far beyond the few hints gathered by Algar, *op. cit.,* 156ff. This important problem will be analysed elsewhere.

65. *Persia and the Persian,* Boston 1887, 365-406 (see 381ff. ; drawing of the 'Takieh or Royal Theatre', 373).

66. *A Year amongst the Persians,* London 1893, 551f.

67. *Ibid.,* 553.

68. *In the Land of the Lion and Sun or Modern Persia,* London 1883, 125ff.

69. *Idem, Persia as it is,* London 1886, 125ff.

70. *Idem, In the Land . . .,* 283.

71. *Trois ans à la cour de Perse,* Paris n.d., 139ff.

72. *La Perse d'aujourd'hui,* Paris 1908 (on *ta'ziya-khânî* and *Takya Dawlat,* see 169ff.).

73. On this *majlis* (Litten, no. 12), see Charles Virolleaud, *Le Théâtre persan ou le drame de Kerbéla,* Paris 1950, 115ff. See also *Elenco,* 364 (with reference to Pelly, Litten and Vatican's collections). There is an obvious evolution of this kind of theme between Chodzko's *Jung* (1830s), Pelly (1860s) and Litten (1920s) : see Virolleaud, *op. cit.,* 116, n.1.

74. Although this is a poor indication, the (British) Imperial Bank of Persia sacrificed a sheep in honour of the passage of the *dasta* of Muharram mourners in Mashhad. God's blessings on the Bank were asked by 'the leading Saiyid in charge of the procession' (see C. E. Yate, *Khurasan and Sistan,* Edinburgh 1900, 144ff.).

75. *Semeiological Aspects of the Ta'ziyeh,* in *Ta'ziyeh,* 32-9.

76. Pelly (1879) ; most of the dramas seem to have been collected in the 1860s from a 'Persian who had been long engaged as a teacher and prompter of actors' (Preface, p.iv) ; in spite of thorough research, I could not find the Persian text of these dramas.

77. Pelly served in Persia first as Secretary of the legation (1859), then as political resident in the Persian Gulf (1862-73) ; see Pelly's Preface (*op. cit.,* I, iii-iv). Litten was German consul in Baghdad (see Litten, Friedrich Rosen's Introduction, iii).

13

Majlis-i Shâhinshâh-i Îrân Nâsir al-Dîn Shah

Ta'ziya is a passion play commemorating the suffering and death of Imâm Husayn and his companions, on the plain of Karbalâ', on the 10th day of the month of Muharram, in the year 61 AH/680 AD. The *Majlis-i Shâhinshâh-i Îrân Nâsir al-Dîn Shah* is a *ta'ziya* play to commemorate the death of Nâsir al-Dîn Shah, who was the patron and prime promoter of the *ta'ziya* drama in Iran.

Scholars believe that the *ta'ziya* as a dramatic-theatrical form is a result of the fusion of the centuries-old mourning rituals for Husayn, such as *rawza-khânî* and *dasta*. What the scholars disagree upon is the date when that fusion finally took place. Now it appears that the birth of this fascinating dramatic form could conceivably be pushed back to the late Safavid period, from the conservative reckoning of the second half of the eighteenth century. The scholars are in complete agreement that this drama reached its fruition during the Qajar period. During the Qajar reign the rapid development of *ta'ziya* occurred in play writing, acting, staging and construction of special theatre buildings.

This flowering was in great measure due to the support and the active interest in the *ta'ziya* by the Qajar shahs. Emulating their monarchs, the well-to-do and the high ranking dignitaries of Iran had helped greatly in the development of the *ta'ziya*. However, this rapid growth would not have been possible if it were not for the great interest in and love for the *ta'ziya* among the people. In addition to its religious significance as an act of expiation – according to the popular religion, participation in the *ta'ziya* is a step towards salvation – *ta'ziya* became a popular form of entertainment. This development encouraged a longer staging of *ta'ziya* – extending it from the first ten days of Muharram until the end of the following month of Safar. By its inclusion in the repertory of plays devoted to the local saints (*Imâmzâdas*) both the time and scope of the *ta'ziya* had been extended. In addition, people wanted the *ta'ziya* to be performed upon successful completion of a pilgrimage or a return to health. *Ta'ziya* became part of a vow or a pious act of gratitude, giving thanks for the answered prayers or simply an entertainment to pass the time. Now it is performed throughout the year.

Ta'ziya plays in general can be divided into two groups: those which belong to the Muharram repertory and those which do not. The former are nevertheless the core of the latter repertory. The non-Muharram plays are never performed during the mourning days of Muharram and they even include comedies. The fact that some *ta'ziya* are of a humorous nature constitutes a contradiction in terms, because the original meaning of *ta'ziya* is condolences, expression of sympathy. As in its European medieval counterpart, *ta'ziya* became an open-ended cycle capable of accommodating into its framework any event occurring between the day of Creation and the day of the Last Judgement. Time and space in *ta'ziya* are dream-like. The events do not necessarily follow chronological order, but each play must be directly or indirectly related to the Karbalâ tragedy. This connection is accomplished by a digression (*gurîz*), which usually appears at the end of the play. This device might take the dramatic form of several bloody scenes of Karbalâ' or a description of those events interjected orally into the play.

During the reign of Nâsir al-Dîn Shah (1848–96) *ta'ziya* reached its zenith. The Shah was a great lover of this art, giving it financial and moral support. He built the great *ta'ziya* theatre, *Takya Dawlat*, the actors and producers of which were paid from the royal coffers. It is therefore not surprising that a *ta'ziya* was composed commemorating his sudden death at the hands of an assassin.

The *ta'ziya* under consideration, *Majlis-i Shâhinshâh-i Îrân Nâsir al-Dîn Shah*, is a non-Muharram play. A manuscript copy of it belongs to the Cerulli collection in the Vatican library and is catalogued under the number 156 by E. Rossi and A. Bombaci in their book *Elenco di drammi religiosi persiani*, Vatican City, 1961. In reality, what appears under this number are two manuscripts of different authorship. One is in the form of a libretto, a *jung*. The other is in the more usual form of *ta'ziya* manuscript in which the part for each character is written separately. The parts are usually connected with the help of an index called a *fihrist*.

Unfortunately, the index to our manuscript is not complete and sometimes does not correspond to the contents. As for the *jung*, it is not complete either.[1] This is not unusual; in fact, it is typical of *ta'ziya* manuscripts. The manuscripts have often been altered and improved upon by actors and producers. Entire sections from plays dealing with the same themes but written by different authors move from one manuscript to another.[2] In our case both manuscripts appear to be copies, probably made by the actors, whose handwriting and spelling were often faulty.

One part of the copy under investigation appears to be a *gusha*, that is, a part which could be added or removed according to the circumstances in which the *ta'ziya* was performed.[3] In this case, the variable part involves the crown-prince, Muzaffar al-Dîn who lives in Tabriz. Upon learning about the assassination of Nâsir al-Dîn Shah, he sets out for Tehran in order to bury the Shah and ascend the throne. In the main text, the prime minister writes a letter to the crown-prince, informing him of his father's death but in the *gusha* the crown-prince receives a telegram. Parenthetically, the fact that the prince was temporarily buried in the huge *Takya Dawlat* reinforces the link between the Qajar shahs and *ta'ziya*.[4]

The play (*majlis*) may be divided into three parts: in the first part Nâsir al-Dîn Shah is suffering from depression. All possible distractions suggested by his prime minister are of no avail. The spell of melancholy is finally broken by a veiled person (*naqâbdâr*) appearing to him in a dream. This common *ta'ziya* device usually occurs in the centre of the acting area, leading the audience to believe that the following scene is the enactment of the dream. The veiled apparition and the sleeping person carry on a conversation. In the case of Nâsir al-Dîn Shah, he is visited by an unidentified apparition. The qualities of the veiled person and the Sûfi undertones of the text suggest that the apparition must be Imâm 'Alî. The first part of the *majlis* ends with the prediction of the Shah's assassination. This is also commonly found in the major *ta'ziya* dramas. The heroes are sometimes aware of their future, at other times they are not.

As in other *ta'ziya* plays, the pace of the first part is very slow with many verbal repetitions. In the second part the pace quickens. The Shah, following the advice in his dream, goes on a pilgrimage to Shâh 'Abd al-'Azîm only to be assassinated there. After the assassination the prime minister tries to conceal the Shah's death as he is afraid of the outbreak of civil disturbances. This is a historical fact which is made obvious in the text. What is interesting in this part is the deep concern of the Shah for his people. This royal benevolence is a result of religious influence.

Philosophically speaking, the first two parts should be considered as a pretext for the third, which is the crux of the *ta'ziya*. The *gurîz*, a digression concerning the martyrdom of Husayn and his companions, takes the form of *rawza-khânî*, which can either entail spoken lines only, or which can be narrated in front of a backdrop of actors representing the Karbalâ' scenes. The Imâm Jum'a addresses the congregation from the top of the *minbar*; the audience becomes the congregation in the mosque. He is both the preacher and the narrator. In the play on several occasions the prayers are performed. This is a very important device in the *ta'ziya* plays to make out of the audience the real participants.

The analogy of the martyrdom of Husayn with that of Nâsir al-Dîn Shah is of great significance. Possibly critical in this analogy is the clerics' identification of the Bâbîs as the Shah's assassins. Nâsir al-Dîn Shah, a victim like Husayn, naturally became an inspiration to the *ta'ziya* playwrights.

The text

At the royal palace in Tehran.

SHAH: A thousand thanks to the Lord of day and night for bestowing the throne of fortune upon the Qajars. Thanks to my efforts and my

231

blessed good offices, to my auspicious endeavours, the land of Iran has been filled with ambergris and sprinkled with the fragrance of the musk of Tartary. But I am sad today; in my sight the day has become tarnished like dark night. There is no desire in me for wine nor for the beloved. I do not want to stroll in the garden or to go hunting. Where is the great man of the court, the famous vizier? Call him to come to me in the utmost urgency.

NÂ'IB (Lieutenant): O illustrious and most famous Vizier of the august Shah, the Shah has ordered that you come to his presence.

SADR-I A'ZAM (from now on called Vizier): Thanks to the eternal creator of day and night for the stability of our fortune. Salutations, O *qibla* of the world, may I be your ransom. O monarch at whose doorstep a hundred emperors act like the lowest servants. Greetings! O Shadow of God! My God, the creator of the universe, be your protector. May the evil eye be kept away from your pure countenance. Enunciate your command to me, O King of Iran, so that I may sacrifice my life for you.

SHAH (to Vizier): O Prime Minister, tell me where you have been, as you have been away from me for quite a while.

VIZIER: I have been occupied with the worship of God. I have been praying, out of my loyalty for the Shah.

SHAH: Meanwhile, O Vizier, grief has entangled me. My heart is bound fast by sorrow and anxiety. O Vizier, take pity on me and find a remedy, because my heart is covered with the rust of grief.

VIZIER: O Owner of the Crown, Throne and Kingdom, one hundred emperors are begging at your doorstep. Should the Shah turn for satisfaction to hunting, let us travel to the plains and spend some days there until the sorrow leaves your mind.

SHAH: O Prime Minister, my faithful Vizier, go and make preparations so that we may go to the plains.

VIZIER (to servants): The order of the Sultan, who represents the strength and the dignity of the state, to the servants of Nâsir al-Dîn Shah is that he desires to make an excursion to the plains for recreation. Alert the guards that the Shah is sad, and that hunting will relieve the sorrow of the Shadow of God. O Shah's brave men, everyone should be aware of this command of the Shah and that he is going on this expedition to hunt in the plains today. All you chiefs, see to it that preparations for the journey are made. Load the provisions onto the backs of the camels. All of you should saddle the horses and start on the journey. Let the beating of the drums be heard everywhere proclaiming readiness for the journey.

VIZIER (to Shah): The travelling party is ready to depart. What is the order of the majestic crown, O Shah?

SHAH: O Prime Minister, order a swift soft-paced horse to be brought so that I may go on the riding expedition.

VIZIER: You obedient servants, bring the horse for the sublime Shâhin-shâh. (To Shah) O King, I have made ready your swift horse. Put your conquering foot in the stirrup.

SHAH: O Vizier, give the command to beat the drums for the departure. Now we go hunting, going towards the plain.

VIZIER (to servants): Announce the marching order of Nâsir al-Dîn Shah by beating the drums.[5]

SHAH: Again thanks be to the Lord of day and night that he bestowed the throne of fortune on the Qajars. O forgiving and merciful One, I do not know why these sorrows do not leave my heart. O kind and good-natured Vizier, where are you? Come close. Melancholy has again overcome me and turned the day into darkest night. I have no desire for wine or the beloved. I have no mind for the garden nor for the pleasures of hunting. This approach to hunting has increased my sadness. I am turning back to the city, towards home. Vizier, order the drums to sound retreat. I am going home with a mournful heart.

VIZIER: Obedient servants, play the drums for retreat. Make haste to turn back to the city.

SHAH (at the royal palace): The sun is setting and my melancholy deepens. Bring me a cup of coffee. (After drinking coffee.) Order the servants to bring the water pipe so that the smoke of my heart may reach the sky. (After smoking the water pipe.) O Vizier, a cloud of anguish covers my heart. Now describe for me the state of affairs of my subjects.

VIZIER: O you, at whose doorstep a hundred Caesars pay tribute, your fame has spread to the east and west. All the people constantly pray for the Shah. All live in dignity at the pleasure of the state.

SHAH (to Vizier): O Vizier, I have the heartfelt wish to resolve my problems by love and loyalty. I will invite all my subjects, old and young, to be my guests so that I can entertain them with kindness.

VIZIER: I cannot disobey your orders, O fortunate and glorious Shah, but I should like to suggest humbly that it is not possible to be the host to all the citizens of Iran, although it is possible for the Sultan to do them a kindness. Should you desire to do all your subjects a favour, then absolve the citizens from paying taxes, such as the tax on slaughtering.

SHAH: Well done. Bravo, O Vizier, you have made me happy. Indeed you have been, are, and will be a real prime minister. Go and announce countrywide that the Shah has absolved all his subjects from the slaughtering tax. Record this, O prime minister, so that the land of Iran will remember me, so that the many citizens will be praying for me. I will always be in their thoughts and memory.

VIZIER: Whatever you command, I am your obedient servant. Your word

and order are a grace for my soul. (Turning to herald.) I am addressing you, O heralds: Carry the order of the Shâhinshâh to the bazaar.
Proclaim to all the people, old and young, that the Shah has made a
great offer to his subjects:

The slaughtering taxes have been removed by order of the *qibla* of
the world who thinks about his people. In return, offer up your
prayers to the Shah since the Shah has made such a magnificent offer
for God's sake.

HERALDS: O people of the city, both young and old, put aside your
sorrows and rejoice.

Women, men, great and minor *shaykh*s, carpenters, citizens and the
poor, listen and know this, so that you can be relieved from suffering
and hardship:

His Majesty, the Shadow of God, our monarch, Nâsir al-Dîn Shah,
has bestowed a favour upon his subjects as a sign of his affectionate
love. The Shah has remitted all slaughtering taxes, so that citizens in
towns and villages will hereafter not be liable for these taxes. In
return, pray for the Shah to free him from his depression.

O merciful God, for the sake of the king of Karbalâ, Husayn, for the
sake of the Prophet, the intercessor for sinners, protect our king
from the wickedness of fate. Keep the evil eye far from our king and
bury his enemy alive. O exalted God, give him victory for the sake of
the five sacred members of the Prophet's Family, keep him in good
health for the sake of the people.

VIZIER (to Shah): O Shâhinshâh, may you always be well and may the
constant flow of sorrow leave you. I have executed your order.

SHAH: Well done! Bravo, O Vizier. Order my supper to be brought. I am
still sad.

VIZIER: Bring supper for the Shah. Singer, release the feelings of your
heart. (To servants.) Then spread his Majesty's bedroll so that he
may rest after the fatigue of the road.

(The Shah goes to sleep surrounded by sentries. The chamberlain tells all
the courtiers to be quiet so as not to arouse him.)

(Enter the veiled dream-apparition, Naqâbdâr.)

NAQÂBDÂR: I stagger under this load of misfortune. I am unable to say
what I foresee, since seeing you means to me that your appointed
time approaches. My heart grieves for the Qajar Shah, as I enter into
his dream, my eyes running with bloody tears. I am going to see him
for the last time because tomorrow he will be bathed in
blood. O king, rest your head in my lap and rid the sorrow from my
soul. My heart burns for you who are in the prime of life.[6] The
heavens glow on your behalf. O king, my heart cries out because of
your predicament, for tomorrow you will be killed at the hand of a
foe. Arise, O source of my sorrows, and look into my tearful eyes.

SHAH: Peace, O Lord of creation and world-keeper.

NAQÂBDÂR: Peace upon thee, O Nâsir al-Dîn Shah Qajar.

SHAH: Where were you, tell me, O king of holy ones? Why, Master, such weeping and lamentation?

NAQÂBDÂR: O king, you do not know about my feelings.

SHAH: Come, come, so that I can console your grief.

NAQÂBDÂR: You don't know what is to befall you.

SHAH: Shall the fire of fate once more afflict me?

NAQÂBDÂR: My heart cries because your life is so short.

SHAH: O diffuser of light, may my soul sacrifice itself for you of the Pure Spirit. May my soul become the ransom for your tearful eyes. Nâsir al-Dîn Shah sacrifices himself for you. I desire that you should consider me one of your slaves, O sublime excellency. I have another wish to ask of you.

NAQÂBDÂR: Divulge your wishes to me.

SHAH: I have a wish, and do not deny it to me.

NAQÂBDÂR: Tell me your wish, O monarch.

SHAH: Wherever you go, take me with you.

NAQÂBDÂR: O do not worry, O Pâdishâh.

SHAH: Truly I want to be your companion.

NAQÂBDÂR: Soon this wish will come true.

SHAH: I have no other wishes to ask of you.

NAQÂBDÂR: Do not grieve and do not weep, Nâsir al-Dîn Shah. Surely I shall accompany you. Sleep, king, I am leaving, goodbye. I am your loving protector. Farewell. If you should have a strong desire to meet me, then come to the shrine of 'Abd al-'Azîm, come in loving friendship.

SHAH (wakes up): The companion of my soul has left me. Now, what is there left to hope for in this world? Announce this to all the viziers and secretaries: They are all to come to me.

SERVANT: Viziers! Secretaries (clerks)! Commanders! The Shah is ordering you into his presence.

VIZIER: Greetings of peace to your Excellency, the shadow of God. Salutations to the sovereign.

AMÎN KHALWAT (courtier): Salutations, O king of destiny and power! Greetings, O glory of the world.

AMÎN AL-MULK (courtier): Greetings, O munificent and liberal king. Greetings, O essence of love and generosity.

SHAH: Since you have sincerely gathered here, I want to say a few words to you. Last night I had a dream which filled me with sorrow. By God, the person whom I am to see in the future I saw in my dream. I pleaded with him, saying, 'Take me with you, O king,' and he said, 'If you really have a strong desire in your heart to see me, then proceed toward the sanctuary of 'Abd al-'Azîm, so we shall meet.'

VIZIER: Praise be to God that the Shah's dream was a good omen, but now we must go toward the plains so that the sadness may leave your heart, O sovereign.

(Several ministers pledge their undying loyalty to the service of the Shah.)

VIZIER: I too am one of the slaves of the royal house. I am ready to sacrifice myself out of loyalty to his Majesty. May my soul and possessions be offered up for the Shah.

SHAH: All your pledges have been made to me, but what do I gain therefrom? Sadness distresses me. Nobody will see what my eyes saw. O magnanimous God, you are the only one who knows the secrets of the heart. What can I do but go on the pilgrimage? O praiseworthy minister, go and make preparations so that we can set out for the shrine of Shah 'Abd al-'Azîm. It will be a good thing to accomplish two wishes at once. I shall make a pilgrimage to 'Abd al-'Azîm and I shall also visit with the beloved.

VIZIER: The word of the Shah is my command. Since the Shah wishes to go on the pilgrimage, all is ready for the journey. Praise be to God that the Shah is content.

SHAH (riding): The foot of endeavour is in the stirrup of the humble pilgrim. In your goodness, O Creator of the World, you promised that you would grant my wish. I am full of pain, please grant me a cure [for it]. (Circumambulating the stage.)

MÎRZÂ RIZÂ (assassin): (Aside.) O forgiving and merciful God, I don't know what to do with my hatred of Nâsir al-Dîn Shah Qajar. Since I have come face to face with unlimited oppression and injustice, I became depressed and tired. I was paralysed by the misfortunes of the world. It suddenly has become possible to do something. I could approach the Shah and revenge myself by doing him in. Then I would always be remembered and until the Day of the Last Judgment, Rizâ will rejoice at his deed. That peerless Shah[7] is making a pilgrimage, so now, God forbid, today I have no alternative than to do my deed. Ever since I became a wanderer from the city of Kirmân I have been wishing a hundred times to complete my deed. It was a lot of trouble to buy this six-shot revolver to kill the Sultan of Iran.

SHAH (still riding): I see the royal sanctuary of his Majesty 'Abd al-'Azîm in the distance, O Vizier. I shall circumambulate the tomb. Come along with me, O excellent Vizier.

VIZIER: Your lunch is ready, O king. After you have eaten, O king of splendour, you may feel inclined to make your pilgrimage.

SHAH (already in the compound of the tomb of the Shah 'Abd al-'Azîm): Before I eat a meal I shall go to the sanctuary, weeping and sighing, 'You are the preserver, my support and a refuge, O God. Even though a thousand enemies have the intention to destroy me, I do not fear them so long as you befriend me.'

NÂ'IB: Make way, O people! Are you not ashamed, creating such a tumult and making so much noise. Go out and be quiet and do not crowd the sanctuary.

SHAH: Vizier, call the servants. There shall be no restricted area today. Nobody should be forbidden to enter, and nobody should interfere with the business of others.

VIZIER: The Shah, generous as he is, has commanded that anybody may enter the sanctuary. In order to preserve our Shah let everyone pray for him with all his heart.

(Responsive shouting.)

MUTAWALLî (custodian of the shrine): May who ever prays loudly be not without words at the time of his own death.

SECOND CUSTODIAN: Repeat these verses in unison: Blessed be the ruby lips of the Prophet.

THIRD CUSTODIAN: May God guard your life.

FOURTH CUSTODIAN: May the Creator of the world assist you. The dust of your court is the collyrium for our eyes. Have the kindness to look after us, the poor. There is no better king than you in the whole world. You are the overlord of all rulers.

(At the sepulchre.)

SHAH: Peace be upon thee, O Prince, far from your own homeland, exiled from your city and your life [there]. I sacrifice my soul to you, O illustrious, your Majesty 'Abd al-'Azîm, O monarch, O sovereign. I came to kiss your feet, the light of God, so that I may reach the object of my desire. May I sacrifice myself in sympathy for your exile, deprivation and misfortunes. O Vizier, spread the prayer carpet so that I may say a compassionate prayer. (He prays.)

MÎRZÂ RIZÂ (soliloquises): God removed the sorrow from my heart by bringing the Shah to me. I am not ashamed of my God any more. The time has come for me to do my work. Now I shall carry a petition to the Shah, and out of rancour, I will do my deed suddenly.

(To the Shah) O King, please attend to my humble petition. I need your help. Free me from being abandoned and oppressed. (Shoots the Shah.)

SHAH (after being shot): O Beloved, I gave up my life and my soul for your sake and I am glad. Thank you a hundred times for granting my wish. (Dies, is left upon the stage.)

VIZIER: Alas, Nâsir al-Dîn Shah Qajar has been bloodied by the deed of this wicked assassin. This dog was the murderer of the Shâhinshâh. Seize him! (Soliloquises.) O God, what shall I do with my heart full of sorrow? Fate has blackened my life. O king, why have you become so quiet? Has resentment stupefied you? Remove all the people. The Shah is weary. This grief is choking me. I do not know

237

what will become of the people.

Step aside, O Sadr-i A'zam and consult with yourself. Sit in the corner with your broken heart and think through this difficult matter. O reason, examine this horrible state of affairs. Stay still while meditating and consulting yourself in this misery. Let us see how you will extricate yourself from this situation. The death of the Shah has broken my back. I am afraid Iran will slip from my grasp. Can you show perseverance in this weakened condition, O courageous Vizier? Do not let the people know what has happened. There would be an uproar if they became aware of the situation. This is not easy but it is a very difficult affair requiring a skilled and wise man. If I were to run away from these circumstances I could be responsible for bloodshed [involving] many people. I have no choice in this world, other than to cry to the son of Zahrâ. O son of Zahrâ, envisage my condition and answer my cry for help, O king of the world. You, the just, pious, and innocent king, must know that I do not have the strength for this difficult task. For the sake of your grandfather, O son of Zahrâ, help me out of compassion. What can I do? I have no choice but to use cunning.

'Praise be to God that the Shâhinshâh of the world is safe and sound and that there is no fear for his health.' (He calls Hâkim Bâshî, a courtier, and says:) It is the order of the *qibla* of the world: Now blow the trumpet and have the servants come to attention. Servants, be ready to bring lunch, sorbet, and two water pipes.

(Later.) Servants, harness the horses as the Shah wishes to travel toward Tehran.

Weeping bloody tears, I write a letter to the Shâhinshâh in the city of Tabrîz: Harm and evil should be far from you, O king. Peace be upon thee, O Shah. May the whole world be at your service. Wishing you good health, I give you bad news. The Shah has been killed treacherously by a certain shameless young man who acted like Ibn Muljam.[8] That scoundrel did his dirty work while the Shah was praying at noon on Friday. [He did it] out of malice. I have arrested the despicable murderer. What do you order me to do? Should I treat him with consideration or cruelly cut off his head? You are urgently needed. Kindly arrive as soon as possible. The country is very much upset. I see trouble all over and I fear there may be disturbances, so please come to Tehran as fast as you can.

(To messenger) Messenger, take my letter to Tabriz quickly. Give it to the Qajar, King of Kings, Muzaffar Shah, the Sultan of the World.

(Messenger departs; to servants) One of you run very fast and bring the Imâm Jum'a [to me]. He is urgently needed.

SERVANT (to Imâm Jum'a): My greetings to you, O exalted among the people of the world, Imâm Jum'a, the light of the eyes of the people.

The prime minister requests your presence to make his humble abode shine with your benevolence.

IMÂM JUM'A (to servant): Go, O servant. I am coming this instant to that blessed prime minister. (Departs.)

IMÂM JUM'A (to Vizier): O Vizier of the Shâhinshâh of Iran, please tell me what is wrong.

VIZIER: How can I tell you? By God, I have no strength to tell you this. May you never meet this fate. The Shah has been killed, his blessed body was rolled in the dust. What can I do, since my day has been turned into night?

IMÂM JUM'A: A thousand times fie upon this careless world. What hatred is shown in this mortal world. How sad for this graceful stature which was as erect as a box tree. May God curse that murderer a thousand times. How can I look upon your body, O Shah? It is time to rend my garments out of grief. This martyrdom reminds me of the martyr of Karbalâ', the exalted Imâm Husayn. If I am not mistaken, the throne of God fell to the ground at the moment when Husayn fell in the dust. The countless armies of the Kufans and the Damascenes rushed to surround Husayn like prickly thorns. Ah, ah, how can I express what they did to my ancestor, what horrible things they have done to Husayn. They have severed his holy head from his body. For three days the corpse of Husayn was lying in the dust of the plain of Karbalâ' unwashed and without a shroud. There was no mother to lift his head from the dirt, no friend to bury his body. Husayn fell without a shroud and had no friend. His body had one thousand, nine hundred and fifty wounds.

VIZIER (while Imâm Jum'a cries): Dear Sir, do not weep bloody tears from both eyes. May the soul of the world be sacrificed for Husayn. Kindly say a prayer for the Shah. (Imâm Jum'a prays in Arabic.)[9]

IMÂM JUM'A: Tell me, O kind Vizier, what should be done in this difficult situation? What I fear is that the populace will get wind of this news and will fight among themselves.

VIZIER: You must go to the mosque, climb up to the minbar, and address the congregation, saying that the Shah was murdered during the noon prayer on Friday and that his honourable soul departed from his body, but tell them that they should not be afraid because Muzaffar al-Dîn Shah has become the Shâhinshâh.

IMÂM JUM'A: I weep as I go to the mosque, thinking of what I must do. O Creator of day and night, I shall climb up to the minbar with the help of God, and I shall tell the story of Nâsir al-Dîn Shah, out of my love for him.

(Four verses of prayer in Arabic.)

May who ever prays loudly be not without words at the time of his death – praise Muhammad loudly. O grieving people in this mosque, listen so that you may hear the whole story, but God forbid that you should be afraid, remember that there is also a pleasant side to life. Be aware that the Shah was killed last Friday and that his blessed body fell into the dust. Despite your grieving and distress [because of him] know that Muzaffar al-Dîn [Qajar] has become your Shah. Keeping in mind this martyrdom remember that martyr of Karbalâ', His Blessed Highness Imâm Husayn. O men and women, beat your heads and breasts while I tell you what happened to my ancestor Husayn. You must participate in the events of the Karbalâ' plain with grief and compassion. Suddenly, when 'Alî Akbar fell to the ground he cried out, 'O beloved father, come!' My ancestor Husayn dashed to his side and with tender love raised the head of his son from the ground, and, weeping, said, 'Alas, that you should be cut down and fall in your youth.' The heavens wept. He sighed and went on, 'Let God be a witness and forgive all the sins of the people of the community of my grandfather and punish the wicked.' How can I truthfuly tell how Husayn stood before those shameless people, shedding tears and saying, 'By God, look at my plight. These blood-thirsty people are killing me while I am thirsty.' Ibn Sa'd cried out to the army, 'O troops, silence that speaker.' My friends, six thousand bowmen fitted arrows to their bows and shot from both sides. So many arrows entered Husayn's body that they stuck on his body like the feather of a *humâ* bird.

[He goes on but the pages are missing in the manuscript.][10]

(In Tabriz.)

CHIEF OF THE TELEGRAPH OFFICE: Long may you live, O Sire. May the Creator of the World be your protector. An urgent telegram has just arrived for you from Tehran.

MUZAFFAR AL-DÎN (reads telegram): Fie upon this unstable world, which rests upon an unstable foundation which allowed the life of the Shah to perish. O God, I do not know how I can help in this difficult situation. There is no other way except to go to Tehran at once. O Vizier, O kind Vizier, see to it that everything should be prepared for the journey. O Vizier, my heart is pierced by wounds. The journey upon which we are embarking will be very difficult. Tell the servants to mount their horses and gallop toward the city of Rayy. O my friends, there is no more time. Direct your steps towards Tehran.

(Soliloquises.) O 'Alî, oh jewel of the sea of light, I need to be inspired by you, O glory of resurrection, O 'Alî, O King of the World, look at my sorry state. O 'Alî, who but you can help me? Who can console Muzaffar al-Dîn Shah? O 'Alî, I am distressed for my subjects. Be generous and have mercy upon them.

O fellow officers, make haste and let the drums and kettledrums signal [our] departure. (After one circumambulation.) The city of

Tehran appears in the distance. I enter the city in deep thought. I shall see the martyred king so that I may utter my mourning.

(Meets Vizier on arrival.) Prime Minister, O vizier of the king. Well done, congratulations, O honourable man. You really have rendered a great service. Bring the robe of honour for the prime minister. Do not grieve. I am your friend in this sad plight. O gallant and vigilant prime minister, tell me where to find the bier [containing] the Shah's body.

VIZIER: May I sacrifice myself for you, Muzaffar al-Dîn Shah, there is the bier with the body of Nâsir al-Dîn Shah.

MUZAFFAR AL-DÎN (to the body): Peace be upon the exalted king. Let my head be an offering to you, Nâsir al-Dîn Shah. How can I bear to look at you, O Shah? I will cut the body of your enemy to pieces. (To Vizier) O industrious vizier of that peerless king, inter the body of Nâsir al-Dîn Shah with proper mourning rites.

VIZIER: According to the order of the *qibla* of the world, Muzaffar al-Dîn Shah, let us set out with the funeral cortege, led by the deceased's horse and dirge singers. [We will go to] the sanctuary of Shâh 'Abd al-'Azîm for the Shah's burial, in the name of the compassionate God.[11]

Acknowledgement

Thanks must be given to Dr B. Warburg and I. Anvar for their assistance in preparing this chapter.

REFERENCES

Bahrâm Bayzâ'î: *Nimâyish dar Îrân*, Tehran 1344.

Jean Calmard, 'Le mécénat des représentations de Ta'ziye', in *Le Monde Iranian et l'Islam*, II, Geneva 1974, 73-126.

Peter Chelkowski, ed.: *Ta'ziyeh: Ritual and Drama in Iran*, New York 1979.

Sâdiq Humâyûnî: *Ta'ziya va ta'ziya-khwânî*, Tehran 1975.

'Abdallâh Mustawfî: *Sharh-i zindigânî man*, Tehran 1334.

Angelo Piemontese, 'La rappresentazione della ta'ziye durante il regno di Nasero'd-Din-Shah (1848-96) secondu lo scrittore persiano 'Abdullah Mostoufi', in *Annuali dell' Istituto Universitario Orientale de Napoli*, new series, vol.13, Rome 1963.

Ettore Rossi and Alessio Bombaci: *Elenco di drammi religiosi persiani*, Vatican City 1961.

NOTES

1. Several sheets of text in the MS seem to be irrelevant to the main body of the text and were therefore not utilised in the translation.

2. Sometimes parts of manuscripts dealing with different themes

have been moved from one MS to another.

3. The author has seen the same *gusha* performed in various *majlis*. *Gusha*s may also be performed as an entity.

4. Muzaffar al-Dîn Shah was buried in the *Takya-yi Dawlat* pending the construction of the real tomb.

5. At the end of the nineteenth century, the *ta'ziyas* prominently displayed pageantry, as is shown by elaborate marches around the central stage. The author of the MS was aware of this processional dramatic feature, and utilised it in his play.

6. Nâsir al-Dîn Shah was 64 years old at the time of his death. Hence, saying that he was 'in the prime of his life' was a typical exaggeration common to all those who are about to become martyrs.

7. It is customary in *ta'ziya* for the villain to extol the virtues of the victim before the murder so that the audience will remember that he is only acting the part but is not himself a bad man.

8. The fact that in the text the assassin Rizâ is referred to as Ibn Muljam is the greatest compliment that could be paid to Nâsir al-Dîn Shah since Ibn Muljam was the murderer of Imâm 'Alî.

9. It is customary for the audience to rise and pray in unison with the actor-preacher.

10. It is quite possible that descriptions of several Karbalâ' scenes are missing in the text of the manuscript. The director of the play is at liberty to expand or contract this part of the play.

11. In the manuscript, there is a passage in which Muzaffar al-Dîn Shah orders the execution of the assassin. There is, however, no appropriate place for it in the text. It was therefore not included.

14

Critical writings on the renewal of Iran

The defeats of Iran during the wars against Imperial Russia (1804–13 and 1828–8) and against Great Britain (1856–7) were alarm signals which shook even some of the nobility and privileged classes, to such an extent that they became aware of the need to take countermeasures. The Shahs and their vassals could not come to terms with the shameful loss of their Caucasian territories sustained during the military conflicts with Russia, whose troops were now coming nearer and nearer to the Iranian border. Moreover, the occupation of Iranian islands and towns by colonial troops under British command constituted another grave danger. They had only recently obtained a foothold in India, and at this time, when Asian and African territories were being colonised, threatened the very existence of Iran as an independent country. Reflection on the causes of the military superiority of Iran's opponents inevitably led to the study of technical achievements, of art and science, and of the advantages inherent in the economy and social structure of Europe. The system of government of the victorious powers, based as it was on law and order, served as a model for the intelligent nobility, who had just awakened from the deepest medieval slumber.

To avert the threatening disaster, the enlightened nobility and bourgeosie were anxious to establish more contacts with Europe, to enlist the help of 'neutral' countries in the reorganisation of their army, to send Iranians to Europe in order to acquire new technical knowledge, and to employ foreign experts in Iran itself. Naturally all these measures remained unsuccessful. The main evil was the absolute monarchy which prevented any democratic change or social reform and the participation of the masses in the country's economic development. In all measures of reform there was no question of any interference with the absolute power of the Shah, the manipulation of the faithful by the clergy, and the income of the princes and governors. Any reformers who exceeded their briefs were beheaded or dismissed. The fate of Amîr Kabîr and of Qâ'im Maqâm may serve as examples.[1]

The Shah was not only the mighty ruler over the life and death of his subjects, he was also wisdom personified, so that all his decisions had to be implicitly obeyed. His courtiers acted even more despotically. They had no difficulty in making use of his easily awakened mistrust to discredit other officials and to have them deposed. These sycophants at the court, entirely motivated by self-interest, intrigued against each other; they instigated disturbances in the capital and in remote parts of the country, and they did not refrain from military conflicts if this would enable them to fill their own pockets.

There were, however, among these functionaries some far-sighted and enlightened men who compared the progress in Europe with the decadence in their own country and who drew the appropriate conclusions. They even dared to record their views on the moral decadence, intrigues, incompetence and corruption of their own colleagues and on the rottenness of the entire system of government. However, their courage seldom extended as far as criticising the monarch, let alone reproaching him for his excesses, outrages and faulty decisions. During their lifetime their memoirs, autobiographies, polemical treatises and critical reflections were kept secret and it was only after the Shah's or their own death that their works were published, either in realistic form or as poems.

Âryanpûr in his literary history *Az sabâ tâ nîmâ*² makes a preliminary observation on the behaviour of the courtiers in the Qajar period. The Russian I. K. Jenikolupov in his book on the poet Mîrzâ Shafi mentions a panegyric from the pen of the poet Fâdil Khan (1784–1829) who in 1829, after the murder of Griboëdov in Tehran, accompanied a prince to St Petersburg in order to appease the Tsar. In this panegyric the poet criticises the villainy of the dignitaries at the court of the Crown Prince 'Abbâs Mîrzâ (1788–1833) who fawned on their master, but who after the Tsar's victory glorified the conquerors like cringing slaves.³

It may be that other poets criticised their contemporaries, though their aggression may not in every instance be attributable to social reasons. One might mention here two contradictory verses of the poet Qâ'ânî (1808–53). On the one hand he talks about his suffering as an individual and on the other hand he deplores the unenviable lot of a court poet in the realm of an autocrat: 'Even if a golden crown were put on my head you would never see me on the threshold of an Amîr's house.' In 1846 when the new governor of Shiraz slighted him and he found himself in dire straits, he wrote: 'I'd better start travelling in search of silver in the hope that by obtaining much of that metal my fate will turn to gold.'⁴ He suffered from melancholia and died mentally deranged in 1853.

When the poet Shaybânî (1856–90) uttered his Cassandra-like warnings they were an expression not only of his pessimistic cast of mind but also of the chaos which rocked the rule of the Qajar dynasty. But those in power took no notice. Notwithstanding his panegyrics on kings and princes, he prophesied that the autocracy of the despots would come to a bad end. He recognised the turbulent state of the country and of the throne when he wrote: 'Surely a clever doctor will be needed to cure the ills of a sick country.' Âryanpûr writes: 'His prophecy was fulfilled; in fact, only a short while later the tottering throne and the crown of the Qajar dynasty collapsed. Never had such views been uttered before the time of Shaybânî; it is obvious that such words could only be published abroad.'[5] What was now needed was not only a complete and drastic change but also a strong ruler who could be master of the situation.

In the course of this process of renewal, prose, hitherto bombastic and overladen with metaphors and parallelisms, underwent certain modifications. It had become simpler and generally more understandable, because the prose-writers could now express their thoughts more directly and, above all, because they did not intend to have their work published during their lifetime. Moreover, they felt that the discontented bourgeosie and poorer classes had to be involved in measures for reform. However, the fear of getting into trouble led them also to make excuses for the Shah and to place the blame for all inadequacies on his advisers and beneficiaries.

Majd al-Mulk, who died in 1881, was one of the first authors to disclose the faults of the government system in his writing. In his tours of duty in Russia and in the Ottoman Empire he became acquainted with European conditions which he compared with the situation in his own country. He scrutinises all sections of the ruling class and characterises them according to their inclinations. He says that the Shah himself is interested in the education and training of his people whom he loves and desires to be treated humanely. He is, however, always surrounded by a crowd of toadies who manage to arouse his interest more in the hunt and in the pursuit of pleasure in preference to affairs of state and to dealing with current problems. The chancellorship is held by a man who is solely interested in his own advantage and who waits to grab the property of those rich subjects who die without heirs. The clergy are afraid that the almighty will afford them no protection if they should champion the cause of those deprived of rights. The worst are the lower clergy, those who from *minbar* and *mihrâb* suppress every call for justice, relying on the support of the rabble. 'The conduct of government in Iran resembles neither the laws of Islam nor the rules and regulations of other nations or states. It is a conglomeration of usages from Turkey, Persia, Tartary, Mongolia, Afghanistan and Asia Minor. These nations conquered Iran over the centuries and left many of their traditions here. These customs have survived right into our own time.' Those educated in Europe also come under attack: 'The Iranian chameleons who have returned from St Petersburg and other foreign cities and for whom the state had to endure many a loss have learned only two things from diplomacy and other branches of knowledge, namely to be contemptuous of the people and to dishonour the nation.'[6]

During the middle of the nineteenth century the socio-economic situation of the population deteriorated more and more. The rivalry between the two neighbouring countries became more pronounced, as one competed with the other in obtaining ever more favours. The Bâbî movement stirred up rebellions and riots, particularly among the poorest classes of the population. This alarmed the ruling class enough to think at long last of some reforms in order to prevent the fall of the dynasty; at the same time sympathisers with change and of course all revolutionaries were being cruelly persecuted.

The nobility and the landowning class who had acquired new incentives by their travels in Europe, and by learning some foreign languages, hoped that they could halt the ruin of the country and prevent the fall of the dynasty by disseminating science and technology. They intended to modernise the country by sending some of their sons abroad and by founding an educational establishment (*Dâr al-Funûn*). Even an uncle of Nâsir al-Dîn Shah, Farhâd Mîrzâ (1818–87), supported the attempt to bring modern knowledge to his fellow countrymen. The king himself, who at first showed great interest in this new school and appointed several European teachers to work in it, soon lost interest in it when he learned that a masonic lodge had been formed within the school which promoted modern ideas and, if not exactly anti-royalist tendencies, certainly markedly anti-despotic ones. The radical minister, Mîrzâ Taqî Khan Amîr Kabîr, was murdered in 1851 on the orders of the ruler.

One of the pupils of the *Dâr al-Funûn* was I'timâd al-Saltana (1843–95). On leaving school he entered the army and rose to the office of minister in charge of printing (*intiba'ât*). Many books, including histories of the Sasanians and Arsacids, were published by him, some of which were written by his staff under his supervision. During his travels to Europe as a diplomat he learned French and probably also English. His interest in ancient and modern history and his positive attitude toward European ways show that he wished to be regarded as a pioneer of progress.[7] A poetic work, entitled *Halsa* (ecstasy) or *Khwâbnâma,* is of some importance. It was later published under the title *A Description of the Decline of Iran.*[8] This work, which also unmasks the miserable conditions at the court of Nâsir al-Dîn Shah, was handed over after the author's death by his widow to the library of the holy shrine at Mashhad.

In this pamphlet, which is like a play, eleven chancellors are called to account, in the presence of mythological as well as historical kings and emperors. In the dock are those who have wielded power since the establishment of the Qajar dynasty. Every one of them is required to admit his deeds and to reveal the intentions which he has cherished and the actions which he has performed, knowingly or unknowingly, causing harm to the country's power and prestige. The rulers ask the questions, whereupon the defendants admit their guilt because of incompetence, weakness or ignorance; judgement is then pronounced by a celestial voice. This trial is initiated by the founder of the Qajar dynasty. He maintains that until 1880 (i.e. until the time when the first concessions were being granted) the news did not engender particular disquiet.[9] In their line of defence certain characteristics of the viziers become clear: one states that when a king succeeds to the throne without any difficulty or trouble[10] – surely an allusion to the pleasure-seeking Nâsir al-Dîn Shah – he does not appreciate the worth of a wise minister and thus his efforts are not recognised; another admits his lack of intelligence and maintains that the Shah has only appointed him in order to consolidate his own position;[11] and a third one stresses that he is suitable only for the teaching profession, lacking all interest in affairs of state, and he says that he does not have the least idea how he has become a minister. Even Amîr Kabîr, who seriously hoped for a renaissance of Iran, confirms that he borrowed 100,000 tûmâns from the Tsar's ambassador which enabled him to pay for the Crown Princes's journey from Tabriz to Tehran.[12]

Within their circle scandalous intrigues dominate the scene. Everyone tries to bring his rival into bad repute with the Shah in order to obtain his position. Nevertheless, eight viziers are acquitted, and they are even honoured by being given a golden crown. One of them, who has provoked the war against England, is condemned for ever to await his fate in limbo between hell and paradise. Another minister, who wanted to sign the contract with Reuter and to subject the whole Iranian economy to the control of a foreign power, is dispatched in chains to hell. In his conduct the last chancellor is utterly merciless, aggressive and malicious; he knows no limits to his greed for power and riches, and he unscrupulously sets the wheels in motion to keep himself at the helm. He intrigues against everybody and never hesitates to play off the Shah against the ambassadors, to lie and to deceive. He entangles the king so deeply in his diabolical machinations that the latter, despite some scruples, grants the concession for the founding of the so-called 'Imperial Bank of Persia', and, in order to preserve political balance and neutrality, makes possible other concessions to the Russians as well. When discussing the problem of this bank the Shah exclaims: 'I expect you to act in such a way that in ten years' time I, your Emperor, won't be execrated by widows and cursed by old men.'[13] And the chancellor replies: 'We have created a bank, an achievement which could hardly be called the act of a traitor.'[14] When there was an epidemic of the plague he did nothing to control it.[15] By bribery he prepared the tobacco monopoly granted to Major Talbot so that the Shah would sign it.[16] By bribes in the form of money or presents it was quite easy to win the favour of foreign diplomats.[17]

As regards the historic accuracy of the events stated, one can only say that I'timâd al-Saltana does not conceal his hostility toward the chancellor. We are dealing here with a poetical work – which is in fact a polemical treatise – in which exaggerations and strongly felt individual antipathies, often overstated, are permissible. The author had the intention of depicting in a poetical dream the causes of the decline – a task which he has convincingly achieved.

I'timâd al-Saltana also translated some tales from French, one of which nearly caused his death. The work, entitled *The Animal's Logic,* describes the fate of a donkey, whose master overburdens it without caring for and feeding it properly, so that it becomes stubborn and unmanageable and breaks its master's neck. The enemies of the author or translator intepreted the story as an incitement to rebellion; and the author believed that the only way he could save himself was to leave his whole property in writing to the Shah. He even feared that this course of action might cause the Shah to execute him. After his death his widow handed the document of the author's testament to the king, who accepted this present.[18]

The same spirit and almost the same contents are found in the *Memoirs of Mîrzâ 'Alî Khan Amîn al-Dawla.*[19] The author and chancellor (1845–1907) was moved, at the time of the efforts by the middle classes to accomplish reforms in the period of Muzaffar al-Dîn Shah (1896–1907), to draft a bill which would remove the economic and social confusion whch had arisen after the murder of his father, and dispel the discontent of the population. But all his efforts to introduce new reforms and regulations were frustrated by the opposition of the clergy, by the greed of those in power and by foreign intervention. He mentions repeatedly in his *Memoirs* that he had never intended to write a history but only to illustrate it by allusion to certain events. He left the book unfinished and it was later completed by others. He makes sometimes biased comments on all the problems of his time. The railways, the construction of which was always obstructed by the two neighbouring countries, the British and Russian concessions, government loans, banking topics, border incidents and adjustments, the dealings with Reuter and the tobacco monopoly are discussed from his own viewpoint and interpreted accordingly.[20] He also suggests that the main cause of the country's decadence is the perpetual struggle for power and prestige, greed and unwarranted ambitions amongst the Shah's officials on the one hand, and the weakness of both Nâsir al-Dîn Shah and his son Muzaffar al-Dîn Shah on the other. His particular interest is the conduct of the kings. Nâsir al-Dîn Shah was a self-seeking, self-willed and obstinate tyrant;[21] once, without first consulting his ministers, he ordered the execution of some soldiers because one of his toadies had alleged that the soldiers had thrown stones at his carriage.[22] He had more confidence in ignorant than in intelligent and experienced men,[23] and he was a slave to his carnal appetites. On his travels in 1873 he had taken so many women with him in his entourage that the Tsar's court did not wish them to have access to the upper storeys of the Kremlin where the Tsarina's bedroom happened to be.[24] He had been so impressed by his travels in Europe that he was willing to accept a number of European institutions. Yet he was so weak that he could not take a stand against those who were opposed to any kind of change. The formation of a number of consultative councils did not produce any effective results.[25] When, after the tobacco strike, the masses urged him to make some concessions to public opinion, he lost all sense of balance.[26] The publication of several Persian newspapers in foreign countries was the penultimate event, which reduced his authority to such an extent that his own chancellor, thinking only of himself, provoked a rebellion of nomadic tribes against the state.[27] He now found his last refuge in his debauchery, and he lost all interest in affairs of state.

The author concludes that the people detested the state so much that they were now determined to rebel.[28] The Shah's inability to surmount the difficulties – especially in the last years of his life – and his conciliatory attitude toward intriguers, as well as his horror of any kind of change, added to his list of failures and encouraged his enemies to put an end to his life by shooting him unexpectedly.

Apart from these critical descriptions in which politicians pinpointed shortcomings, there were also efforts aimed at remedying wrongs. Mustashâr al-Dawla wrote down the experiences and thoughts which he had collected during his three years' stay in Paris[29] in the booklet *A Word*. Opinions as to how the country should be reorganised differed widely. Some believed that this should be done by disseminating and promoting science and technical knowledge. Others, including the author, maintained that only the just treatment of all citizens based on law and order – in other words, on justice alone – could bring about any renewal of Iran. All citizens, whether Muslims or non-Muslims, should have the same rights, and should be treated before the judge fairly and without any clerical interference. He was convinced that all power derives directly from the people. In a letter to Muzaffar al-Dîn Shah he criticises the despotism and corruption of the courtiers, and confirms his demands for equality, liberty and legality; and he prophesies that even if rulers formed no government based on law the course of events would force it upon them.[30]

The work *True Dreams* is of special significance for these changing times. Its authors did not belong to the ruling class but to the middle class – the bourgeoisie who were responsible for the revolution of 1905–11. In contrast to other writers who either kept everything they wrote completely secret or perhaps let it be read by only a very few, these tried to have their work published. The authors of the booklet are resolute young men from Isfahan who do not conceal their anti-imperialist and anti-royalist convictions and who are anxious to become the leaders of the revolution. The most prominent of these are Sayyid Jamâl al-Dîn (1862–1908) and Malik al-Mutakallimîn. Both were murdered by Muhammad 'Alî Shah. As regards the content of the poem, it is not dissimilar to

Dreams by I'timâd al-Saltana. However, the sinners are not in the presence of kings, but before God. On Judgement Day the dignitaries, clergymen, governors and policemen have to account for the sinful deeds which they have committed against their fellow human beings on earth.

The poetic significance and historical value of the work lie in the fact that the guilty are not only reproached in a general way for deeds of brutality, wilful interference in community affairs, fraud and greed, bribery and nepotism, ambition and lust, but also individual cases are examined, which offer an authentic picture of the miserable conditions in Isfahan in the 1880s during the reign of the despot Zill al-Sultân, a brother of Nâsir al-Dîn Shah.[31] At that time, authors chose a dream-story as a safer medium to describe events which they would not have dared to make known openly. When the authors pretend to have seen a dreadful vision, they describe in reality their own and other people's experiences. The culprits admit to having stirred up trouble against speculators, so that they can make common cause with the governor and bring about the ruin and death of many people. The clergy are only concerned with their own advantage. Small pieces of land which belong to poor peasants have been appropriated by rich landowners through fraudulent machinations. Hundreds of clergymen await their fate, which is to be consumed by hellfire. God is amazed at the inordinate number of clergy who make a nuisance of themselves in the town. The hallmark of spiritual dignity for these *mullâs* consists in wearing a huge turban, in pronouncing Arabic gutturals in a croaky manner, and in dressing in a slovenly manner, in order to give an overall impression of holy isolation from the world. Scholarship and erudition are things of the past. When the Almighty examines their documents it becomes obvious that they have exchanged each other's signatures on testimonials, and have in the same way given each other honorific titles like Âyatallâh. They are against new schools, reject progress in any form, and defame their opponents as Bâbîs and atheists. The character sketch of the Governor-General who came to Isfahan with a huge moustache and shabby coat, and left his post as one of the richest landowners, is not worth repeating. This description is similar to the behaviour of other potentates known to us from other works. In his book on the revolution in Iran, Dr Mahdî Malikzâda says: 'The publication of *True Dreams* made a great stir, and thousands of handwritten copies were produced in Iran.'[32]

An apt illustration of the chaotic mismanagement at the Qajar court is found in the autobiography of 'Abbâs Mîrzâ Mulkârâ (1839–98), the elder brother by nine years of Nâsir al-Dîn Shah,[33] who, even if not openly, was secretly hoping for the fall of the Shah, and considered himself a claimant to the throne.[34] The intrigues of their mothers and the interventions of the three neighbouring countries made the situation even worse. There is strong evidence of his hostility towards the Shah, his half-brother, and also toward the princes and courtiers who supported him, a hostility which the sons had inherited from their mothers. The author acquired his democratic views during his 27-year exile in the Ottoman Empire, and through social contact with Turkish democrats who laid the ground for the bourgeois revolution in their own country.

He records his own experience at court. When Muhammad Shah died the mood of the people had become so incensed that the court personnel, at the Queen Mother's instigation, looted the Imperial larder, and the young prince and his family had nothing to eat for 24 hours.[35] Through the machinations of the followers of the new Shah, who was then still at Tabriz, the Crown Prince's residence, a plan was set afoot to blind and then to kill 'Abbâs Mîrzâ. When one of his servants refused to give false witness, according to which his master had had foreknowledge of a plan to assassinate the new king, he was tortured. 'Abbâs Mîrzâ owed his life to the British and Russian ambassadors, who intervened and demanded that he be spared and exiled to Iraq.[36]

It is true that Nâsir al-Dîn Shah at a later date rendered homage to his half-brother, but this only happened because of special political circumstances prevailing at the time. During the war between Iran and Britain (1856–7) his brother showed him special favour by giving him a post and more money, but only out of fear of the British, who might otherwise be provoked to an act of revenge. Likewise his nomination as the representative of Iran at the coronation festivities of Tsar Nicholas II was due to the support which the Tsar's representative showed him.

'Abbâs Iqbâl is of the opinion that the protection granted by the two great powers was aimed at having at their disposal an even more pliable tool before deposing the king. The main part of his book deals with the unmasking of those in power, with the chaos at court, the administrative confusion created by provincial governors, with contradictory and arbitrary edicts, unauthorised powers of the clergy, and, finally, with the weakness and barefaced mendacity of the Shah and the princes. As a keen observer who even took notes during his travels[37] the author could also give an eye-witness account of the lavish life-style of the king,[38] of the bedraggled army,[39] and of the empty promises made by the authorities. His characterisation of his half-brother is unique. In a conversation in French with a French doctor, the latter compliments him on his good command of the language, but he advises him not to reveal this to his royal brother who is full of envy and does not like others to possess any qualities superior to his own.[40] The violation of human rights, above all as regards pleasure-seeking and depravity, is not only the prerogative of the Shah but is aped very quickly by his confidants and other privileged men. Mulkârâ mentions only the orgies of one of the Shah's favourites, an uncivilised owner of a tea-house, who had been promoted by the Shah to a very high position, and to whose wishes even the chancellor and ministers had to attend.[41] He further writes about the licentiousness of another prince whose passions were limitless.[42] It was the privilege of those in power to rob others of their goods and property. The case of one royal Master of the Hunt will serve as an example.[43] From other works there is information about the intrigues of the dignitaries against each other,[44] but it is striking to read of the mutual suspicion of the Shah and his chancellor Mîrzâ Husayn Khan Sipahsâlâr (d.1873). During a journey in the Shah's carriage he, the highest official of the state, insults his king in the most obscene manner. He tells the Shah that he does not possess one single quality from his father, and that he has inherited everything from his pleasure-seeking, promiscuous (*qahba*) mother. He cannot speak the truth, he does not like anyone, he cannot bear to see anybody happy, he spends his time mostly with vulgar, common people, he despises reasonable men, and is disorganised in every sphere except hunting and eating. The joint must always be well cooked, and mandarins and oranges must be available. He never acknowledges services rendered to him. The chancellor concludes that he will kill him and anyone else who serves him well.[45] Mulkârâ is so amazed at this outburst that he says to himself: 'This man is a close confidant, holds the highest position in the state, earns more than 200,000 *tûmân*s (almost £200,000), and yet he is full of anxiety and even fear. Woe unto me, his old enemy whom he has hated since the death of the late king!'[46]

There are no doubt other memoirs of this period which have not yet been published or which are inaccessible to me. The autobiographies, which were published after the establishment of the dictatorship of Rizâ Shah and his son, were composed or formulated more or less according to the prevailing political situation and more often in conformity with the wishes of the ruler at that time. Mukhbir al-Saltana Hidâyat, the Prime Minister of Rizâ Shah for many years, considers it quite normal that applicants for government posts offer the king a valuable present. The fact that the author, when playing chess with Nâsir al-Dîn Shah, always had to lose in order not to risk the ruler's disfavour is an example of the mentality which motivated the Shah's subjects at that time.[47] Noteworthy too is the interpretation of the order made by Nâsir al-Dîn Shah that boxes should be placed in the town so that everyone could put complaints against the government into them. These boxes were soon full of 'silly jokes by rowdies and trouble-makers', so that this initiative caused only annoyance and the order had to be revoked. The whole thing was very amusing. The author therefore concludes as follows: 'A good example is the press at the time of the Constitutional Revolution. It was never to allow freedom of speech.'[48] Apart from glorifying the potentates, most memoirs at the time of the dictatorship consist of self-praise and the enumeration of their authors' merits.[49]

Even if the critical writings discussed above do not have the same

252

importance for the awakening of the Iranians from their medieval slumber, as the literary endeavours of the pioneers of progress at the beginning of the twentieth century – mainly because they usually remained unpublished – they nevertheless reflect the feelings of some intellectuals, who recognised the evil of the country's backwardness but were powerless to remove the causes. One can certainly say that their way of thinking contributed, if only in a small way, to the fall of the Qajar dynasty in 1925.

NOTES AND REFERENCES

1. Qâ'im Maqâm was killed in 1835; Amîr Kabîr was killed in 1851 on the orders of Nâsir al-Dîn Shah.
2. Y. Âryanpûr, *Az sabâ tâ nîmâ*, Tehran 1971, 55.
3. *Ibid.*
4. *Ibid.*, 95 and 98.
5. *Ibid.*, 141.
6. Majd al-Mulk, *Risâla-yi majdiyya*, Tehran 1942.
7. E. G. Browne, *A Literary History of Persia*, iv, Cambridge 1924, 454-6.
8. *Khwabnâma*, Mashhad 1945.
9. *Ibid.*, 12.
10. *Ibid.*, 14.
11. *Ibid.*, 15.
12. *Ibid.*, 24.
13. *Ibid.*, 67.
14. *Ibid.*, 76.
15. *Ibid.*, 114.
16. *Ibid.*, 96.
17. *Ibid.*, 62.
18. Âryanpûr, *op. cit.*, 267.
19. Amîn al-Dawla, *Khâtirât-i siyâsî-yi Mîrzâ 'Alî Khân Amîn al-Dawla*, ed. by H. Farmânfarmâyân, Tehran 1952.
20. P. M. Sykes, *A History of Persia*, London 1915, ii, 373.
21. Amîn al-Dawla, *op. cit.*, 24.
22. *Ibid.*, 25.
23. *Ibid.*, 32.
24. *Ibid.*, 46.
25. *Ibid.*, 80-2.
26. *Ibid.*, 163-4.
27. *Ibid.*, 183.
28. *Ibid.*, 243.
29. Mustashâr al-Dawla, *Yak kalâm*, Tehran 1325.
30. Nâzim al-Islâm Kirmânî, *Târîkh-i bîdârî-yi îrâniyân*, Tehran 1332, 186.
31. *Ru'âyâ-yi sâdiqi*, Tehran 1321. The manuscript available to me consists of 30 sheets of A4 paper each with 35 typewritten lines. It was probably written in the 1930s, based on a text unknown to me. It was unfortunately not possible for me to compare the manuscript with the printed text. Cf. B. Alavi, *Geschichte und*

Entwicklung der modernen persischen Literatur, Berlin 1964, 71-5.
32. M. Malikzâda, *Târîkh-i inqilâb mashrûtiyyat-i Îrân*, ɪ, 196 and 208; Alavi, *op. cit.*, 81
33. *Sharh-i hâl-i 'Abbâs Mîrzâ Mulkârâ*, Tehran 1946.
34. *Ibid.*, 93.
35. *Ibid.*, 2.
36. *Ibid.*, 3.
37. As 'Abbâs Iqbâl writes in the preface to the edition of 'Abbâs Mîrzâ Mulkârâ's work.
38. 'Abbâs Mîrzâ Mulkârâ, *op. cit.*, 10-11.
39. *Ibid.*, 12.
40. *Ibid.*, 60.
41. *Ibid.*, 111.
42. *Ibid.*, 58.
43. *Ibid.*, 61.
44. *Ibid.*, 89.
45. *Ibid.*, 65-6.
46. Another politician, Mahdî Qûlî Khan Hidâyat, maintains that Nâsir al-Dîn Shah was an outstanding politician. Hidâyat wrote his biography during the lifetime of the king and of the dictator Muhammad Rizâ during which anti-monarchical thoughts were not permitted. Cf. *Khâtirât va Khatarât*, Tehran 1950, 90.
47. *Ibid.*, 97.
48. *Ibid.*, 103.
49. An exception may be the work written down by the defence counsel during the proceedings of the military tribunal in 1953, cf. *Taqrirât-i Musaddiq dar zindân*, Tehran 1980. This work was written down by Jalîl Buzurgmihr and edited by Îrâj Afshâr. Of especial interest to us is the passage which deals with the de-thronement of the last Qajar king and the accession of Rizâ Shah in 1925, *ibid.*, 105-13.

15

The Qajar period: an epoch of decadence?

1. First of all we should define what we mean by 'decadence'. The *Century Dictionary* (II, 1478) defines the term as follows: 'A falling off or away; the act or process of falling into an inferior condition or state; the process or state of decay; deterioration . . . *The Decadence* specifically, the last centuries of the Roman empire'.[1] It is fashionable now to accept the idea of a complete relativisation of cultural values: it is common now to consider Dakota thought or Dogon culture as equivalent in value to European culture, the only difference being a difference in *quality* and not in 'value': no primitive or superior cultures exist. I am ready to accept all this, only if it is meant as a weapon against certain forms of exasperating colonialism. But I am not ready to accept it in general. In spite of the danger of being considered a reactionary, I think that there is a practical standard of measurement of progress or regression in culture (I speak of course of a *practical,* empirical standard, not of a *moral* standard). To express it in its simplest and most traditional terms, it is the standard proposed by the Bible in Genesis (Gen. I, 28) when, having created men, '. . . God blessed them, and God said unto them: Be fruitful, and multiply, and replenish the earth *and subdue it: and have dominion over* the fish of the sea, and over the fowl of the air, and over every living thing that moveth upon the earth'. It is not a purely abstract standard, nor a standard too unilateral or 'European' to be accepted. It is accepted – as facts show – even by those cultures that seems to reject its religious or metaphysical origins. Hindu culture, for instance, does not reject tanks, aeroplanes and even (recently) the atomic bomb, in spite of the fact that the general attitude to which we owe all these blessings (or curses) of modern civilisation is metaphysically and theoretically rejected by Hindu philosophers. A further point: the curve progress or regression is not always the same for all domains of a culture. Sometimes a period of decline in political history can coincide with a period of progress in scientific achievements or vice versa. The problem is, as we see, rather delicate and complicate.

2. What is, now, the Qajar period? More or less precisely it is the period of Iranian history going from the advent of the Qajar dynasty (more or

less 1800), up to the advent of the Pahlavi dynasty (1925). It is the nineteenth century, one of the most brilliant in Western history and, allegedly, one of the least brilliant in Iranian history. But is this really so? The Qajar period suffered especially from sharp criticism levelled against it by two trends, very important in the West, Bahât criticism and Pahlavi criticism. It is quite customary in the Bahâ'î circles, mindful of the harsh persecutions against the new faith brought about by the Qajar sovereigns, to define it as a special period of decadence in Iranian culture, and this is partly justified. It is sufficient to read the introduction, written by Shoghi Efendi in English, with many quotations from Lord Curzon's *Persia and the Persian Question*, to the *Dawn Breakers* by Nabîl Zarandî[2] to understand what I mean. Moreover, one of the best connoisseurs of Iran, E. G. Browne, in his various books, insisted on the bad state of clerical and political power in that period, oblivious probably of the fact that the Persian constitutional revolution (1906) which he loved so much, happened just during Qajar times, even if against the despotic Qajar kings.[3] It is enough to quote a single passage of Lord Curzon's above-mentioned book to understand what I mean. 'In a country so backward in constitutional progress, so destitute of forms and statutes and charters and so firmly stereotyped in the immemorial tradition of the East . . . the government of Persia is little else than the arbitrary exercise of authority by a series of units in a descending scale from the sovereign to the headman of a petty village'. From this a certain Victorian prejudice against the so called 'unlimited sexual freedom of the Moslems' is not absent. The same Lord Curzon says with horror that 'Colonel Stuart, who was in Persia in the year after Fath-'Alî's death, gives him 1000 wives and 105 children . . .'.[4] It is clear that all this afforded a good pretext to British and to foreign colonialism in general for intervention in Persia, to save the poor Persians from such a horrible 'backward' state, this being perhaps the real cause of Persia's decadence. But let us now study the different fields of Qajar culture in order to assess whether such a harsh judgement is justified by facts.

3. *Literature.* Even such a sharp critic of Qajar Persia as Browne, admits that[5] 'Qâ'ânî is one of the most melodious of all the Persian poets and his command of the language is wonderful'. He adds immediately after '. . . but he lacks high aims and noble principles'. Apart this moral judgement (which is in my opinion probably true of all the Persian poets, excluding perhaps only Nizâmî) we must say that Qâ'ânî, who was the leading poet of Qajar Iran, is one of the greatest poets of the entire Iranian literature. The fact that he was active especially during Qajar times points to a lack of 'decadence', at least in this sense, in the Qajar period. His originality is also indisputable, and the Victorian judgement on his 'immorality', typical of Browne and certain 'orientalists' is totally out of place.

It is true that in the Qajar period in Iran the so-called 'Indian style' or, to put it better, 'Sâ'ibian style' was abandoned to return again to a 'classical' or even 'pre-classical' decorative style[6] of the Ghaznavid ancient pleiad, but we must not forget that this was also the style of Manûchihrî Dâmghânî,[7] and this last did not lack a powerful originality in expression similar to that exactly demonstrated by Qâ'ânî. Therefore, in literature at least, the Qajar period must not be labelled as a period of decadence. Nor should we forget that, together with the formation of the rather clumsy and Europeanised style of Persian journalism (Persian modern journalistic style was born, we should always recall, in the Qajar period), this is also the epoch of the wonderful 'Sa'dian' style, of the writings of an 'Abd al-Bahâ' or the simple and colloquial style of Nâsir al-Dîn Shah's travelogue in Europe.

4. *Theology and philosophy*. This leads us to speak briefly of the style of the theological and philosophical treatises. Browne himself speaks of the 'popularising treatises [of Shi'i theology] in simple Persian prose'. Actually, the Qajar period is a period of the popularisation of Shi'i theology, introduced by the Safavids in the sixteenth century, with the great Arabic treatises like those of the two Majlisîs or the philosophical Arabic works of Mullâ Sadrâ Shîrâzî, so intelligently studied by Corbin.[8] This popularisation brings with itself a simplification and clarification of the style. In reality, the *'Aqâ'id al-Shî'a* summarised by Browne[9] and composed during the reign of Muhammad Shah (1834–48) is far from being a complicated and difficult treatise, but presents itself as a clear outline of the current popular creed of the Shi'a. Works like those of the great philosopher of the Qajar period, Mullâ Hâdî of Sabzawâr (1798–1878), called by Browne[10] 'the last great Persian philosopher', are certainly of remarkable interest from the point of view of the history of Muslim philosophy, and have been studied by M. Iqbal[11] and partly by me;[12] this author surely writes in a clear and comprehensible Arabic. These modern philosophers were highly revalued and esteemed by Corbin, and their works were recently republished with commentaries by the Imperial Academy of Philosophy (*Anjuman-i Falsafa-yi Îrân*).

The Qajar period also marks the birth of a new religion, though one starting as a Muslim 'heresy', the Bâbî and Bahâ'î movements. Much has been written on it,[13] but it is sufficient to state that this new monotheistic religion, which has recently gained adepts even in Indian villages of South America, in the Pacific Ocean archipelagos, in Vietnam and Laos, not to speak of Europe and the USA, was born in this period and aims at the unification of mankind! Its importance, apart the pretensions of its adepts, is therefore objectively great, and it is not the least boast of the Qajar period.

5. *Science and travels (geography).* Here the decadence is certainly more marked. Modern science, in spite of certain Islamic roots, is chiefly Western, though, as I said in the concluding remarks of my Amsterdam lecture, *Islam as an essential part of Western culture,* '. . . not the least privilege of the catholicity of modern Western science is that of being able to accept as "its own" an Archimedes as much as a Biruni or an Einstein, and also, if it is not corrupted by a basically unhistorical anti-religious prejudice, to admit that Moses, Christ, and Muhammad also contributed to its own most ancient origins'.[14] Only in this sense, that of a broader tolerance and catholicity, may we say that modern science is Western. And really, we find very few traces of all this in Qajar scientific treatises, with their traditional Neoplatonic considerations and their lucubrations on the astrolabe and similar medieval instruments, etc.

But we should not forget the travelogues, a literary and scientific genre in which the Qajar period excelled. I have studied this subject elsewhere, and I hope the reader may know my article of 1953.[15] Relations of travels to Europe or generally to Western countries written in Iran in this period are often little masterpieces of simple (if sometimes naïve) prose: see the travelogue of Nâsir al-Dîn Shah, that by Garmrûdî on the travels of the Âjûdânbâshî in Europe in the years 1838–9, recently published in Iran,[16] and the travel account of Muzaffar al-Dîn Shah in 1900, examined elsewhere in this present volume by Professor G. M. Wickens.

6. *Politics and the press.* It is in this period that the Constitutional movement arose, a movement that finally led to the constitution of 1906; an Iranophile like Browne even went so far as to say that, according to him, the Persian Parliament was even better than the British one! In his book *Press and Poetry in Modern Persia,*[17] and in the fourth volume of his *Literary History of Persia,* he gave numerous examples of late Qajar satirical and political prose, which is the direct ancestor of its modern equivalent. We should not forget that it is just in the Qajar period that we find the kind of 'Muslim progressive' thinker like the novel writer Mîrzâ Tâlibov (1834–1910), the dramatist Âkhûndzâda (second half of the nineteenth century), or the Egyptian historiographer al-Jabartî (1754–1825) who are (for me at least) the most attractive writers of the pre-colonialist period. Influenced by the broader aspects of Islamic tolerance, and already sympathetic (for this very reason) to European political freedom and its (then) moderate nationalism, they tried to create a new political life in their countries, a life that later (in Iran just in the Pahlavi period) degenerated into forms of extremer nationalism of the worst European Fascist type. As Professor D. Ayalon has aptly said of al-Jabartî:'The great process of westernisation which commenced in Egypt in the early nineteenth century, and the beginnings of which our author

still witnessed, made it all the more difficult for the new generation of Egyptian historians to become the continuators of al-Jabartî, who wrote in the Muslim traditional historical style. In its attempt to write history, this new generation suffered from the weakening of its ties with the old Muslim civilization on the one hand, and from the difficulty in adopting the new European civilization on the other'.[18]

Similar statements could be made for Iran. Actually, it should not be forgotten that the best aspects of modern Persian nationalism (often considered a special characteristic of the Pahlavi régime) were born not in that epoch but in the Qajar period. Even the revaluation of the ancient glories of pre-Islamic Iran, that assumed in the neo-Achemenianism of the Pahlavis its worst aspect, had started in Qajar times, perhaps already at the time of Fath 'Alî Shah, though, more wisely, the Qajars preferred the Sasanian empire, better known to Muslim Iran and whose continuity with post-Islamic Iran could perhaps be more easily demonstrated, to the Achemenid one, which was after all discovered chiefly by Western orientalism.

7. Concluding these rather haphazard remarks, we might say that, far from being an epoch of decadence, the Qajar period in Iran is culturally the last flourishing period of Shi'a Islam. After this, alas, short-lived period, Iran (and the Muslim world at large, perhaps), instead of giving new contents to methods only formally traditional, under the influence of the new thought and forms brought by the West (a West that in ancient times had been in its turn influenced by Islamic culture), often preferred to 'throw away the baby together with the bath water' and, renouncing some formally obsolete traditional appearances, renounced also certain positive contents of these. Or, as it is demonstrable now in Iran, in an (initially positive) reaction to all this, Iran has fallen again into the forms and contents of the traditional (and now obsolete) culture. The real decadence in Iran started therefore just in the Pahlavi régime, so much extolled even by certain Western orientalists.[19] The reaction to the Pahlavis should not mean a reversion to a hardly existing Utopian 'Medina state', but rather, perhaps, to Tâlibof or to Âkhûndzâda in modernised forms.

NOTES AND REFERENCES
1. *The Century Dictionary. An Encyclopedic Lexicon of the English Language,* London 1899, II, 1478.
2. *The Dawn Breakers. Nábil's Narrative of the Early Days of the Bahá'í Revelation,* New York 1932, pp.XXXVIII, XLVIII.
3. Browne expresses this view in all the works cited in this chapter.
4. This is quoted in *The Dawn Breakers, p.*XL.
5. Browne, *A Literary History of Persia.* IV. *Modern Times (1500-1924),* Cambridge 1924, 329.

6. A. Bausani, 'Letteratura neopersiana' in A. Pagliaro-Bausani, *Storia della letteratura persiana*, Milan 1960, 318ff.
7. *Ibid.*, 329ff.
8. H. Corbin, *En Islam iranien*, Paris 1972, IV, 54-122.
9. *Op. cit.*, 381-402.
10. *Ibid.*, 411.
11. M. Iqbal, *The Development of Metaphysics in Persia*, Cambridge 1908, ch.VI.
12. Bausani, *Persia religiosa*, Milan 1959, 403.
13. See the bibliographical summary in Bausani's articles 'Bâb', 'Bâbîs', 'Bahâ'u' llâh', 'Bahâ'îs' in *Encyclopaedia of Islam*, new edition, Leiden 1954.
14. *Idem*, 'Islam as an essential part of Western culture' in *Studies on Islam*, Amsterdam 1974, 36.
15. *Idem*, 'Un manoscritto persiano inedito sulla ambasceria di Husain Hân Moqaddam Ağûdânbâšî in Europa negli anni 1838-39', in *Oriente Moderno*, XXXIII (1953), 485-505.
16. M. Mushîrî, *Sharh-i ma'mûriyyat-i Âjûdânbâshî . . . dar safârat-i Otrîsh, Farânsâ, Inglistân . . .*, Tehran 1347 Sh./1968.
17. Cambridge 1914.
18. D. Ayalon, 'The historian al-Jabartî', in *Historians of the Middle East*, eds B. Lewis and P. M. Holt, London 1962, 391ff.
19. G. Lenczowski (ed.), *Iran under the Pahlavis*, Stanford, Calif. 1978.

16

Some remarks on the early history of photography in Iran

1. The introduction of photography to Iran
Contemporary accounts. Among the documents from the reign of Nâsir
al-Dîn Shah, perhaps the earliest information about the introduction of
photography to Iran is the extensive account in the section dealing with
the events of the year 1280 AH/1863–4 in the third volume of the *Mir'ât
al-buldân-i Nâsirî*[1] written by I'timâd al-Saltana (Sanî' al-Dawla). The
relevant pages are as follows:

> . . . One of the new sciences belonging to and branching from the
> natural sciences which has found currency and shown advancement
> during the reign of the present Shah is photography. [Here the writer
> inserts material dealing with the principles of photography, its tech-
> nique and history] . . . Towards the end of the reign of that pious
> King and Fighter for the Faith, Muhammad Shah, may The
> Almighty clothe him in light, Monsieur Richard Khan[2] who at
> present teaches English and other languages at the Dâr al-Funûn
> used, with much toil, to take pictures on silver plate. In the early part
> of the reign of our present Shah, may our souls be sacrificed for him,
> when the Dâr al-Funûn was built, Monsieur Krziz[3] the Austrian
> artillery instructor, made some photographic experiments on paper.
> Monsieur Focchetti, the biology teacher, was the first person to use
> the collodion process at the Tehran College; and Monsieur Carlian
> [?][4] who had accompanied Farrukh-Khân Amîn al-Dawla[5] from
> Paris to Tehran in order to propagate the science and methods of
> photography, made the use of the collodion process widespread. . . .[6]

The next source of information is from the same author's *al-Ma'âthir
wa 'l-âthâr*[7] where, under the heading 'The promotion of the science and
craft of photography' he writes,

> This craft, which is a branch of the natural sciences, has gained
> currency and become widespread during the present reign, although
> an example of it can be found in the latter part of the reign of
> Muhammad Shah in the work of Monsieur Major Richard Khan, the
> teacher of French and English, etc. But the origin of the propagation
> and the process of perfecting the craft and disseminating the art of
> taking pictures which is called photography is one of the great

contributions of the present reign; for hitherto the instruments and equipment for taking pictures which Monsieur Richard Khan had brought used silver plate and the process was called the Daguerreotype one after the name of its inventor.[8] Nowadays the very number of photographers and their workshops in the capital Tehran and other major cities of Iran would make their enumeration a most arduous task.

From 1839, when the details of the daguerreotype method were officially published, until 1851 when the collodion process was invented, the science of photography made much progress.[9] Most of the new instruments and equipment were given to the Persian Court as presents and found their way there two or three years after their invention and first production. Richard Khan, whom we have already seen mentioned by I'timâd al-Saltana as the pioneer of photography in Iran, has left a diary, parts of which have been published. In this published section he refers to taking pictures on silver plate in 1260 AH/1844 for the Crown Prince, Nâsir al-Dîn Mîrzâ, at Tabriz:

> 5 December 1844. Through Madame 'Abbâs,[10] I had an audience with the Crown Prince [i.e. at Tabriz] in order to take his picture on silver plate. Two sets of equipment using metal plates have been brought for the Shah. One is a gift from the Queen of England and the other from the Emperor of Russia. Although the operating instructions have been sent in accompanying leaflets, up to now no single European or Persian has been able to operate them and take pictures. When they realised that this task was within my scope, they approached me and first summoned me to take pictures of the Crown Prince and his sister. The Crown Prince is about thirteen or fourteen years old.[11]

Three years later, in the last months of Muhammad Shah's reign, he again refers to taking pictures of the King:

> 23 February 1847. The King has asked me to take pictures of him and his household (*andarûn*) and the princes.[12]

Again, it must be emphasised that by photography it is the daguerreotype process which is meant here. And it is to the same process that I'timâd al-Saltana refers to in his *Iksîr al-tawârîkh*[13] as one of the new sciences of the reign of Muhammad Shah and as 'a kind of painting'.

The first European photographers of Iran. Turning from Qajar documents to present-day research, we will briefly refer to two sources of valuable information about French and Italian photographers in Iran, the former active in the years 1274–7 AH/1857–63 and the latter dating from 1277–9 AH/1860–3.

For our information about the French photographers, we are indebted to an article by J. Qâ'im-Maqâmî[14] based on documents in the French military archives at Vincennes (no.1673) containing reports by the head of the French military mission in Iran. These mention that in 1274/1857 two photographers named Carlhiée and Blocqueville accompanied the mission. According to the same report, while photographing the Turcoman revolt of 1277/1860 in Khurasan, their equipment was smashed and Blocqueville was taken prisoner. These are therefore perhaps the first European photographers to have entered Iran, although we have no examples of the photographs that they may have taken during their stay.[15]

For our information on Italian photographers in Iran, we are indebted to Angelo M. Piemontese's valuable study, 'The Photograph Album of the Italian Diplomatic Mission to Persia (Summer 1862)'.[16] The article deals in a comprehensive manner with the background of the Mission and its members, including the two photographers Montabone and Pietrobon. It places this particular mission and album within the larger context of the early history of photography in Iran and provides succinct commentaries on individual photographs.[17]

Another valuable collection of photographs of Iran which has recently been discovered is that of Ernst Hoeltzer (1835–1911) who worked in the Persian Telegraph Department from 1863 to 1890.[18] These photographs were first described and discussed in the journal *Kâveh* by the editor of the journal, Muhammad 'Âsimî, who later produced an edition of them.[19]

Finally, it must be pointed out that the contemporary worldwide interest in early photographs has led to a series of books and exhibitions on the history of photography in the Middle East and these often contain sections on the works of other slightly later photographers in Iran.[20]

2. Persian words for photography

The word '*aks* has long been used in Persian in the general sense of the reflection of objects in water, mirrors, etc.; and the clicking sound made when pictures are taken suggested the compound verb '*aks andâkhtan* to denote the verb 'to photograph'. The older generation of Iranians may remember the following bawdy doggerel inscribed on the shop sign of a lower-class photographer:

From you a penny, from us a photo
You dish it out, we slot it in.

The terms '*aks* and '*akkâs* have also a more technical use in two sixteenth-century texts dealing with miniatures and illustrations. Both passages refer to the same artist, Mawlânâ Kepek of Herat. The first is from an introduction to an album in the Topkapi Museum (dated 984 AH/1576–7) published under the title of *Bustân-i khatt*:[21]

The other rare talent of the era was Mawlânâ Kepek the '*Akkâs* of Herat, who made '*aks* (stencils) of pictures and line drawings, and in the making of coloured stencils and gold sprinkling and the use of different colours and artistic designs (*tarrâhî*) and calligraphic copying (*muthannâ*) has excelled all human beings.

The same artist is also mentioned in a treatise by Qâdî Ahmad, son of Mîr-Munshî (*circa* 1015 AH/1606–7) published under the title of *Gulistân-i Hunar*:[22]

> Maulana Kepek . . . was good at '*aks,* and in mastering that art made new discoveries. . . . He created curious images, wonderful designs, rare colourings. His '*aks* made people free from (their former use of) gold sprinkling.

3. A philosopher's first encounter with photography

Although Iranians had soon become acquainted with photography and some knowledge of it must have reached provincial cities, Hâjjî Mullâ Hâdî Sabzavârî seems to have been completely unaware of it until 1286 AH/1869–70 (i.e. almost 20 years after it had first gained currency), when Nâsir al-Dîn Shah ordered his picture to be taken while on a visit to Sabzavâr, thus causing the Hâjjî much astonishment and surprise. There are two accounts of the episode. The first is from Nâsir al-Dîn Shah's travel diary written by Hakîm al-Mamâlik:

> Âghâ Ridâ, the court photographer, who had been commissioned by His Majesty to take a picture of His Excellency the Hâjjî, performed his allotted task and was received in audience by His Majesty. Having brought for royal inspection the photographic plate of the said Excellency which he had taken in a most accomplished manner, he was praised and rewarded. He begged to inform His Majesty that because the Hâjjî had not hitherto seen the instruments and tools of this craft and had not observed the reflection and imprint of images of objects on external surfaces, he marvelled greatly when he encountered it and pondered a while; and when he became completely acquainted with its essence, he pronounced it a useful device in the demonstration of the science of perspective.[23]

The second passage is from I'timâd al-Saltanâ's *Mir'ât al-buldân*:

> Âghâ Ridâ, the Court Photographer and household attendant, by order of His Majesty took a picture of His Excellency the Hâjjî Mullâ Hâdî; and because until then His Excellency the Hâjjî had not witnessed the action of photography and considered it against the laws and scientific proofs of previous sages, he was infinitely surprised.[24]

The significance of this anecdote, as already realised by Mr 'Abbâs Zariyâb-Khôî, is that when the Hâjjî heard that an instrument existed which could produce pictures on paper, he thought that this was an impossibility, and his reasoning was based on the psychological aspect of the problem; for the ancients believed that it was only the human spirit which was capable of imprinting and recording images, and this faculty was beyond the scope of any man-made machine.

4. Photography at court

Another social problem was that of taking pictures of women; as it was unlawful for the male photographer to enter the *harem* and take pictures, the photographing of women was almost impossible. It was for this reason that Nâsir al-Dîn Shah would personally take pictures of the members of his seraglio. Underneath most pictures of the women of his seraglio which exist in the collection of his photographs in the royal collection, he points out in his own handwriting that he has personally taken the pictures. One can safely say that these are the earliest portrait photographs of Iranian women that we possess, and they include a picture of Nâsir al-Dîn Shah's mother, the famous Mahd-i 'Ulyâ. In fact, Nâsir al-Dîn Shah had become so interested in photography that part of the royal buildings became known as 'Akkâs-khâna, the abode of photography.

Both in his *Mir'ât al-buldân-i Nâsirî* and in his *Diaries,* I'timâd al-Saltana makes observations on this pastime of the Shah. In his *Mir'ât al-buldân* he writes:

When the comprehending mind of His Majesty became interested in the progress and propagation of this science and his own angelic and imperial essence was fully acquainted with this science, His Majesty decided that one of the servants and private attendants of the Imperial Court should also become thoroughly skilled in this craft so that at home or on travels, he might, acting on the august commands of His Majesty, take pictures of strangers and acquaintances, of buildings and old monuments; and with these amuse His Majesty in times of relaxation ... [here he gives some information about Âgâ Ridâ, the court photographer] ... And in order to propagate this science and expand its scope of operation, one of the royal private buildings was designated as an 'akkâs-khâna so that at times when His Majesty sought relief from matters of state, he would honour that place with His Presence and observe its operation and progress. In important expeditions such as the journeys to Khurasan and Mazandaran and the exalted shrine of Karbala, the photographs of all ancient and distant and unusual places and monuments would be taken and made into an album and presented to His Majesty, and they still are in His Majesty's possession.[25]

Owing to the shortage of space at a time when the construction of a new building for the seraglio was in progress, the building that the Shah had designated for his 'Akkâs-khâna was placed at the service of his harem. This is referred to in I'timâd al-Saltana's entry in his diary for 29 Dhu'l Hijja 1299 AH/11 November 1882:

The building of the Shah's seraglio is not finished and the members of the harem have been split up and housed in the rooms used for the pantry, stores and photography.[26]

It seems that the first photographic apparatus which was imported into Iran was for the court of Nâsir al-Dîn Shah, and that the king was very interested in this art and made it into one of his favourite pastimes. Some of his photographs exist in the royal collection and some have been reproduced in Dr J.B.Feuvrier's *Trois ans à la cour de Perse*. Under many of the photos there are notes in his own handwriting, and to these we shall later refer in greater detail. The Shah would sometimes abandon this hobby, only to return to it later. Thus in his entry for 4 Shawwâl 1306 A H/3 June 1889, I'timâd al-Saltana writes:

> In the past few days the Shah has been taking pictures, with 'Azîz Khan the Eunuch as his apprentice. For sometime now His Majesty had lost interest in this, but he has started again.[27]

Nâsir al-Dîn Shah's intensity of interest in this art resulted in the creation of the office of Photographer to the Court (*'Akkâs-bâshî*). The details are given in the *Mir'ât al-buldân-i Nâsirî*:

> Âqâ Ridâ, the private attendant, who is now an aide-de-camp of His Majesty and the Keeper of the Royal Purse and is held by the most perfectly virtuous essence of His Majesty in a position of trust and confidence, and is one of the truly genuine and home-bred and nurtured products of this august reign, was commissioned by Royal order to learn this noble science. Before long, and blessed by the care bestowed by His Majesty on him, he became proficient in this science and acquired complete knowledge. This pleased His Majesty who honoured him with royal favours . . .[28]

In his *al-Ma'âthir wa l-âthâr*, too, I'timâd al-Saltana refers to Âqâ Ridâ under the heading of photographers, and besides him, also mentions the name of Mîrzâ Husayn 'Alî. The latter had beautiful handwriting and signed under his photographs 'the work of the loyal servant Husayn 'Alî'.[29] Apparently, these two were the first photographers who were officially engaged by the Court. Examples of their work can be seen in the albums of the royal collection.

Nâsir al-Dîn Shah's interest in photography also encouraged others to take pictures of important ceremonies and to send them to the Shah. Thus I'timâd al-Saltana writes in his *Diaries*:

> Sha'bân 1299. Nusrat al-Dawla had sent gifts on behalf of his father (*sic*: text, 'son') Nâsir al-Dawla. He had also sent a photo of Nâsir al-Dawla holding a tome (*sic*) in which there was some money. It made me laugh a lot, for nothing could be more vulgar than this photograph. It implied that the money which he was holding was for royal offering.[30]

It was also because of Nâsir al-Dîn Shah's interest in photography that a department in the Dâr al-Funûn College was assigned to photography, and under some of the photographs of the time are the following labels: 'The Royal Photography Office' and 'The Photography Atelier of the Dâr al-Funûn College', thus indicating that there were two different centres of photography, one for the court, and the other for government business.[31]

The descriptive labels under the photographs were printed on cardboard pieces, on to which the photographs were then pasted. These backings were printed outside Iran and then imported, and were imitations of what was then customary among photographers in Europe, the Caucasus, Ottoman Turkey and India. It is from these backings that the names of some of the pioneers of photography in Iran have reached us. The names of those whose work is included in the royal collection of albums are cited in Mrs Badrî Atâbây's valuable work.[32]

Last but not least, mention should be made of those early photographs of Iranian scenery and portraits of eminent people which were printed on postcards.[33]

5. Famous photographers

Photography gradually became a profession, but as it was not a lucrative business, photographers would sometimes combine it with another trade. Among these photographers, according to Mr 'Abdallâh Intizâm, were those whose major profession was dentistry. They would also take photographs as a side-line and the title of both professions would be inscribed on their shop window. An example of these was the Musannan Photographic Studio on Nâsiriyya Street in Tehran.

The names of those who chose photography as a profession in the first years of its introduction into Iran have not been recorded (especially in the provinces), except for the cases of Âqâ Ridâ Iqbâl al-Saltana and Mîrzâ Husayn 'Alî Khan, who had the title of photographers to the Court, and whose names, as we have already noted, were recorded in contemporary Qajar sources. The names of the other photographers must be extracted from the information in the pieces of cardboard on to which photographs were pasted. Thus, for example, Mr Abdallâh Intizâm's oral report that he had heard of an early photographer called Mîrzâ 'Abdalghânî or Mîrzâ 'Abdalbâqî can be confirmed by photograph no.622 in the collection of the Central Library and the Centre for Documents of Tehran University which has the label: "Abdalbâqî's Photograph Studio'.

The most famous photographer in the history of Iranian photography was 'Abdallâh Qâjâr (died in 1326 AH/1908–9). He took many pictures of landscapes and notables and underneath most of the pictures his title and rank are recorded, for example: 'Special Photographer to His Imperial Majesty, and His Humble Servant, 'Abdallâh Qâjâr – Tehran' or 'The Photographic Department of the Dâr al-Funûn College – 'Abdallâh Qâjâr'. The Royal Library contains many examples of his work.[34]

The best source of information about him is his own account (written in 1314 AH/1896–7), which is reproduced in Mr Iqbâl Yaghmâ'î's article

'The beginnings of the craft of photography and stereotyping in Iran':
This slave, 'Abdallâh Qâjâr, Private Photographer to the Martyred
King Nâsir al-Dîn Shah – may God shed light upon his resting-place –
went to Europe, at the time when the Prince I'tizâd al-Saltana was
Minister of the Sciences, and with much encouragement from his
most exalted excellency Mu'îr al-Mamâlik, may God prolong his
blessed fortune. I spent about a year and a half in Paris, learning
photography and the art of retouching photographs; but as the
school of photography there was not entirely adequate, my friends
and acquaintances advised me to go to Vienna and wrote a letter of
recommendation to Loucard, Photographer to His Imperial Majesty,
the Emperor of Austria and First Secretary to the Viennese Photographic Association. As I had intended to stay in Europe for two or
three years, I went to Vienna and gave the letter of introduction to
Loucard. After bestowing much kindness upon me, he sent me to the
Salzburg polytechnic, where all aspects of photography are studied.
He also wrote a letter or recommendation to Professor Jourda, who
was then the teacher of photography there. I took Loucard the
photographer's letter to the state polytechnic at Salzburg and presented it to Professor Jourda. The kindnesses of Professor Jourda
towards me are beyond description and in the nature of miracles. In
brief, on my first day, the head of the school, and the teachers, all
formally presented themselves and showed me all the examples of
different types of photography which existed in the school. After
coffee, Loucard's letter was read and the Professor was extremely
pleased, and said that the arrival of a student from the East, and
specially from a royal family, was a source of honour to them. Then
he turned to me and said that it would be better if I resided in his
house, and he gave me his own drawing-room with two other rooms,
and I was employed for three years and began to work and study. At
the beginning of the work and for the first six months, according to
the usual requirements of training, I was engaged in taking photographs from photographs. The mastery of this is a requirement of the
craft and I progressed in a most satisfactory manner and obtained the
school certificate. I then started on photolithography and was engaged in that noble task for a year. Photolithography consists of
taking pictures of photographs from designs on lithographic stone.
After the completion of my study of photolithography, I was engaged for a year on phototypy. Phototypy is the process of printing
pictures from photographs on glass plates of scenes, or people or
whatever one can imagine and take on glass. In a sense it can be seen
as an improvement and perfection of the process of photolithography. Both processes, photolithography and phototypy, can produce up to one thousand and two hundred prints in about fourteen

hours. It is not possible to produce more unless one has several plates and there is a reason for this which need not be gone into. Anyway, given several plates and a steam wheel, one can produce ten thousand prints a day. After completing these two subjects, I embarked on zincography. This too is an improvement on photolithography in the sense that by photolithography one cannot produce more than two or three thousand satisfactory prints, but using zincography, one can print thousands and these last for years. But like lithography, it is limited to engravings and lithographs. Now we turn to the process of phototypy, where one can take pictures with or without engraving or etching on metal plates. For a short time I was engaged in this process which involves galvanoplastic plates. Then I turned to colour photography, but did not complete its study, only attaining some rudimentary knowledge of it. Having overstayed the three years by ten months and lacking the financial means for staying any longer, I had to go to Vienna, where I received maximum co-operation and assistance from His Excellency Narimân Khan Qavâm al-Saltana, our minister plenipotentiary at that capital.

To put it briefly, after a great deal of trouble and hardship and after waiting two months at Odessa because the sea was frozen and there were no means of transport, I came to the capital city of Tehran via Sebastopol, having undergone much toil and penury. Having reached Iran, after a few months, I saw that the best means of seeking audience was through His Excellency the Minister of Interior. Through his good offices an audience with the Martyred Shah (i.e. Nâsir al-Dîn Shah) – may the almighty lighten his resting-place – became possible. After royal favours bestowed upon me, I was entrusted to the care of His Excellency, and it was ordered that all the operations which I had presented to his royal favour should be carried out at the Dâr al-Funûn School.

Now I had to set up the equipment. I borrowed the printing apparatus which His Excellency Qavâm al-Saltana had sent to Jahângîr Khan, the Minister for Crafts, and began to work. Every day, while I worked, their Excellencies Nâyir al-Mulk, the Minister for Sciences, and Hâjjî Najm al-Dawla and other teachers of the School would come to watch me at work in the photo printing-house. I printed a map of Ahwaz and some other regions in front of their Excellencies and presented these to them. About this time, the royal visit to the School took place. On the day of the visit, the various processes were paraded in front of His Majesty who ordered the purchase of the printing equipment. But the precondition for the advancement of this matter was through referring work for illustrations of books and newspapers, and no decree was issued regarding this matter, and I too had no strength and means left and so the matter was delayed. Although later on I tried to activate the matter on several occasions, single-handed I could not do much. This is why I have described the position and appeal to those interested in such matters, and I promise that if a benefactor provides the tools and completes the necessary equipment, I shall in the space of twenty days print the required picture and present it to him.

I would like to point out that I regard myself a mere servant and I only expect enough help and co-operation not to be stuck by over-work. While I can, the entrusted work is carried out by me night and day without interruption; and if after the provision of the required tools I am found to be incompetent and unable to carry out the tasks, I should be given the most severe punishments so that others may be prevented from making unjustified claims. Your humble servant, 'Abdallâh Qâjâr.[35]

'Abdallâh Qâjâr, the son of Jahângîr Mîrzâ, was born around 1266 AH/1849–50, and after this return from Europe was placed in charge of photography in Dâr al-Funûn. Later, in the reign of Muzaffar al-Dîn Shah, he became the head of the Imperial Printing Press and his name-stamp can be seen at the end of some of the books printed in that press.

'Abdallâh Mîrzâ accompanied Muzaffar al-Dîn Shah on his first journey to Europe (1317 AH/1899–1900). His ancestral family name is Jahânbânî. Mr 'Abdallâh Intizâm recalls that 'Abdallâh Qâjâr had a photography shop in the upper storey of a building next to the Dâr al-Funûn. Three students of 'Abdallâh Qâjâr's studio became famous photographers. One was Ivanov, known as 'Roussie Khan'; we shall refer to him later. Another was Mâshâ'allâh Khan, examples of whose work are in the photograph collection of the Central Library and the Centre for Documents of Tehran University (no.694). The third was Khâdim the Photographer.

In order to find out the names of all the photographers of the reign of Nâsir al-Dîn Shah and the early years of his son's rule, one must examine all the old Nâsir photographs in different collections. Fortunately, Mrs Badrî Atâbây has made a list of the names in the Royal Collection.[36] These names belong to the years between 1282–1331 AH/1865–1912. It must be pointed out that, almost certainly, not all those listed were professional photographers. Some must have taken pictures as a hobby and thus their names must have survived and were then recorded by Mrs Atâbây. The names of those recorded by her are as follows (I have placed my own notes and observations in brackets):

Âqâ Ridâ Iqbâl al-Saltana (already referred to above). A great number of his pictures are in the Royal Albums, including the following albums: 112–17, 143, 161, 168, 171, 325, 331–2, 340, 342, 363, 382 and others. In many of these albums, he has signed his name as 'Ridâ the Court Photographer of His Majesty's Photographic Studio', or 'Ridâ'.

Hâjjî Mîrzâ 'Alî, the Court Photographer (*'Akkâs-bâshî*).

'Alî Nâghî.

'Azîz the Eunuch (I'timâd al-Saltana's sarcastic comment on him in his *Diaries,* is quoted on p.266).

'Abdallâh Qâjâr, the Dâr al-Funûn Photographer, already discussed above.

'Abbâs-'Alî Bîk, administrator of the Royal Photographic Studio (see Album no.133 for his photograph).

Amîn Hadrat, head of the office of the Royal Photographic Studio.

Husayn 'Alî, Court Photographer (he had studied photography in Europe, and examples of his work can be seen in the following albums: 160, 201, 236, 257, 266, 267, 283, 286, 295).

Mîrzâ Ahmad, the Court Photographer. (His own photograph appears in Album no.156 and is also reproduced in this article. He is mentioned by Kamâl al-Mulk Ghaffârî in his autobiography, where he refers to his title of Sanî' al-Saltana.)[37]

Mîrzâ Ibrâhîm Khan, Court Photographer. (He is the son of Mîrzâ Ahmad the Court Photographer. Mîrzâ Ibrâhîm had the title of Court Photographer in the court of Muzaffar al-Dîn Shah; and in the 1317 AH/1899–1900 trip to Europe he accompanied the Shah. The first ciné-camera bought by Muzaffar al-Dîn Shah was placed at his disposal. In his account of his travels under the entry for 21 Rabî' II 1318, describing the journey to Ostend, Muzaffar al-Dîn Shah writes: 'Today there is a festival of flowers . . . the Court Photographer is busy taking pictures and photographs' (Album no.441 contains an example of his work).)[38]

Muhammad Husayn Qâjâr.

Mîrzâ Jahângîr.

Manûchihr Khan.

Abu 'l-Qâsim, son of Muhammad Taqî Nûrî (the date 1323 AH/1905–6 is inscribed on some of his photographs, and they are mostly pictures of scenery and buildings).

Aghayantz the Armenian. (He has a picture of the port of Anzali in Album no. 292 and under it has written 'The Photographic Studio of Aghayantz'.)

Dûst Muhammad Khan the Photographer.

Other photographers whose names I have seen in the Royal Collection are as follows:

Sayyid 'Alî. His photographs were pasted on cardboard. On it, his name 'M. Seid Ali' and 'Teheran' are printed in Latin script and between them there is the emblem of the Lion and the Sun (done three different ways). On one batch, the crown of Nâsir al-Dîn Shah can also be seen. His photographs can be seen in album no.278, which contains mainly pictures of clerks and accountants.

Khânbâbâ-yi al-Husaynî.

'Yûsuf'. Albums 109–11, belonging to the years 1312–13 A H/1894–6.

Among the last of the first generation of photographers Antoin(e) Sevruguin, an Armenian who was popularly known as 'Antôn Khan', occupied an important place. He was alive until about 1920 and had a shop in 'Alâ' al-Dawla Street (Firdawsî Avenue) near Zahîr al-Dawla's house. At the time of the bombardment of the Majlis in 1908, when Zahîr al-Dawla's house was looted, his shop also suffered damage and part of his collection of glass plates was destroyed. After his death, his wife and daughter managed the shop for a few years.[39] Apparently, he must be the same 'Antovân Khan' who wrote a treatise on photography for Muzaffar al-Dîn Shah in 1295 A H/1878, when he was in Tabriz. We shall refer later to this treatise.

Another photographer contemporary with Antoin(e) Sevruguin was 'Roussie Khan' who had been a student of 'Abdallâh Khan Qâjâr and later opened a shop in 'Alâ' al-Dawla Street. His real name was Ivanow, but he was usually known as Roussie Khan. He travelled to Russia in 1326 A H/1908 and signed a contract with a firm in Odessa called Bomer to send him paper, glass and cardboard for his photography. Many pictures of notables of the Constitutional period are his work. He accompanied Muhammad 'Alî Shah after his abdication to Europe, but his shop still functioned under the management of Mihdî Musawwir al-Mulk until 1299 (Sh. or A H?).[30]

Musawwir al-Mulk (son of Mîrzâ Hasan Gul-i Gulâb, the Calligrapher and the father of Husayn Gul-i Gulâb) had his photographic studio in 'Alâ' al-Dawla Street. He was also skilled in stereotyping and drawing. Some of the drawings in the newspaper *Sharâfat* are his work. At present, Tahâmi Photographic Shop in Tehran (near Bahâristân Square) has a collection of original plates of the Nâsirid and Muzaffarid era. Another collection which contained valuable old plates was that of M. Rahmânî.

6. The teaching of photography

When photography was first introduced, some Iranians went abroad to study it; but gradually its teaching became established in Iran itself.

In his autobiography, which is of value for the study of cultural history, Fursat al-Dawla Shîrâzî, writing about the time when he was eighteen years old (1289 A H/1872–3) and in connection with a painting which he had done of Husâm al-Saltana, the governor of Fars, writes:

> At that time photographs were not so common in Iran, and those that did exist were so bad that they were of no interest at all.[41]

The same writer, while giving an account of the life of Sayyid Muhammad 'Alî Dâ'î al-Islâm Tihrânî who had studied English and founded the

Safâ-Khan association in Julfâ, Isfahan, writes that 'Among the sciences, he had studied photography'.[42] This indicates that at the beginning of the fourteenth century AH/early twentieth century photography was still considered a science, worthy of mention and note, rather than a universal pastime. Fursat himself, who was a painter, began to learn photography from 'Abdallâh Mîrzâ while he was staying in Tehran:

> During my stay in Tehran, 'Abdallâh Mîrzâ Qâjâr, the Court Photographer, told me that it would be a good idea for some one who had mastered the art of painting to know photography as well. He insisted upon this and taught me the craft of photography. I bought some instruments and equipment and busied myself at times with photography until I had mastered it.[43]

The study of photography was so highly esteemed and prestigious that a person who had studied it might call himself *muhandis* 'engineer'.[44] Sometimes Iranians would earn their living as photographers abroad. I have seen an example of this in the family collection of the Afshâr family of Yazd. This was the work of M. 'Abd al-Rahîm Shîrâzî, who worked in Cairo about a hundred years ago and had a shop. His photograph emblem was the lion and the sun. Hâjjî Mîrzâ Muhammad Sâlih Yazdî, who worked in Bombay, also used this emblem, and it was commonly used by photographers working in Iran itself. For example, Sayyid 'Alî and Antoine Sevruguin both used it on mounts which had been printed outside Iran (apparently in Russia).

In the provinces too, there were photographers, but unfortunately we have no information about their names and work. Efforts must be made to gather old photographs in provincial towns as well as the names of their photographers. Fortunately, there is a succinct article by Karâmat Ra'nâ Husaynî dealing with one of the photographers of Shiraz. He was known as Mîrzâ Hasan the Photographer, and came from Kâzarûn. He also wrote poetry with the *takhallus* of *'Kâtib'*. His house was also his studio and was still standing until recent years; on its walls hang some of his photographs. He learnt photography in India and came to Bushire and Shiraz and began practising his trade there in 1312 AH/1894–5.[45] On a journey to Shiraz, accompanied by Dr Asghar Mahdawî, I had the good fortune to visit this house through the good offices of Karâmat Ra'nâ Husaynî. One of the rooms in the house looked like a museum of photography. As far as I remember, some of the framed photographs were placed on the ceiling in place of joists.

From Hamadan too we have some information. This comes from about one hundred photographic plates which belonged to Dr Taqî Razawî. With Mr 'Abdallâh Intizâm's help and encouragement, I obtained these for the Central Library and Centre for Documents and they are now kept in that library. Prints have been made from the plates. The name of the photographer is 'Abd al-Bâqî Mubarqa'.

Among the family photographs of the Afshâr family of Yazd, a picture was found in which the local photographer had placed his own name at the feet of the people whose photograph he was taking, so that his name would be preserved on the picture itself. As this device was not found anywhere else, I have reproduced it here.

7. Photographic manuals

It is appropriate here to give a list of treatises on photography in chronological order:

The oldest treatise describing the art of photography and how to develop pictures and make copies, as far as we know, was written by Muhammad Kâzim b. Ahmad Mahallâtî[46] by order of Nâsir al-Dîn Shah. It contains a preface, three chapters and a coda. A manuscript of this, in the author's own hand and dated 1280 AH/1863–4 is in the Library of the Sipahsâlâr Madrasa. Other copies exist in the I'timâd al-Dawla Collections (Hamadan) and the National Library.[47]

Another treatise is *Fann-i 'akkâsî, The Art of Photography*. This is a translation made by Antovan Khan in 1295/1878 for Muzaffar al-Dîn Shah when he was the Crown Prince at Tabriz. A copy of it is in the National Library.[48]

In Vol. III of the *Mir'ât al-buldân-i Nâsirî* about two pages are given to the operation of photography, its principles and history.[49]

Another treatise called *Qavâ'id-i 'aks va tiligrâf*, 'Principles of photography and telegraphy', was written by Hasan b. 'Alî Ridâ Lâhijî Najafî and dedicated to Muhammad Taqî Mîrzâ Rukn al-Dawla, Governor of Khurasan and to Hâjjî Mihdî-Qulî Khan Sahâm al-Mulk in 1298 AH/1880. I have seen a copy of this in the Central Library of Isfahan University when I was engaged in cataloguing the manuscripts there with the help of my colleague Muhammad Taqî Dânish-Pazhûh.

A copy of a translation from French on photography dated 1301 AH/1883–4 in 18 chapters and translated by a certain Mahmûd[50] is in the Central Library.[51]

Another treatise, dated 1313 AH/1895–6, was prepared by Nawwâb Muhsin Mîrzâ[52] for Mîrzâ Ismâ'îl, the aide-de-camp for artillery, and is in the Malik National Library.

In the Library of the Sipahsâlâr Madrasa there is a treatise in 74 folios on photography which begins with a description of the various chemicals used in photography.[53] Prescriptions of chemicals used in photography can also be found in Nâsir al-Dîn Shah's notes which contain instructions on how to develop pictures in the Shah's own hand.[54]

In the end of the book entitled *Majmû'at al-sanâ'i'*, 'A compendium of crafts', which is a treatise on different crafts and sciences, there is a chapter on photography. The book was printed in India, but manuscripts of it are also in existence.[55]

*8. The collection of the office of crown goods (*Buyûtât*)*

From the court of Nâsir al-Dîn Shah and Muzaffar al-Dîn Shah (and also partly from the reign of Muhammad 'Alî Shah and Ahmad Shah) a great number of albums and individual photographs have survived which were previously kept in the Office of Crown Goods and are now in the (former) Royal Library. Most of the pictures are from Nâsir al-Dîn Shah's era and are collections of his memorabilia. The following points about them are worthy of note:

(1) They are about 20,000 in number.

(2) The majority of the photographs are in valuable albums. Badrî Atâbây gives the number of the albums as no.42132.

(3) Some of the photographs were taken by Nâsir al-Dîn Shah himself.

(4) Some are photographs of individual notables and *'ulamâ',* and some are of groups.

(5) Among the pictures, there are some of historical monuments, royal buildings, views of towns and houses of the notables and given the fact that many monuments have been since destroyed, they are of historical importance. Among these are the buildings in the gardens of Mu'ayyir al-Mulk, Amîn al-Dawla and the several gates of the city of Tehran. I'timâd al-Saltana alludes to this point in his *Diaries*: '21 Rabî II 1305. By the order of the Shah, they had taken some photographs of the buildings and monuments of Azarbaijan. This is a very good idea'.[56]

(6) Some of the photographs are of royal tours and hunts.

(7) There are also pictures of shop-keepers and the professional classes, as well as pictures of clowns, buffoons, dervishes, hired musicians and calligraphers.

(8) There are also a number of European postcards and photographs sent from Europe.

(9) On the margin of some of the photographs (whether taken by him or by others) Nâsir al-Dîn Shah has written notes and comments, which contain matters of historical interest; they also shed light on the Shah's mentality and are of help in identifying the subjects.

(10) One of the oldest photographs which carries a date is the photograph of Hâjjî Ridâ, the household footman to Fath 'Alî Shah, taken by Nâsir al-Dîn Shah himself in 1278 AH/1861–2, indicating that the Shah had been interested in this hobby for a long time.

Some examples of the type of notes and comments made by Nâsir al-Dîn Shah are: 'This photograph of me was taken by me in the *andarûn* (women's quarters)'; 'taken by me in Niyâvârân'; 'taken by me in Tehran'; and 'I took these two pictures with the instant photographic apparatus which I had bought from Europe. It was the 8th Sha'bân 1307 (30 March 1890), eight days after the New Year (Naw-rûz), the Year of The Leopard. I was feeling most depressed and ill and bad-tempered'.[57]

Nâsir al-Dîn Shah also took two photographs of two of the illustrations in Prince Alexis Soltykoff's *Voyage en Perse,*[58] and these are preserved in one of the albums. As they contain descriptions of the subjects in the illustrations, which are not identified in Soltykoff's own account, they deserve attention. Under the picture of Soltykoff's audience with Nâsir al-Dîn Mîrzâ (i.e. when he was the Crown Prince), he writes:

> I have written these lines on 18 Jumâdâ I 1307 (10 January 1890)...I am sitting in the top floor of the Tehran *andarûn.* Thank God I am physically fit but have 'flu. All the harem are ill and have 'flu. I had toothache a few days ago. Thank God it is gone now. But every day I have discharge from my haemorrhoids. It hasn't stopped yet. Lots of snow yesterday. The whole world is covered in white. Praise be to God, we are now fifty-eight years old, and, praise be upon Him, from the time when we were seven and this picture of us was drawn, I have had two molar teeth extracted, one upper and one lower, on the left side and, praise be upon Him, I am in the peak of health and strength. I must be very thankful to God, I always thank Him and always shall. In this year – praise be upon Him – in all the provinces of Iran there is abundance of provisions, low prices and security. God willing, may it always be thus. It is two months now since I returned from my third [journey] to Europe.

9. The collection of photographs from the Office of Crown Goods
When I was in charge of the Office of Publications of the Libraries of Tehran University (including the Central Library), I arranged for about 20,000 photographs of the Office of Crown Goods to be microfilmed. Some of them were then printed (20–30 cm. format) for an exhibition in Tehran University. Later, these photographs were bound in covers and kept in the Library. I also wrote a report on the exhibition.[59] The work of cataloguing the microfilms was began by me, but was later taken up and completed in a most thorough manner by the late Dr Husayn Mahbûbî Ardakânî. I hope that this catalogue will soon be printed and made generally available. Along with this, more work was carried out in printing copies, so that at present, the Central Library has a set of microfilms and two complete folio-size series of photographs of the collection. The majority of those photographs which are of historical importance have been reproduced (in 30–20 cm. format) and bound in covers. They have been used by scholars and reprinted in their works. The most notable example is M. Bamdâd's well-known *Biography of Iranian Notables* which contains many of the photographs without, unfortunately, acknowledging the source or listing the catalogue numbers.

10. Other collections in the Central Library
The activities of the Library in this context can be briefly listed:
(1) The purchase of old photographs from booksellers and antique-

dealers in Kirman, Isfahan, Yazd and Tehran. These photographs have been numbered and kept in separate files. The work of cataloguing and making alphabetical and subject indices has been carried out by Dr Asghar Mahdawî and is available for reference in the Library. As in the case of the Catalogue of the Collection of the Office of Crown Goods by Dr Ardakânî, it is hoped that this catalogue too will be published one day.

(2) The purchase of old photograph plates. Some were bought in Tehran from Manûchihrî Bookshop. Some were given free by Dr Taqî Razawî Hamadânî. These are mainly of Hamadan.

(3) The purchase of postcards. Most of them belonged to Dr Kamâl Janâb, who presented them to the Library.

(4) The preparation of microfilms of politicians and men of letters through their family albums. So far the following have been collected: Muhammad 'Alî Furûghî, Malik al-Shu'arâ' Bahâr, Mushîr al-Dawla Pîrniâ, Abû Nasr Husâm al-Saltana, Dûst-'Alî Khan Mu'ayyir al-Mamâlik, Sa'îd Nafîsî Sâdiq Hidâyat, Ibrâhîm Pîr-Dâvûd, Mujtabâ Mînuvî, 'Alî Akbar Dihkhudâ, Sayyid Hasan Taqîzâda, Jalâl Âl-i-Ahmad, 'Abd al-'Azîm Gharîb, 'Abbâs Iqbâl Âshtiyânî, Badî' al-Zamân Furûzanfar.[60]

(5) The preparation of microfilms of albums belonging to the following families of the Qajar period: Sâhib Ikhtiyâr, Mu'âwin al-Dawla and Iqbâl al-Dawla Ghaffârî. This is the most important section, apart from the Crown Collection.[61]

On the history of photography in Iran, Khusraw Mir'ât and Yahyâ Zukâ' have gathered valuable information, and it is to be hoped that they will publish this. Finally, I must thank Mr Karîm Imâmî for preparing the photographs which have been printed in this article.

NOTES AND REFERENCES

1. *Mir'ât al-buldân-i Nâsirî*, Tehran 1295 AH, iii, 20-1; see Storey *PL*, i/1, 344, no.444(1), ed. (2).

2. Jules Richard, who became known in Iran as Ridâ Khan Richard. Gobineau makes oblique references to him in *Les Nouvelles Asiatiques (Histoire de Gambèr Ali)* under the name of M. Brichard; also in C. J. Wills, *In the Land of the Lion and Sun or Modern Persia*, London 1883, 36-7. See Bâmdâd, ii, 44.

3. August Křziž (b. in Tabor 1814, d. in Chrudim 1886), in Persian service 1851-9. Taught at the Dâr al-Funûn and did pioneering work in mapping Tehran and its surroundings. See *Plan von Teheran* of August Křziž, ed. Helmut Slaby, Graz 1977.

4. Presumably Monsieur Carlian is the same as Monsieur Carlhiée mentioned by J. Qâ'im-Maqâmî, see n.14 below.

5. Farrukh-Khan Amîn al-Dawla.

6. The collodion process was invented in 1851, see Helmut and Alison Gernsheim, *A Concise History of Photography*, London 1965.

7. *Al-Ma'âthir wa 'l-âthâr* was written on the occasion of the fortieth year (1304 A H/1886-7) of Nâsir al-Dîn Shah's reign, and published in 1306/1888-9. See Storey, *PL*, i/1, 344, no.444(2), i/2, 1174-5, no.1661. Browne, *LHP*, iv, 456.

8. See Helmut and Alison Gernsheim, *L. J. M. Daguerre: the History of the Diorama and the Daguerreotype,* New York 1968.

9. Including the invention of the calotype in 1841 and the first practicable method of photography on glass, the albumen process, in 1848. For a short introduction, see *A Concise History of Photography,* cited in n.6 above.

10. Madame 'Abbâs, wife of Hâjjî 'Abbâs Gulsâz, on whom see 'Abbâs Iqbâl's article in *Yâdgâr,* iii/6-7, 106-9. Daryûsh Gul-i Gulâb in his *Barrasî-yi fanni-i 'akkâsî* ('A technical study of photography'), Tehran 1360 Sh., 13, states that Madame 'Abbâs was responsible for some of the pictures of Nâsir al-Dîn Shah's wives.

11. Dr Khalîl Khan 'Alam al-Dawla Thaqâfî, *Maqâlât-i gûnâgûn* ('Diverse essays'), Tehran 1322 Sh., 113.

12. *Ibid.,* 47.

13. *Iksîr al-tawârîkh,* ms. in the Law Faculty Collection of Tehran University in the Central Library of the Univ., 487. I have given a list of the contents of the book relating to industry and crafts in a brief notice in *Âyanda,* v/4-6 (Summer 1979), 326-7.

14. J. Qâ'im-Maqâmî, *Wurûd-i san'at-i 'akkâsî ba-Îrân* ('Introduction of the craft of photography to Iran'), in *Yâdgâr-nâma-yi Habîb Yaghmâ'î* ('H. Y. Memorial volume'), Tehran 1356 Sh., 279-82.

15. [*Translator's note:* The above article contains a number of errors and omissions. The name Blocqueville is given throughout as Aloqueville and no mention is made of important references to him and his subsequent adventures as a prisoner, given in the standard works of the nineteenth century. I have not been able to consult the French archives. But see G. N. Curzon, *Persia and the Persian Question,* London 1892, i, 277-8 and 586; Arminius Vámbéry, *Travels in Central Asia,* London 1864, 19; and *idem, The Story of My Struggles,* London 1905, 181.

   According to Curzon, Blocqueville wrote the history of his adventures as a prisoner in the journal *Tour du Monde* for April 1866 (incidentally, one of the journals regularly translated and read to Nâsir al-Dîn Shah by I'timâd al-Saltana). Blocqueville also published accounts of his adventures in a separate format; the following book is cited in the Catalogue of the Bibliothèque Nationale: H. de Blocqueville, *Notice sur les nomades du Turkestan,* Paris 1865. There is also a reference in Sir Arnold T. Wilson's *A Bibliography of Persia,* Oxford 1930, 25: Blocqueville de Couliboeuf, *Quatre mois de captivité chez les Turkomans aux frontières du Turkestan et de la Perse (1860-1),* Paris 1866.]

16. *East and West,* n.s. xxii (Sept.-Dec. 1972), 249-311.

17. Piemontese's references to the existence of copies of the Italian photographs in Iran can be confirmed; there is a copy with a

descriptive commentary in Italian which had been sent to Nâsir al-Dîn Shah and is now in the Royal Collection (Album no.374). A few of the photographs have been reproduced by Badrî Atâbây in her *Catalogue of the Albums in the Royal Library*, Tehran 1977.

18. See Helmut Wietz's foreword to Jennifer Scarce's 'Isfahan in camera: 19th century Persia through the photographs of Ernst Hoeltzer, *Art and Archaeology Research Papers (AARP)*, London 1976, 1. The article provides a succinct commentary of Hoeltzer's work and reproduces many of his photographs.

19. *Îrân dar yak sad-u-sîzdah sâla pîsh* ('Iran, one hundred and thirteen years ago'), Part I: *Isfahan*, Tehran 1355 Sh. (Publications of Centre for Anthropological Studies, no.13).

20. [*Translator's note:* E.g. Paul E. Chevedden's *The Photographic Heritage of the Middle East: an Exhibition of Early Photographs of Egypt, Palestine, Syria, Turkey, Greece and Iran, 1849-1893*, Malibu, Calif. 1981, which contains reproductions of photographs taken by Isabella Lucy Bishop in 1890 in Iran. It also has an excellent bibliography of other related works, to which the following should be added: Louis Vaczek and Gail Buckland, *Travellers in Ancient Lands, a Portrait of the Middle East, 1839-1919*, Boston 1981.

Besides these modern works, a great deal of information on photography can be gathered from diaries and travel books of the period. Thus, bearing in mind that the Eastman Co. produced the first mass-produced Kodak camera with nitrocellulose roll-film in 1889, it is interesting to find Curzon taking pictures of 'Turkomans which I took with my "Kodak" at Imam Kuli', *Persia and the Persian Question*, i, 119. He also provides very useful information on various aspects of photography, its use by archaeologists, the price of cameras, etc.; see i, 146, 277-7, 495; ii, 122, 132, 150, 211, 213, 312, 565 (n.2); and also C. J. Wills, *op. cit.*, 237-8, 331. A. M. Piemontese also gives a partial list of books containing 'photographs of Persia that can be termed old', *op. cit.*, 263 (n.80). Persian catalogues of foreign libraries should also be consulted, e.g. see Rieu's *Supplement to the Catalogue of the B.M.*, no.412, which contains some early photographs.]

21. *Bustân-i khatt*, published by Mustawfî Bookshop, Tehran 1358 Sh., 11-12.

22. *Gulistân-i hunar*, ed. Ahmad Suhaylî Khwânsârî, Tehran 1359 Sh., 157, English tr. V. Minorsky, *Calligraphers and Painters: a Treatise by Qadi Ahmad, Son of Mir-Munshi*, Washington 1959, 192-3. For the various interpretations of *'aks* in this context see Minorsky, *op. cit.*, 160 (n.568), which gives Zakhoder's interpretation, and 193 (n.691), which gives that of Dr Bayânî. See also Khwânsârî's preface to his edition cited above, 43, which also gives an account of *'aks* and agrees with Dr Bayânî's suggestion that it denotes stencil work.

23. *The Diary of Nâsir al-Dîn Shah's Journey to Khurasan (Safar-*

nâma-yi Khurasân) written by Hakîm al-Mamâlik, lith. ed. Teh-ran n.d., 132 (the Shah's journey took place in 1286 AH/1869).

24. *Mir'ât al-buldân*, iii, Tehran 1295 AH, 74.

25. *Ibid.*, 21-2.

26. *The Diaries of I'timâd al-Saltana (Rûz-nâma-yi khâtirât)*, ed. Îraj Afshâr, Tehran 1345 Sh., 225.

27. *Ibid.*, 653.

28. *Mir'ât al-buldân*, iii, *loc. cit.* Âqâ Ridâ the Court Photographer later obtained the title of Iqbâl al-Saltana and became Minister for Munitions. See Bâmdâd for further biographical details.

29. *'Amal-i khâna-zâd Husayn 'Alî*, lit. 'The work of the humble family protégé Husayn 'Alî. (*Khâna-zâd* = born to a servant in a notable's house, here, however, merely a general expression of loyalty.)

30. *The Diaries*, 201.

31. [*Translator's note:* 'The chemistry branch has included the teaching of photography, and several of the best illustrations in these two volumes are from photographs taken by pupils of the Royal College.' Curzon, *op. cit.*, 495.]

32. *Fihrist Albumhâ-yi Kitâb-khâna Saltanatî* ('The catalogue of the albums in the Royal Library'), Tehran 1357 Sh.

33. I have obtained a fairly representative collection of the earliest postcards of Iranian scenery and notables for the Central Library and the Centre for Documents of Tehran University. Some of them are gifts from Kamâl Janâb. Mr Khusraw Mir'ât has made some notes and research about postcards.

34. *Translator's note:* An example of his work, a photograph of the *walî-'ahd*, the future Muzaffar al-Dîn Shah, with the tag 'The Dâr ul-Funûn College, Tehran, 'Abdallâh Qâjâr' is reproduced in Curzon, *op. cit.*, i, 416.

35. In the journal *Âmûzash va Parwârash*, xxxviii/1-2 (1347 Sh.), 90-7. The source of the extract is not recorded in the article, and the writer has personally informed me that he took it from a newspaper of the time of Muzaffar al-Dîn Shah but forgot to indicate the source.

36. *Op. cit.*, n.32.

37. *The Memoirs of Dr. Ghassem Ghani*, London 1981, v, 28.

38. *Chihrawhâ-i az pîshrawân-i hunar va adabiyyât-i Mu'âsir-i Îrân* ('Sketches of the forerunner of contemporary art and literature of Iran'), publ. by Farhang-Saray Niâvarân, Tehran 1357 Sh., 18.

39. I have obtained this information from Mr 'Abdallâh Intizâm; the occasion was a letter to me in November 1980 from Mr H. Edwards of the Freer Gallery of Art (Washington) informing me that Mrs M. Smith had had in her possession some of the original photograph plates of Antoine Sevruguin, that these had now become the property of the Gallery, and that they intended to set up an exhibition.

40. From the notes in Gul-i Gulâb's book, where on pp.13-15 a brief history of photography in Iran is given.

41. This autobiography is printed in Fursat's preface to his *Dîwân*,

Bombay 1332 AH, 21.

42. *Ibid.*, 140.

43. *Ibid.*, 147.

44. For example, Sayyid Hakîm Ashraf 'Alî Razavî Nâsir al-Dawla who, as is apparent from his name, was an Indianised Iranian, in his book entitled *Amîn al-Akhbâr* (a personal account of the years between 1274-1313 AH), calls himself *Muhandis 'Akkâsî.* See ms. no.2957 in the Malik Library.

45. *Mûza-yi 'aks wa khatt* ('A museum of photography and calligraphy'), *Yaghma*, no.27 (1353), 336-43.

46. Mahallâtî (1250-1313 AH) was the chemistry teacher at the Dâr al-Funûn, and because of this was known as Mîrzâ Kâzim Khan Chîmî (see Khânbâbâ Mushâr, *Authors of Printed Books*, v, 44.

47. *The Catalogue (Fihrist) of the Sipahsâlâr Library*, ed. M. T. Dânish-Pazhûh and A. Munzavî, v, Tehran 1356 Sh., 425.

48. The Catalogue (Fihrist) of Manuscripts in the National Library, ed. A. Anvâr, Tehran 1350 Sh., iv, 154.

49. *Mir'ât al-buldân*, iii, 21-2.

50. This 'Mahmûd' is perhaps either Mahmûd Khan Mâzandarânî (Miftâh al-Mulk), who was educated in Europe and wrote on telegraph codes (see *Authors of Printed Books*, vi, 62), or else Mîrzâ Muhammad Khan Qummî (Mushâr al-Mulk) who studied astronomy in Europe. See Bamdâd, *Biography of Iranian Notables*, iv, 45.

51. *The Catalogue of Manuscripts in the National Library*, ed. Anvâr, iii, Tehran 1351 Sh., 113.

52. Muhsin Mîrzâ was the son of Shams al-Shu'arâ', poet and man of letters, who died in 1315 AH/1897 (see *Authors of Printed Books*, v, 226). There is a photograph of him in the Royal Collection on which there is a note by Nâsir al-Dîn Shah, with the date 1281 AH/1864.

53. *The Catalogue of the Sipahsâlâr Library*, v, Tehran 1356 Sh., 425.

54. *The Catalogue of Albums in the Royal Library*, ed. B. Atâbây, Tehran 1357 Sh., 10-12 (preface).

55. Calcutta 1295 AH, 103-10.

56. *Rûz-nâma-yi khâtirât I'timâd al-Saltana*, ed. I. Afshâr, 1st impr., 606.

57. This photograph has been reproduced in Badrî Atâbây's *Catalogue of the Albums in the Royal Library.*

58. Prince Alexis D. Soltykoff (or Soltykov), *Voyage en Perse*, Paris 1851, 1853, translated into Persian as *Musâfarat ba-Îrân* by Dr Muhsin Saba in the B.T.N.K *Îrân-shînasî* series, Tehran 1337 Sh. The book is of importance for its accurate and precise illustrations of Muhammad Shah's Court and for the Iranian landscapes.

59. *Râhnamâ-yi Kitâb* (1347 Sh.), 664-6.

60. These photographs were exhibited in memorial exhibitions.

61. Examples of them can be seen in *Makhzan al-waqâ'i'* by Husayn Sarâbî, Tehran 1344 Sh.

PLATES

1. Majd al-Dawla. This is one of the photographs taken by the Italians and given to Nâsir al-Dîn Shah as part of the album. The note is in Italian, and Nâsir al-Dîn Shah has written the names of three of the figures in his own hand.
2. Hâjjî-Âqâ Ridâ, private footman to Fath 'Alî Shah. The note underneath is by Nâsir al-Dîn Shah and dated 1278 A H/1861-2, but the photograph itself might be earlier. This is one of the oldest dated photographs.
3. Nâsir al-Dîn Shah in European dress. Taken by himself. 1284 A H/1867-8.
4. By Nâsir al-Dîn Shah himself of a group of women and maids of his harem. He has called this 'a group of women'.
5. Perhaps by Nâsir al-Dîn Shah. It is of one of his wives.
6. Mîrzâ Ahmad, Court Photographer. From the Collection of the Office of Crown Goods.
7. The photograph of one of Nâsir al-Dîn Shah's Court Photographers. From the Collection of the Office of Crown Goods. It dates from before 1313 A H/1895-6.
8. The figure on the left is 'Abbâs 'Alî Khân the Director of the Royal Photographic Studio. From the Collection of the Office of Crown Goods.
9. Two unidentified portraits. An example of the work of 'Abdallâh Qâjâr in the Collection of the Office of Crown Goods.
10. The drawing-room of Mu'âwin al-Dawla Ghaffârî. Photographed by Antoine Sevruguin. 1319 A H/1901-2.
11. Hâjjî Muhtasham al-Saltana Isfandiârî. Photographer: Hâjjî Mîrzâ Sâlih Yazdî in Bombay, c.1900.
11. Verso.
12. Safâ 'Alî Zahir al-Dawla. Photographer: Antoine Sevruguin. 1316 A H/1898-9.
12. Verso.
13. Mîrzâ 'Alî Muhammad Khân Tarbiyat. One of the conquerors of Tehran in the Constitutional Revolution. Photographer: Roussie Khan in 1327 A H/1909-10.

1

2

3

4

5

6

7

8

9

10

13

14

17

Persian royal portraiture and the Qajars

Till the recent political upheavals, Iranians have been staunchly consistent monarchists throughout their long history. Monarchy relies to a considerable extent on public relations, and before the advent of wireless, television, and the popular press, these were achieved by royal portraits and other graphic representations by which the monarch was displayed to his admiring subjects in the most impressive and favourable guise possible. Hence we find plentiful bas-reliefs of the Achaemenids, for which Darius the Great set the tone on the Rock of Bîsutûn: 'I am Darius the Great King, the King of Kings, for long King of this great earth . . . a Persian, son of a Persian, an Aryan of Aryan descent.' This tradition was carried even further by the Sasanians: 'The Ormuzd-worshipper, the God, Shâpûr, King of Kings Aryan and non-Aryan, of the race of the Gods.' On the cliff-face of Naqsh-i Rustam, not far from Shiraz, can be seen a veritable panorama of the Persian monarchy from the Elamites through the Achaemenids and Sasanians almost down to the Arab conquest. It is the most numinous spot in the whole of Iran.

During the first six centuries of Muslim rule Iran lost much of her political identity, though the practical business of government under a succession of alien overlords was mostly carried out by Iranians, who always retained a lively consciousness of their heroic past. This consciousness was further quickened by the appearance of the *Shâh-nâma*, Firdawsî's great national epic, at the beginning of the eleventh century, in which all the old national traditions were brought together and, as it were, codified. In it the monarchy was consistently held up as the ideal, divinely appointed, form of government, sanctified by the presence of the *farr*, or royal splendour.

But Muslim orthodoxy frowned on human or animal representation; sculptures in the Achaemenid and Sasanian tradition were unthinkable, and the art of painting, by which such representations could be discreetly confined between the covers of a book, had not yet reached the requisite stage of development for royal portraiture. But at last, at the beginning of the thirteenth century, we come upon the earliest identifiable Islamic painted royal portraits that have come down to us. Badr al-Dîn Lûlû was Atabeg of Mosul from 1218 till 1259; he seems to have been something of an artistic patron, and several fine pieces of inlaid metalwork are known, bearing dedications to him. But the important fact for our present purpose is that he commissioned a twenty-volume manuscript collection of songs, the *Kitâb al-Aghânî,* and all but one of the seven surviving volumes contain frontispieces in which he is portrayed.[1] Writers on Islamic painting have been strangely reluctant to recognise these for what they obviously are. 'Such depictions should not be regarded as portraits, but as ideal effigies of rulers' says the *Catalogue* of the Arts of Islam Exhibition. But Islamic painters had a strictly practical approach to their art, and it seems highly doubtful that such an abstract and sophisticated idea would ever have entered their heads. The name of Badr al-Dîn Lûlû is inscribed on the arm-bands of these figures; he was the patron (the copyist uses the epithet of *al-Badrî*); and it is no more than natural that he should wish to emphasise that fact by the inclusion of his portrait in the manuscripts he commissioned.

Several frontispieces survive from the thirteenth and fourteenth centuries in which rulers are depicted, but it has not been possible to identify the subjects.[2] The *Anthology of Dîwâns* of 1315 in the India Office Library contains a large number of stereotyped miniatures representing the various poets presenting their works to their respective patrons, but these cannot be regarded as true portraits.[3] To be really convincing a portrait should be as nearly as possible contemporary with its subject.

It is in the Timurid period of the fifteenth century that the royal portrait really comes into its own, though no authentic representation of the great conqueror himself seems to have survived. Martin published what purported to be a contemporary portrait from his own collection, and it was reproduced as such by Sir Percy Sykes in his *History of Persia.*[4] It is admittedly a fine portrait of a dark-skinned bearded warrior in armour, seated on a camp-stool, and it fits one's mental image of Tîmûr very well. But, apart from the fact that it cannot, stylistically, be earlier than the mid-sixteenth century, it bears no inscription to identify the sitter, and one strongly suspects that the idea sprang from Martin's own fertile brain, like the alleged 'Portrait of Saladin' (a Mamlûk automaton figure) which forms the frontispiece of his great work. This fine portrait made a sad last appearance at the Sevadjian sale.[5] It had been reduced to a mutilated fragment, the figure having been clumsily cut out with scissors and all the scrolled background lost – possibly the work of a former owner's mischievous children. In this connection a certain copy of the *Shâh-nâma,* formerly in the Kevorkian collection, is worth a passing glance, as it was formerly thought to contain a contemporary portrait of Tîmûr.[6] But the fact is that the manuscript is of the normal Turcoman commercial type, the original date, 891/1486, having been altered in the colophon to 791/1389. The circumstantial inscription round the border of the carpet on which the ruler is seated in the frontispiece is a palpable later addition, and also contains the earlier date.

The first of the great succession of Timurid bibliophiles was Tîmûr's grandson Iskandar Sultân, but it does not appear that any of the surviving paintings executed for him contains his portrait. After his fall and miserable death in prison his mantle fell on his cousin Bâysunghur Mîrzâ, whose lavish Herat establishment for the production of fine manuscripts is well known to all students of the subject. His two most impressive volumes, the Tehran *Shâh-nâma* and the Topkapi *Kalîla wa Dimna,* both contain double-page frontispieces depicting the prince, round-faced and with a small moustache, hunting and holding outdoor court respectively. He was of notoriously bibulous habits, and any doubt of his identity is instantly dispelled by the cup of wine which he holds in both representations. It seems certain also that he had himself portrayed in some of the miniatures in the Vienna Khwâjû Kirmânî and the Berenson Anthology.[7]

Many other members of the family are to be found portrayed in fifteenth-century manuscripts. The *Shâh-nâma* of Bâysunghur's brother Ibrâhîm Sultân, who ruled at Shiraz, contains no less than four double-page miniatures in which he is shown holding court indoors and out, hunting, and in battle.[8] Ulugh Beg, another grandson of Tîmûr, being the eldest son of Shâh Rukh, is portrayed seated in state under an awning inscribed with his name and titles, in the right-hand half of a detached frontispiece (probably from a *Shâh-nâma*) now in the Freer Gallery, Washington.[9] Muhammad Jûkî, a younger son of Shâh Rukh, had himself depicted as the hero-prince Isfandiyâr in the double-page battle-scene in the Royal Asiatic Society's *Shâh-nâma* of c.1440.[10] This miniature is an adaptation of the battle-scene of Ibrâhîm Sultân in the Bodleian *Shâh-nâma,* noticed above. Finally, at Herat in the late fifteenth century, Sultân Husayn Mîrzâ is vividly portrayed in several well-known manuscripts illustrated by Bihzâd and his school.[11] These examples are sufficient to demonstrate that royal portraiture was a flourishing art under the Timurids, and that, consciously or unconsciously, the Sasanian tradition of representing the monarch hunting, holding court, or in battle, was maintained or revived.

During the second half of the fifteenth century the Timurids were ousted from most of their dominions by the Turcomans of the Black and White Sheep clans, pushing in from the west, and centres of painting such as Baghdad, Tabriz, and Shiraz fell into Turcoman hands. Only Khurasan and its capital, Herat, remained to the Timurids (with an interlude in 1458 when Herat itself was occupied for a brief period by the Black Sheep Turcoman chief Jahânshâh). The greatest bibliophile among the Black Sheep princes was Pîr Budâq, son of Jahânshâh, and among the White Sheep the brothers Khalîl and Ya'qûb Beg. Nothing identifiable as a portrait can be found among the surviving manuscripts commissioned by Pîr Budâq during his successive governorships of Shiraz and Baghdad, unless we accept as his (as we well may) the celebrated Tehran *Kalîla wa Dimna,* which contains a fine double-page frontispiece of a young prince holding court.[12] Like his Timurid predecessor Iskandar Sultân, Pîr Budâq was a persistent rebel and trouble-maker, and this brought him to a similar untimely end. Khalîl and Ya'qûb Beg were sons of the great White Sheep chieftain Uzun Hasan (who is probably portrayed in a double-page hunting-scene in Leningrad),[13] and the former succeeded his father on the latter's death in 1478. But he had been on the throne for less than a year when he was defeated and killed by the troops of his younger brother. However one small but extremely fine manuscript survives from his brief reign, the *Dîwân* of Hidâyat in the Chester Beatty Library. This contains four exquisite little miniatures, each portraying Khalîl in a characteristic situation: holding court out-of-doors, on a hawking expedition, listening to a suppliant from his palace balcony, and relaxing in a vinery.[14] These are far more informal in atmosphere than the Timurid paintings we have been considering, and are, indeed, wholly delightful, prompting the thought that, had he survived, Khalîl would have occupied a high place amongst Islamic patrons of culture and the arts. Several portraits of Ya'qûb Beg are to be found in the Topkapi albums,[15] but the finest paintings produced under his patronage are in a magnificent manuscript of the *Khamsa* of Nizâmî in the same library, where the young prince is depicted as Bahrâm Gûr in the various coloured pavilions.[16]

Two examples from outlying seats of Turcoman rule are worth noticing before we pass on to the Safavid period. The first is the frontispiece of a beautiful little Anthology in the British Library.[17] The colophon gives the date 873/1468 and the place as Shamakhâ (Shîrwân) on the west coast of the Caspian Sea; the scribe uses the epithet *al-Sultânî* (written in gold). It therefore seems not unreasonable to identify the prince in the frontispiece as the Shîrwânshâh Farîdûn b. Farîburz, who must by this time have been a tributary of Uzun Hasan. This frontispiece, incidentally, is a reduced and simplified version of that in the Tehran *Kalîla wa Dimna,* which we are inclined to associate with Pîr Budâq. The second is in a remarkable copy of the *Shâh-nâma* written for Sultân 'Alî Mîrzâ, who ruled in the Caspian province of Gilan. The colophon gives the date as 899/1494. This manuscript is in two volumes, both in Istanbul, Volume I in the Museum of Turkish and Islamic Art, and Volume II in Istanbul University Library. There must originally have been something like 350 miniatures (the two volumes combined at present contain 311), but a number of them were extracted and stolen earlier in this century, the double frontispiece itself having been divided; the right-hand half (containing the prince's portrait) is still in the Museum of Turkish and Islamic Art's volume, but the other has found its way into the Keir collection.[18] In accordance with a personal idiosyncrasy of one of the painters employed on it, this manuscript is familiarly known as the 'Big Head *Shâh-nâma*'.

The Safavids swept to power under Shah Ismâ'îl at the turn of the fifteenth-sixteenth century. Only one portrait of Isma'îl himself has been credibly identified, represented in the guise of Bahrâm Gûr hunting, by the great painter Sultân Muhammad in the Paris Nawâ'î manuscript, executed two or three years after his death.[19] But his successor Tahmâsp appears in several manuscripts and separate miniatures and drawings of his period. Mr Cary Welch sees him as one of the attendant pages in the miniature of Firdawsî and the three court poets illustrating the Preface in the great Houghton *Shâh-nâma*.[20] This identification, however, remains controversial. But he is more plausibly recognisable in the double-page frontispiece of a Jâmî manuscript in Leningrad, where he is shown shooting various game driven towards him in a *battue*.[21] He is also to be found in another Leningrad manuscript to which he himself contributed.[22]

The next Safavid monarch, Ismâ'îl II, succeeded in 1576. He was a man of culture and sensibility, though with a pronounced vein of cruelty, and his reign was terminated after no more than eighteen months, probably by an assassin's dagger. However, he had attempted to restore the royal atelier, which had fallen into a depressed state in Tahmâsp's latter years of bigotry and intrigue, by commissioning a large and magnificent copy of the *Shâh-nâma*.[23] Only about half of the illustrations for this were completed before Ismâ'îl's untimely death, and the manuscript was eventually acquired and broken up by the notorious dealer Demotte early in the present century. Among the separated miniatures, however, is a large double-page frontispiece, perhaps by 'Alî Asghar, father of Rizâ-i 'Abbâsî, which almost exactly reproduces, on a rather enlarged scale, that of Tahmâsp in the Leningrad Jâmî which we have already noted. The prince is depicted in conventional style, clean-shaven and with no particular individual features, but the artist must have intended to represent Isma'îl II.[24]

After the short and inglorious reign of the invalid Muhammad Khudabanda the throne was won by Shah 'Abbâs the Great. In his time the painter Rizâ overshadowed all his contemporaries, and altered the basic character of Persian painting from the courtly formality of the Timurids and early Safavids to a style of mannered elegance and erotic languor in which the beginnings of a moral and spiritual decline are clearly reflected. Portraits of 'Abbâs are not infrequent, and are easily recognisable by the immense handlebar moustache which he affected. Many of these portraits stem from the visit of the Mughal ambassador Khan 'Âlam in 1618, and the meeting between the envoy and the monarch was recorded by both Rizâ and the Mughal painter Bishan Dâs, who accompanied the embassy. Many versions of both compositions have survived.[25] In addition, 'Abbâs appears in the double-page frontispiece of a number of manuscripts, a characteristic example being that in a fine copy of Nizâmî's

Khamsa in the John Rylands Library.[26]

No authenticated portraits of 'Abbâs' successor Shah Safî are known, but there are one or two of the next king, 'Abbâs II, though not of very high quality; one of them is in the Victoria and Albert Museum. This monarch followed an established tradition by commissioning a copy of the *Shâh-nâma* at his accession in 1642; it must be the largest copy of the epic in existence, and is now in the Leningrad Public Library.[27] Its enormous bulk is swollen by the inclusion in the text of several passages from apocryphal epics composed by later imitators of Firdawsî and celebrating the fictional exploits of heroes connected with the main narrative of the *Shâh-nâma*. It comprises no less than 875 folios with 192 miniatures, but curiously enough there is no double-page frontispiece; whether this omission was due to the modesty of 'Abbâs II or to some other cause we have no means of knowing.

The last Safavid monarch, Shah Sultân Husayn, is realistically portrayed in a miniature in the British Museum which shows him presiding at a New Year *salâm*.[28] This miniature, by Muhammad 'Alî, son of Muhammad Zamân, is in the thoroughgoing westernising style of the end of the seventeenth century, and is dated to the year before the abject collapse of the dynasty before the Afghan attack in 1722.

This westernising style was to dominate Persian painting for the following two centuries. It may have had its origins in oil portraits of European royalty brought as presents to Shah 'Abbâs the Great and his successors, or to the influence of European painters such as 'John the Dutchman' resident at Isfahan during the seventeenth century, which can be clearly seen in the Chihil Sutûn frescoes. In any case, the emphasis in Persian painting shifted from miniatures illustrating the classical poets to large oil paintings, mostly in the form of portraits. Two of the earliest of these depict the great soldier Nâdir Shah, who freed Iran from the horrors of Afghan rule, and went on to invade India and sack Delhi in 1738. These portraits, one in the Victoria and Albert Museum[29] and the other in the Commonwealth Relations Office,[30] are very strongly influenced by contemporary European portrait-painting; but through this veneer the Persian miniaturist can often be perceived, as in the treatment of jewellery, and especially the enamelled gold dagger and sword-hilt in the Victoria and Albert portrait.

After Nâdir Shah the only period of comparative tranquillity in eighteenth-century Iran was between 1750 and 1779, when the shrewd and genial Karîm Khan Zand ruled at Shiraz. A painting of his court, signed by Ja'far, is in the Pars Museum, Shiraz, and a very inferior copy in the Museum of Decorative Arts, Tehran. The characterisation is admirable, with a striking contrast between the stiff line of formal courtiers and the easily lounging central figure of Karîm Khan, contentedly pulling at his *qayiân,* and looking out of the picture in a very knowing manner, almost as if he were winking at the spectator. A water-colour of him in the Churchill album in the British Museum is less lively.[31] But the Zand dynasty was short-lived. Its last representative, the heroic Lutf 'Alî Khan, was betrayed after a gallant struggle and foully murdered by the unspeakable eunuch Âqâ Muhammad Khan Qajar. A portrait of Lutf 'Alî Khan, perhaps somewhat idealised, was engraved from an apparently lost original for Sir Harford Jones Brydges, who made it the frontispiece to the account of his mission.[32]

So we arrive at the Qajar dynasty in the person of its odious founder. Many stories are told of the cold and implacable cruelty of Âqâ Muhammad which it would be out of place to retail here.[33] He had the hairless emaciated face of the eunuch, and naturally these features are brought out in all the surviving portraits. The most impressive seems to have been that in the palace of Karaj, not far from Tehran. It was the work of 'Abdallâh Khan, a court painter who lived on till almost the middle of the nineteenth century, and is thus described by Lady Sheil: 'It represented Agha Mahommed Khan, the founder of the Kajjar dynasty, surrounded by the chiefs of his tribe who helped him to the sovereignty of Persia. . . . The likenesses of the chiefs are said to be excellent, and that of Agha Mahommed Khan himself inimitable. The former are fine, sturdy, determined-looking warriors. Agha Mahommed looks like a fiend. The atrocious, cold, calculating ferocity which marked the man is stamped on his countenance.'[34] Another excellent portrait of Âqâ Muhammad, in miniature, is in the richly decorated manuscript of poems by Fath 'Alî Shah sent by that monarch as a present to the Prince Regent (George IV) and now in the Library of Windsor Castle. It is by Mîrzâ Bâbâ, first among the early Qajar court painters, who was already in the service of the family at Astarabad before they attained supreme power.

With the accession of Âqâ Muhammad's nephew, Fath 'Alî Shah, in 1798 we enter a pleasanter atmosphere. All accounts are agreed that he was inordinately handsome, and his fine eyes, wasp-like waist, luxuriant beard, and dazzling jewels are unfailingly noted by travellers and envoys who had the privilege of an audience. He was himself by no means unaware of these personal attractions, and a number of court painters were kept busy transferring them to canvas. We have already had occasion to mention Mîrzâ Bâbâ and 'Abdallâh Khan, but they were rivalled, and indeed sometimes surpassed, by Mihr 'Alî, whose masterpiece, formerly in the Amery collection and now the show-piece of the Nigaristân Museum, Tehran, has often been reproduced, and is perhaps the finest Persian oil painting in existence.[35] It would be tedious to enumerate all the surviving portraits of this picturesque monarch; Mihr 'Alî alone has left at least ten.[36] But it is interesting to compare them with that drawn from life by Sir Robert Ker Porter, and subsequently engraved as the frontispiece of his *Travels*.[37] They agree remarkably well.

Fath 'Alî Shah reigned till 1834, and it seems certain that both Mîrzâ Bâbâ and Mihr 'Alî predeceased him by some years. But two good portraits of him were painted in the 1820s by Ahmad, who may well have been a pupil of Mihr 'Alî. One of them hung in the British Embassy in Tehran for most of the nineteenth century, and was still there a few years ago, though what its recent fate may have been, none can say. The other, in a private collection, is remarkable in depicting the monarch in full armour, seated on a chair-like throne known as the *Takht-i Nâdirî* (not squatting, as usual, on a carpet or on the more normal Persian *takht,* which resembles a bed). Unfortunately the face of this latter portrait has been completely repainted.[38] It may also be noted here that Fath 'Alî Shah was the first Persian monarch since the Arab conquest whose portrait appeared on the coin of the realm, and that he even imitated the Achaemenid and Sasanian practice of having himself portrayed in rock reliefs, though it must be admitted that these do not seriously rival their prototypes in dignity and impressiveness.

Fath 'Alî Shah was succeeded by his grandson Muhammad Shah, a man of unattractive appearance – short and fat, and with a fairly short round beard and a permanent scowl. Portraits of him are numerous, a good and typical example, by Muhammad Hasan Afshâr, being in the Churchill album in the British Museum.[39] Several oil portraits, two of them by Ahmad, whose style had by this time become much more westernised, are in the Gulistân Palace, Tehran. It was during the reign of Muhammad Shah that the greatest Persian painter of the Qajar period began to make his name. This was Abu'l-Hasan Ghaffârî, the descendant of a line of artists in Kashan, who began as a pupil of Mihr 'Alî, and was later known by his title of *Sanî' al-Mulk*. The king was evidently impressed with his work, and sent him to Italy to study the works of Raphael and other Italian masters. But by the time he returned Muhammad Shah was dead, and his son Nasr al-Dîn had begun his long reign.

The reign of Muhammad Shah saw an alteration in male costume that had a sad effect on royal portraiture. Whereas Fath 'Alî Shah is always portrayed in rich flowing robes of brocade, his grandson affected the contemporary fashion of frock-coat and trousers, which by no means flattered his plump figure. This semi-European vogue became the norm, though in the early years of his reign Nasr al-Dîn had himself painted in frock-coats of Kirman shawl-work trimmed with fur, his tall astrakhan cap at a rakish angle, and, not infrequently, a long dagger of Cossack type (*qamar*) at his waist. There is quite a group of water-colour portraits of this type in which the king is shown indolently lounging on a sofa of florid Victorian design.[40] Three large oil portraits of Nasr al-Dîn from the 1850s and 1860s are worth remarking. The first, in the Gulistan Palace collection, is signed by Ja'far (not, of course, the same Ja'far who painted Karîm Khan), and depicts the monarch wearing the state crown and a long robe of Kerman shawl; it is an impressive piece of work. The second, in the Vienna Kunsthistorisches Museum (Inv. No. 1230), is by the Armenian painter Ovnatanian, whose meticulous style is more European than Persian. It shows Nasr al-Dîn beside a cannon, a telescope in his hand; his frock-coat of Kerman shawl and trousers are of European type, and his high astrakhan cap is adorned with a diamond aigrette.[41] The third is an impressive and highly 'atmospheric' full-length by Muhammad Hasan Afshâr.

But the most notable example of royal portraiture in the 1850s is to be found in the set of seven large panels executed by Abu'l-Hasan Ghaffârî and his assistants for the Nizâmiyya Palace. Based on 'Abdallâh Khan's celebrated Nigaristân frescoes of Fath 'Alî Shah and his court, they show, in the central panel, Nasr al-Dîn enthroned and flanked by his sons and chief ministers. The other panels contain portraits of courtiers and foreign envoys. Among the latter is the Comte de Gobineau, whose *Trois Ans en Asie* (Paris 1859) gives such a vivid picture of mid-nineteenth century Iran. But Great Britain is not represented, Mr Murray having been recalled on the eve of the brief Anglo-Persian war of 1856–57. The portraits are in Abu'l-Hasan's best style, and some preliminary studies for them are preserved in the Iran Bastan Museum. The paintings themselves are also there, in the Treasure Room, having been saved some fifty years ago from being transported *en bloc* to Turkey.

Later portraits of Nâsir al-Dîn are dull by comparison. The royal costume became completely Europeanised after the king's foreign tours, and the tall rakish astrakhan cap, worn with such panache in the 1840s and 1850s, was reduced to little more than a pill-box set square on the head. Photography took over to a great extent, and there was already a court photographer (*'akkâs-bâshî*) in the 1860s. His portrait (his name was Âqâ Rizâ) appears with many others, of various princes and celebrities, skilfully executed in lithograph by Abu'l-Hasan in the Government periodical which he edited till his death in 1866. Abu'l-Hasan's nephew, Muhammad Ghaffârî, generally known by his title of Kamâl al-Mulk, painted at least one excellent portrait of the king towards the end of his reign (he was assassinated by a deranged fanatic in 1896), but this can be regarded as the swan-song of Persian royal portraiture.

Nasr al-Dîn's son and successor, the feeble Muzaffar al-Dîn, occasionally appears in various media, including painted enamel, with his melancholy features and long moustaches. After him came the obese and repulsive Muhammad 'Alî Shah, whose portrait appears, wearing the towering Qajar crown, on certain higher value postage-stamps; these were of European manufacture. His son Ahmad Shah, the last Qajar monarch, inherited his father's tendency to over-weight, and after his abdication in 1925, when he spent all his time in Europe, he became quite gross. He was the only Qajar (apart from the eunuch Âqâ Muhammad) to appear clean-shaven. I have not seen any painted portraits of him, but he was often depicted more or less crudely on rugs which can sometimes still be seen in the windows of West End carpet-dealers, and which, strangely enough, seem to command high prices.

So the splendid tradition of Persian royal portraiture petered out in meretricious incompetence; it had been continuous from Darius the Great – a period of over 2,400 years – though sometimes interrupted, and manifesting itself in many different forms. Its golden age was undoubtedly the reign of Fath 'Alî Shah, which saw the ideal combination of a strikingly handsome monarch whose vanity ensured a spate of portraits of the highest standard possible at the time, with a group of artists of undeniable skill, though perhaps of restricted scope, in whose works he has achieved immortality. And of all these there can be little doubt that Mihr 'Alî's great portrait of 1813 in the Nigaristân Museum is the finest. Fath 'Alî Shah may have been incompetent, vain, avaricious, and vacillating, but we like to remember him as Mihr 'Alî has depicted him, 'every inch a king'.

NOTES AND REFERENCES

1. *The Arts of Islam,* ed. D. Jones and G. Michell, London 1976, nos 515-17, and further references there quoted.
2. For example M. S. Ipşiroglu, *Painting and Culture of the Mongols,* tr. E. D. Phillips, London 1967, pl.11.
3. B. W. Robinson, *Persian Paintings in the India Office Library,* London 1976, nos 1-53.
4. F. R. Martin, *The Miniature Painting and Painters of Persia, India and Turkey,* London 1912, I, fig.17; Sir Percy Sykes, *A History of Persia,* London 1921, II, opp.p.120.
5. Paris, Hôtel Drouot, Salle No.10, 23.xi.1960, Lot 1.
6. Eric Schroeder, *Iranian Book Painting,* New York 1940, Fig.2; Phyllis Ackerman, *Guide to the Exhibition of Persian Art,* New York 1940, Gallery IV, Case 6, C.; Sotheby and Co., 2.v.1977, Lot 172.
7. (Tehran *Shâh-nâma*) L. Binyon, J. V. S. Wilkinson, and B. Gray, *Persian Miniature Painting,* London 1933, No.49, pl. XLIV; (Topkapi *Kalîla wa Dimna,* R.1022) *Ars Islamica* I (1934), 199, fig.10; (Vienna Khwâjû Kirmânî); Ivan Stchoukine, *Les Peintures des Manuscrits Tîmûrides,* Paris 1954, pl.LV; (Berenson Anthology) R. Ettinghausen, *Persian Miniatures in the Bernard Berenson Collection,* Milan 1961, pls II, III.
8. Bodleian Library, MS Ouseley Add.176. Binyon, Wilkinson, and Gray, *op. cit.,* pl.XXXVIII; Stchoukine, *op. cit.,* pl.XXII; *Apollo Miscellany* 1951, 23.
9. Freer Gallery of Art, 46.26.
10. Robinson, 'The *Shâhnâma* of Muhammad Jûkî, in *The Royal Asiatic Society: its History and Treasures,* London 1979, 83-102, especially fig.23; Stchoukine, *op. cit.,* pl.LXVII.
11.. Especially the Cairo *Bûstân*; Binyon, Wilkinson, and Gray, *op.*

cit., pl.LXVIII. See also, *ibid.*, pl.LXVII.

12. Robinson, 'The Tehran Manuscript of *Kalîla wa Dimna*: a Reconsideration', in *Oriental Art* IV (1958), 3-10, fig.1.

13. Martin, *op. cit.,* Vol.II, pl.60, 61; O. Akimushkin and A. Ivanov, *Persidskii Miniatyuri XIV—XVII vv,* Moscow 1965, pls 18, 19; B. Gray (ed.), *The Arts of the Book in Central Asia,* Paris and London 1979, figs 140-1.

14. CB Library MS 401. Robinson, *Persian Drawings,* New York 1965, pl.80; *idem, Persian Miniature Painting from Collections in the British Isles,* London 1967, No.126, pl.41.

15. See, for example, *Arts of the Book* (note 13), fig.147.

16. *Arts of the Book,* pl.LXVII.

17. MS Add.16561; Stchoukine, *op. cit.,* pl.XLV.

18. A. Sakisian, *La Miniature persane,* Paris and Brussels 1929, fig.42; *Arts of the Book.* pl.LXIX.

19. MS Sup. ture 316. E. Blochet, *Musulman Painting,* London 1929, pl.CXXIV.

20. S. C. Welch, *A King's Book of Kings,* New York 1972, 83.

21. Martin, *op. cit.,* pl.116, 117.

22. *Gûy u Chawgân* of 'Ârifî, Leningrad Public Library Dorn 441; cf. Welch *op. cit.,* 52.

23. Robinson, 'Isma'îl II's copy of the *Shâhnâma'* in *Iran,* XIV (1976), 1-8.

24. *Ibid.,* pl.I; Messrs Colnaghi, *Persian and Mughal Art,* London 1976, 116, 117.

25. Robinson, 'Shah 'Abbâs and the Mughal Ambassador: the pictorial Record', in *Burlington Magazine,* February 1972, 58-63.

26. *Idem, Persian Paintings in the John Rylands Library,* London 1980, No.669 (p.233).

27. Leningrad Public Library, Dorn 333. L. Gyuzalian and M. Diakonov, *Iranskiye Miniatyuri,* Moscow and Leningrad 1935, pls 35-45.

28. Robinson 1967 (note 14), No.88; R. Hillenbrand, *Imperial Images in Persian Painting,* Edinburgh 1977, No.107.

29. Robinson, *Persian Oil Paintings* London 1977, pl.1.

30. Sykes, *op. cit.,* Vol.II, opp.p.254.

31. E. G. Browne, *A Literary History of Persia,* IV, Cambridge 1924, pl.V (see also pl.IV).

32. Sir Harford Jones Brydges, *An Account of the Transactions of His Majesty's Mission to the Court of Persia,* London 1834; Sykes, *op. cit.,* II, opp.p.284.

33. For example, *ibid.,* 288, 294; Sir John Malcolm, *History of Persia,* London 1815, II, 198, 200, 290.

34. *Glimpses of Life and Manners in Persia,* London 1856, 115.

35. S. J. Falk, *Qajar Paintings,* London 1972, frontispiece and pl.15.

36. Viz: Victoria Memorial Hall, Calcutta (1), Hermitage, Leningrad (2), Gulistan Palace, Tehran (2), Museum of Versailles (1), Ethnographical Museum, Tehran (1, *eglomisé*), and three or four more in private hands.

37. *Travels in Georgia, Persia, etc.*, London 1821.
38. International Exhibition of Persian Art, Burlington House, 1931, *Souvenir*, 49; it was also reproduced in colour as a card by Messrs Colnaghi in 1976.
39. British Museum Or.4398. Robinson 1967 (Note 14), No.102 (2).
40. See Robinson, 'A Lacquer Mirror-case of 1854', in *Iran* v (1967), 3.
41. For further information on Akop Ovnatanian see M. Kazarian, *Khudozhniki Ovnatanian,* Moscow 1968, which illustrates another portrait of Nasr al-Dîn, and one of Muzaffar al-Dîn as Crown Prince, both mounted.

1

2

4

5

6

7

8

9

10

18

Qajar metalwork: a study in cultural trends

Metalwork, abundant at all times in the Iranian world, appears to have been produced in vast quantities during the Qajar period. Tens of thousands of nineteenth-century brass and tinned copper wares are to be seen in Iran, Afghanistan and parts of Iran occupied by Russia – northern Azerbayjan in 1828 or the northern areas of Khurasan around Marv, in 1885–6. In out-of-the-way places many are still in daily use. Steel vessels and utensils likewise survive in large numbers. Ironically, hardly any attention has been given to that ultimate phase of Iranian metalwork, partly, perhaps, because metalwork has only just begun to be the object of systematic investigation, but also because Qajar metalwork has elicited little interest from Western collectors and museums.[1] Typologies have yet to be worked out in every category, making generalisations very hazardous at this stage.

The dearth of published material is all the more frustrating as few periods in Iranian history witnessed the rapid development of so many styles. The mere characterisation of the various schools that came into being would far exceed the scope of a general paper.[2] Nevertheless, even in the absence of much needed monographs, it is obvious at a glance that the Qajar period was one of considerable change reflecting the impact of foreign cultures.

This made itself felt in all forms of metalwork, including the most widespread and most traditional of all, tinned copper with engraved decoration. Yet, the pace of change was far from uniform. It varied according to geographical location. In as much as it is possible to localise objects, the eastern areas appear to have been if not more conservative than western Iran, at least less inclined to adopt Europeanising or Hindustani motifs. Furthermore, within each area, the pace of change differed greatly according to which aspect of the art is considered. Compared to Safavid metalwork, many Qajar wares display drastic alterations in shape or decoration, or sometimes both. In sharp contrast to the visual element, the conceptual heritage of the Safavid past, i.e. the symbolism as expressed in the iconography and the literary texts engraved on the objects remained surprisingly unchanged both in eastern and western Iran. This is particularly apparent on tinned copper wares, a category that lends itself well to comparison with pieces from earlier periods thanks to the large numbers that have come down to us from Safavid times. These alone will therefore be considered in this paper.

1. Eastern Iranian metalwork

Three dated pieces, all in the reserve collection of the National Museum at Kabul, may serve to illustrate the main trends of the hitherto unknown Khurasan school from the late Zand period down to the mid-nineteenth century.

The earliest piece is a household vessel or *tâs* executed in 1200/4 November 1785–23 October 1786 (fig. 1) a decade or so before the Qajars finally established their authority over Khurasan.[4] Its profile is unlike that of any Safavid bowl even though parts of it can be traced back to the earlier répertoire. The broad neck, waisted and flaring slightly, closely compares with that of a bowl in Moscow, dated 1774 and the upper section with its rounded shoulders is essentially similar to that of an earlier bowl in the Victoria and Albert Museum.[5] But the lower section with its flaring, slightly concave sides rising at a low angle has no precedent. The overall shape, while in no way a revolutionary one, may thus be characterised as the logical sequel to an earlier type. It testifies to the vitality of the art, which is thoroughly original and yet shows no break with the past.

Much the same may be said of the engraved decoration. The fundamental rules governing Safavid composition are respected. An epigraphic frieze runs on the neck as is usual and is broken up into eight sections, a common occurrence as early as the sixteenth century.[6] The formal pattern is strictly symmetrical. Individual motifs – the trilobate cusped escutcheons, the half palmettes, etc. – are nearly all borrowed from the Safavid répertoire although they are used differently. To mention but one example, no Safavid designer would enclose a three-blossom spray within a trilobate escutcheon such as may be seen in the main decorative border on the sides.

The calligraphic frieze written in fine *naskhî* from a master's hand reproduces two poems of two distichs each that I have not encountered previously. But the symbolism of the metaphors is traditional. One compares the sky with the upturned bowl, an age-old image in the Iranian répertoire.[7]

In short, this bowl, commissioned by one Ghulâm Rizâ, whose name is engraved with the date 1200 AH/4 November 1785–23 October 1786 within one of the eight trilobate escutcheons, shows that in Khurasan creation continued to develop along traditional lines on the eve of the advent of the Qajar dynasty.

This went on in the early years of the Qajar period.

A circular tray also in Kabul reproduces a well-known Safavid type (fig.

2).[8] The flat shallow well and the broad, slightly flaring rim, terminated with a grooved edge, shows no change from the earlier period. The composition follows traditional rules. Strictly symmetrical, it is arranged in concentric areas. Innovation essentially affects details – the markedly waisted cartouches are typical of their time. So is the handling of the zodiacal sign Leo dominated by the planet Sun in the central roundel. On the other hand, the Indianising fashion of the previous century has left its mark on the blossoms with downturned petals in Mughal fashion to be seen on the rim within one of the cartouches.[9] A marked weakness can be detected in the figurative element – the lion is clumsily drawn. This is hardly surprising given the decadence of manuscript painting at that time. A certain stiffness is beginning to be apparent in the abstract pattern, again matching the wane of the illuminator's craft.

As on the bowl dated 1785–6, the name of the man who commissioned the tray, one 'Muhammad Bâqir in the year 1200/1 April 1805–20 March 1806', appears in one of the eight cartouches otherwise filled with ornament. The epigraphical tradition of much earlier times, already well established in Khurasan by the late sixteenth century[10] thus continued unchanged. Indeed the poem in the *hazaj* metre enclosed within four cartouches engraved in the central area frequently occurs in Safavid metalwork:[11]

ای آنکه تراست در جهان هوش

در صحبت أهل بزم میکوش

بر دار ز روی قاب سرپوش

تا یار کند طعام را نوش

You whose judgement in this world is sound
  Endeavour to stay in the company of revellers
Lift the cover from the bowl
  That the Companion may quaff the beverage

The poem appears here with two variants – *ahl-i bazm* in the second distich and *zi rûy-i qâb*, 'from the bowl (*qâb*)' – usually found in Qajar times. In keeping with Safavid norm, reference is made to the object, identified as a *qâb*.[12]

Forty years later, signs of drastic change were beginning to appear, as may be inferred from a bowl of heavily cast copper, tinned and decorated with engraved designs (fig. 3).[13] The shape with fully rounded sides rising from a short tapering ring foot, while unknown in earlier times, is not unexpected. The composition shows two late innovations. On the outside, the main field is covered by a continuous repeat-pattern for which there is no precedent in earlier metalwork. The inner surface (fig. 4) is also decorated, an unprecedented occurrence concerning bowls of that type in Safavid and Zand times.

New motifs are to be seen. The bands of interlacing scrollwork framing the main field on the outside carry blossoms which, their simplicity notwithstanding, are unmatched in earlier metalwork. Below the lower band, the motif of circular interlacing arches resting on a horizontal fillet is equally new in its overall appearance. Most striking, however, is the inside with its rosette or *shamsa* enclosing calligraphy on a ring-matted ground. It is framed by two narrow bands of radiating strokes and a broader band of scrollwork that goes back to the thirteenth century.[14] These would appear to be the result of a Revivalist strain that made itself felt in Iranian art from the very beginning of the Qajar dynasty – if we are to go by so-called lacquerwork, i.e., cardboard and wood objects with painted decoration covered with several layers of transparent varnish.[15] Indeed, the idea of a rosette on the inside of the bowl harks back to fourteenth-century – and earlier – metalwork. Alternating cartouches and sprays lightly incised on the sides belong to the fashionable répertoire adopted in western Iran in contrast to the more traditional motifs, despite the innovative composition on the outside.

Most innovative of all, however, is the inscription engraved within the *shamsa*. Unparalleled in Safavid metalwork, it strikes a new tone of strident Shi'ite militancy well in tune with the development of the *ta'ziya* or religious Passion:

سلام على الحسين   ١ ﻋﻰ ١٢

لعنت على قاتل الحسين

Peace upon Husayn 1261(?)// curse upon
the murderer of Husayn

This text indicates that the bowl was originally intended for *ta'ziya* performances. These religious passions recount, among others, the stages of Husayn's tragic end. The bowl would have been used during the episode in which Husayn is denied water.

Similar bowls without inner decoration or calligraphy of any kind were presumably intended for more general use. A typical specimen was formerly part of the Arfa' al-Dawla collection in the Villa Isfahan (fig. 5).[16]

Despite innovations in the decorative composition, such pieces still belong to the mainstream of the Iranian tradition going back to the middle Safavid period. The very technique – champlevé engraved patterns with black composition overlay on hatched ground to set them off – emphasises their link with the past. They suggest that in Khurasan, the impact of new fashions was, on the whole, moderate by the mid-nineteenth century and the introduction of foreign-born motifs virtually non-existent.

2. Western Iranian metalwork

The contrast could not be greater with contemporary wares from the Western areas.

A bowl acquired in Qazvin by its Tehran owner illustrates the western equivalent of the bowl dated 1785–6 in the Kabul National Museum (fig. 6).[17] Comparison with dated material suggests that it was made at a somewhat later date, probably in the second quarter of the nineteenth century. This might account for variations in the shape – the neck is broader and shorter, the sides are more bulging, the stepped rim at the top unlike the moulding that terminates the lip on the Kabul piece. Above all, the decoration is drastically different. There is no calligraphy. A repeat pattern runs on the neck and on the sides, creating a different rhythm. The main motif is borrowed from a new répertoire shared with textile designers – the bean-like motif, which is actually one half of a two-petal lotus-blossom. Commonly found on so-called cashmere silks, the time and location of its first appearance have yet to be determined.[18]

A closely related bowl-cover (fig. 7) formerly in the Raymond Jones collection may well have originated in the same workshop.[19] This is suggested by the nearly identical border of bean-like motifs with the same tiny rosettes in between.

In shape, the cover derives from a shorter and more sinuous eighteenth-century type.[20] The elongation and greater rigidity appears to betray a western Iranian penchant for exaggeration in a sort of Baroque mood. This is also reflected in the decoration, despite a deliberate attempt at following Safavid rules of composition on bowl covers. The top is chamfered and carries radiating decoration in vertical-oriented downward cartouches as it might on a Safavid dish-cover.[21] A tripartite division has been observed on the main part as on many middle Safavid vessels. On the other hand, the bean-like motifs are outsized although not quite so much as on the bowl. The calligraphy itself, with its thick and rigid lettering, expresses the same trend towards Baroque exaggeration.

In sharp contrast to the shape and decoration, including the calligraphy, the textual context is as conservative as it would have been on an eastern Iranian object. Indeed it slavishly adheres to the Safavid tradition.

In the upper calligraphic frieze, the first four cartouches enclose two much-repeated distichs from Sa'dî's preface to the *Gulistân* – *gharaz naqshîst*, 'Our yearning is a design etc.'[22] The fifth cartouche encloses the first hemistich of a one-liner – in Persian, *fard* or *mufrad* – also by Sa'dî which is remarkable only for being transcribed in abbreviated form:

الهی عاقبت (محمود کن ا) ن

O God, make the issue a felicitous one!
The latter often occurs on Safavid metalwork.[23]

In the lower border, two poems succeed each other. The first one is the poem in the *hazaj* metre already noted on the Kabul tray dated 1805–6, which, as has been said, is often found on Safavid bowl-covers (above, p.313). It is noted with precisely the same variants – *ahl-i bazm* is spelt as a single word. The second poem, a quatrain in the *rubâ'î* metre, begins:

سریوش بقاب تا هم آغوش نشد

یکلحظه دلش ز غم فراموش نشد

As long as the cover-bowl did not embrace the bowl
His soul would not forget sorrow for one moment[24]

I have not encountered this poem before, which, given the limited number of recorded bowl-covers, does not allow one to draw any conclusion.

Both poems are consistent with the standard rule whereby the object is named in the poem(s) engraved on it. In this case, the object-name is *sarpûsh*.[25]

Precisely the same contrast between modernity in design and traditionalism in the literary heritage is presented by a small bowl dated 1242/5 August 1826–24 July 1827 (figs 8–9).[26] The simple shape reproduces an age-old type well-known in Safavid times and closely resembles that of a Victorian and Albert bowl dated 1243.[27] The piece was cast, tinned and engraved. On the outside, six cartouches enclose calligraphy from a great master's hand in the midst of scrollwork derived from the European répertoire via its Hindustani rendering.[28] On the underside a large rosette, each of its radiating lobes filled with formalised floral patterns, is framed by a band or radiating triangular arches, each one enclosing a floral spray, and two narrower bands of ornament no longer to be made out. The carpet effect closely compares with that of the Khurasan bowls even though the répertoire is different. Inside, a calligraphic frieze of 17 cartouches separated by interlacing lobed rosettes runs along the rim emphasised by a festoon of arch-like pendentives. On the bottom, another frieze of 7 cartouches separated by similar rosettes is emphasised by an identical festoon of pendentives.

While the decoration is entirely original, the texts could not be more traditional. Inside, the upper border encloses a famous *ghazal* by Hâfiz (*Ân kas ki bi dast jâm dârad,* 'He that holds a bowl in his hand,' etc.),[29] followed by a simply hemistch – *dil ki dar band* (fig. 9), etc. – from a distich which is fully written on the outside. In the lower border, two distichs often encountered on Safavid metalwork – *Ay sâhib-i tâs gham farâmûshat bâd,* 'O master of the bowl, may you forget every sorrow, etc.'[30] are still legible. They are followed by another hitherto unrecorded poem, much erased by wear, that should eventually be deciphered.[31] On the outside, a distich and a quatrain both unrecorded but well in tune with traditional verses on Safavid metalwork must be traced to their source before any comment can be made.

Too little is known about eighteenth-century metalwork to even venture a guess as to whether the verses by Hâfiz and others reflect a return to the earlier Safavid epigraphical tradition or simply, as I suspect, the continuity of that tradition. Future investigation will eventually provide the answer. Whatever the case, however, the contrast remains between the literary conservatism and the breakdown of the aesthetic continuum.

Awareness of this breakdown might account for a Revivalist trend in the decoration that became increasingly perceptible in the Qajar period.

A typical case is that of a small casket made of beaten copper, tinned and lightly engraved with a figurative pattern on the ring-matted ground (figs. 9, 10).[32] The shape of the casket is a pure product of its time. The lower part designed like a bowl with tapering, incurving sides, continues earlier models. Not so the cover with its dome modelled after the many northern and north-western tomb-towers with chamfered conical roofs. True, the idea of a casket shaped like a mausoleum goes back to early times[33] but the choice of the architectural model, with the marked contrast between the lower and the upper shape, is typical of Qajar aesthetics.

However, the artist has attempted to decorate his casket in the Safavid taste. The subject matter itself is Safavid – animals in the open country or bâdiya,[34] a lion, a hare, etc. So is the handling of the formalised plants which the artist has attempted to render in sixteenth-century style with some success.

Revivalism even left its mark on abstract patterns. A wine bowl of traditional Safavid shape is decorated with a frieze of interlacing circles that goes back to tenth–eleventh-century design.[35] The use of architectural motifs again harks back to very early times.[36]

These were the last tenuous links with a dying tradition. In the second half of the century, the attempts at copying the past became inept, aesthetically and technically. Motifs borrowed from Europe or, sometimes, the pre-Islamic past as seen with European eyes, swept aside most of the traditional répertoire. Most telling of all, the century-old link between the visual and the conceptual, between destination and decoration on one hand and literary excerpts on the other hand was cut off. Persian poetry was no longer calligraphed on objects that had stopped bearing any relationship to the living culture. They were reduced to the level of bazaar curios for foreign visitors and for Iranians who had become tourists within their own environment.

NOTES AND REFERENCES

1. The first historical outline of Iranian metalwork in Islamic times has only just been published: A. S. Melikian-Chirvani, *Islamic Metalwork from the Iranian World,* London 1982, 446 pp. On Qajar metalwork see A. Pope, ed., *A Survey of Persian Art,* Tokyo-London-New York 1965², vol.XII, where two tinned copper objects of the Qajar period are illustrated, a bowl dated 1243/25 July 1827–13 July 1828 in plate 1387c (caption reversed with plate 1387D) and a late nineteenth-century lantern (with a wrong eighteenth-century dating in plate 1388A). Steel objects and enamelled gold are shown further. Other tinned copper wares have been reproduced in general books or catalogues although never published in the scholarly sense, i.e. with due attention paid to the shape, designs and inscriptions. A large group of bowls, trays, ewers and bowl covers must be mentioned among others: R. Efendi, *Azerbayjan dekorativ tatbiqi san'atlari (orta asirlar),* ('The Decorative Arts and Crafts of Azarbayjan in the Middle Ages'), Baku 1976, pls 142-59. A few monographs have appeared in scattered publications e.g. A. A. Ivanov, 'Dannie epigrafiki i voprosi datirovki iranskih mednikh i bronzovikh izdelij XIX v.' ('Epigraphic and dating problems concerning Iranian copper and bronze wares of the 19th c.'), *Epigrafika Vostoka,* XVII (1966), 65-771 and U. Scerrato, 'Coppia di candelabri di Isfahan di epoca Qagar' ('A pair of Isfahan candlesticks from the Qajar period') in *Arte Orientale in Italia* II, Rome 1971, 27-48.

2. This writer is currently gathering material for a 'Survey of Qajar Metalwork'.

3. Many steel objects referred to as 'Safavid' pieces actually belong to the Qajar period. We lack at present a substantial body of steel pieces that may be dated to the Safavid period beyond reasonable doubt. I will show in a future paper that a *kashkûl* published three times as a Safavid piece on the basis of what is clearly an apocryphal date – 1015 H – is thoroughly Qajar in shape and decoration and even technique. See latterly J. W. Allan, *Islamic metalwork in the Nuhad Es-Said Collection,* London 1982, 114-17, no.26.

4. Heavily cast copper, tinned and engraved with designs partly inlaid with black composition. Height: 12.6 centimetres. Diameter of opening: 19.5-20.4 centimetres. Diameter of body: 25.5 centimetres.

5. The bowl dated '1774' was illustrated by S. Maslenitsyna, *Persian Art in the Collection of the Museum of Oriental Art/Iskustvo Irana v Sobranij Gosudarstvennovo Museya Iskusstva Narodov Vostoka,* Leningrad 1975 pl.65. English caption p.193. The Hijra date is not given, the only date quoted being this slightly inaccurate Christian era. The Victoria and Albert Museum equivalent is published in *Islamic Metalwork from the Iranian World,* 338, pl.156. See pp.337-9.

6. E.g. the Khurasan bowl dated 1013/1604-5 in the Kabul Museum: see *ibid.*, 277 n.43 and illustration, 269, fig.68. Note also the mid- to late-sixteenth-century bowl, possibly from Khurasan, in the Victoria and Albert Museum – *ibid.* 295-6. A western Iranian example will be found on p.293.

7. See Melikian-Chirvani, 'Conceptual Art in Iranian Painting and Metalwork' in *Akten des VII. Internationalen Kongresses für iranische Kunst und Archäologie*, Berlin 1979, 393. The concept can be traced back to the late Buddhist period – see *ibid.*, 399, n.6 and *idem*, 'Recherches sur l'Architecture de l'Iran Bouddhique' in *Le Monde Iranien et l'Islam*, III (1975), 39. There is good reason for believing that this concept was actually developed as early as the Achaemenid period as I hope to show soon. It is one of the – perhaps *the* – longest surviving metaphors in the Iranian répertoire.

8. Inventory 58.2.156. Cast copper with engraved decoration on hatched ground – the hatching not so fine and regular as on Safavid wares. The tinning, now decaying, has gone greyish in parts. No visible trace of black composition over hatched areas as on Safavid vessels. Height: 4.4-4.6 centimetres. Diameter: 35.2-35.4 centimetres.

9. These must have first become familiar to Iranian designers through the Mughal miniatures that reached Iran. They are often to be seen in illuminated margins of the Shah Jahân period, e.g. a leaf from a *muraqqa'* in the Edwin Binney 3rd collection in M. C. Beach, *The Grand Mogul*, Williamstown (Mass.) 1978, 173, pl.70, bottom corner right. The motif otherwise appears everywhere including architectural decoration: A. Volwahsen, *Islamisches Indien*, Fribourg 1969, 108, showing a detail of the Taj Mahal.

10. *Islamic Metalwork from the Iranian World*, 301. The fourth cartouche with the patron's name appears in pls 131, 301.

11. *Ibid.*, 34 (on a late sixteenth-century tray-cover from Western Iran) and 321 (on a bowl-cover of the same period).

12. *Qâb* considered by Steingass (*A Comprehensive Persian-English Dictionary*, London 1957⁴) as a Turkish word is glossed 'a vessel or case'. It actually occured on trays – as here – and on bowls as implied by the bowl-covers on which they appear – e.g. Efendi, *Azerbayjan dekorativ tatbiqi san'atlari*, pl.158. Its spelling suggests that it is a Turkicised rendering of Persian *kâp*, a word recorded in the late eleventh century by Zamakhsharî, *Pîshraw-i Adab ya Muqaddimat al-Adab*, ed. Sayyid M. Kâzim Imâm, Tehran 1342 s./1963, 146. Arabic *'azz* is glossed *kâp-i buzurg*, 'a big *kâp*'. *Ghumr* is a *kâp-i khurd*, 'a small *kâp*' and *qa'ba kâp-i chûbîn*, *kâp-i khurd* 'a wooden *kâp*, a small *kâp*'. What is clearly a derived form, *kâpa*, renders Arabic *qadah*.

13. Inventory 58.2.132. Heavily cast copper, tinned with engraved decoration. Height: 9.4-9.6 centimetres. Diameter of opening: 19-19.2 centimetres. Diameter of foot: 10.4-10.9 centimetres.

14. Compare the sketchily trilobate leaf with trilobate elements in

the design engraved on a Khurasan bowl published in Melikian-Chirvani 'Les Bronzes du Khorâssân – V', *Studia Iranica* 6 (1977, 2) pl.x – on the cover, centre left – and xi – petals forming part of the central blossom.

15. The earliest attempt at Revivalism in papier-mâché objets d'art may have been the neo-Moghul manner favoured by artists such as Muhammad Sâdiq as early as 1194/1780, well before the Qajars. See Melikian-Chirvani, 'Objets peints d'Iran', *Connaissance des Arts*, nr.302 (April 1977 pl.415, 6).

16. Tinned copper, cast, with engraved decoration. Height: 14.2 centimetres. Diameter (measured at opening from outer edge to outer edge): 26.5-26.5 centimetres. Diameter of foot: 15.3 centimetres. Formerly in the Villa Isfahan. Sold at Montecarlo by Sotheby's on 28 July 1983; see Sotheby Parke Bernet Monaco sa, *Collection de la Villa Ispahan, Monte-Carlo*, first item in lot 1625, p.49, all described as 'Iran 19th century', without any further characterisation.

17. Raised copper, tinned and engraved. Height: 14.5-14.6 centimetres. Diameter of opening: 27.4-27.6 centimetres. Diameter of body: 31.3-31.4 centimetres. Diameter of flat circular base: 12.5 centimetres.

18. Large size single bean-like motifs do not seem to have been recorded on any work of art predating the nineteenth century. However small-size motifs of this type occur as early as the eleventh century in manuscripts – e.g. in the manuscript dated Ramadân 507/9 February–10 March 1114 of the *Kitâb Tarjumân al-Balâgha*, ed. A. Ateş, Istanbul, 1949, heading of page 33 (facsimile) where the 'bean-like' motifs are seen to be the components of the stylised lotus-blossom. They are engraved as single elements on a silver bowl in the Freer Gallery datable to the eleventh century: Melikian-Chirvani 'La coupe d'Abu Sahl-e Farhad-jerdi', *Gazette des Beaux-Arts,* vi per. lxxi (1968), 130, fig.1.

19. Hammered copper sheet with cast finial riveted through a narrow circular opening at the top. Tinned, with engraved decoration. Height: 25.3 centimetres. Diameter of – slightly distorted – base including flat rim: 24.4-25.4 centimetres.

20. Efendi (see note 1) *op. cit.*, pl.156.

21. Compare *Islamic Metalwork from the Iranian World*, pl.145.

22. The earliest occurrence of the two distichs on metalwork is on the water-tank in the Masjid-i Jâmi' at Herat, completed in 776/1374-5: Melikian-Chirvani 'Un bassin iranien de l'an 1375', *Gazette des Beaux-Arts* 6e pér. lxxiii (1969), 7-8.

23. *Islamic Metalwork,* 321. I have also encountered it on a wine-bucket dated Muharran 828/23 November-22 December 1424 to be published soon.

24. I have failed to read the third hemistich.

25. From inkwells – *Islamic Metalwork,* 284 – to bowls, *ibid.*, 304. *Sarpûsh* is an early word – *ibid.*, 396. It also occurs in Safavid poetry.

26. Height: 44.65 centimetres. Diameter of opening: 14.65-14.75 centimetres.
27. *Islamic Metalwork*, 295, no.295.
28. Here again one may assume that illuminated margins were the source for such designs on metalwork,
29. Often found on Safavid metalwork. For text, see: *Dîvân-i Khwâja Hâfiz-i Shîrâî*, ed. Sayyid A. Anjavî ('Injû'î') Shîrâzî, Shiraz 1346 s./1968², 46-7.
30. The first occurrence known to me is on the wine-bucket dated 1424 mentioned in note 23.
31. The distich reads:

دل که در بند زلف دلدار است

به بلای سیه گرفتار است

> The heart that is trapped in the hair of its Beloved
> Is caught in dire calamity

32. Beaten copper, tinned, with engraved decoration on ring-matted ground. Height with cover: 8.6 centimetres. Diameter of base: 8.9-8.95 centimetres.
33. Compare *Islamic Metalwork from the Iranian World*, 150, fig.56 – casket from Fars, fourteenth century – and 32, fig.7, stupa-shaped incense burner from Khurasan, probably ninth century.
34. On the *bâdiya* theme the punning reference to the *bâdiya*-type of bowl on which it appears in Safavid times, see Melikian-Chirvani, *Islamic Metalwork from the Iranian World*, particularly 330-1.
35. Height: 10.6-10.7 centimetres. Diameter of opening: 20-20.2 centimetres. Diameter of ring foot: 8.4 centimetres. Its dating in the Qajar period is established by certain typical motifs as the clumsy quatrefoils in a row (compare with pl.148 in Efendi, *Azerbayjan dekorativ tatbiqi san'atlari*). The technique is poor. Too thinly cast, the walls have been pierced in several areas by the engraver's chisel. Compare the interlacing roundels on the eleventh-century Khurasan candlestick in Melikian-Chirvani, 'The candlestick as a symbol of the cosmos' in *Proceedings of the Edinburgh symposium on Seljuk art and culture*, edited by R. Hillenbrand (in press).
36. A typical architectural motif is the band of square tiles resting on their tip. Architectural motifs on early pieces – so far unpublished; several are recorded in the writer's archives – include concave discs in bas-relief of the type found inside the anonymous mausoleum at Bukhara traditionally associated with Ismâ'îl the Samanid.

1

2

3

4

5

6

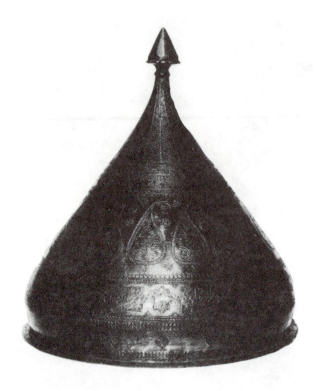

7

8

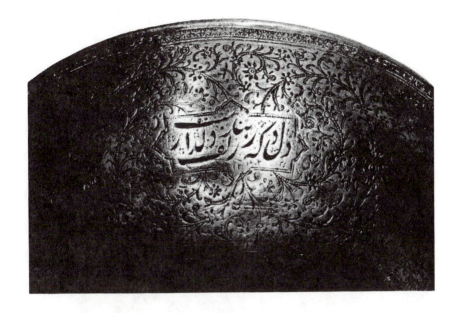

9

10

11

12

19

The royal palaces of the Qajar dynasty; a survey

'It stands on an eminently pleasant point of the adjoining mountains, being built on a detached and commanding hill, on the great slope of the Elborz. The edifice is lofty, and when seen from a distance, presents a very magnificent appearance. The stateliness of the structure itself, is very much increased in effect, by the superb range of terraces, which connect its spacious gardens, as they diverge from the base of the building downwards, towards the bottom of the hill.'[1]

Sir Robert Ker Porter's description of Fath'Alî Shah's summer palace of Qasr-i Qajar (figs 1 and 2) located in the hills north of the capital Tehran, whch he saw during his years of travel in the east from 1817 to 1820, reveals that he was more discerning and appreciative of the merits of Qajar architecture than later scholars who either ignore it entirely or dismiss it as unworthy of thoughtful attention. There is for example no mention of any building later in date than the Madrasa-yi Madar-i Shah of Isfahan built between 1706 and 1714 in Arthur Upham Pope's standard *Survey of Persian Art*[2] and indeed no monograph devoted to any systematic examination and recording of eighteenth- and nineteenth-century buildings. Qajar buildings are mentioned in gazeteers and guidebooks but the coverage is uneven so that several sources have to be consulted in order to compile a reliable handlist of surviving monuments.[3] The Qajar period, was, however, remarkably stable and peaceful by the standards of Persian history, creating an environment favourable to the encouragement of extensive architectural programmes. Buildings have survived in relatively large numbers, naturally concentrated in and around Tehran, but also in Isfahan, Kashan, Kirman, Qazvîn, Rasht, Shiraz and Zinjan. Especially important are the secular buildings which include the palaces and country residences of the Qajar rulers and their extensive families. Here first hand examination of the monuments themselves can be supplemented by the wealth of information available in such secondary sources as the many contemporary European travel accounts and official reports, Persian language chronicles and archives, and the illustrations provided by European paintings and sketches and later photographs.

The fall of the Safavids in the early eighteenth century initiated a period of political chaos and civil war in which Karim Khan Zand's comparatively tranquil interregnum should be regarded as only a temporary suspension of hostilities. Finally, Persia was reduced to a state of exhausted peace by the triumph of Agha Muhammad of the Turkish speaking Qajar tribe based in Mazandaran, who captured and murdered the last Zand ruler Lutf 'Alî Khan at Kirman in 1794. Agha Muhammad had already consolidated his power base in north Persia by establishing his capital at Tehran in 1786 and while his personal supremacy was shortlived as he was assassinated in 1797, his successors ruled until the deposition of the last Qajar Shah, Ahmad, in 1924. During the Qajar period Persia was still ruled as a traditional society and regarded very much as a personal possession of the royal family. Provincial governorships, for example, were divided between members of a very extended Qajar family and consequently a distinct class of officials developed which through patronage and connections amassed an enormous amount of influence. Despite these conservative pressures, however, the Qajar rulers were concerned to maintain internal peace; they also made efforts to resist the conflicting influences of British and Russian foreign policy, and made intermittent attempts at military and administrative reform and economic development.

In such a personalised society the ruler's influence extended through all levels of activity. This becomes very clear when examining visible expressions of this influence such as architecture, and here the two outstanding personalities of the Qajar Dynasty were Fath 'Alî Shah (1797–1834) Agha Muhammad's nephew, and Nâsir al-Dîn Shah (1848–96), Fath 'Alî Shah's great grandson. Fath 'Alî Shah's reign was marked by his efforts to maintain a stable country despite the loss of Georgia, the Caucasus and north Azerbaijan to the Russians formalised at the treaties of Gulistan in 1813 and Turkomanchai in 1828, and the renewal of diplomatic relations with Europe, especially Britain and France. In his style of rule he was well aware of the importance of keeping up an impressive appearance. His elegant figure resplendent in tight-waisted brocade robes and his personal beauty zealously maintained by hair dyes and cosmetics until his death at 68 was represented many times by his court painters (see fig. 4 in Chapter 17) and overwhelmed European visitors such as Ker Porter:

> He was one blaze of jewels, which literally dazzled the sight on first looking at him; but the details of his dress were these; a lofty tiara of three elevations was on his head, whch shape appears to have been long peculiar to the crown of the great king. It was entirely composed of thickly-set diamonds, pearls, rubies, and emeralds so exquisitely disposed as to form a mixture of the most beautiful colours in the brilliant light reflected from its surface. Several black feathers, like the heron plume, were intermixed with the resplendent aigrettes of this truly imperial diadem, whose bending points were finished with pear-formed pearls of an immense size. The vesture was gold tissue,

nearly covered with a similar disposition of jewellery; and crossing the shoulders were two strings of pearls, probably the largest in the world. I call his dress a vesture, because it set close to his person, from the neck to the bottom of the waist, showing a shape as noble as his air.

His mind was equally well-dressed,[4] as he patronised literature and the arts, writing poetry himself and commissioning a splendid illustrated manuscript of the *Shâhanshâh-nâma*.[5] In other leisure pursuits such as hunting he also followed Persian royal tradition.

The short reign of his grandson Muhammad Shah (1834–48) was notable for a change in certain outward aspects, at least to a more European style of rule. Henry Rawlinson was employed to modernise the Persian army which included adopting European uniforms, while the court abandoned the traditional long-skirted robes and beards for frock coats and trousers. Nâsir al-Dîn Shah's long reign witnessed an acceleration of European influence, as diplomats, soldiers, technicians and missionaries came into Persia. Increased competition from cheap manufactured imports threatened local manufactures. Surviving portraits and impressions of Nâsir al-Dîn Shah (fig. 3) show a change in personal style from the elegance of Fath 'Alî Shah. Apart from his habit of decorating his lambskin hat with diamonds or wearing jewelled epaulettes his clothes were quite sober reflecting contemporary European tailoring. 'Lady Durand then sat beside His Majesty on a gilded couch, and they chatted in French, while I observed the splendid rubies and diamonds decorating the front of the Shah's uniform, the well-known diamond aigrette, and his trick of pushing up his spectacles on to the front of his *kulâh*.'[6] While still pursuing the traditional royal sport of hunting his interests were more modest than those of Fath 'Alî Shah. Instead of composing grandiose verse he was busy keeping a prose diary especially after the first of his three visits to Europe in 1873, 1878 and 1889,[7] and was an enthusiastic amateur photographer.[8]

Qajar buildings, despite their inventive flamboyance, are firmly rooted in the principles and methods of Persian architectural tradition. While therefore disappointingly few examples of pre-Qajar palace architecture have survived, it is necessary to review them, as they furnish an essential background against which the Qajar structures can be interpreted and understood. The two cities of Persia in which royal buildings have survived in any discernible quantity are Isfahan and Shiraz, capitals respectively of the Safavid dynasty (1501–1722) and of the shortlived Zand dynasty (1750–1794) where ambitious town planning schemes were initiated under Shah 'Abbâs I (1588–1629) and Karîm Khan (1750–79). Shah 'Abbâs's Isfahan is still dominated by the enormous square – the Maydân-i Shah – begun in the late sixteenth century, each of whose four arcaded sides is dominated by an imposing building. Here the only example of palace architecture is the 'Âlî Qapu built in 1598 which is basically an unsatisfactory construction, as it poses questions of function and deployment of space to which reasonable answers are difficult to find. A compact box-like structure of five storeys, it is probably best regarded as a monumental portal to now destroyed palace buildings which would have occupied gardens between the Maydân-i Shah and the north-south thoroughfare of the Chahâr Bâgh, as it is clearly too cramped and small to have functioned as a palace in its own right. Its most striking architectural features are the juxtaposition of levels within the building expressed most clearly in the several storeys of low rooms grouped around the main portal all interlinked by open arches, and the large columned porch – *talâr* – on the second storey open on three sides and with a recess at the back to take a large throne. Clearly the most important considerations were to create continuous and varied space and a close relationship between internal and external environments. The same principles are seen in the Chihil Sutûn palace situated well behind the Maydân-i Shah north-west of the 'Âlî Qapu and completed in 1647 for Shah 'Abbâs ii. Here the open columned *talâr* is, however, at ground level and on a larger scale . . . Behind the *talâr* is a large reception hall flanked by a split-level honeycomb of small rooms. In comparison with the 'Âlî Qapu the function of the Chihil Sutûn is less ambiguous; it was reserved for the reception and entertainment of distinguished guests. Other independent buildings now vanished set within the palace garden would have functioned as administrative units or as private quarters for the ruler and his household. The third surviving royal building, the Hasht Bihisht, which was built c.1670 by Shah Sulaymân, south of the Chihil Sutûn as a graceful octagonal kiosk with open columned porches on four sides, also illustrates the concept of a palace as a group of independent buildings set within a garden. Essentially the Safavid palace structures are best understood as a series of additions within an extensive royal administrative and residential area. In Europe, expansion of a palace would have been made by firmly building extensions to the original structure, whereas in Persia the problem was solved by constructing independent, relatively small buildings. This solution was more intimate, convenient from the point of view of climate and aesthetically pleasing.

Karîm Khan Zand's buildings in eighteenth-century Shiraz continued these basic principles of palace architecture. Like Shah 'Abbâs he planned an imposing Maydân-i Vakîl with secular and religious buildings grouped around it. The Maydân which was noted by European travellers[9] in the nineteenth century no longer exists, as buildings of the Karîm Khan Zand avenue contructed in the 1930s now traverse its site. Certain palace buildings have survived, however, whch indicate that traditional forms continued and functions were divided between different types of structure. Unlike Isfahan, the main building whch served both as a defensive citadel and administrative centre – the *Arg* – has survived though much altered. It consists of a large square enclosure built of brick with a tower at each corner and two storeys of apartments built into the walls facing an open interior courtyard. Outside the citadel an adjacent building with a columned open *talâr* functioned as a public audience chamber, while for more private occasions a garden on the south side of the Maydân contained individual pavilions, of which one – a graceful kiosk – has survived, repeating on a smaller scale the elegance of Isfahan's Hasht Bihisht and continuing the close relationship between internal and external environment.

As Fath 'Alî Shah and Nâsir al-Dîn Shah had the longest reigns of the Qajar dynasty, they naturally had the time and scope to embark on extensive building programmes in which the construction and embellishment of palaces concentrated at Tehran played a significant role. Here they continued the use of traditional building materials – brick for the structure, and stone, wood, stucco, ceramic tile and painting for decoration. Despite the shortness of his reign, Agha Muhammad established what was to become the Qajar tradition of migrating from winter palaces in Tehran to summer palaces in its environs or further afield. Before he formally established Tehran as his capital in 1786 the city had enjoyed a reputation as a reasonably prosperous and spacious settlement famed for the excellent produce of its orchards and market gardens. The Safavids had built an *Arg* or citadel surrounded by a wall which was further augmented by Karîm Khan Zand before he decided to base himself at Shiraz. In 1759 he commissioned the architect Ustâdh Ghulâm Rizâ Tabrîzî to rebuild the walls of the town and to erect an audience chamber, administrative buildings and private quarters within the *Arg*. On these foundations Agha Muhammad was able to begin the establishment of a full-scale palace which was to become the Gulistân Palace of Fath 'Alî Shah and his successors.[10] As Agha Muhammad's original buildings in Tehran were adapted and augmented by his successors a clearer idea of his palace architecture is obtained by examining the summer palaces which he built at Astarabad and Sari in Mazandaran. Although the original buildings have long since vanished there are reliable contemporary accounts of them. According to Binning, who visited Astarabad in 1851, the foundation date 1791 was still clear over the entrance, although the palace was in a very dilapidated condition. James Morier who visited it in 1815 gives a clear description:

We were lodged in the palace built by Aga Mahomed Khan, which considering the comparatively decayed state of the province is still an excellent building, even superior to the palaces of Teheran. It is entered as usual by a maidan or square that leads to the principal gate, which is lofty and well ornamented with gilding and paintings. Here we remarked two or three old howitzers, and one long gun, bearing an inscription of Aurungzebe, all brought hither by Nadir Shah. From the gate we entered into a large well paved court, planted with orange trees, now loaded with fruit. The furthest end of the court is occupied by a very lofty Dewan Khaneh or hall of audience, supported by two immense wooden pillars, and painted all over with the portraits of the old Persian heroes. On the sides are large rooms, also very curiously painted, from which I copied the picture of a woman playing on a stringed instrument, and over them are suites of upper apartments, from the windows of which a great tract of the country surrounding the town is to be seen. Behind the Dewan Khaneh is a large anderoon, or the women's apartment, strongly secured by very massive doors.'[11]

This is in turn supplemented by Hommaire de Hell's drawing of 1848,[12] which shows that Morier's 'portraits of the old Persian heroes' was a lively tilework panel depicting the combat of Rustam and Isfandiyâr.

The palace at Sari was visited and described by James Baillie Fraser in 1821:

The palace, which was built by Aga Mahommed Khan, makes no great appearance externally; but I have been told that it formerly contained much comfortable accommodation; certainly those parts of it which I saw were far from magnificent. The chief dewankhaneh, or hall of audience, was once fitted up with paintings and mirrors, after the usual Persian taste, but the former are defaced or faded and the latter are broken or in disrepair. One painting, representing Shah Ismail cleaving in twain the Aga of the Janissaries before the Turkish emperor Sultan Solyman, a favourite subject of the Persian pencil, certainly possesses considerable merit. Some of the groups fighting and struggling in the foreground are drawn with a degree of spirit and execution not often to be seen in Eastern pictures. The walls of the principal public rooms, for three or four feet above the floor, are lined with Tabreez marble, painted with flowers, and certain rooms of the more private apartments in the interior, into which I was afterwards admitted, were finished in the same taste. All was clean and tolerably spacious but without any splendour whatever. The whole of this palace, though not regularly fortified, is surrounded by a wall, and capable, to a certain extent, of defense.[13]

By 1836 it had been destroyed by fire.[14]

The accounts of the two palaces show, however, that their plan and style of decoration were similar, namely walled enclosed gardens dominated by an audience chamber at one end featuring the columned *talâr* noted in Safavid buildings, and ornamented with striking narrative paintings and title panels. Nearer to Tehran, twelve miles beyond Damâvand, Agha Muhammad had built a more modest structure, the Bâgh-i Shâh, noted by Morier in 1815[15] as basically an orchard containing a small pavilion which functioned as a hunting lodge.

The task of developing the city of Tehran was continued by Fath 'Alî Shah. Plenty of contemporary accounts give a picture of a polygonal enclosure surrounded by a turreted brick wall and a deep moat (e.g. fig. 4). Six gates pierced the wall – the Dawlat and Shemiran gates to the north, the Shâh 'Abd al-'Azîm and Naw gates to the south, and the Dawlâb and Qazvîn gates to east and west respectively. All were flanked by pairs of brick towers and decorated with gaudy tiled panels depicting such favourite themes as Rustam combating the White Dîv and other heroic deeds. Within (fig. 5), the city was cramped with newly built bazaar and residential quarters and dominated by the sprawling complex of the *Arg* or Gulistân Palace in the south, which functioned as both administrative centre and residence for Fath 'Alî Shah and his family. Today, disappointingly little of his work has survived, since Nâsir al-Dîn Shah drastically remodelled and rebuilt it as part of his ambitious reconstruction programme for Tehran begun in 1867. Apart from contemporary written and pictorial sources, a map of the palace drawn by Dr J. Feuvrier, who was Nâsir al-Dîn Shah's private physician from 1889 to 1892,[16] enables the surviving structures to be identified (fig. 6). Only two remain of Fath 'Alî Shah's scheme – the *talâr* of the Divânkhâna – audience chamber or *Takht-i Marmar* – the Marble Throne as it is more popularly named, and the *'Imârat-i Bâdgîr* – Building of the Windtower – on the north and south sides respectively. From contemporary descriptions, however, it is clear that the basic principles of Safavid and Zand palace architecture of enclosing independent structures within an extensive garden were followed. The account of the French traveller Pierre Amedée Jaubert makes it clear that by 1806 Fath 'Alî Shah's additions to Karîm Khan Zand's and Agha Muhammad's buildings were complete, as he described them in considerable detail.[17] He entered the palace through an elaborate gateway, the *Dar-i Sa'âdat,* also known as the 'Âlî Qapu, which opened into a spacious garden court. Passing through another gate, he was taken down a long avenue towards an open porch which from his description of its pair of twisted green marble columns and the throne on which Fath 'Alî Shah was seated is identifiable as the *Takht-i Marmar* (fig. 7).[18] After his audience, Fath 'Alî Shah had him escorted through luxuriant gardens containing ornamental pools and pavilions which no longer survive. The *Takht-i Marmar* is directly related in function to the columned *talârs* of Isfahan's 'Âlî Qapu and Chihil Sutûn although in structure it is more of a chamber open on one side only. Its interior, lavishly decorated with carved stone friezes, mirrorwork inlaid woodwork, and large scale oil paintings of Fath 'Alî Shah, his courtiers, and European figures, which frame the green marble throne, is both a dictionary of Qajar taste and a possible indication of the degree of luxury which may once have adorned the Isfahan palaces.

Fath 'Alî Shah did not reside only in the Gulistân Palace, but kept several establishments divided between the city and country for the court's winter and summer migrations. This habit was to be maintained by all the Qajars, a nomadic custom preserved from their tribal past as well as a sensible measure designed to cope with seasonal variations of climate. In practice, the distances travelled were small since most of the summer residences were located in the Shemiranat – the villages of Shemiran, Gulhak and Tajrish which today are northern suburbs of Tehran. One of Fath 'Alî Shah's favourite summer residences, the Nigaristân Palace, situated then to the north-east of the town was completed by 1810.[19] Today only one structure survives, a vaulted pavilion decorated in white and mauve stucco, now functioning as the Museum of National Arts, surrounded and dwarfed by buildings of the Plan Organisation.[20] Fortunately, the Nigaristân was much visited by European travellers whose accounts enable its appearance and plan to be reconstructed. It is interesting as an example of a private informal palace in comparison with the Gulistân. 'Its near neighbourhood, as well as superior beauty, often attracts the Shah to walk to it from the ark and to pass hours there, in the most delightful relaxation of mind from the cares or ceremonies of state . . .' observed Sir Robert Ker Porter.[21]

It consisted of three separate buildings[22] situated within a beautiful garden 600 paces long by 300 acres wide planted with poplars and roses and entered by a large portal. The first building encountered was the one whch survives today described by Jeanne Dieulafoy in 1885 as a large domed pavilion in the form of a Greek cross with a group of smaller rooms in each arm.[23] The most flamboyant building was situated at the end of the garden, an octagonal audience hall decorated with paintings of Fath 'Alî Shah and his sons receiving foreign ambassadors which were noted by a series of European visitors from William Price in 1811[24] to Curzon writing in 1889.[25] The remaining building was the *andarûn* – the women's quarters – a closed rectangular structure without external windows built around an inner courtyard. The comparison with earlier royal buildings such as the Hasht Bihisht at Isfahan and the Karîm Khan pavilion at Shiraz set within a garden is obvious, but no parallel exists for the plan of the *andarûn*. The disintegration of the Nigaristân began early, as George Keppel in 1824 noted that the summer houses are dirty and already decaying,[26] a state confirmed by Binning in 1850 – 'The apartments are all dirty and dingy; the present Shah rarely comes hither and the place is consequently neglected.'[27]

Nothing now remains of Fath 'Alî Shah's summer residences in the Shemiranat, though the ruins of Qasr-i Qâjâr, the most splendid of them, did survive until the 1950s. Sufficient descriptions, drawings and plans, however, exist, so it is possible to understand its original appearance. It was completed by the early nineteenth century, as Tancoigne seeing it in

1807 located it four miles north of Tehran[28] and described its stucco-covered brick buildings set like an amphitheatre against a rock. William Price in 1812 was full of admiration for its setting:

> The Takht-i Kajar, or Palace of Kajar, is a noble pile of building situated on an eminence, about half way between Tehiran and Shemran, surrounded by beautiful gardens, to which an aqueduct conveys water from the mountains. The beauties of nature and art, richly blended, make this one of the most delightful residences in Persia. . . .[29]

The most informative source is provided by the plan and meticulous drawings (see figs. 1 and 2) of the French architect Pascal Coste who visited Persia from 1839 to 1841.[30] Two features are especially striking. The palace was constructed as a series of symmetrical ascending terraces, each contained within an arcaded brick wall finally reaching the royal apartments at the summit which were decorated with portraits of Fath 'Alî Shah and his family. The proportion of open space far exceeds that allocated to the buildings, especially in the enormous garden preceding the columned pavilion which forms the first gatehouse. In terms of architecture the rectangular double-storeyed building of the royal apartments is directly comparable to the *andarûn* of the Nigaristân Palace, as they were both constructed without windows to open on to an interior garden court. The gatehouse also with its central two storeyed entrance and upstairs *talâr* is in direct line of descent from Isfahan's 'Âlî Qapu.

Another favourite summer palace of Fath 'Alî Shah was the Sulaymâniyya built in 1808 at Karaj, once a small village west of Tehran. From travellers' accounts it was a less formal structure than Qasr-i Qâjâr consisting of a series of garden courts containing a tower, audience hall and andarûn. Only the audience hall which was remarkable for the profusion of its decoration has survived today as one of the buildings of the National School of Agriculture. According to Lady Sheil's account:

> It was decorated in the usual style of Persian taste – abundance of gilding, varnish of all colours, looking glasses covered the walls and ceiling; fresco paintings of damsels of Europe and Persia were interspersed, all scantily attired, but particularly the former, who were invariably represented as if in the fullest or rather the scantiest dress for a ball. . . . At one end of the apartment was a large fresco painting, full size, of Fetteh Ali Shah, in regal array, with a numerous party of his sons standing around him. . . . At the other extremity of the room was another painting of still greater attraction. It represented Agha Mohammad Khan, the founder of the Kajjar Dynasty, surrounded by the chiefs of his tribe who helped him to the sovereignty of Persia.[31]

Not content with the environs of Tehran, Fath 'Alî Shah had summer palaces situated at a greater distance in the north at Sultaniyya[32] on the route to Tabriz which was completed by 1806 and in the east at Chashma-yi 'Alî near Dâmghân. Sultanîyya has disappeared completely, while at Chashma-yi 'Alî (fig. 8) only an octagonal pavilion with deep inset columned *talâr*s on four sides has survived.[33] Contemporary travel accounts indicate that both palaces were originally large terraced complexes comparable to Qasr-i Qâjâr.

Most of Fath 'Alî Shah's migrations alternated between a winter base in Tehran and various summer residences spread over a wide north-east radius. When he travelled to the south of Persia, apart from the Bâgh-i Takht[34] which he had constructed in Shiraz in 1798, he was prepared to use renovated Safavid palaces, notably at Isfahan and Kashan. At Isfahan he chose the Hasht Bihisht, where he redecorated the columned octagonal kiosk with gilded stucco and large-scale portraits of himself and his court so successfully that the building was frequently mistaken for a Qajar original.[35] The Bâgh-i Fîn just outside Kashan had been built by Shah 'Abbâs I as a summer retreat on the plan of separate pavilions set within a garden enclosed by a high wall and monumental gateway. Fath 'Alî Shah made extensive additions here including an octagonal kiosk, *andarûn* and bathhouse.[36]

The number and extent of Fath 'Alî Shah's palaces were a direct result of his migratory way of life. This was governed not only by a nostalgia for the Qajars' tribal customs or the seasonal requirements of climate but also by the practicalities of internal policy. The migrations followed by long stays in summer encampments meant that Fabh 'Alî Shah could check local conditions and renew alliances with tribal chiefs. His buildings were traditional in their basic plan and arrangement with changes evolving at a natural pace rather than as a result of external influences. His restoration of the Hasht Bihisht shows, for example, how easily his architects and decorators could add to the seventeenth-century foundation. Where foreign elements appeared, notably the paintings of Europeans, they were blended into the Persian scheme. Against this traditional background, however, a strong individual taste emerged. Normally it was a ruler's custom to abandon his predecessor's buildings and construct his own, as is shown by the neglect and decay into which Agha Muhammad's Mazandaran palaces were allowed to fall. Fath 'Alî Shah seemingly liked Safavid buildings as he went to considerable effort to renovate the Hasht Bihisht and the Bâgh-i Fîn. His contemporary architecture has as common themes a preference for a generous allowance of garden space in proportion to that allocated to buildings and a taste in decoration for grandiose painted compositions centred on himself surrounded by family and courtiers.

Nâsir al-Dîn Shah built as extensively as his great grandfather but introduced new influences which resulted in a notably different style of architecture. He maintained the Qajar customs of abandoning his predecessors' buildings and of migrating from winter to summer residences but on a more modest scale. The long journey to such places as Sultâniyya was abandoned and he concentrated on a series of residences in the Shemiranât. His horizons had been broadened by contact with European ideas of architecture, both from seeing imported drawings and plans, and from 1873 onwards by direct observation during his travels. His palace buildings therefore present a rich amalgam of Persian tradition and European innovation. As a beginning he embarked in 1867 on a drastic reconstruction programme for Tehran by demolishing congested areas of the city and building large squares and broad boulevards and eventually introducing street lighting. He enlarged the area to four times that of Fath 'Alî Shah's city and encircled it with a splendid new set of walls complete with towers and moat and twelve tile-decorated gates. These walls were designed and constructed by General Buhler to a plan based on Vauban's fortifications of Paris.[37]

Within the newly extended Tehran the Gulistân Palace was now centrally positioned. Nâsir al-Dîn Shah continued to use it as his winter residence and administrative centre, but so transformed it that as it stands today it is essentially his work; of Fath 'Alî Shah's buildings only the *Takht-i Marmar* and the much restored 'Imârat-i Bâdgîr remain. Altogether Nâsir al-Dîn Shah spent twenty-six years from 1867 to 1892 rebuilding the Gulistân Palace to a plan which still maintained the traditional segregation of public and private areas. The work was divided into three phases – 1867–73, 1873–82, 1882–92.

Nâsir al-Dîn Shah's first project was the construction of the *Shams al-'Imârat* – the Sun Building – on the east side of the palace area which was completed in 1867. Apparently he had been studying pictures of European architecture and had decided that he wanted a tall building which looked out over Tehran, and commissioned his chief architect Dûst 'Alî Khan, Nizâm al-Dawla, to design and supervise the work. The resulting building, which served as Nâsir al-Dîn Shah's private quarters, is a multi-storeyed tower with two turrets with balconies. An outstanding feature is the flamboyant decoration in polychrome ceramic tile using such motifs as the lion and sun emblem of the Qajars, and Victorian garlands of roses intertwined with Persian arabesque strapwork. In contrast to Fath 'Alî Shah's taste for painting as architectural decoration Nâsir al-Dîn Shah's preference was for massed highly coloured tilework[38] which covers the outer surface of the Gulistân Palace, ornate carved stucco and mirror inlay reflecting in their designs the influence of contemporary European fashion. Other buildings constructed up to 1873 were a *takya* – a round building with a central stage for the performance of religious spectacles, especially the Muharram passion plays – in the south of the palace area, and *andarûn* quarters behind the Takht-i Marmar.

From 1873 to 1882 Nâsir al-Dîn Shah concentrated his attention on the north side of the palace where he pulled down all Fath 'Alî Shah's buildings. Under the supervision of Mîrzâ Yahyâ Khan, Mushîr al-Dawla, a spacious new series of buildings was erected in their place (figs 9–11) entered by a mirror-decorated stair which leads to a tiled vestibule from which access is gained to the audience hall and other reception rooms. All these buildings are linked externally by an impressive double-storeyed façade which combines such European features as tall windows and semi-engaged classical columns alternating with continuous tilework decoration in which repeated geometrical motifs are mixed with designs of flowers and scrolling foliage. At the same time the *Nâranjistân* – Orangery – was built and the retaining walls of the palace completed and decorated with tiles.

During the third phase two buildings were added. A new *andarûn* was built in 1882 behind the audience hall on the north side on the plan of a rectangular enclosure around a garden court. A few years later the private quarters were extended as a European style *Khwâbgâh* – Sleeping Place – two storeyed with windows surmounted by classical pediments and a continuous balustrade running along the roof, was built within the *andarûn*'s garden.[39] The last building erected in 1891 was small, rect-angular and two-storeyed – the Kakh-i Abyad – the White Palace – on the south side to the right of the present entrance to the palace gardens. Comparatively little of Nâsir al-Dîn Shah's work in the Gulistân Palace has survived, about a quarter of the buildings shown on Dr Feuvrier's plan. On the west side, the guardhouses and stables have been demo-lished and the formerly private street Khiyabân-i Nâ'ib al-Saltana is now the public Khiyabân-i Davâr. While Fath 'Alî Shah's Takht-i Marmar survives on the north side only, the building housing the audience and reception halls remain from Nâsir al-Dîn Shah's reign as the *andarûn* behind was pulled down in the early 1960s to make room for the Ministries of Finance and Justice. The *takya* and neighbouring buildings have been replaced on the south side by offices allocated to the Ministry of Information, but the Kakh-i Abyad has been converted into an ethno-graphical museum. The *Shams al-'Imârat* on the east side has been preserved.

Nâsir al-Dîn Shah's summer palaces built in the Shemiranat share architectural features common to the Gulistân Palace. Parts of two palaces, Ishratabad and Sultanabad, both built in 1888 respectively below and above Qasr-i Qajar, have survived and apart from continuing the traditional scheme of a garden containing independent buildings they exhibit a marked eccentricity and irregularity of plan and decoration in comparison with the graceful symmetry of Fath 'Alî Shah's designs.

At 'Ishratâbâd[40] the main surviving building is a four storeyed brick tower, the *Khwâbgâh* or private apartments of Nâsir al-Dîn Shah (fig. 12). Three of the storeys are decorated with polychrome tile panels with gaudy floral designs while the top storey has an open colonnade running around all sides. In style and construction it is comparable with the *Shams al-'Imâra* and now destroyed *Khwâbgâh* in the Gulistân Palace. The remaining buildings are devoted to the *andarûn* apartments and here instead of a single structure whose rooms discreetly face on to a closed garden a more open plan was adopted. Apartments were still focused on an ornamental centre but they took the form of seventeen separate chalets grouped around a lake (fig. 13). A complete *andarûn* plan is found at Sâhib Qirâniyya[41] the northernmost of Nâsir al-Dîn Shah's Shemiranat palaces at Niyâvarân. At Sultanatâbâd separate buildings were again constructed in a garden of greater extent than that of 'Ishratâbâd.[42] The two which have survived are at *Khwâbgâh* – here a five- storeyed tower of polygonal shape and a rectangular building with a deep colonnaded porch running around it which functioned as a public audience hall (figs. 14 and 15). Its most notable feature is a superb reception room with painted ceiling and dado of polychrome tiles whose range of motifs varying from traditional Persian subjects to whimsical copies of Europeans are unequalled. The *andarûn* quarters have vanished completely so that there is no way of knowing if they resembled the chalets of 'Ishratâbâd and Sâhib Qirâniyya or the traditional plan. Dr Feuvrier does not comment on this in his account of Sultanatâbâd, being more interested in describing a clock tower which Nâsir al-Dîn Shah had built based on an original at Nîmes.[43]

Nâsir al-Dîn Shah's summer palaces represent the apogee of Qajar secular architecture on the grand scale. From his few successors only Muzaffar al-Dîn Shah (1896–1907) attempted any building schemes, though on a much reduced scale. In the Gulistân Palace, for example, his work is seen only in some tilework friezes lining a hall leading out of the entrance vestibule of Nâsir al-Dîn Shah's buildings on the north side; these tiles were installed in 1899.[44] Here the techniques and subject matter blend ancient and modern, as the tiles depict rulers of Persia including the Parthians and Sasanians and such notables as Shah 'Abbâs I and Nâdir Shah, and views of Persian and European monuments but all worked in a stippled and hatched sepia and white colour scheme inspired by contemporary lithographs and photographs. In the Shemiranat, Muzaffar al-Dîn Shah in 1940 built one palace – Doshantepe[45] – east of Tehran, where the traditional garden of generous proportions harmonises with a white domed and balconied building supposedly inspired by the Trocadero in Paris and a collection of wrought iron greenhouses, pavilions and arbours to produce the last extravaganza of late Qajar Euro-Persian architecture.

NOTES AND REFERENCES
1. Sir Robert Ker Porter, *Travels in Georgia, Persia, Armenia, Ancient Babylonia . . . during the Years 1817, 1818, 1819 and 1820*, London 1821-2, I, 335.
2. Pope (ed.), *A Survey of Persian Art*, Oxford 1938, II, 1213-5, IV, pls 501-6. The eighteenth and nineteenth centuries are dismissed in Vol.II, 1216-18; *idem., Introducing Persian Architecture*, Oxford 1969. A very brief and unsatisfactory paragraph on p.115.
3. Certain buildings are listed in the following: Laurence Lockhart, *Persian Cities*, London 1960; Roger Stevens, *The Land of the Great Sophy*, London 1979; Nosratollah Meshkati, *A List of the Historical Sites and Ancient Monuments of Iran*, Tehran 1974.
4. Porter, *op. cit.*, I, 325-6.
5. *Shâhanshâh-Nâma 1225 H-1810*, India Office Library Persian MS 3442.
6. Ella Sykes, *Through Persia on a Side-saddle*, London 1901, 19.
7. Nâsir al-Dîn Shah Qajar, *The Diary of H.M. the Shah Of Persia during his Tour of Europe in A.D. 1873* (translation by J. W. Redhouse), London 1874.
8. Angelo M. Piemontese, 'The photograph album of the Italian Diplomatic mission to Persia (summer 1862)', *East and West*, NS XXII, 3-4, Rome 1972, 261-2.
9. See J. A. Lerner, 'British travellers accounts as a source for Qajar Iran,' *Bulletin of the Asia Institute of Pahlavi University*, nos 1-4, Shiraz 1976, 205-74, for a reconstruction of Karîm Khan's plan and for a survey of comments.
10. For a detailed account of the Gulistân Palace, see Yahya Zoka, *A Short History of the Buildings of the Royal Citadel of Tehran and a Guide to the Gulistân Palace*, Tehran 1349.
11. *A Second Journey through Persia, Armenia and Asia Minor to Constantinople between the Years 1812 and 1816*, London 1818, chap.XXIII, 376-7.
12. Xavier Hommaire de Hell, *Travels in the Steppes of the Caspian Sea, the Crimea, the Caucasus etc.*, London 1847, IV, pl.LXXXIV.
13. *Travels and Adventures in the Persian Provinces on the Southern Banks of the Caspian Sea*, London 1826, chap.IV, 41-2.
14. Charles Stuart, *Journal of a Residence in Northern Persia and the Adjacent Provinces of Turkey (in 1835-36)*, London 1854, 266.
15. *Op. cit.*, chap.XXIII, 361.
16. *Trois ans à la cour de Perse*, Paris 1899, 160.
17. *Voyage en Armenie et en Perse fait dans les années 1805 et 1806*, Paris 1821, chap.XXVI, 202-9.
18. See A. D. Tushingham, 'The Takht-i Marmar (Marble Throne) in Teheran', in *Iranian Civilisation and Culture* (ed. Charles J. Adams), Montreal 1972, 120-7, for a detailed study of the throne's structure and symbolism.
19. J. M. Tancoigne, *A Narrative of a Journey into Persia and*

Residence at Teheran, London 1820. Letter X X, 179-80. Tancoigne accompanied General Gardane's mission of 1806-7.

20. Today located near the junction of the streets Avenue Istanbul and Avenue Kurush above the Maydân-i Bahâristân.

21. Porter, *op. cit.*, vol.1, 337.

22. Tancoigne, *op. cit.*, 19.

23. *La Perse, la Chaldée et la Susane . . . ,* Paris 1887, chap.vii, 129.

24. *Journal of the British Embassy to Persia,* London 1825, 29; entry for 9 December 1811.

25. G. N. Curzon, *Persia and the Persian Question,* London 1892, 1, 338-40.

26. *Personal Narrative of a Journey from India to England in the Year 1824,* London 1827, 2, 129-30.

27. Robert Binning, *A Journal of Two Years Travel in Persia, Ceylon etc.,* London 1857, 2, 221.

28. Tancoigne, *op. cit.*, Letter x x, 180-3. Its site is now to be located on the Old Shemiran Road in the Abbasabad district.

29. Price, *op. cit.*, 38-9, entry for May 1812.

30. *Monuments Modernes de la Perse,* Paris 1867, 42 and pls l v i i i-l x i.

31. *Glimpses of Life and Manners in Persia,* London 1856, 115-16.

32. Gavin Hambly, 'A note on Sultaniyeh/Sultanabad in the early 19th century', *A A R P* (Art and Archaeology Research Papers) 2, 1972, 89-98.

33. The author visited Cheshmeh Ali in summer 1974 and found that this pavilion was under restoration.

34. Lerner, *op. cit.*, 218-24.

35. Binning, *op. cit.*, 1202-4; Coste *op. cit.*, pls.x x x v i-i x for excellent drawings showing both the original structure and Fath 'Alî Shah's renovations.

36. Curzon, *op. cit.*, ii, chap.x i x, 16.

37. A detailed survey of Nâsir al-Dîn Shah's newly built Tehran was made between 1868 and 1888 by the students of the Dâr al-Funûn College at Tehran under the supervision of 'Abd al-Ghâfir Najm al-Mulk, astronomer and professor of mathematics, and published as a map in 1892.

38. Jennifer M. Scarce, 'The tile decoration of the Gulestan Palace at Tehran – an introductory survey', *Akten des VII Internationalen Kongresses für Iranische Kunst und Archäologie, München 7-10 Septembre 1976,* Berlin 1979, 635-41.

39. Feuvrier, *op. cit.*, 160.

40. 'Ishratâbâd is situated on the Old Shemiran Road at the end of the former Takht-i Jamshîd Avenue. It was recently an army barracks. For an earlier description see Curzon, *op. cit.*, 1, 342.

41. Sâhib Qirâniyya was formerly one of the residences of the Pahlavi rulers and therefore inaccessible to visitors. The account is based on Feuvrier, *op. cit.*, 201-2.

42. Sultanatâbâd is also situated on the Old Shemiran Road well north of the site of Qasr-i Qâjâr and 'Ishratâbâd. It was at the centre of a large army complex including a munitions factory.

343

For an earlier description see Feuvrier *op. cit.*, 260-4.

43. *Ibid.*, 262.
44. Scarce, *op. cit.*, 640-1.
45. Donald Wilber, *Persian Gardens and Garden Pavilions*, Vermont 1962, 155-60.

1

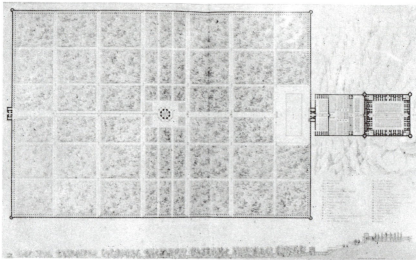

2

3

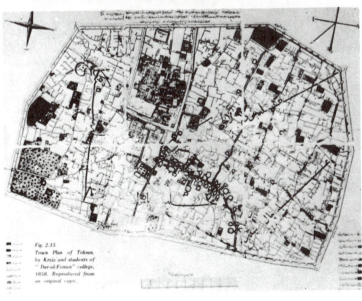

Fig. 2.15
Town Plan of Tehran,
by Krzis and students of
"Dar-ol-Fonun" college,
1858. Reproduced from
an original copy.

4

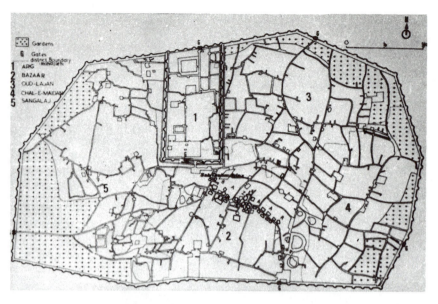

5

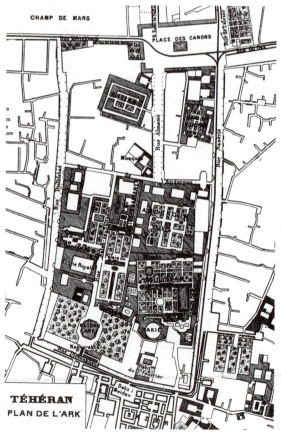

TÉHÉRAN
PLAN DE L'ARK

6

7

8

9

10

11

12

13

14

15

20

The role of tradition in Qajar religious architecture

Qajar religious buildings, like Victorian architecture not so long ago, have had a bad press. The reasons for this are not far to seek. Certainly the architects of the time were in a sense unfortunate in that they were working at the tail end of a distinguished but by this stage quite exception- ally immobile tradition. As early as the Timurid period a certain tiredness can be detected in the way that already long-familiar architectural forms are manipulated, and in many Safavid buildings this tiredness degener- ates into full-scale decline. The immutable norms of mosque layout which constrained Qajar architects are readily summarised – courtyard, two or four *îwâns*, arcades to link these *îwâns* and a *pîshtâq* to serve as entrance. This fossilised schema virtually excluded the experiments with other types of mosque that had enriched Iranian architecture in earlier periods, such as single dome chamber mosques, multi-domed mosques, and others of hypostyle or single-*îwân* type. The problem, then, was not simply conservatism – a feature rightly or wrongly regarded as immanent in Iranian art – but conservatism of a peculiarly rigorous kind, which had somewhat arbitrarily fastened upon the courtyard mosque with *îwâns* in cruciform disposition as the classic expression of Iranian religious architecture, and which tolerated no fundamental departure from that ideal. It was no mean achievement on the part of Qajar architects that, working within such narrowly defined limits, they were able nonetheless to attain a respectable degree of variety in the mosques which they built. It is also a tribute to the flexibility of the schema they used that it could accommodate such variations without surrendering its intrinsic monu- mentality, amplitude and dignity. Such a reflection might suggest that conservatism was not such a dead weight on these architects as would at first appear.

A *coup d'œil* over Qajar art in general, indeed, very quickly reveals that conservatism was not the last resort of a bankrupt imagination but an active principle deliberately applied in all sorts of contexts.[1] In archi- tecture it could be explained as a natural reluctance to stray far from the obvious successes of the fairly recent Safavid past. The palace of Sar- hangâbâd near Zavâra, a miniaturised Chihil Sutûn, shows that this attitude was not confined to religious architecture. In metalwork, however, it could result in downright archaism, for example in the copying of twelfth-century objects.[2] Even more remarkable is the Qajar propensity to revive Sasanian modes. This is most apparent in the unheralded appearance of the first large-scale figural rock reliefs produced for well over a millennium; their imperial iconography leaves no room for doubt that Sasanian themes were deliberately copied or adapted. These Qajar reliefs may even be placed right next to their Sasanian forebears, as the case of Tâq-i Bustân shows.[3] Such Qajar wall paintings as the series in the Nigaristân, which depict long files of courtiers at attention,[4] are also most conveniently explained as calques of Sasanian reliefs, such as those of Bîshâpûr, while the figural stone reliefs in Qajar palaces in Shiraz[5] and elsewhere echo models which are chronologically yet more remote, namely the Achaemenid sculptures of Persepolis. Stone reliefs with vegetal motifs, such as the lotus[6] or the 'tree of life',[7] used in orthostat fashion, occur in both Achaemenid and in Sasanian art and then, after many centuries of disuse, are revived in Qajar mosques. Finally there is the evidence of Qajar figural tilework, in which portraits of pre-Islamic Iranian monarchs abound. Clearly, then, this was an age whose art had a pronounced retrospective quality. 'Traditionalism' is somewhat too feeble a term for this carefully directed re-use of the past.

Yet another dimension of this discriminating but somewhat eclectic revival of selected elements from the Iranian architectural heritage deserves discussion here. This is the Qajar predilection for building on to established sites. In earlier periods it was standard practice to carry out running repairs to religious buildings, especially mosques, and to add new elements – an entrance, an îwân, a dome chamber, a pair of minarets and the like. Most shrine complexes in Iran illustrate this process. It results in the major religious buildings of the land becoming palimpsests in which the principal styles of the past can be read in almost stratigraphical fashion. The Qajar approach to this well-established custom is not consistent. While piecemeal repairs and additions no doubt predominate statistically, they are overshadowed by the much bolder and more thoroughgoing approach typified in some of the major congregational mosques and shrines in the land: Burujird, Gulpâygân, Qazvîn, Qum and Mâhân among others. In these and similar cases the earlier buildings often constitute no more than the core; the whole nature and structure of the monument has been transformed. In the Friday mosques of Burujird[9] and Gulpâyagân,[10] and in the Haydariyya at Qazvîn,[11] a Seljuq dome chamber is virtually all that remains of the pre-Qajar mosque. An entirely new and very much larger structure – complete with entrance, arcaded courtyard and subsidiary chambers and halls – has been grafted on to this nucleus. In the absence of excavations it is impossible to tell for sure whether such a radical reshaping of these mosques typically entailed the destruction of earlier work or whether a reverential desire to conserve prevailed. The evidence, such as it is, seems to favour the former hypothesis. At Burujird and at the shrine of Shah 'Abd al-'Azîm at Rayy, for example, Seljuq inscriptions have been covered by whitewash[12] and by later decoration[13] respectively. Similarly, Qajar tilework now covers the exterior of the great Seljuq dome in the Qazvîn *jâmi'*, a dome which was in all probability intended by its builders to be bare, and much of the courtyard façade seems to have met the same fate.[14]

In the case of a well-established shrine like that of Shah Ni'matallâh Walî at Mâhân,[15] where most of the extant buildings seem to have been in excellent repair, the question of destruction probably did not even arise. Thus the major nineteenth-century contribution to the shrine is a couple of self-contained extra courtyards, the rear one complete with a monumental entrance. Seen in the context of the shrine as a whole, which already had a courtyard and a sufficiently imposing entrance, such an addition may at first appear superfluous. But its spatial and scenic, not to say theatrical, advantages leap to the eye even if they do not command general admiration. The Timurid and Safavid structures on the site, embowered in gardens and pools, and set against a matchless backdrop of mountains, blended unobtrusively with the landscape (fig. 1). This happy symbiosis, which can still be enjoyed from selected vantage points, was not to last. The Qajar architects took the site in hand and made it more assertively a monument. Whether they also improved on nature is an open question, but certainly by adding further courtyards they greatly intensified the spatial drive along the major longitudinal axis, and thus tied the building together. Quite possibly the monumental entrance to the rear courtyard was conceived in the same spirit (fig. 2). It tidies up the ensemble and prevents it from petering out. Moreover, it allows the building to make its proper impact from the reverse direction, giving it a rear facade as well as the one to the front. But this is not the only possible interpretation. The sprawling dimensions of the Qajar rear courtyard, its stridently colourful interior and exterior tilework, the *îwân* which marks the transition to the inner Qajar court and emphasises the processional axis towards the dome chamber, and perhaps principally the almost preposterous height of the multi-tiered minarets flanking the entrance – all these factors invite the suspicion that the Qajar architects were trying to modify if not reverse the previous spatial emphasis of the building, and at the very least to make their facade compete with the earlier one. Perhaps the self-same desire to compete with earlier work helps to explain the remarkable similarity between the Qajar and Safavid vaulting inside the shrine.

These reflections highlight a further constant of Qajar architecture – its emphasis on exterior façades. This goes far beyond the decoration of external perimeter walls with tilework, an idea which centuries earlier had grown naturally out of the decorated brick façades of Seljuq Iran and was first employed on the grand scale in the Timurid period, for example in Samarqand.[16] Similarly, the notion that the façade is pre-eminent underlies the device of leaving the rear and side walls bare of tilework while decorating every inch of the main façade. This practice too is not a Qajar invention; perhaps the most celebrated example of it in earlier times is the Masjid-i Shah in Isfahan, whose public face turned towards the *maydân* contrasts most forcibly in its incrustation of technicolour tilework with the homely quality of the plain brick exteriors visible from the back and the sides.[17] Since the idea of a strongly emphasised façade, then, was in itself nothing new, the main achievement of Qajar architects in this field was to devise hitherto unexploited methods of realising that emphasis. This is the period when the minaret takes on a new importance only vestigially related to its religious significance. When minarets proliferate beyond any conceivable functional need for the *adhân*, their paramount role is clearly as an articulating element, even though their presence in a religious building does suggest a secondary role as markers proclaiming from afar the sacred nature of the monument (fig. 3). The minarets which festoon the shrine at Qum or numerous lesser Qajar shrines throughout the country, like the Shâhzâda Husayn at Qazvîn,[18] can admittedly be interpreted in this sense. Even so, there can be no doubt that the minaret suffered a decisive secularisation in this period. The city gates of Tehran, Qazvîn, Isfahan, Shiraz, Simnân and other large cities provide clinching evidence to this effect.[19] Liberally sprinkled as they are with diminutive, excessively slender minarets distributed promiscuously along an undulating façade, these gates typify the eccentric originality of which Qajar architects were capable. Some palaces of the period, especially the Bâgh-i Takht at Shiraz with its seemingly endless sextuple terrace,[20] carry the concept of the façade to heights unsurpassed in Persian architecture. Such buildings have a quality of relentless monotony and assertion for which such late Islamic Indian buildings as the Hall of Winds in Jaypûr offer the best parallel;[21] they carry unmistakable undertones of megalomania. Nor is this a chance connection, for eighteenth- and nineteenth-century Muslim architecture in Iran and India has a common source in the Timurid style (to look no further back into the past), and the Timurid penchant for façade architecture, involving as it does not only gigantic size but also repetition as a deliberate aesthetic principle, is clearly discernible beneath the later accretions of local tradition and contemporary taste. This topic will be discussed in more detail later in this paper.

Not nearly enough fieldwork has been done to permit generalisations about the link between the main façade and its immediate urban context. Thus it is an open question whether the sites of these large new mosques were deliberately chosen so as to allow their façades to make the maximum impact on their surroundings. Very often, however, it seems that lack of space was one problem with which the architects did not have to grapple. Thus at Gulpâygân, Burujird and the Haydariyya at Qazvîn the relatively small Saljûq structures were vastly expanded by the addition of an arcaded courtyard. Internally this courtyard was, moreover, at once symmetrical and rectilinear, and its exterior too incorporated long unbroken wall surfaces. This is in strong contrast to the sense of untidy, unplanned but nevertheless organic growth which characterises the exteriors of most earlier Iranian mosques. Even so, the traditions of mosque design set by earlier generations were not entirely reversed and the concept of imposing upon the mosque an ordered exterior façade to match the order which reigned within never took root. Contemporary caravansarais had far more developed façades,[22] which suggests that the absence of this feature in Qajar mosques is deliberate. Clearly, the immemorial custom which dictated that mosque exteriors should not be emphasised by decorative means was observed. Elaborately tiled portals were not considered a violation of this custom, and had indeed been a common feature from late Saljûq times onwards. It is therefore not surprising that they should occur frequently in Qajar mosques and *madrasas* (fig. 4). There was no predetermined location for such portals. It is noticeable that in some cases the portal is sited so as to coincide with the end of a street (e.g. Masjid-i Shah, Qazvîn, fig. 5) and thereby exerts maximum visual impact. The absence of published cadastral surveys carried out in Qajar times makes it impossible to discover whether it was the street or the portal which was built first, or whether they were planned as a unity. Such dovetailing does however suggest – especially when the portal is placed off-axis in relation to the rest of the mosque – that Qajar architects were not averse to employing directed vistas, or even perspectives with a vanishing point, when opportunity offered.[23] Whether European influence was active in such cases remains to be seen.

At first sight a discussion of building materials and their uses does not offer the prospect of remarkable insights into Qajar architecture. After all, in an architecture as traditional as that of Iran it would be unreasonable to expect any marked divergences from long-established custom in the type of building materials used or even perhaps in the way that they were employed, particularly when the period in question – in this case the Qajar era – is in general not noted for the excellence or for the originality of its art. The basic building material, therefore, continued to be baked brick. It was, however, used in somewhat unexpected ways – though there is not space to discuss these here[24] – and was supplemented, even more unexpectedly, by stone and marble used for both structural and decorative purposes. The glass mirror-work which was such a feature of Qajar palatial architecture was employed only sparingly in religious buildings such as the Shah Chirâgh in Shiraz or the shrine of Fâtima at Qum. This is scarcely surprising; indeed, the evidence of Qajar archi

tecture in general suggests that architects had substantially more leeway
in the building of palaces than in building mosques. Religious architecture, by adhering more closely to the norms laid down in preceding
centuries, avoided the ranker effusions of Qajar domestic buildings – the
sentimental pseudo-Alpine landscape panoramas executed in a garishly
oleographic style better suited to a chocolate box than to a wall. These
obscure descendants of the Victorian picture postcard did, however,
exert a passing influence on mosque decoration in the tiny vignettes of
buildings set in sketchy landscapes which at intervals relieve the panels of
densely floral tilework ornamenting Qajar mosque interiors (figs 6 and
7).[25] While the immediate inspiration for these clichés probably comes
from contemporary European popular culture, a collateral source in
Islamic art itself must also be examined – the pictures of the Holy Places
of the Hijâz, especially the Prophet's Mosque in Medina and the Ka'ba
itself.[26] These had long been a stock-in-trade of Ottoman tilework, although their origins can be traced as far back as the Great Mosque of
Damascus in the early eighth century. Even if no direct connection with
such specifically Islamic prototypes can be sustained, it is clear that the
idea of representing architecture on mosque walls was deeply embedded
in Islamic culture long before Qajar times. The novelty lay in giving the
theme such trivial expression. Shortage of space forbids a more detailed
account of Qajar mosque tilework here; this is a study in itself,[27] and
reveals a wide range of innovations.

This is by no means an isolated instance of the new uses to which
tilework was put in the Qajar period. After all, this medium provided the
principal decorative theme in Qajar architecture. Properly to assess the
changes in the motifs and colour schemes of tilework, and the changes in
how it was used, between – say – the closing years of the Safavid period
and the end of Qajar rule would require a separate treatise. Happily this is
the aspect of Qajar architecture which has received the most scholarly
attention to date, though even here the sheer bulk of unexploited
material is daunting. Valuable conclusions have been reached on matters
of technique, subject matter and colour schemes. Even so, much remains
to be discovered about such topics as the proportion of glazed to unglazed
surfaces, the interaction with other materials and finally the location of
such ornament.

These remarks suggest that the decoration of Qajar buildings may be as
useful in determining the individual nature of this architecture as are its
spatial and architectural qualities. While the present paper stresses these
latter qualities, it may be useful as a corrective to purely architectural
analysis to investigate at relatively close range at least one aspect of Qajar
decoration. It seems appropriate to choose inscriptions, not only because
this is a much-neglected subject but also because the norms governing the
types and uses of epigraphy had become almost fossilised over the pre-

vious centuries. The unobtrusive originality of Qajar inscriptions is thus all the more remarkable.

For many centuries lengthy inscriptions had been a hallmark of mosque decoration in Iran. Fashions in monumental epigraphy changed slowly, and in the absence of major advances in calligraphic art during the Qajar period it would be reasonable to expect a continuation of earlier modes throughout the nineteenth century. The reality is quite different. While traditional doubledecker inscriptions in *thulth* remained popular,[28] much more use was now made of *nasta'līq* in monumental epigraphy (e.g. Masjid-i Sardâr, Qazvîn). Calligraphers also rang the changes on the format of these inscriptions, in that they often replaced a continuous text by a series of adjoining epigraphic cartouches. Lobed or hexagonal forms, distantly derived from the *tabula ansata*,[29] were preferred. Sometimes these cartouches were laid out in a double row, one above the other, as in the Masjid-i Sardâr, Qazvîn, or the Masjid-i Âqâ Buzurg, Kâshân (fig. 8) – a recycling of the doubledecker inscription in a new idiom. The convention which had hitherto generally confined lengthy courtyard inscriptions to the *îwâns* was now set aside, and extensive epigraphic bands formed a continuous coping around the courtyard (rear court in the Mâhân shrine; Masjid-i Nasr al-Mulk, Shiraz (fig. 9)). This use of inscriptions to knit together a courtyard façade – or, in the case of the Sipahsâlâr mosque, Tehran, to separate the first from the second storey – was a notable advance on earlier experiments in the articulation of façades by means of epigraphy.

These major changes in the script, format and location of epigraphic bands by no means exhaust the tally of Qajar innovations in this field. New colour combinations abound, as in the *mihrâb* of the Ibrâhîm Khan *madrasa* in Kirman, where a yellow inscription weaves its way through green foliage set against a white ground; closed letters have infills in a variety of colours; vegetal scrolls now sprout blooms in full flower. The Qajars continued the earlier custom of placing the ruler's name and titles directly above the crown of an arch and executing this section in a different colour so that it stands out from its surroundings; but they chose new locations for such inscriptions, even though the portal arch remained the preferred site. Thus the name of Fath 'Alî Shah is blazoned forth in yellow letters above both the east and the west *îwân* in the Masjid-i Shah at Simnân. At the Kirmanshah *jâmi'* and the Sipahsâlâr mosque the imperial theme is expressed in different guise, for there the Qajar crown is depicted enclosing an inscription. But in this field of royal iconography pride of place must go to a splendid cartouche in the Madrasa-yi Khan at Shiraz (fig. 10). The panel is in the name of Nasir al-Dîn Shah and is dated 1279. On either side of it is an inscription in white on dark blue, but the multifoil cartouche itself is outlined in carmine and has a light turquoise background with yellow letters. It might well be argued that this panel raises epigraphic homage to the sovereign to new heights.[30]

Two other *tours de force* of Qajar epigraphy deserve brief mention here. In the Sanandaj *jâmi'*, within the *qibla îwân* – which is itself a farrago of conflicting accents, colours and motifs – the dominant feature is a huge blank arch enclosing a replica of itself and placed directly above the *mihrâb*. All four of the major areas into which this arcuated scheme is divided have epigraphy as their leitmotif, and each is differentiated from the next in size or style of script and in colour or background (fig. 11). In another *qibla îwân*, that of the Masjid-i Shah at Simnân, the entire framework of the *îwân* arch is occupied by an unbroken maze of cramped square Kufic inscriptions. Nothing comparable on this scale survives from earlier Iranian architecture. These angular inscriptions form an appropriate counterpoise to the overridingly geometrical bias of the other tilework in the mosque and to the rectilinear patterning of the courtyard paving.

The earlier parts of this paper have sufficiently emphasised the conservative nature of Qajar religious architecture. It is now time to identify its originality. This lies partly, as hinted above, in the type of tilework developed in this period, which greatly expands a thematic repertoire already foreshadowed in the previous century. But a rather more profound originality may be detected in the way that familiar architectural elements are employed. This is a matter of ensemble rather than of structural details. Occasionally, it is true, a mosque may contain a particularly complex set of vaults, like the array of five domical vaults in cruciform design in the Masjid-i Nasr al-Mulk at Shiraz (fig. 12); but this is the exception. Secular buildings tell a different story. The Qajar *tîmchas* at Qum, Kâshân[31] and Kirman among other cities offer perhaps the finest sustained display of *muqarnas* vaulting on the grand scale that is to be found in Iran. There was no intrinsic reason why such expertise should not have been deployed in mosques and *madrasas*. That such vaults are conspicuously absent in religious architecture must therefore be a matter of deliberate policy. The vaulting in Qajar mosques and *madrasas* is sober, restrained and of high technical precision – but it does not seriously attempt to innovate. It is an instrument of the architect's purpose rather than a focus of display in its own right.

If, then, neither decoration nor structural features adequately reflect the individual character of Qajar architecture, in what sense can the ensemble itself be claimed to do so? The key seems to lie in a new interest in articulating the inner façades. No longer is this a matter of architectonic ornament; the imaginations of the Qajar architects tended to express themselves on a more ample scale. The main focus of experiment was the *îwân*. In earlier periods the principle that the *îwân* should dominate the façade of which it was part, and that this was best done if it were centrally placed, had won general acceptance. But the increasing height and breadth[32] of these *îwâns* had resulted in the façade as a whole acquiring a lopsided appearance with the *îwân,* inordinately top-heavy, incapable of being fully integrated with it. Quite frequently the contrast between the *îwân* and the surrounding single-storey arcades was extreme, involving a ratio of the order of 4:1 in height.[33] This trend reached its apogee in the Ilkhanid and Timurid periods.[34] Such a use of the *îwân* as an isolated marker and as an obvious pivot of the design has little in common with the way it functioned in the pre-Islamic architecture where it originated. In Parthian and Sasanian buildings the *îwân* is integrated into the façade in a way that excludes the disequilibrium of later architecture. However large it is in relation to its adjoining facade, it is not allowed to break the roof-line of that façade. This generalisation certainly holds good for the largest of Sasanian (and for that matter subsequent) *îwâns,* namely that of Ctesiphon.[35] Thus the size of the *îwân* grew in direct proportion to the size of the façade of which it was a part. This rule was, however, broken quite early in Islamic times, for at Ukhaidir[36] and presumably at the Târî Khâna mosque in Dâmghân,[37] both conventionally dated in the late eighth century, the central *îwâns* – though in absolute dimensions much smaller than some of their immediate Sasanian forerunners – do project above the roof-line. The next stages of the process are hard to trace for lack of surviving structures, but certainly by the twelfth century the principle that the *îwân* should tower above its adjoining arcades was well established.[38]

It is precisely this time-honoured principle that Qajar architects were concerned to modify. Such was the weight of accumulated tradition that they were powerless to eradicate it entirely, but they consistently attempted to reverse the earlier trend. It is indeed tempting to speculate that this unexpected development should be interpreted in the wider context of the Qajar fascination with the distant past. It would certainly be wrong to attribute a composition such as the *qibla* façade of the Masjid-i Sardâr in Qazvîn (fig. 13) or the lateral portal to the Kirman *jâmi‘,* where the *îwân* is kept within the roof-line of the façade in approved Sasanian fashion,[39] to a deliberate attempt to revive Sasanian modes. Qajar architects, after all, were not art historians. Moreover, conscious antiquarianism is much harder to demonstrate in Qajar architecture than in the rock reliefs of the period, nor could buildings serve the purposes of royal propaganda as efficiently as the reliefs. The overall picture is rendered still more complicated by the fact that some Qajar buildings continue to emphasise the dominance of the *îwân* in the traditional way;[40] moreover, attempts to diminish the *îwân*'s role are already sporadically encountered in pre-Qajar architecture. Even so, the trend in Qajar times was clearly to bring the *îwân* into a more rational and visually closer relationship with the façade to which it belonged.

How was this done? The simplest method, which would have been to reduce quite markedly the absolute height of the *îwân,* was by and large rejected. Yet to add an extra one or even two storeys to the entire façade was generally not feasible either; there was no functional imperative to that effect and it would incur substantial additional expense. Qajar architects therefore chose a middle way by concentrating their attention on the area of transition between the façade and the *îwân.* Hitherto the *îwân* had risen cliff-like at right angles to the roof-line of the courtyard façade. Attempts were now made to modulate the harshness of this juxta-position.

Various bridging devices were employed to this end. One method was to flank the *îwân* arch with two superposed niches or bays per side.[41] The double storey formed by these openings equalled the *îwân* arch in height and therefore effectively doubled the width of the *îwân* 'unit'. The *îwân* complex thus created proved more amenable than an isolated *îwân* in formulating a suitably accentuated but nevertheless harmonious façade (fig. 14). In most Qajar mosques where it was employed this *îwân* complex resulted in a division of the appropriate façade into three approximately equal parts, though the *îwân* itself ensured that the central portion received the necessary extra emphasis even if its breadth was slightly less than that of the flanking blocks.

Another method of mitigating the stark contrast between diminutive arcade and towering *îwân* was to flank the *îwân* by a narrow niched panel on each side; this rises to a point roughly midway between the height of the main arcade and that of the *îwân* frame, thereby creating a stepped silhouette (fig. 15).[42] This idea proved capable of very varied application. Its impact could be changed decisively by quite minor adjustments in the height of the *îwân* relative to its flanking panels or in their breadth *vis-à-vis* the arches of the main arcade. The Masjid-i Shah at Qazvîn shows how these ideas were applied to achieve different ends in separate parts of the building. The west *îwân* stresses the breadth of the whole *îwân* complex, for the *îwân* proper barely projects above the roof-line of the flanking panels (fig. 16). The *qibla îwân,* by way of contrast, rises markedly above its flanking sides and thus an even, well-defined, triply-stepped centrepiece is created (fig. 17). Nor did the steps have to be of even height or width. Indeed, in a multi-stepped silhouette – which was the obvious development after triple stepping – the horizontals and verticals may be prolonged or reduced for extra visual interest, as in the lateral *îwâns* of the Qazvîn *jâmi'* or the *qibla îwân* of the Kirmanshah *jâmi'* (fig. 18). The Nasr al-Mulk mosque in Shiraz illustrates in its *qibla* façade a well-scaled diminuendo of arch sizes, from the gigantic arch of the *qibla îwân* itself via the lesser arches of the flanking bays down to the smallest arch at the furthest extremity of the *qibla* façade (fig. 19). It is noticeable that the entire façade, not just the *îwân* complex, is encompassed in this carefully orchestrated scheme. Such progressive stacking of volumes (often geared to the climactic *qibla* dome, as at the Masjid-i Âqâ Buzurg, Kâshân (fig. 20)) allowed the architect to build his *îwân* as high as ever without incurring the risk of leaving it marooned amidst its surroundings by virtue of that very height. There is more than a touch of theatre in such assertive centrepieces, whose outstanding representative in secular architecture is perhaps the entrance portal of the Yazd bazar.[43] Here the central section alone – to say nothing of the array of flanking arches in several tiers – consists of three superposed arches, each larger than the one below, whose soaring impetus is further accentuated by a pair of slender flanking minarets. Typically enough these have no religious function.

A third – and novel– means of highlighting the *îwân*, encountered only rarely because it requires a double row of arcades along the façade, consists of setting the upper arcade well back from the lower one, and thereby leaving the *îwân* to stand out on its own (e.g. Masjid-i Sayyid, Isfahan, fig. 21; and Masjid-i Shah, Simnân, fig. 22).

Underlying all these experiments in the size of *îwâns* and in the areas immediately surrounding them is a powerful commitment to the concept of façade architecture. The various *îwân* compositions just discussed are of course not two-dimensional but in some respects they operate as if they were. This was in itself nothing new in Iranian architecture. Safavid architects in particular had renounced earlier preferences for high-quality decoration and elaborate vaulting in favour of marshalling large spaces. Their lead was eagerly followed by their Qajar successors. In the great royal mosques of the nineteenth century the innate advantages of sheer size are exploited to the full. It is the ensemble that counts. For this reason it is often as well not to examine the decoration very closely. A bird's-eye view of the building, on the other hand, often reveals how naturally the architect thought big. Thus it is standard practice for the east and west sides to take second place to the north-south axis, as in the Masjid-i Shah at Zanjân (figs. 23 and 24). They may be deprived of *îwâns* altogether, or their *îwâns* may be palpably reduced in scale *vis-à-vis* their counterparts to north and south; the lateral façades may comprise, in addition to the *îwân*, a single arcade while the corresponding arcades on the north and south sides take up two storeys. These arrangements suggest a broad-brush approach to the problem of mosque design, an ability to compose the layout in blocks quite independent of the detailing subsequently applied. Hence the harmony and rhythm of these courtyard façades.

These broad expanses of wall, when viewed within the context of large open courtyards, ran the risk of stressing size at the expense of all other aspects of the design. The need to humanise this daunting sense of scale was evidently felt, and nature itself was imaginatively used to this end. Accordingly, when the important role allotted to pools, flower beds and trees is taken into account it will be realised that the architect of such a mosque was also something of a landscape gardener. The pools, for example, may be circular, square or polygonal (usually octagonal) and thus emphasise centrality; cruciform, reflecting the disposition of the *îwâns*;[44] or rectangular, thereby highlighting one axis at the expense of another.[45] The combination of water, trees and greenery with a spacious geometrically conceived layout cannot fail to bring to mind the Persian garden and the 'garden' rugs which are its symbolic equivalent. Nor can the evocative paradisial connotations of the garden in Islamic theology and popular culture alike be overlooked in this context. As with so much else in Qajar mosque design, this use of water and growing things is not in itself new, but the emphasis laid upon it in nineteenth-century religious architecture is unprecedented. The mosque without a pool in the court-yard is an exception in this period, and trees in the mosque are also found far more frequently than before (e.g. Masjid-i Shah, Qazvîn; Masjid-i Jâmi', Kirmanshah; Masjid-i Sipahsâlâr, Tehran (fig. 25)). In the Masjid-i Shah at Simnân there are actually groves of trees in the corners of the courtyard (fig. 26), and the same is true on a smaller scale of the Masjid-i Âqâ Buzurg in Kâshân (fig. 27) and the Madrasa of Ibrâhîm Khan in Kirmân. The Masjid-i Shah at Zanjân, on the other hand, has flower beds in the corners of the courtyard and two pools in the middle of it (figs. 23 and 24). Sometimes, as at the Masjid-i Jâmi', Kirmanshah, the pool is displaced so as to make room for a central dais for open-air devotions (fig. 18). Yet another solution is adopted at the Masjid-i Shah at Simnân, where the channel of water feeding the central pool follows the east-west axis rather than the *qibla* axis and is lent further emphasis by its border of vegetation, which cuts a swathe of vivid green across the vast courtyard. It seems justified, then, to interpret such landscaping devices as attempts to soften the austerity of very large open spaces which characterised Qajar religious architecture, even if the paradisial associations of shade, run-ning water and greenery operated at no more than a subliminal level.

Another popular means of articulating a façade was the kiosk or turret form. This did not of course exclude the use of full-scale minarets in traditional fashion, as the Masjid-i Sipahsâlâr in Tehran shows. Yet even here the decoration is different from earlier norms, including as it does vignettes of Muslim buildings rendered in tolerably accurate European-style perspective, while in the *madrasa* of the same name the minaret to the right as one enters the building has an upper inscription in the 'dumb Kufic' (*Kûfî-yi gung*) style normally reserved for domes and curtain walls. Other forms of tower were also employed. In the Masjid-i Âqâ Buzurg, Kâshân, for instance (fig. 27), the north façade is closed at each corner by a *bâdgîr* (wind-catcher), which performs the visual function normally associated with minarets. It is a pity that this imaginative transposition of a vernacular form into public architecture should be so exceptional.[46] A much more familar addendum to Qajar mosques is the clock tower. This feature is encountered as early as Safavid times, when an Englishman named Feste made a clock for Shah 'Abbâs I which was placed in a tower over the bazar entrance in Isfahan. But the attention which it excited indicates how unusual it was at that time.[47] In Qajar times these towers are usually truncated. Indeed, their location forbids them to act as towers, for they are almost invariably placed at the crowning central point of an *îwân*. Thus they are subsumed, by form and placing alike, to an already long popular form – the *guldasta*. This was typically a square[48] open-plan kiosk, made of wood and with a pyramidal roof, which with the decline of the minaret came to be used for the call to prayer. It quickly established itself, too, as one of several articulating – usually centering – devices used in composing the screen-like interior façades of the time. At need it could be broadened so as to emphasise mass as well as centrality; thus on the north *îwân* of the Madrasa-yi Sultânî at Kâshân it extends to almost the entire width of the *îwân* arch (fig. 28). Another contrivance with the same purpose was a two-dimensional trefoiled tympanum, a standard fixture on Qajar palace façades[49] but only seldom encountered in mosques (e.g. Masjid-i 'Atîq, Shiraz). Occasionally and unexpectedly, as on the south-west façade of the Masjid-i Mushîr in Shiraz, a quirky hybrid of this form and the clock-tower was devised, perhaps for fun (fig. 29). The abbreviated clock-tower was a further means of articulating the central point of a façade. Since it was a more monumental form than the *guldasta* it was well suited to emphasise portals – as in the Kirman *jâmi'* – or the *îwân* opposite the *qibla*. It therefore had a vital role in identifying the major axis of the building and setting it visually apart from the transverse axis. Sometimes, as at the Masjid-i Sayyid in Isfahan, the same axiality is secured by means of a shortened clock-tower on the north *îwân* (fig. 30) and a standard *guldasta* on the opposite *îwân* (fig. 31), with no comparable crowning element on either of the lateral *îwâns* (fig. 21). It will be clear from these remarks that the articulating function of the clock-tower was paramount, and for this reason it could be used with more freedom than the minaret. Nevertheless, it is a first cousin of that form, and this kinship reflects itself in various ways. Being devoid of religious significance, clock-towers could not very well be used in pairs to flank *îwâns* in the fashion of minarets. Even so, the location of single clock-towers above the centre of an *îwân* shows that architects were just as concerned to use them, too, for articulation as to avoid the danger of having them mistaken for minarets. In its form and decoration the massive octagonal brick clock-tower which rises above the north *îwân* of the Masjid-i Imâm al-Dawla at Kirmanshah could very well be a minaret (fig. 32). Indeed, the decorative arch profiles let into its plain brick surface, with their tiled fields, find their closest parallels in earlier minarets such as the octagonal examples at the Wazîr

Khan mosque in Lahore.[50]

This connection with Mughal architecture, though initially unexpected, is by no means an isolated phenomenon in Qajar architecture. Further examples of it have been noted *en passant* elsewhere in this chapter, but among its most consistent expressions are the turrets or *guldastas* which diversify the roof-lines and are typologically indistinguishable from the *guldastas* of Qajar religious buildings. The issue may therefore briefly be examined in microcosm in that context. While it might be superficially attractive to interpret the connection as exemplifying the influence of Mughal upon Qajar architecture, such a theory will not bear close examination. The two periods are badly out of phase chronologically, and the distance between the two areas would have constituted a further and powerful inhibiting factor. Above all, it was traditionally Persian that influenced Indian culture, not vice versa, and it is – to say the least – unlikely that Qajar Iran and British India had enough common ground politically and culturally to allow much artistic cross-fertilisation.[51] The collateral descent of Qajar and Mughal architecture from the Timurid style seems, as suggested elsewhere in this paper, the most convincing explanation for the intermittently close relationship between them. Within that somewhat nebulous context the striking resemblance between Qajar turrets and Mughal *chhattris* can be put down to coincidence. In both traditions these Islamic gazebos often functioned visually as surrogate minarets, notably when placed in pairs on either side of an *îwân* (as in the Nasr al-Mulk and Mushîr mosques (fig. 33) both in Shiraz; cf. the Sanandaj *jâmi'* (fig. 34)) or at the corner of a building. Sometimes, as in the Sipahsâlâr mosque in Tehran, the connection is reinforced by the location of the turret on a clock-tower or even on an actual minaret. It is an apt comment on the tenacity of architectural tradition in the eastern Islamic world that there should be so little difference in form between the *guldasta* of the north *îwân* of the Masjid-i Shah, Qazvîn, and the turrets on the mausoleum of I'timâd al-Daula, built in Âgra two centuries earlier.[52] Moreover, the well of Ahmet III, built in Istanbul in 1734 and therefore chronologically equidistant between these two buildings, shows how a similar form could be put to yet another use.[53]

This paper has tried to show that the idiosyncratic blend of tradition and innovation which distinguishes Qajar religious architecture finds perhaps its most mature and noteworthy expression in the articulation of façades. The approach of Qajar architects and craftsmen to other elements of mosque design and decoration which were less susceptible to change is of course also worth investigation, but shortage of space forbids more than a glancing reference to these matters here. This chapter will have served its purpose if it has helped to quash the cliché that Qajar religious architecture is nothing but plagiarism. The Qajar commitment to courtyard mosques incorporating *îwâns*, although it admittedly closed the door to experimentation with other mosque types, did not *ipso facto* imply a derivative style of building. How, then, was the danger of undue dependence on the past averted? The creative energies of Qajar architects, though funnelled into a relatively confined sphere of operations, found expression principally in one element of the standard plan: the *îwân* in the context of its associated façade. It is not hard to understand why this was so. In an architectural style which brought its façades within the building and for the most part underplayed external ornament, the means chosen to articulate these interior façades were of crucial importance. Vaulting, extra domes and minarets, contrasting planes, applied ornament, the rhythmic alternation of open and closed spaces or of bays and niches of varying dimensions – all played their part, and deserve detailed discussion in due course. But it is the *îwân* that is pre-eminent. Against all odds Qajar architects managed to make this, the most hackneyed element in the Iranian mosque, the vehicle for unexpected spatial groupings which rejuvenated the millennial cruciform layout. In this new use of old forms lies the key to Qajar religious architecture.

Acknowledgement

I would like to record my deep appreciation of the generosity of Miss Jennifer Scarce in allowing me free access to her magnificent photographic archive of Qajar architecture. Without her assistance in this respect the present article could not have been written. I am also very much obliged to her for giving me permission to reproduce her photographs in this article. I hope these pictures bring back to Laurence Elwell-Sutton abundant happy memories of the Iran he loves, and they are dedicated to him with fondness and thanks for many a pleasant hour spent in his company.

NOTES AND REFERENCES

1. A textbook case of this process is the mosque at Istahbanât (fig.35). Its carved stucco *mihrâb* seems to be a serviceable imitation of the Ilkhanid style. Its *maqsûra,* with its three aisles parallel to the *qibla* and its multiple bays, belongs typologically with such early 'Abbasid work as the *jâmi'* of Shustar; there is no *îwân.* Inside the *maqsûra,* all is of stone; some of the columns have chamfered shafts and brutally simple dosserets abound. Such characteristics link the mosque not with any Qajar building but with medieval work in this area, as at Darâb, Sarvistân, Ij and the *khudâkhâna* in the Masjid-i 'Atîq at Shiraz.

2. See E. Baer, 'Traditionalism or archaism? – reflections on a 19th century bronze bucket', in *Islam in the Balkans. Persian Art and Culture of the 18th and 19th Centuries,* ed. J. M. Scarce, Edinburgh 1979, 87-93. Cf. also the article by A. S. Melikian-Chirvani in the present volume.

3. E. Herzfeld, *Am Tor von Asien. Felsdenkmale aus Irans Helden*

zeit, Berlin 1920, pl.xxxi.

4. B. W. Robinson, 'The court painters of Fath 'Ali Shah', *Eretz Israel* vii *(L. A. Mayer Memorial Volume)*, 1964, 102-3 and pl.xxxiii and *idem, Persian Paintings in the India Office Library*, London 1976, 250-1.

5. D. N. Wilber, *Persian Gardens and Garden Pavilions*, Rutland, Vermont 1962.

6. E.g. on the tomb of Cyrus at Pasargadae (D. B. Stronach, *Pasargadae*, Oxford 1978, fig.19).

7. As at Tâq-i Bustân (A. U. Pope and P. Ackerman, eds, *A Survey of Persian Art from Prehistoric Times to the Present*, London and New York 1939, pl.168c).

8. Cf. J. M. Scarce, 'The tile decoration of the Gulestan palace at Tehran – an introductory survey', in *Akten des VII. internationalen Kongresses für iranische Kunst und Archäologie, München 7-10 September 1976*, Berlin 1979, 640-1 and fig.5.

9. M. Siroux, 'La mosquée djum'a de Bouroudjird', *Bulletin de l'institut français d'archéologie orientale* xlvi (1947), 239-58.

10. A. Godard, 'Les anciennes mosquées de l'Iran', *Athar-é Iran* i/2 (1936), 193 and fig.132.

11. *Ibid.*, 198 and fig.137.

12. An article by Sheila Blair on this inscription will appear in the proceedings of the symposium on the Art of the Saljûqs held in Edinburgh in August and September 1982 (in press).

13. M. K. Pirniya, 'Dargâh va katîba-yi âstâna-yi hadrat 'Abd al-'Azîm', *Bâstân shinâsî va hunar-i Îrân* ii (1348/1969), 4 and 6.

14. D. N. Wilber, 'Le Masgid-i Gami' de Qazwin', *Revue des études islamiques* xli (1973), 199-229.

15. M. E. Bastani-Parizi, *Râhnamâ-yi âthâr-i târîkhî-yi Kirmân*, Tehran 1335/1956, 74-95; A. M. Hutt and L. W. Harrow, *Iran 2*, London 1978, pls.72-3, 93-5.

16. E.g. the Shîr Dar and Tilla Kârî *madrasas*; see the unnumbered plates of these buildings in A. M. Pribytkova, *Pamyatniki arkhitekturi Srednei Azii*, Moscow 1971.

17. See G. Zander (ed.), *Travaux de restauration de monuments historiques en Iran*, Rome 1968, 174, fig.37, and Hutt and Harrow, *Iran 2*, pl.61. For the parallel case of the Yazd *jâmi'*, see *Survey*, pl.438.

18. Sir Roger Stevens, *The Land of the Great Sophy*, London 1971, pl.4b.

19. Cf. *Survey*, pl.472a (Qazvîn).

20. Wilber, *Persian Gardens*, fig.92.

21. W. Speiser, *Oriental Architecture in Colour*, London 1965, pl.72.

22. M. Y. Kiani, *Iranian Caravansarais with Particular Reference to the Safavid Period*, Tokyo 1978, pls.13, 14, 18, 22, 30 and 45.

23. E.g. the portal of the Yazd *jâmi'*, which, before its urban context was recently changed, blocked off the end of a narrow street (M. Siroux, 'La Masjid-e-Djum'a de Yezd', *BIFAO* xliv (1947), pl.v/3). The surroundings of the mosque in the 1930s are of course no reliable guide to its original environment.

24. I hope to take up this subject elsewhere.
25. E.g. at the Masjid-i Sipahsâlâr, Tehran.
26. R. Ettinghausen, 'Die bildliche Darstellung der Ka'ba im islamischen Kunstkreis', *Zeitschrift der deutschen morgenländischen Gesellschaft* 87 (1934), 111-37.
27. Even here the emphasis has been predominantly on secular tilework; but happily a recent article by J. M. Scarce has outlined the major aspects of this area ('Function and decoration in Qajar tilework', in *Persian Art*, 75-85).
28. As on the west *îwân* of the Madrasa-yi Sultânî, Kâshân.
29. See E. Herzfeld, 'Die Tabula ansata in der islamischen Epigraphik und Ornamentik', *Der Islam* VI (1916), 189-99.
30. The basic form of the cartouche is in fact a star-shaped hexadecagon formed by rotating one square over another, but at every obtuse angle of the figure is a convex lobe. The total effect is therefore lobed. In addition, the outline is lightly serrated which gives the cartouche a nimbed effect, and the solar image is further enhanced by the predominant yellow tonality of the letters within the cartouche.
31. See M. Foroughi *et al.*, *Masterpieces of Iranian Architecture*, Tehran n.d., 218-21 and 228-31.
32. E.g. the *îwân* at Nîrîz (A. Godard, 'Le Masdjid-e Djum'a de Niriz', *AI* I/1 (1936), 166-7.
33. As in the Simnân *jâmi'*.
34. As in the Friday Mosques of Yazd and Ashtarjân, the shrines of Turbat-i Jâm and Gazûr Gâh and the *buq'a* at Tâybâd.
35. This can best be seen in a photograph taken while the façade was still largely intact (*Survey*, pl.149).
36. O. Reuther, *Ocheidir*, Leipzig 1912, pls. XVII and XXIV.
37. The present state of the mosque (see O. Grabar, 'The visual arts', in *The Cambridge History of Iran* IV, ed. R. N. Frye, Cambridge 1975, pl.2) is deceptive, for it shows an *îwân* absent in earlier photographs (e.g. in Pope, *Persian Architecture*, London 1965, pl.71). An examination of the ground plan, however, shows that the central bay on the *qibla* side is indeed wider and would have called for some corresponding emphasis in the elevation. Perhaps the *îwân* should nevertheless have been restored to be a trifle lower, as in the example at the Nâ'in *jâmi'* (Grabar, *op. cit.*, pl.3).
38. E.g. the Firdaws *jâmi'* (A. M. Hutt and L. W. Harrow, *Iran 1*, London 1977, pl.78).
39. *Eidem, Iran 2*, pl.125.
40. E.g. the Masjid-i Shah, Simnân, or the Masjid-i Shah, Tehran (for the latter, see L. Lockhart, *Persian Cities*, London 1960, plate between pages 2 and 3).
41. E.g. the Masjid-i Sayyid, Isfahan.
42. E.g. the Masjid-i Shah, Qazvîn.
43. Hutt and Harrow, *Iran 2*, pl.137.
44. E.g. the Madrasa-yi Sultânî, Kâshân.
45. E.g. the Masjid-i Mushîr, Shiraz.

46. A *bâdgîr* is incorporated into the *madrasa* of Ibrâhîm Khan at Kirmân, but it does not perform a significant articulating role there (fig.36).
47. For a discussion of this clock see Sir Roger Stevens, 'European visitors to the Safavid court', *Iranian Studies* VII/3-4 (1974), 435.
48. Octagonal examples are also known, as in the Masjid-i Sultân at Burujird.
49. E.g. the Dîwân Khâna at Shiraz (Wilber, *Persian Gardens*, pl.102).
50. J. Burton-Page, 'Wazir Khan's Mosque', in *Splendours of the East*, ed. M. Wheeler, London 1965, 96-7, 99.
51. Domestic architecture in southern Iran was perhaps the exception that proved the rule; see the article by Bakhtiar and Hillenbrand in the present volume, below.
52. Speiser, *Oriental Architecture*, pl.30. A whole range of other Mughal buildings could have been cited with almost equal relevance (*ibid.*, pls.18, 20, 22, 32 and 33).
53. *Ibid.*, pl.34.

1

2

3

4

5

6

7

8

9

10

11

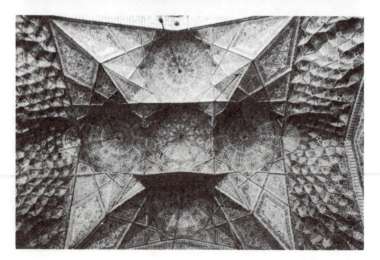

12

13

14

15

16

17

18

19

20

21

22

23

24

25

26

27

28

29

30

31

32

33

34

35

36

A. A. BAKHTIAR and R. HILLENBRAND

21

Domestic architecture in nineteenth-century Iran: the Manzil-i Sartîp Sidihî near Isfahan

Qajar domestic architecture is still very imperfectly known, although paradoxically a great deal of it has survived. Not even a handlist of the important buildings in this field has been published. Thus there exists no framework within which to place a given specimen of the genre. The dearth of published plans is especially serious. It is true that some sporadic discussion of Qajar houses – principally palaces – occurs in a few studies whose prime concern lies in other aspects of contemporary culture such as urban development,[1] gardens[2] or photography.[3] The accounts of nineteenth-century European travellers in Iran often mention Qajar domestic architecture *en passant,* but these references have yet to be systematically collated and exploited.[4] Other sources of information are the detailed accounts of Qajar tilework published in recent years, which necessarily contain some material on the architectural context of this decoration,[5] and the gazetteers of the various *ustâns* of Iran.[6] The latter aim to record most monuments of importance but it must be admitted that in general they give short shrift to the Qajar period.

The net result of this sparse and motley publication is to convey the impression that much Qajar domestic architecture is on a grand scale, bears decoration of sometimes overpowering richness, attests the strength of foreign influences, and is to be found in profusion in major cities like Tehran, Qazvîn, Shiraz, Kâshân and Isfahan. However, it is only in the latter city and its neighbourhood[7] that an attempt has been made in recent years to survey and record at least a representative sample of such buildings.[8] The present study is merely a small part of that project, but it indicates the quality of the material available. It is not only academically desirable but also urgent that such work should be published, since Qajar domestic architecture has been a prime victim of modern urbanisation projects, and outstanding examples of this style have been suffered to decay all over the country. This article is a memorial to such buildings, and its purpose will have been achieved if it stimulates interest in them and thereby helps to avert the threat to those which still survive. But it must be emphasised that the spade-work of recording the finer Qajar houses and palaces with a view to establishing typologies of plan, local style and the like has barely begun.

The building under discussion here is locally known as Manzil-i Sartîp Sidihî (fig. 1). It is located in the settlement of Sidih – 'three villages' – now known as Humâyûnshahr, some 18 kilometres northwest of Isfahan. The nucleus of this prosperous and well-populated satellite town comprises the three hamlets of Adiryân – the largest and most important village and the site of the house itself – Khizûn, and Parishûn. In the later Qajar period this area formed part of the vast domains administered under the Crown by Mas'ûd Mîrzâ, otherwise known as Zill al-Sultân (1850–1919),[9] the first child and eldest son of Nâsir al-Dîn Shah. Since his mother was not of royal blood, Zill al-Sultân could not be crown prince, an honour reserved for his brother Muzaffar al-Dîn. As consolation prize, so to speak, he was awarded a provincial governorship from the age of eleven onwards, and for forty years he was the *de facto* ruler of most of southern Iran with Isfahan as his seat. His brief – to maintain law and order and to remit government taxes on time – was not so onerous as to prevent him from amassing a fabulous personal fortune. In the absence of conscription his army consisted of volunteers and of tribal and district levies.

One such levy came from Sidih, and in 1870, when a new commanding officer – Sayf Allâh Khan, a native of Adiryân – was appointed, he decided to mark the occasion of his investiture by inviting the Zill al-Sultân and his entourage to visit him at his estate for a few days. The exact form of the house, or rather compound, at that time cannot be reconstituted with certainty. All that remains of it is the *andarûn*, or women's quarters, dated to 1820 and located southwest of the main entrance; the niched octagonal vestibule or *hasht* immediately inside the entrance, with the long corridor leading almost due south of it; and at least four of the six rooms directly to the east of that corridor, which were used to store and prepare food and drink. This earlier house naturally had a *bîrûnî*, or male compound, too but this was pulled down in 1870 since it was regarded as not grand enough for the proposed festivities. The large courtyard on the eastern side of the complex, with its encircling portico and suites of rooms to the north and east, was built in its place. This section is without doubt the jewel of the building and the discussion which follows will therefore deal only glancingly with the other parts just mentioned. The latter will, however, be considered first.

The powerfully accentuated entrance complex gives promise of a substantial building to come. It is flanked by a pair of projecting piers on each side which enclose a deep niche, and a similar niche opens immediately within the entrance porch. The widely splayed wings of this portal recall mosque architecture – for example the Masjid-i Shah in nearby Isfahan. So too does the busy profile of the entrance porch, with its multiple projections and recessions. It finally narrows to funnel one into the *hasht,* a cool room in the summertime and well suited to informal male gather ings. A staircase to the roof leads off on the east side while the long corridor mentioned previously (fig. 2) gives access to the rooms used by servants and to the *andarûn*. The corridor is roofed by a series of more than a dozen roughly hemispherical transverse vaults, a technique used in Iran from at least the Sasanian period.[10] Their diminishing perspective and play of light and shade have a sculptural impact.

Rather more than halfway down the corridor a passage opening to the east gives access by a somewhat roundabout route to a suite of three rooms to the south. The chamber adjoining the corridor was a kind of scullery where tea, coffee and cold drinks were prepared; the other two rooms were for the use of servants, which with an admirable economy of design opened directly into the portico of the *bîrûnî* and therefore allowed the servants maximum ease of access to the men there. North of the passage was another group of three rooms somewhat differently laid out. Once again, the room adjoining the corridor had a service function, being used to store fruit and vegetables. The other two rooms, arranged *en suite* with the smaller room opening off to the south of the larger one, together constituted a *hawzkhâna,* or summer sitting room – literally a place containing basins of water with fountains. In layout the main section (fig. 3) is essentially a four-*îwân* plan, though in fact the lateral '*îwâns*' have flat not vaulted roofs.[11] The illusion is strengthened by the fountain and octagonal pool with scalloped sides which form the central element of the deeply sunken floor.[12] In the manner of many a Qajar open-air façade in palace and mosque alike, the dadoes which border the floor are stone orthostats carved with floral designs in horizontal cartouches. The second storey is also of open-plan design, though in a different idiom; it is articulated by a continuous succession of arches. The central trio of arches on either side is filled with latticed glass, with a restricted use of stained glass in the tympana. The *hawzkhâna* is ventilated by a wind-tower or *bâdgîr*. The feeling of light, air and spatial freedom thus created brings into this room a sense of the world outside. The light tonality of the decoration fosters the same illusion. Somewhat harder to assess, however, is the subject-matter of that decoration. Undertones of manuscript illumination may be detected in the ansate cartouches, and the emphasis on ewers and chalices may readily be paralleled in glazed tilework. But the flavour of the ensemble is emphatically not Iranian; the dripping and slightly decadent ormolu suggests rather the Second Empire style or some derivative of it. With its high ceiling, fresh ventilation and running water this *hawzkhâna* was an ideal place for relaxation on a hot summer's day.

The southern end of the corridor led, via a right-angled turn, to the *andarûn*. This comprised suites of rooms laid out on three sides of a courtyard with a pool. The place of honour was the hall in the centre of the north side. Here the ladies would entertain company. Smaller adjoining rooms to each side were suitable for smaller gatherings of the same kind. Two store-rooms occupied the rest of the northern side. The central block of the similarly arranged western side featured a living-room flanked on each side by a bedroom, which could double as an anteroom and as a storage space for bedding. Easily the most complex arrangements are those on the south side, which is divided into four roughly equal groups with an additional narrow central section acting as a caesura. Proceeding from west to east, the first group has a cool room to the north and a store to the south. The second and third groups are identical; they total four rooms which are intended for younger children. Those rooms which gave onto the courtyard were for summer use while the more sheltered rooms behind were occupied in the winter. The central section, though somewhat narrower, was obviously more appropriate for communal use: it served as a covered veranda with a view over the courtyard garden, which was itself sunken. The last group to the east in this block comprises three rooms; the two to the south were used both as storerooms and as places where the ladies of the house could prepare light snacks or sweets and roasted nuts. The narrow room to the north served as a cloakroom and a recess at the back of it contained a lavatory.

Nothing remains of the areas north and east of the *andarûn*, though the expanse to the north formerly contained stables and probably servants' quarters. Directly south of the *bîrûnî* was the main garden of the residence. Southwest of the *bîrûnî* and adjoining the *andarûn* to the east was the kitchen court, now destroyed. Here were sited stores for grain and other food, and also a home bakery. Either in this area, or alternatively in the now empty tract of land north of the *andarûn*, there was in all probability a bath-house complete with drying yards so that water used for bathing purposes could evaporate in the sun and would not penetrate to the wells of potable water. Fuel was also prepared and stored in the area of the *hammâm*. From early spring onwards, quantities of thorns would be brought in from nearby fields on donkeys or mules and would be dried in the yards. They would then be stacked on the domes of the hot rooms in the baths and their multiple layers would provide excellent insulation. Later in the year, before autumn was over, foliage from the gardens and orchards would be added. Further fuel was provided by cow dung formed into round cakes and dried in the sun. This was especially suitable for stoves.

So much, then, for the many component parts of this Qajar *manzil*. The *pièce de résistance* of the entire building is, as noted above, the *bîrûnî*; and it will be convenient to preface a detailed discussion of it by identifying the functions of the rooms not mentioned so far. The cynosure of the whole is assuredly the central chamber on the north side, the audience hall with its *shâh nishîn*.[13] This was used for formal audiences or meetings. It was flanked on either side by smaller rooms intended for more intimate gatherings or for less important guests. It will be seen that this tripartite arrangement is simply a more elaborate version of the corresponding section in the *andarûn*. The extremely lavish decoration in a range of media leaves no doubt that the *shâh nishîn* was the place of honour in the entire residence.

The east side consists of four separate elements. Proceeding from north to south, one encounters first an unusually small room (c.3.6 × c.4.3 m.) which functioned as a combined cloakroom and lavatory. Its humble function explains well enough why it is tucked away in such a discreet manner and its doorway is appropriately narrow. The three rooms to the south of this are of unequal size and layout. The first two, however, were despite these differences intended to serve the same purpose – as a place for informal gatherings either on winter afternoons when the rays of the sun would play directly on these areas, or on summer mornings when it was especially refreshing to sit on its veranda. The first of these two rooms doubled – as did the room at the centre of the opposite side – as a classroom for the children of the house and their tutors. The last room on this eastern side is also the largest. It is a continuous space but a long narrow pier projecting into that space conveys the impression that it is partitioned into two sections of unequal importance. The idea is similar to that of the *hawzkhâna* though the idiom in which it is executed is different. As in the *hawzkhâna* the room focuses on a pool with a fountain, while a polygonal niche replaces the principal *îwân* of the *hawzkhâna*. This room was intended principally for summer use; its amenities could be enjoyed by the rest of the household while the notables were occupying the two adjacent rooms to the north.

The individual functions of the various rooms comprising the *bîrûnî* have now been enumerated. What of the architecture of this section of the house? Not surprisingly, the *bîrûnî* is incomparably more splendid than the *andarûn*; after all, the principal *raison d'être* of the new construction was to house male rather than female notables. For all the traditional nature of the building as expressed in the functions allotted to the rooms and in the emphasis on a cruciform plan centred on a courtyard, the dominant style is modernised Iranian. In place of axial *îwâns* are simply recesses whose breadth on the courtyard façade is marked simply by the gap in the colonnade and then by the four recessed columns screening the room behind. The architecture throughout this façade is essentially trabeate but for the arcuated tympanum found at the upper centre of the dominant northern *corps de bâtiment* (fig. 4). Some of the column shafts have spiral grooving (fig. 5) obviously related to, though different in detail from, the 'barley-sugar' columns of the Zand period in Shiraz, as found in the Masjid-i Vakîl for example.[14] Indeed, some of the columns at Sidih would not be out of place in that monument (fig. 6). Other variations on the leitmotif of the spiral column display rosettes of the kind familiar from Persepolis (fig. 6) or have a spiral with a more horizontal emphasis, like a loosely coiled spring, with depictions of living creatures occupying the field (fig. 5). Such shafts bring to mind the historiated columns of imperial Rome, and that may indeed be their ultimate source even though the mode of transmission – possibly photographs or engravings – remains obscure for the moment. Other columns are fluted in a passable imitation of the classical manner, and debased Corinthian capitals abound (fig. 6). But it is the eastern, western and especially southern courtyard façades that most strongly reflect the fundamental ideas of classical architecture, though at several removes. On the south side the very long and plain architrave, which functions visually as a single beam (fig. 4), illustrates the same point. Perhaps the most likely source for these pseudo-classical features is Russian, or more specifically Caucasian, architecture. Several buildings with such features were erected by the Russian-influenced architects in Tehran and may have been the intermediaries for this outbreak of European influence at Sidih. Subsequent buildings in Tehran aped this Caucasian architecture, a development which is scarcely surprising in view of the strength of Russian influence in northern Iran following the treaties of Gulistân (1813) and Turkomânchây (1828). By contrast, the more southerly areas of Iran were apt to look for inspiration to the architecture of the neighbouring British Raj in India.

The spatial variation in planes and levels which is used with such success in Qajar religious architecture[15] is also found here. The vaguely classical idiom of the *bîrûnî*, with its emphasis on columns and architraves, excludes the use of the traditional 4-*îwân* plan in the courtyard. Nevertheless, as already noted above, on three of the four sides a central splayed recess defined by columns breaks the even tenor of the colonnade. Thus the articulating function of the *îwân* is maintained in an alien idiom. These recesses are, moreover, raised. In each case four steps with broad treaders and short risers bearing shallowly carved horizontal medallions lead up from the courtyard to give access to the buildings around it. A stone dado of orthostat slabs carved with vases of flowers and cartouches marks off the colonnaded portico from the courtyard proper.[16] Thus the courtyard is palpably sunken. With the courtyard itself, moreover, are set a pair of long, shallow, sunken plots or beds, laterally placed, which flank the central octagonal pool to north and south.[17] They create yet another level. So too, incidentally, does the now neglected garden to the south, which is sunk below the level of the walkway surrounding it. This garden is irrigated by underground conduits. The courtyard is further landscaped in that each bed has six trees planted in pairs and so placed that when the *bîrûnî* is seen from a central vantage-point in the garden they neatly fill the inter-columniations of the south façade. At the same time they have been trained so as to function as bushes complementing the façade rather than obscuring it by excessive height. Finally, the courtyard as a whole follows a formula repeated several times and on various scales within the residence: an open space with a pool is set in the midst of densely planned structures, to powerful spatial effect.

The *shâh nishîn* dominates this whole courtyard by its massive two-storeyed façade. An imposing sextet of columns rising to the full height of the two storeys, and thus towering above the other columns of the courtyard portico, is set before the richly fenestrated façade of the *shâh nishîn* complex. The two-storeyed arrangement here sets the northern section apart from the rest of the *bîrûnî* and underlines its place of honour. At the centre of this ensemble there breaks through the roof-line the characteristic Qajar tympanum. Unlike most others of its kind, it is decorated in stucco rather than in tilework.[18] Indeed, tilework is conspicuously absent throughout the compound. Conversely, however, stucco is paramount, probably because workers from Tehran, where this was a common contemporary form of decoration, were employed. Plaster ornament of this type was otherwise still uncommon in the Isfahan area at this time.

The interior of the *shâh nishîn* comprises a hall divided by a pair of columns and a narrow platform into two distinct sections. The rear section has a lower ceiling and ends in an arched recess containing a fireplace (fig. 7). The walls are festooned with blind arched recesses containing carved and painted plaster with themes such as medallions, chalices and flowers. The fireplace itself sparkles with cut-glass mosaic and floral frescoes whose delicacy is worthy of a manuscript (fig. 8). This luxuriant decoration is set off by plain plastered dadoes. Chairs were widely used in Iran by this time, as contemporary portraits and other evidence show,[19] but there is no reason to doubt that the more traditional custom of taking one's ease sitting cross-legged against the wall persisted. A plain dado, against which mattresses and cushions could be arranged, best suited this custom.

Local and family traditions concur in asserting that the *bîrûnî* was built in the remarkably short time of six months by dint of round-the-clock labour. Such speed imposed certain economies in the building materials used. The relative barrenness of the surrounding countryside and the dearth of timber meant that it was costly and difficult to provide enough kiln fuel to make substantial quantities of baked brick. The use of baked brick was therefore kept to a minimum. Much the same is true of stone; thus the stone used for the columns (especially plinths) and pool in the *bîrûnî* was taken from the Âtashgâh outside Isfahan. Most of the *bîrûnî*, therefore, is of mud-brick which was made *in situ* and thereby contributed incidentally to the lowering of the garden area. Once the mud-brick walls had been raised they were given an extra coating of clay and straw and then plastered over. The façades of the rooms behind the courtyard portico are of this type and are left plain. When the walls of a room had reached the desired height they were roofed with rafters consisting of poplar trunks. These slender trees would be felled, stripped of their bark and left to dry in the sun for a few months before use. Upon this framework would be laid rough-cut planks which would be covered with layers of clay and straw. In covering the underside of such a ceiling planewood with high relief decoration would be used, thus creating a kind of coffering, the whole painted with intricate friezes and medallions (fig. 7).

The Persian rococo of the *shâh nishîn* is only one aspect of this residence, and it is liable to give a distorted impression of the design priorities in the building. This was essentially a house to be lived in as well as looked at. In subsequent years, it must be admitted, the *bîrûnî* was used only on special occasions such as feasts, marriages and other ceremonies, and it is only the *andarûn* which is still in use. Even so, the flexibility of the architectural planning is an ingenious response to the taxing climatic conditions of the region. Solar energy is exploited wherever possible. The house had to be comfortable in two extremes of temperature – five months of heat and three months of penetrating cold. One solution was to design rooms with verandas in front. This not only kept away rain and snow but also brought in the comparatively feeble rays of the sun in the winter months while providing agreeable shadows in high summer. Most rooms had fireplaces intended for occasional heating and barbecuing. Every flue had a stopper that in winter when the fire had died down could be shut to keep the heat in while in summer it could be opened to let a breeze pass through. In houses which, like the one discussed here, were intended for the wealthy, some rooms were designed for use during a specific season of the year. Low roofs were appropriate for rooms intended for winter use, while high ceilings were the optimum solution for summer weather. Colonnades on the north side to keep the sun out of the rooms behind in summer, and also to protect them from winter weather, were a common feature of domestic architecture in this period, though the *bîrûnî* at Sidih is unusual in that the colonnade is extended to surround the entire courtyard.

What conclusions may be drawn from the material presented here? First of all, the house at Sidih conforms to an ancient custom of Iranian domestic architecture in that the total destruction of serviceable earlier buildings to make way for more splendid new ones was regarded as preferable to piecemeal repairs and improvements. The *bîrûnî* shows how very quickly (with influence and ready money) such new work could be erected. It is worth noting, too, that the compound was intended for communal living as a virtually self-contained entity. Most of the food was prepared, and some herbs and vegetables even grown, on the spot; servants lived within its walls; its single entrance was eminently defensible; bath, stables, bakery and gardens were all incorporated. The emphasis on lavish stucco decoration is unusual for Isfahan but fits neatly within the architectural style of contemporary northern Iran. This stucco and the debased classical idiom of the *bîrûnî* attest the strength of European influences at this time. Nevertheless, such influences are powerless to dislodge the immemorial traditions of Iranian domestic architecture so far as the overall layout is concerned. Indeed, it is above all in its many ingenious shifts to accommodate the climatic extremes of the Iranian plateau that the building repays study and commands admiration.

NOTES AND REFERENCES

1. E. Pakravân, *Vieux Téhéran*, Tehran 1962.
2. D. N. Wilber, *Persian Gardens and Garden Pavilions*, Rutland, Vermont 1962.
3. J. M. Scarce, *Isfahan in Camera – 19th Century Persia through the Photographs of Ernst Hoeltzer*, London 1976; A. M. Piemontese, 'The photographic album of the Italian diplomatic mission to Persia (summer 1862)', *East and West*, New Series, XXII/3-4 (1972), 249-311.
4. Their utility is well demonstrated in the article by J. M. Scarce in the present volume.
5. Scarce, 'Ali Mohammad Isfahani, tilemaker of Tehran', *Oriental Art*, New Series, XXII/3 (1976), 278-88; *eadem*, 'Function and decoration in Qajar tilework', in *Islam in the Balkans. Persian Art and Culture of the 18th and 19th Centuries*, ed. Scarce, Edinburgh 1979, 75-86; *eadem*, 'The tile decoration of the Gulestan palace at Tehran – an introductory survey', *Akten des VII. internationalen Kongresses für iranische Kunst und Archäologie, München 7.-10. September 1976*, Berlin 1979, 635-41; S. R. Peterson, 'Painted tiles at the Takieh Mu'avin ul-Mulk (Kirmanshah)', *ibid.*, 618-28.
6. For a representative list of these see *Bibliographical Guide to Iran*, ed. L. P. Elwell-Sutton, Brighton 1983, 306.
7. E.g. the area of Zavâra where the palace of Sarhangâbâd, currently being published by Ingeborg Luschey-Schmeisser, is to be found.
8. A thorough survey of these buildings by A. A. Bakhtiar and J. Donat awaits publication.
9. For a brief biography, see A. R. Sheikholeslami, 'Zill al-Sultan: political leadership', in *Islam in the Balkans. Persian Art and Culture*, 95-7.
10. E.g. at Îwân-i Kirkha (G. Herrmann, *The Iranian Revival*, Oxford 1977, 107).
11. Such roofed-over 4-*îwân* plans are common enough in medieval *madrasas* in Anatolia and Egypt.
12. Slightly sunken courtyards are characteristic of Iranian caravansarais from the Safavid period onwards, and are also common in Qajar mosques.

13. According to F. Steingass, *A Comprehensive Persian-English Dictionary*, London n.d., 728, the literal meaning of this word is 'The seat of the King, i.e. a gallery or balcony projecting from the palace, where the King shows himself to his people; a balcony, gallery, portico, or similar projection; a costly carpet'. It will be noted that the central section does indeed project deeply into the back wall.

14. Cf. A. U. Pope, *Persian Architecture*, London 1964, fig.319.

15. E.g. in the mosque of Âqâ Buzurg in Kâshân (Scarce, *Isfahan in Camera*, fig.24).

16. This is a standard feature of Qajar mosques and palaces alike.

17. The idea of incorporating such beds in a courtyard may owe something to garden architecture; whatever its source, it was a leitmotif of Qajar mosques.

18. Tilework is used for such tympana in the city gates of Qazvîn, Tehran and Simnân as well as in palaces (Wilber, *Persian Gardens*, figs.61, 94 and 102).

19. S. R. Peterson, 'The chair in Qajar Iran', in *Modern Iran. The Dialectics of Continuity and Change*, eds. M. E. Bonine and N. Keddie, Berkeley 1981.

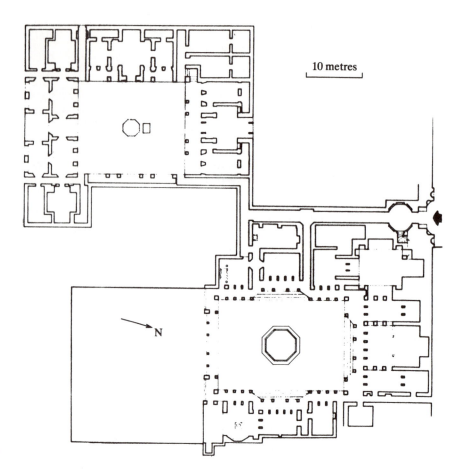

1

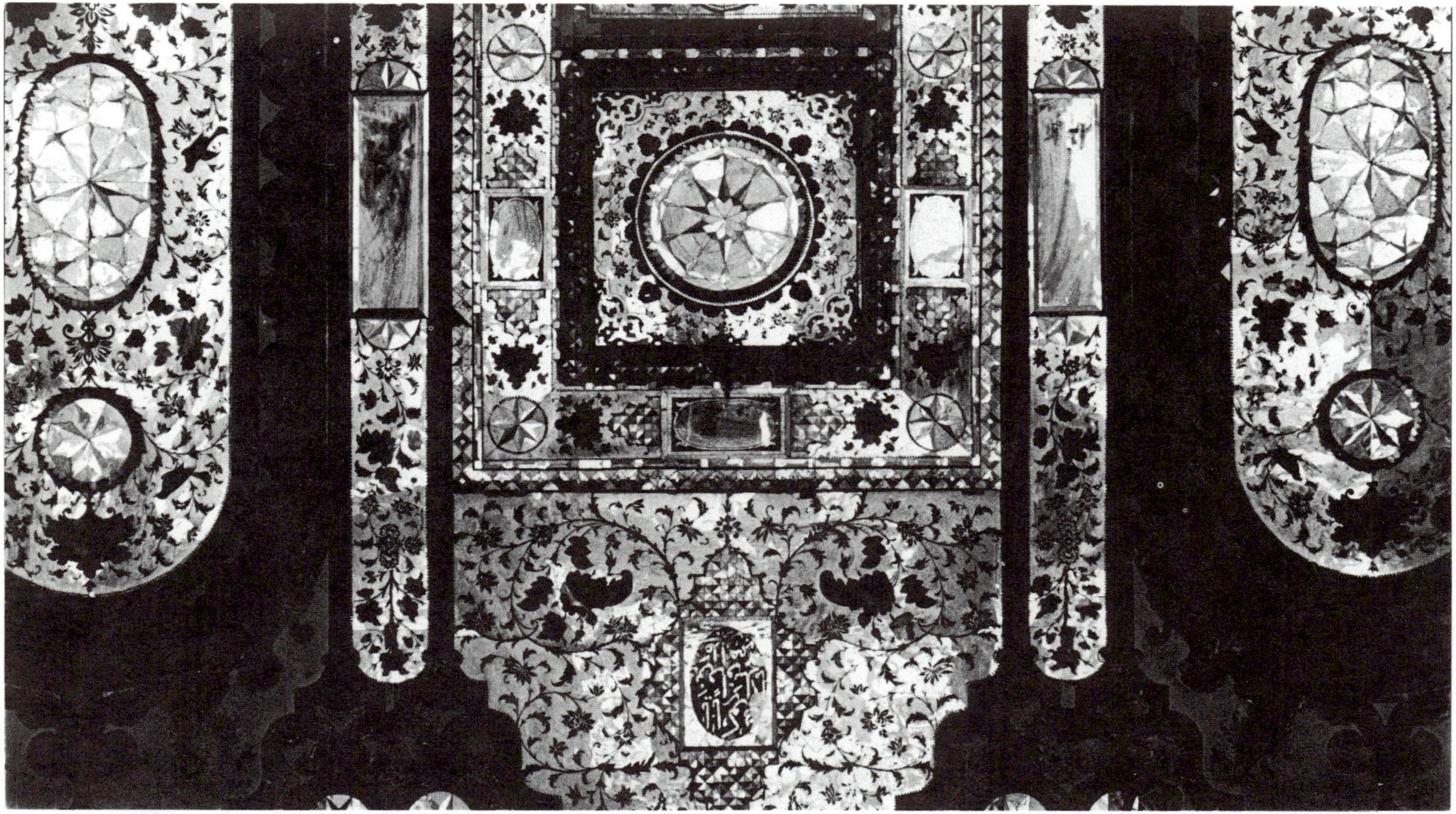

Index

Index

403

Index

Index

Index